The Golden Chain

John Dillon

The Golden Chain

Studies in the Development of Platonism and Christianity

VARIORUM

British Library CIP Data

Dillon, John *1939–*
The Golden Chain : studies in the
development of Platonism and
Christianity. – (Collected Studies
Series ; CS 333)
1. Platonism
I. Title   II. Series
184

ISBN 0–86078–286–7

Published by

Variorum
Gower House,
Croft Road, Aldershot
Hampshire GU11 3HR
Great Britain

Gower Publishing Company
Old Post Road
Brookfield
Vermont 05036
USA

Printed in Great Britain by

Galliard (Printers) Ltd
Great Yarmouth, Norfolk

COLLECTED STUDIES CS 333

CONTENTS

Introduction   ix–xi

Acknowledgements   xii

I   What Happened to Plato's Garden?   51–59
        Hermathena CXXXIII.
        Dublin, 1983

II   Self-Definition in Later Platonism   60–75
        Notes   197–9
        Self-Definition in the Greco-Roman
        World (Vol. 3 of Jewish and Christian
        Self-Definition), edd. Ben E. Meyer and
        E.P. Sanders. Co-pub London: SCM Press
        Philadelphia: Fortress Press, 1982

III   The Academy in the Middle Platonic Period   63–77
        Dionysius III.
        Halifax, Nova Scotia, 1979

IV   Female Principles in Platonism   107–23
        Itaca I.
        Barcelona, 1986

V   Tampering with the Timaeus:
        Ideological Emendations in Plato   50–72
        American Journal of Philology 110.
        Baltimore, Md., 1989

VI   Speusippus in Iamblichus   325–32
        Phronesis XXIX.
        Assen, 1984

VII   "Xenocrates" Metaphysics: Fr. 15 (Heinze)
        Re-examined   47–52
        Ancient Philosophy 5.
        Pittsburgh, 1986

VIII "Metriopatheia and Apatheia":
Some Reflections on a Controversy in
Later Greek Ethics 508–17
Essays in Ancient Greek Philosophy II,
edd. Anton and Preus. Albany: SUNY Press,
1983

IX The Transcendence of God in Philo:
Some Possible Sources 1–8
Center for Hermeneutical Studies
Protocol of the 16th Colloquy (April 1975),
Vol. 16. Berkeley, Ca., 1975

X Philo and the Stoic Doctrine of *Eupatheiai*
(with Abraham Terian) 17–24
Studia Philonica 4.
Chicago, 1976–1977

XI Ganymede as the Logos: Traces of a Forgotten
Allegorisation in Philo? 183–5
Classical Quarterly, n.s. 31.
Oxford, 1980

XII The Descent of the Soul in Middle Platonic
and Gnostic Thought 357–64
The Rediscovery of Gnosticism, Vol. 1,
ed. B. Layton. Leiden: E.J. Brill, 1980

XIII Plutarch and Second-Century Platonism 214–29
Classical Mediterranean Spirituality:
Egyptian, Greek, Roman, ed. A.H. Armstrong
(World Spirituality Vol. 16). New York:
Crossroad Publishing Company, 1986

XIV Harpocration's Commentary on Plato:
Fragments of a Middle Platonic Commentary 125–46
California Studies in Classical Antiquity 4.
Berkeley, Ca., 1971

XV A Date for the Death of Nicomachus
of Gerasa? 274–5
Classical Review n.s. 19.
Oxford, 1969

XVI   The Concept of Two Intellects: A Footnote
        to the History of Platonism   176–85
        Phronesis XVIII.   .
        Assen, 1973

XVII   The Platonising of Mithra   79–85
        Journal of Mithraic Studies, 2.
        London: Routledge and Kegan Paul, 1977

XVIII   Plotinus, Philo and Origen on
        the Grades of Virtue   92–105
        Platonismus und Christentum: Festschrift
        für Heinrich Dörrie, edd. H-D. Blume and
        F. Mann (Jahrbuch für Antike und
        Christentum, Ergänzungsband 10). Münster:
        Aschendorffsche Verlagsbuchhandlung, 1983

XIX   *Aisthêsis Noêtê*: A Doctrine of Spiritual
        Senses in Origen and in Plotinus   443–455
        Hellenica et Judaica: Hommage à Valentin
        Nikiprowetsky, edd. A. Caquot et al.
        Leuven–Paris: Editions Peeters, 1986

XX   The Theory of Three Classes of Men in
        Plotinus and in Philo   69–76
        Scholars, Savants and Their Texts:
        Studies in Philosophy and Religious
        Thought, Essays in Honor of Arthur Hyman,
        ed. R. Link-Salinger. New York etc.:
        Peter Lang Publishing, Inc, 1989

XXI   Origen's Doctrine of the Trinity and
        Some Later Neoplatonic Theories   19–23
        Notes   239–40
        Neoplatonism and Christian Thought
        ed. D.J. O'Meara (Studies in Neoplatonism,
        Vol. 3) International Society for
        Neoplatonic Studies. Norfolk, Va., 1982

XXII   Looking on the Light: Some Remarks on the
        Imagery of Light in the First Chapter
        of Origen's *Peri Archôn*   215–230
        Origen of Alexandria: His World and His
        Legacy, edd. C. Kannengiesser and
        W.L. Petersen. Notre Dame: University of
        Notre Dame Press, 1988

XXIII   The Magical Power of Names in Origen and
         Later Platonism   203–16
         Origeniana Tertia, edd. R. Hanson and
         H. Crouzel. Rome: Edizioni dell'Ateneo,
         1985

XXIV   Plotinus and the Transcendental Imagination   55–64
         Religious Imagination, ed. J.P. Mackey.
         University of Edinburgh Press, 1986

XXV   Plotinus, *Enn*. III 9, 1 and Later Views
         on the Intelligible World   63–70
         Transactions of the American
         Philological Association 100. New York, 1969

XXVI   Iamblichus and the Origin
         of the Doctrine of Henads   102–106
         Phronesis XVII.
         Assen, 1972

XXVII   Proclus and the Parmenidean Dialectic   165–75
         Proclus, lecteur et interprète des anciens
         (Colloque international CNRS, 1985),
         ed. J. Pépin et H–D Saffrey. Paris: Editions
         du CNRS, 1987

XXVIII   Image, Symbol and Analogy: Three Basic
         Concepts of Neoplatonic Exegesis   247–262
         The Significance of Neoplatonism, ed.
         R. Baine Harris (Studies in Neoplatonism,
         Vol. 1) International Society for
         Neoplatonic Studies. Norfolk, Va, 1975

Addenda and Corrigenda   1–3

Index   1–4

This volume contains xii + 322 pages

INTRODUCTION

The publication of this selection of articles, covering the twenty years from 1969 to 1989, gives me the opportunity to review, and introduce corrections and modifications into, essays some of which were composed at a much earlier stage of my career. My primary concern throughout this period has been with the history of Platonism, beginning with the Old Academy, but circumstances dictated, strangely enough, that I work my way *backwards*, from Iamblichus, on whom I did my doctorate, and Proclus, through that period commonly known as 'Middle Platonism', on which I was then invited to write a book, to the Old Academy and Plato himself. Even Plotinus I initially skirted round, and only now am coming to concentrate on intensively, while that other great figure of the later period, Origen, I am still nibbling at tentatively, conscious of the vast amount of patristic scholarship still to be absorbed. The same is true, unfortunately, for such figures as Damascius, Simplicius, John Philoponus, Pseudo-Dionysius, John Scottus Eriugena, Salomon Ibn Gabirol, and the Renaissance Platonists. What we have here, meanwhile, if it be not thought too irreverent an image, are merely some pulls on the Golden Chain.

I have arranged the essays in roughly historical order, but I have begun with a number which concern a question of continuing interest to me, namely the nature of the Platonic school at various stages of its development, and the conditions under which instruction and research may have been carried on over the centuries between Plato and Proclus. This is a subject on which all too little evidence is available, so that one is driven to making conjectures on the basis, largely, of scraps of anecdote. I tend, as will be seen, to a minimalist position as regards the physical plant and degree of formal organisation of the 'Academy'. This I do not see as destructive of the great tradition, the 'Golden Chain' which I have taken as the title of this collection; it rather seems to make it more marvellous that the whole edifice survived as it did. I conclude that in the case of the Greek intellectual world (as, indeed, would have been the case in mediaeval Europe, or in the mediaeval Arab world) we are dealing with a fairly small coterie of people, most of whom at any given time were personally known to each other, and so problems of identification and accreditation which would be characteristic of the modern world would not obtain. Questions of orthodoxy and heresy, again, though they can arise, have a fuzzier aspect in such an environment than would be the case were there a central validating authority, such as there came to be in the Christian Church as it developed over the first few centuries of its existence.

Apart from this topic, I have presented a series of studies on figures from Speusippus and Xenocrates in the Old Academy, through Philo of Alexandria and Origen (neither of these strictly Platonists, of course, but rather honorary members of the Golden Chain), to Plotinus, Iamblichus and Proclus, together with some more general issues, such as *metriopatheia* versus *apatheia*, or the fall of the soul, which span all or much of the period under review. Some of the positions advanced I recognise as being rather speculative, but in no case am I convinced in retrospect that they are definitely wrong (otherwise, of course, they would not appear here). For instance, I cannot really be sure that there is a lacuna in Xenocrates, Fr. 15 Heinze (Essay VII), but I still feel that *something* is seriously wrong, and that Xenocrates cannot be maintaining what he is there presented as maintaining. Nor would I still care to assert that I have discovered the date of Nicomachus of Gerasa's death (XV), but I still have a soft spot for that comparatively youthful squib. Why, after all, did Proclus choose *Nicomachus* from whom to be reincarnated? He was well respected in later times, certainly, but not the *first* person one would choose to be a reincarnation of.

Again, on the question of the Iamblichean origin of the doctrine of henads (XXVI), one must take account now of the arguments against my position given by Saffrey and Westerink in the Introduction (ch. 1) to Vol. III of the Budé edition of Proclus' *Platonic Theology*, but I still think that Iamblichus proposed something like the later (Syrianic) doctrine of henads, though he certainly also saw them as objects of some level of intellection. My conviction that this is so has been strengthened by the recent researches of Dominic O'Meara, in his book *Pythagoras Revived* (Oxford, 1989), which reveal the contents of Book VII of Iamblichus' work *On Pythagoreanism*, in which precisely these entities, 'divine numbers', are identified with the gods (cf. in particular pp. 76–85, and Appendix I).

Finally, the concluding essay of the collection (XXVIII), on 'Image, Symbol and Analogy', should have taken account also of an important passage in Proclus' *Platonic Theology*, I 4, in which symbolic and iconic exegesis is distinguished very clearly, the former being declared Orphic, the latter Pythagorean. The myth of the *Gorgias*, the myth of Poros and Penia in the *Symposium*, and Protagoras' myth in the *Protagoras* are declared to be symbols, while the *Timaeus* and the *Politicus* are identified as using icons in many places. The passage fortunately reinforces rather than contradicts my position, but I should not have overlooked it (I am grateful to Prof. Werner Beierwaltes for having pointed it out to me at the time), and am glad to be able to draw attention to it now.

One paper I have included although I am only part-author of it, 'Philo and the Stoic Doctrine of *Eupatheiai*', since it involves a piece of detective work that I am rather pleased with (although, as will be seen, I had to modify my conclusions even before the paper was published). I am most grateful to my collaborator, the distinguished Armenian scholar Abraham Terian, for making the study possible in the first place (I was, and still, alas, am quite ignorant of Armenian), and for allowing me to republish it now.

I am most grateful to the various publishers and learned journals listed in the Table of Contents for permitting me to republish the essays first published under their imprint, and to the editor of this series, John Smedley, for his guidance and encouragement.

I have appended some Addenda and Corrigenda to the various essays, at the end of the volume. These are indicated by asterisks in the margin at the relevant places.

JOHN DILLON

Trinity College,
Dublin

ACKNOWLEDGEMENTS

Grateful acknowledgement for permission to reproduce the articles included in this volume is made to those responsible at the following journals, societies and publishers:
Hermathena, Trinity College, Dublin (I); SCM Press, London (II); *Dionysius* and the Dalhousie University Press, Halifax, Nova Scotia (III); *Itaca*, Societat Catalana d'Estudio Clàssics, Barcelona (IV); to the Editors for Johns Hopkins University Press, *American Journal of Philology*, North Carolina (V); *Phronesis*, Van Gorcum Publishers, Assen (VI, XVI, XXVI); to the Editor of *Ancient Philosophy*, Duquesne University, Pittsburgh (VII); SUNY Press, Albany (VIII); the Center for Hermeneutical Studies in Hellenistic and Modern Culture (IX); to the Editor *Studia Philonica* and Scholars Press, Atlanta (X); Oxford University Press, Oxford (XI, XV); E.J. Brill, Leiden (XII); Crossroad Publishing Company, New York (XIII); University of California Press, California (XIV); Routledge, London (XVII); Aschendorffsche Verlagsbuchhandlung, Münster (XVIII); the Editors *Hellenica et Judaica*, Editions Peeters, Leuven–Paris (XIX); Peter Lang Publishing, Inc., New York (XX); International Society for Neoplatonic Studies, Norfolk, Virginia (XXI, XXVIII); University of Notre Dame Press, Notre Dame (XXII); Edizioni dell'Ateneo, Rome (XXIII); University of Edinburgh Press, Edinburgh (XXIV); American Philological Association, New York (XXV); CNRS, Paris (XXVII).

PUBLISHER'S NOTE

The articles in this volume, as in all others in the Collected Studies Series, have not been given a new, continuous pagination. In order to avoid confusion, and to facilitate their use where these same studies have been referred to elsewhere, the original pagination has been maintained wherever possible.

Each article has been given a Roman number in order of appearance, as listed in the Contents. This number is repeated on each page and quoted in the index entries.

I

What happened to Plato's garden?

Investigations into the nature of the Platonic School in later antiq-uity[1] have led me to take a closer look at the nature of the School at an earlier period, back to and even including Plato's lifetime. I was stimulated initially to these investigations by the work of John Lynch, in his excellent book, *Aristotle's School*,[2] and, more recently, by that of John Glucker, in *Antiochus and the late Academy*,[3] both of whom have shed much light on the true state of affairs in the early Academy. There remain, however, some questions to be cleared up. I am not confident of solving these questions on this occasion, but a determined teasing out of the wretchedly inadequate evidence that we have may be made to yield some further results.

The (largely unexamined) consensus of past scholarship has been that Plato returned from his first visit to Sicily in 386 and 'founded the Academy'. If this statement is carefully qualified and its sphere of reference delimited, it may be accepted, but the picture which it generally conjures up is, I think, delusive. There are three passages in Diogenes Laertius' *Life* of Plato and one from Aelian's *Varia historia*, which are worth looking at in this context, and I will examine them in turn.

The first two, in the form in which Diogenes presents them, are irrelevant, but, on close examination, they can be made to yield some useful evidence. First, *D. L.* III. 5: 'At first he (Plato) used to study philosophy in the Academy, and afterwards in the garden near Colonus, as Alexander states in his *Successions of philosophers*, according to the doctrine of Heracleitus.'

This ostensibly in Diogenes' narrative refers to a time before Plato has fallen under the influence of Socrates, and so before his twentieth year, or 407 B.C. It would thus have nothing to do with any founding of the Academy. This would be the time when, as Aristotle tells us (*Met.* A 6, 987a32), he was under the influence of the neo-Heraclitean Cratylus. But it has been suggested, with what I regard as great plausibility, that the central part of this sentence, '. . . in the Academy, and afterwards in the garden near Colonus', was inserted into his source by Diogenes, who is trying to be helpful, and, as so often, with disastrous results. The original report from Alexander would then have told us simply that Plato originally followed the philosophy of Heracleitus, a true statement. The central statement is also true, but misplaced. Detached from its context, it gives us valuable information about this *kēpos* of Plato's: it was *para ton Kolōnon*. We may note that the *kēpos* has the definite article; it is the well-known *kēpos* of Plato near Colonus.

The second passage is also overtly irrelevant, but still interesting. (*D.L.* III.7): 'Having returned to Athens' (from journeys to Megara, Cyrene, Italy and Egypt in the years immediately after the death of Socrates, i.e. the early 390s), 'he lived in the Academy, which is a gymnasium' (or 'place of exercise') 'outside the walls, in a grove, named after a certain hero, Hekademos . . .'[4] The public park and the exercise-place dedicated to the hero Hecademus had been a haunt of sophists and philosophers long before Plato's time, and in betaking himself there he was only following a pattern. Cratylus, indeed, may well have taught there. But this has nothing to do with founding an academy in the modern sense.

That belongs to a later stage of his life, which is described in our third passage (*D.L.* III. 18–20). This is the most circumstantial of our reports, and it alone is relevant as it stands. Diogenes takes it from the 2nd century A.D. sophist Favorinus of Arles' *Pantodapē historia*, or *Omnifarious history*, and it is connected with the extra-ordinary story of Plato's falling out with Dionysius I of Syracuse, his being given by Dionysius to the Spartan admiral Pollis, who happened to be on official business in Syracuse at the time, to be sold into slavery, and his being duly sold by Pollis in Aegina. The Aeginetans, it seems, who were at war with Athens, had actually vowed to put to death the first Athenian (or, more possibly, all Athenians) who set foot on their shores, but when they heard that Plato was a philosopher, they resolved to sell him instead. There happened to be in Aegina one Anniceris of Cyrene, who was on his way to Olympia to compete in the chariot race (this would place the incident, presumably, in early summer of 386). He bought Plato, and duly repatriated him to Athens.

This is the part of the story that really concerns us.[5] When Plato reached home, his friends held a collection to repay Anniceris the 20, or, some say, 30, minae he had expended on Plato, and conveyed it to him. Anniceris refused the money, saying gallantly that 'the Athenians were not the only people worthy of the privilege of providing for Plato'. (He is also reported to have said that freeing Plato was a greater honour than winning the chariot race at Olympia, which would indicate that he did so!) There is, it seems, however, an alternative story, according to which Dion of Syracuse, who had to some extent got Plato into this mess in the first place,

What happened to Plato's garden?

produced 30 minae to repay Anniceris, and this money Anniceris would not accept, 'but bought for Plato the little garden (*kēpidion*) which is in the Academy'. '*En Akademeiāi*', we may note, does not * have to mean 'in the public precinct of the Academy', but only' in the area of the Academy'. I do not see how Anniceris, or anyone else, could buy for Plato a piece of an Athenian public park. Anniceris was on his way to Olympia (though why he was going there by way of Aegina is not explained). However, we find a story in Aelian (*VH* 2. 27) and Lucian (*Demonax* 23) of Anniceris giving an exhibition of chariot-driving in the Academy, and the assumption that Anniceris visited Athens on his way home after the Games would make more credible the second version of the end of the story, that Dion sent the repayment of the ransom-money to Anniceris, who declined it, and used it to buy Plato the *kēpidion*. The whole thing still has an uncomfortably anecdotal ring about it, but one cannot positively assert that such a sequence of events could not happen. At least I think we may accept that a property was purchased for 20, or more probably 30, minae, and made over to Plato and his companions.

Another anecdote of considerable significance, it seems to me, is relayed to us by Aelian (*VH* 3.19)—it casts light on the relationship between this *kēpos* and Plato's stamping-ground in the public park: 'Once, when Xenocrates went off on a visit to his homeland (i.e. Chalcedon) Aristotle set upon Plato, surrounding himself with a gang of his own partisans, including Mnason of Phocis and people like that. Speusippus at that time was ill, and for this reason was unable to stand by Plato. Plato was by now eighty years of age and at the same time, because of his age, was to some extent losing his memory. So Aristotle devised a plot and set an ambush for him, and began to put questions to him very aggressively and in a way 'elenctically', and was plainly behaving unjustly and unfeelingly. For this reason, Plato left the concourse outside (*tou exō peripatou*), and walked about inside with his companions (*endon ebadize sun tois hetairois*).'

After an interval of three months, Xenocrates arrived back from abroad and came upon Aristotle perambulating where he had left Plato. When he observed that he with his cronies did not go back to Plato's (*ou pros Platona anachōrounta*) from the *peripatos*, but was going off to his own place in the city, he asked one of those who had been in the *peripatos* where Plato was, for he suspected that he was not well. The other replied, 'He is not ill, but Aristotle has been giving him a bad time, and has forced him to retire from the *peripatos*, so he has retired and is philosophising in his own garden (*en tōi kēpoi tōi heautou*).

The rest of the story concerns us less. Xenocrates scolds Speusippus, gathers the loyal forces, and reinstates Plato in his usual haunts, (*apodounai to sunēthes chōrion tōi Platōni*). This story is no doubt biased, gossipy and tendentious, but it is unreasonable, I think, of its latest commentator to dismiss it as spurious, as being 'unworthy of the little we know about Plato and Aristotle'.[6] It sounds very like a Hellenistic gossip-monger's anti-Aristotelian distortion of an actual incident, and the circumstantial detail it provides is most valuable, since it plainly emanates from someone, such as Antigonus of Carystus, who was familiar with the conditions under which the 'Academy' operated. It is these details, not the story itself, that must concern us. Note first that the only two entities concerned are the *peripatos* and Plato's own *kēpos*. I have refrained from translating *peripatos*, as I am wary of giving it the wrong connotation. It could be a formal 'walk', even with colonnades, or it could be just a part of the Academy where the group normally walked. Either way, that is plainly where Plato's normal activity is centred. When discomfited there, he leaves the Academy altogether and returns to his *kēpos*. Then in the story, Xenocrates comes first to the *peripatos*, not to Plato's house, and Aristotle, at the end of the day, is heading back into town to go home (*kath' heauton eis tēn polin*) instead of calling in on Plato on the way and perhaps staying for a *syssition* or a *symposion*. Xenocrates is surprised, not that he should be going home, but that he should do so without calling in first to the *kēpos*. But plainly neither Xenocrates nor Aristotle *lives* there. This anecdote, then, seems to me to reveal, artlessly and incidentally, the true state of affairs obtaining in Plato's 'Academy' and properly evaluated, should serve to dissipate much windy speculation on its physical aspect.

What, then, are we to imagine this *kēpos* to have consisted of? Is it to be thought of as what later ages spoke of as Plato's Academy? This is a question that I find to be systematically ignored by the authorities who describe to us the workings of the Academy. A *kēpos* is not necessarily just a garden. Epicurus' *kēpos*, after all, included a suburban villa of considerable proportions as well as a garden, enough to hold a community. We could, therefore, imagine living-quarters for Plato himself and at least a few companions, with room, also, for an ever-growing library; but as I shall explain presently, I doubt that there was even that.

What happened to Plato's garden?

It is not my concern to speculate yet again on the system of study and other activities pursued in the Academy; I am concerned simply with the nature and fate of the physical plant; but I will give an example—a reasonably sober and well-informed one, indeed—of the sort of systematic ambiguity that surrounds talk of the Academy. Here is W.K.C. Guthrie, in Vol. IV of his *History of Greek philosophy* (pp. 19–20):

> The Academy of Plato does not correspond entirely to any modern institution, certainly not a university of modern foundation. The nearest parallels are probably our ancient universities, or rather their colleges, with the characteristics that they have inherited from the medieval world, particularly their religious connexions and the ideal of the common life, especially a common table . . . . The institution takes its name from its site, nearly a mile outside the walls of Athens, supposedly sacred to a hero Academus or Hecademus, and including a grove of trees, gardens, a gymnasium and other buildings. The sanctity of the place was great, and other cults, including that of Athena herself, were carried on there.

Already, I think we are getting into trouble. Guthrie knows perfectly well the story of the purchase of the garden, but in speaking of the 'site', he carries on here as if the garden and the Academy were the same thing. He goes on:

> To form a society owning its own land and premises, as Plato did, it appears to have been a legal requirement that it be registered as a *thiasos*, that is, a cult-association dedicated to the service of some divinity, who would be the nominal owner of the property. Plato's choice was the Muses, patrons of education , not so much, perhaps, because he believed that 'philosophy was the highest "music"' (Phaedo 61A), as because a Mouseion or chapel of the Muses was a regular feature of the schools of the day.

He goes on to mention the attested common meals or *syssitia*, famous for their moderation and philosophic quality. Things now seem to me, however, to be thoroughly mixed up. John Lynch has effectively disposed of what was simply Wilamowitz's assumption that the Academy must have been a thiasos dedicated to the service of the Muses.[7] The evidence does not support this at all. What we know is that Plato dedicated a shrine to the Muses in the Academy grove, and that his successor Speusippus added to it statues of the Graces (*D.L.* IV. 1). This shrine may indeed have provided a focal point for the group's perambulations in the Academy grove, but it does not require the postulation of a *thiasos*; it is more the staking of

55

a claim, in so far as that is possible on public ground. As for the *syssitia*, they would have been held in the *kēpos* or in some other suburban villa nearby, as no doubt was a fair amount of the activity of the group. It is plain, however, that a certain proportion of the day was spent in the park, either in an alcove in the gymnasium, or walking about among the trees (the *peripatos*), in full view of the public. We have enough contemporary evidence from comic poets, Epicrates and Alexis, for example, to attest this.

We have, then, two separate entities, both important to the life of the school, the *kēpos* and the public park, with its gymnasium and walks. The problem that now arises is, what ultimately happened to this *kēpos*, and what entity is it that in later times came to be known as 'Plato's Academy'?

If this garden was presented to Plato by Dion or Anniceris, then, one would think, it should appear in some form in Plato's will, of which Diogenes preserves what seems to be the complete text.[8] There are two estates mentioned in this will, the estate in Iphistiadae and the estate in Eiresidae, and neither of them sounds unequivocally like the *kēpos para ton Kolōnon*. They are both given a careful legal description, in terms of the estates or landmarks bordering upon them, and neither of them is described as bordering either upon the Academy or upon Colonus. Nor is there any mention, as there is in the wills of the scholarchs of the Lyceum later, of any school property or books. The estate at Iphistiadae is left to Adeimantus, who is either a nephew or a grandnephew—perhaps a son of Plato's half-brother Glaucon, or a grandson of Adeimantus—with the provision that it is not to be sold or alienated. What is to happen to the other estate is not said, but this one at least is bounded on the west by the river Cephisus, which puts it in the approximate vicinity of Colonus and the Academy. On the other hand, Plato declares that he bought this estate off one Callimachus, so that it cannot be the one that Anniceris bought for him, unless, of course, he is choosing to draw a veil over how he came to buy it. I dwell upon this, because John Glucker, in his recent study of the later Academy, plumps for this second estate as necessarily being the *kēpos*, though he admits that the bequest is in that case phrased rather perversely. He blames this on the exigencies of the Athenian law of succession and wills. I find this difficult to swallow.

An alternative has been proposed: Plato's will contains no reference to the school, because he bequeathed the estate near the Academy to the School already in his lifetime. This rather desperate

What happened to Plato's garden?

proposal runs up against certain awkward pieces of evidence from the period after Plato's death, to which I wish now to return.

First of all, where did Speusippus live? He was one of the executors—with six others, admittedly,—of Plato's will, and may have been able to take possession of the estate at Eiresidae, but he is strangely not mentioned in a passage of Plutarch (*De exilio* 10), which talks of Xenocrates and Polemon living in Plato's house after him, and indeed very rarely leaving it. Now we know from Plutarch's *Dion* (17), that Dion, during his period in Athens, purchased a country estate (*agros*), 'for his leisure moments', and when he went out later on his expedition to Sicily (in 357), he bequeathed this estate to Speusippus. Presumably in view of Dion's interests, such an estate would not be too far from the Academy or Plato's *kēpos*, so we may assume I think, that Speusippus was able to base himself there.

There is on the other hand a story in Diogenes Laertius (IV. 3) which presents Speusippus as being driven to the Academy in a small carriage, because of his arthritis, and meeting Diogenes the Cynic on the way. To do this, one would naturally suppose that he came from the direction of the city, not the Cephisus, since Diogenes was very much of a city person. This is mildly troublesome, but one cannot hang much on such an insubstantial anecdote.

Xenocrates is reported by Diogenes (IV. 6–7) to have spent the great part of his time *en Akademiāi*, which, once again, need mean only, 'in the area of the Academy', the point being made that he hardly ever came into town. On the other hand, there is an anecdote involving the notorious courtesan Phryne, who tried to make his acquaintance, and, pretending she was being chased by some people, took refuge in his *oikidion*, 'his little house'. He admitted her, and since there was only one couch (*klinidion*), he permitted her to share it with him, but she totally failed to seduce him. The story, whether we believe it or not, implies an acceptance that Xenocrates lived in something like a one-room cottage—not, one would think, proper lodgings for the Scholarch of the Academy. This seems rather to undermine Plutarch's remark.

Again, Xenocrates' successor Polemon, according to his near-contemporary Antigonus of Carystus (*ap. D.L.* IV. 22), who should have known, lived, along with his colleagues Crates, in the house of one Lysicles, while Arcesilaus and Crantor, two other colleagues, shared a house, presumably all in the vicinity of the Academy, but no one, apparently, living in Plato's *kēpos* or house. We hear also of Polemon's students (*D.L.* IV. 19) who, since he never went abroad but spent all his time *en tōi kēpōi,* 'in the Garden', made themselves little huts nearby, and lived not far from the shrine to the Muses (*mouseion*) and the *exedra*—that is, the alcove or arcade in the gymnasium where Polemon was accustomed to lecture.

All this is most troublesome. The garden pops up again, though it is not quite clear whose garden. Polemon 'spends his time' (*diatribei*) there, but he did not exactly live there, but rather in the house of Lysicles. And his students encamped somewhere, not far from various landmarks in the public park. We are invited to assume that they camped either in the Academy or in the *kēpos.* I am not familiar with the regulations about overnight camping in Athenian public parks in the 3rd century B.C. Perhaps philosophic squatters were tolerated, as long as they cleaned up after them. At any rate, though there is a mention of a garden, even of *the* garden, there is no sign of living accommodation, even for members of the faculty.

Lastly, a peculiar remark about Arcesilaus, again from Diogenes (IV. 32): 'he would seem to have held Plato in admiration, and had obtained a set of his works' (or 'had acquired his books'—*ta biblia autou ekektēto*). Either way, a curious thing for the Head of the Platonic Academy to have to do. Arcesilaus, we may note, left all his property in his will to his brother Pylades (*D.L.* IV. 43)—no mention of any school property, or of anything left to the school.

I am driven to draw some rather radical conclusions from all this confusion. It seems to me that the confusion actually dissolves to some extent if one abandons certain presuppositions which were never supported by evidence anyway. One solution is to assume that the Platonic Academy in the accepted modern sense is a non-entity, that the Academy is more a state of mind than a place. Let us assume that there was this garden, purchased by Anniceris and/or Dion for the use of Plato and his associates, but not exactly belonging to Plato, or to anyone in particular—I do not think that in Classical Athens we have to postulate formal ownership by a corporation or *thiasos,* whatever about the situation in the Roman Empire. It sounds as if this garden, unlike Epicurus', was just a garden, although students of scholarchs could erect huts in it if they wished, but most scholarchs lived in their own houses, or in houses lent to them, in the vicinity of the Academy. The main philosophic activity of the school took place in the grounds of the Academy. There was sand in the gymnasium on which to do geometry or geography, and shady walks and groves in which to pursue ethical or metaphysical questions. Communal meals could be held in the

What happened to Plato's garden?

garden, or more probably at the house of the scholarch—in Plato's case, probably in his house at Eiresidae, which must have been in easy walking distance of the Academy. What held the institution together was a shared tradition and a permanent base in the Academy park. As for the garden, it remained at least till Cicero's time. At the beginning of *De finibus* V, he makes Piso stand in the Academy and point to it not far off—*illi propinqui hortuli*—but by that time the Academy as a tradition had moved elsewhere, into the centre of town, and the Academy groves were deserted by philosophers.

I cannot claim to have solved all the problems connected with Plato's Garden—the available evidence does not, I think, permit this—but I think that my minimalist proposals clear the air a little. If we are left without an imposing portico on which to inscribe the motto MĒDEIS AGEOMETRĒTOS EISITŌ, then that just has to be one of the casualties. We can inscribe it on our hearts.

Notes

1. 'The Academy in the Middle Platonic period', *Dionysius* III (1979), 63–77. I am indebted to the useful collection of all the relevant passages by Alice Swift Riginos, *Platonica: The anecdotes concerning the life and writings of Plato* (Leiden, 1976).

2. John Lynch, *Aristotle's School* (Berkeley and London, 1972).

3. *Hypomnemata*, Heft 56 (Göttingen, 1978).

4. This is followed by a quotation from Timon the Sillographer (Fr. 30D) showing that Plato operated in the Academy grove.

5. All the relevant passages are gathered in Riginos, *Platonica*, ch. 8.

6. Leonardo Taran, *Speusippos of Athens* (Brill, Leiden, 1981), 221.

7. Cf. *Aristotle's School*, 108–127.

8. DL. III. 41–2.

9. *Antiochus and the late Academy*, 229–233.

II

Self-Definition in Later Platonism

Self-definition by contrast to other groups

A terminological problem must be faced at the outset of this paper: self-definition in relation to what? An individual or an organization must define itself in relation to whatever stands over against it as 'other' at any given stage of its existence. During its long history, Platonism had to define itself in relation to various opponents, and I shall try to discuss all of them adequately, ending with Christianity, its last and most formidable adversary.

From the beginning of the Platonic School, as soon as a rival establishment was set up by Aristotle in the Lyceum, Platonists were under the necessity of defending themselves by defining themselves. Under the pressure of well-aimed attacks from Aristotle, himself a Platonist, Plato's successors Speusippus and Xenocrates had to hammer out a dogmatic system from the plethora of interesting suggestions and baffling puzzles which Plato had bequeathed to them. Responding to this challenge, Xenocrates in particular, through a large corpus of treatises on almost every area of philosophy (all of which are lost), became the true founder of Platonism as a system. Questions such as the nature of God, the Forms and their relation to the physical world, or the definition and role of Pleasure and Happiness, receive definitive treatment from Xenocrates, mainly in response to polemical assaults from Aristotle.

In the process of polemical self-definition, a notable phenomenon is the extent to which one finds oneself borrowing concepts and formulations from one's opponents. There is nothing very surprising about this process, which is just as much a feature of modern, as it was of ancient, ideological conflict. One's opponent, ruffian and charlatan though he may be, almost invariably scores a point or two in the controversy which one is forced to counter.

Self-Definition in Later Platonism

Aristotle scored a good many. The result for Platonism was that, although Aristotle himself remained beyond the pale, Aristotelian logic quickly superseded *diaeresis*, the Aristotelian doctrine of the mean became a basic feature of ethical theory, and God came to be accepted as a mind thinking itself, its contents being the Forms. A host of technical terms and concepts were taken on as well, 'matter', 'potential/actual', the four causes, the categories. It might be argued – and it was argued, vigorously, in later times – that most of these doctrines and formulations were not original to Aristotle, but arose in the Academy before he broke with it. There may be some truth in this. Later tradition (which we can see at work, for instance, in Albinus's *Didaskalikos*) managed to identify traces of these doctrines at one point or another in the dialogues (most varieties of syllogism in the *Parmenides*, all the Categories in *Timaeus* 37AB – this from Plutarch, *An. proc.* 23, *Mor.* 1023E), but the adoption of these concepts into the Academy, in their fully-fledged form, is, I would maintain, the direct result of inter-school polemic.

In the course of the next century or so, from Arcesilaus's accession to the headship of the school in about 270 BCE to the death of Philo of Larissa in the 80s, Platonism ceased to be on the defensive, and, sheltering behind a cloud of scepticism, went onto the attack. Their chief enemy, or rather victim, in this period was the Stoic school, and their dogmatism in the area of epistemology. While not necessarily abandoning the conceptual baggage which it had inherited from the Old Academy and Peripatos, the Academy concentrated its efforts on undermining Stoic claims to certainty, and the ethical and physical superstructure based on this. For the majority of the Hellenistic age, 'Academic' meant sceptical, and this terminology persisted in later times, *Akadēmaikos* remaining distinct from *Platonikos*, as an epithet of members of the New Academy[1]. The advocacy of *epochē*, 'suspension of assent', and of *to pithanon*, 'the plausible', as a standard of conduct, became the hallmarks of a Platonist during this period, and left their mark later on Platonists such as Plutarch.

Identity crises and self-definition

At the turn of the first century BCE, however, there began a development away from scepticism, under the scholarchate of Philo of Larissa, which culminated in a return to dogmatism and the assimilation of much Stoic doctrine. This came to a head in the

80s, with Philo's dissident pupil, Antiochus of Ascalon, who broke away from the sceptical tradition to found what he defiantly termed 'the Old Academy', thus putting the intellectual world on notice that he was restoring the 'true' teachings of Plato and his immediate successors. This development brought on something of an identity crisis in the Platonic tradition, the reverberations of which continued for centuries, in the form of a running argument as to whether the New Academics were truly part of the Platonic tradition, and it is at this point that we may begin a closer examination of the process of self-definition.

What exactly the new position in epistemology taken up by Philo was is a matter of controversy, on which much light has been thrown recently by the exhaustive investigations of John Glucker.[2] Philo appears to have accepted the Stoic claim that things are knowable in themselves (*enargeia*), while rejecting the Stoic claim about certainty, that the mind can perceive impressions which are such as could only come from the object in question (*katalēpsis*).[3] Fortunately, the only aspect of his innovation which really concerns us here is the consequences it had for the self-image of the Academy. For it is with Philo, and his pupil Antiochus, that the controversy about the unity of the Academic tradition first arises, a controversy that was to remain active for the next few hundred years.

The New Academy, despite its sceptical stance, seems to have had no problem about claiming Platonic ancestry for itself. Arcesilaus, we learn from Diogenes Laertius, 'seems to have held Plato in admiration, and possessed his works' (4.32). However, it stressed, inevitably, the Socratic and aporetic element in Plato's works. Whether or not Arcesilaus or Carneades accepted the Theory of Ideas in any form is not clear, but as regards the possibility of certainty on the basis of sense-perception, which was what the Stoics were claiming, they could claim Plato as a sceptic, even in such a work as the *Theaetetus*.[4] When Philo veered back towards dogmatism, he was faced with a problem. If Plato was a dogmatist, as a reading of, say, the *Phaedo*, *Republic* or *Timaeus* would tend to suggest, did the sceptical Academy then constitute a deviation from true Platonism?

This was the second considerable crisis of self-definition in the Platonic school after the initial confrontation with Aristotle and Theophrastus. (Arcesilaus does not seem to have gone through a comparable crisis on taking over from Polemon and Crates, though his description of these distinguished predecessors as

Self-Definition in Later Platonism

'sort of gods, or left-overs from the Golden Race' may in fact conceal a measure of irony, such as would naturally escape Diogenes Laertius [4.22]). Philo tried to solve the crisis (perhaps in response to prodding by his Roman patrons, after his retreat to Rome in face of Mithridates in 89 BCE) by composing a treatise in which he argued that neither Plato nor the New Academics were thoroughgoing sceptics. He may simply have wished to claim that the principle of probability (or better, 'plausibility') involved no more than a relative scepticism (denying only the Stoic criterion) which was compatible with Platonic doctrine, but it is possible that he went further. Augustine, in his *Contra Academicos* (3.20.43), reports a statement of Cicero's in his *Academica* to the effect that the New Academy 'had a habit of concealing their opinions, and did not usually disclose them to anyone except those that had lived with them right up to old age'.[5] If Cicero got this notion from anyone, the only man one can imagine him getting it from is Philo – certainly not from Antiochus, who would have no interest in making such a claim – but if Philo said such a thing, what did he mean? Not necessarily, I think, that the New Academy preserved a whole system of dogmatic Platonism which they only revealed to trusted initiates; he need have meant no more than that in public Arcesilaus or Carneades would maintain total scepticism, simply posing difficulties for the Stoics, but in private they were prepared to express views on how to live to their permanent pupils. This would relate, perhaps, to the dispute that seems to have arisen in the school about Carneades's personal beliefs in the generation after his death, Clitomachus (his most authoritative exegete) maintaining that he had never been able to discern what the Master really believed about anything, whereas Metrodorus and Philo claimed that Carneades had held that the Wise Man would form opinions on the basis of *pithanotēs*.[6]

At any rate, Philo was concerned to maintain the unity of the Academic tradition. This aroused the indignation of Antiochus, who in these same years (the late 90s and early 80s) seems to have been provoked by Philo's rather vacillating stance in epistemology to a wholehearted acceptance of the Stoic theory of knowledge, and with it to a quite different view of the development of Platonic doctrine. Cicero makes Lucullus (*Luc.* 11) give a vivid description of a session in Alexandria in the winter of 87–6 BCE, in which Antiochus gives a heated refutation of Philo's position, which he is presented now as hearing for the first time. This circumstance is best explained, as Glucker has persuasively argued,[7] if we take it that Antiochus had not followed Philo to Rome in 89, but had stayed on somewhere in Greece, until picked up by Lucullus, who wanted him for diplomatic missions, in 87. This scene is probably taken by Cicero from a prefatory section of a treatise in dialogue form, the *Sosus*, which Antiochus is reported to have composed in refutation of Philo's position, dedicating it, significantly, to a Stoic philosopher of that name from Antiochus's home town of Ascalon.

Antiochus in this work makes a clear break between the Old Academy down to Polemon, and the New, from Arcesilaus to Philo, condemning the latter as being untrue to the position of Plato. This is a significant development, but he does more. First, he declares that there is no essential difference between the Old Academy and the Peripatos; they are both equally parts of the great tradition. This is fully expounded by Varro, Antiochus's 'mouthpiece', in Cicero's *Acad. post.* 15ff., and more succinctly at *Fin.* 5.7, where Piso, the spokesman of Antiochus, speaks of

> the Old Academy, which includes, as you hear Antiochus declare, not only those who bear the name of Academics, Speusippus, Xenocrates, Polemon, Crantor and the rest, but also the early Peripatetics, headed by their chief, Aristotle, who, if Plato be excepted, I almost think deserves to be called the prince of philosophers.[8]

This unity was that much easier to maintain before the rediscovery of Aristotle's esoteric works, which only saw the light (whether or not they had in fact been immured in a cellar in Scepsis) in Andronicus's edition somewhat later in the century,[9] but even so it must seem to us to gloss over a good deal. On the theory of ideas, after all, Aristotle had been pretty severe even in his exoteric works, such as the *Peri Ideōn*. Antiochus will presumably have taken such criticisms to refer only to early versions of the theory, or to perversions of it.

On the other hand, Antiochus sought to bring the Stoics into his new synthesis. For him, Stoicism was essentially an updated Platonism. Only in certain respects (such as making virtue alone sufficient for happiness, for example) did Zeno deviate from the Old Academy and these details can easily be isolated and corrected. At *Fin.* 4.3, Cicero says, speaking in his own person to the Stoic Cato:

> My view, then, Cato, is this, that those old disciples of Plato, Speusippus, Aristotle and Xenocrates, and afterwards their pupils Polemon and Theophrastus, had developed a body of doctrine that left nothing to be desired either in fullness or finish, so that Zeno, on becoming a

pupil of Polemon, had no reason for differing either from his master himself or from his master's predecessors.[10]

Antiochus thus staked out his base, pleasing nobody but himself (certainly not either Stoics or Sceptics), but defining a position for the Platonist school from which it did not deviate radically for the rest of antiquity. For the next few hundred years, Platonism moves between the opposing poles of Aristotelianism and Stoicism, different Platonists taking up different positions on the spectrum in accord with their personal predilections and the exigencies of inter-school warfare.

Almost immediately after Antiochus's synthesis, however, Platonism was forced to re-define itself to some extent. The rediscovery of Aristotle's esoteric works already alluded to, and Aristonicus's edition of them and commentaries upon some of them, led to defections from the school of Antiochus in the direction of Aristotelianism. Antiochus's pupil Cratippus appears in the 40s teaching in Athens as an Aristotelian, but he is a fairly harmless figure. More significant was Antiochus's pupil in Alexandria, Ariston, who wrote commentaries on the *Categories* and probably on the *Prior Analytics*, contributing a certain amount to the later development of Aristotelian logic.[11] It is probably in reaction to his activity that the Alexandrian Platonist Eudorus (who was probably not a pupil of Antiochus, but quite possibly of his pupil Dion),[12] in the 20s gave Platonism a distinct anti-Aristotelian turn, by initiating a series of polemical commentaries on the *Categories* which continued down to Plotinus (in *Enn.* 6.1–3). He also criticized Peripatetic ethical theory (and implicitly that of Antiochus) from a Stoic perspective.[13]

The other important contribution of Eudorus to the self-definition of Platonism was the revival of the Pythagoreanism which had been fostered by the Old Academy (or at least by Speusippus and Xenocrates). Making use of a host of Pythagorean pseudepigrapha which had sprung up, in mysterious circumstances, in the third and second centuries BCE,[14] Eudorus reintroduced a transcendental element into Platonism, rejecting Stoic materialism in physics, which Antiochus had admitted into the tradition. Eudorus's first principle is a One above a pair of Monad and Dyad, a thoroughly immaterial, not to say ineffable, entity.[15] With Eudorus, indeed, we begin to find that constellation of doctrines which are generally thought of as Middle Platonist – such characteristics as a belief in the transcendence and immateriality of

God, and the existence of immaterial substance in general, as well as a vivid interest in mathematics, and in particular in mystical numerology; and, in ethics, an ascetic, world-negating tendency, which takes 'likeness to God' as its slogan rather than the Stoic 'conformity with Nature', adopted by Antiochus. All these characteristics we see reflected in such a figure as the Jewish thinker Philo of Alexandria, who, while not himself to be reckoned as a member of the Platonist *hairesis*, certainly reflects to a large extent the state of contemporary Platonism.

Self-definition without institutional supports

Mention of a Platonist *hairesis*, or 'school', raises an important question in connection with Platonist self-definition in this period. It is relatively easy to define oneself if one has an institution to relate to, with all the physical plant, communal memory, and accreditation system that that might be taken to involve. Until recently, it was almost universally assumed, on the basis of the exhaustive researches of Carl Gottlob Zumpt (1792–1849), issuing in his study of 1844, entitled *Über den Bestand der philosophischen Schulen in Athen und die Succession der Scholarchen*,[16] that the Platonic Academy survived, albeit in great obscurity for much of the time, all through antiquity, until it was finally closed by Justinian in 529 CE. The excellent study of John Lynch, in the course of his book *Aristotle's School*,[17] and now the magisterial work of John Glucker,[18] have finally, I think, disposed of that comfortable illusion, and have revealed something much more interesting, a tradition maintaining itself unofficially, by word of mouth, without official certification, but yet preserving, in the process of transmission from master to pupil, a communal memory and consciousness. What one finds, in fact, is a series of individual schools, sometimes being handed on from a founder to his successor, as was the case with Antiochus, Gaius (to Albinus), or Plotinus (to Porphyry), but sometimes apparently going no further than their founder, as seems to be the case with the schools of Plutarch's mentor Ammonius, or Aulus Gellius's teacher Taurus. All these men, however, knew that they were Platonists. They knew where they came from, and had some sense, at least, of belonging to a 'golden chain' of philosophers (though this actual expression may only date from Neoplatonic times). Unlike the Epicureans (or the Christians), but like the Stoics, they imposed no rigid requirements for orthodoxy, though a belief in the transcendence of God,

Self-Definition in Later Platonism

the theory of ideas, and the immortality of the soul is certainly a distinguishing mark of Platonists of this period. On the other hand, on such questions as the temporal creation of the world, the self-sufficiency of virtue, or the best system of logic, a wide measure of latitude was permissible, even though a man like Atticus, in a polemical mood, might castigate fellow-Platonists for being soft on Aristotelianism,[19] and Plutarch condemn his predecessors for their misunderstanding of Plato on the question of the creation of the world.[20]

Indeed, a running polemical battle was kept up throughout this period with the other schools, in which the Christians, as we shall see, were presently granted the compliment of being included. Eudorus, as I have noted, attacked Aristotle's *Categories*, and in this he was followed by the shadowy figures Lucius and Nicostratus (first to second centuries CE), by Atticus, and by Plotinus. Plutarch was friendly to Peripateticism, but aimed a number of polemical treatises at the Stoics (*SR*, *CN*) and at the Epicureans (*Non posse*, *Adv. Col.*, *Lat. viv.*). Taurus wrote against the Stoics (Aulus Gellius, *NA* 12.5), and Atticus, as mentioned above, violently attacked the Peripatetics. All this activity, which is generally conducted on a disedifyingly low level, has the purpose rather of 'self-definition' (and the collection and preservation of pupils) than the disinterested search for the truth. It certainly did not prevent Platonists from borrowing terminology freely from both Peripatos and Stoa, presumably on the grounds that all this was common philosophical currency.

While on the subject of inter-school rivalry, it is necessary to raise again a topic which I discussed earlier, in connection with the quarrel between Antiochus and Philo, namely the unity of the Platonic tradition. This question was not finally settled by Antiochus's disowning of the New Academy. A nostalgia for the sceptical tradition of the Academy still lingered in certain Platonist breasts, notably in that of Plutarch, who wrote a work (now lost) *On the Unity of the Academy since Plato* (Lamprias Cat. no. 63), which perhaps recapitulated the arguments of Philo of Larissa, and the sophist Favorinus of Arles, who affected a New Academic stance when dealing with philosophical questions.[21] Plutarch found the arguments of Carneades and Clitomachus of great assistance in attacking the Stoics, but in his positive doctrine Plutarch was no sceptic. We do not even know the grounds on which he maintained the unity of the Academy. Very possibly he subscribed to the notion that from Arcesilaus to Carneades the positive doctrines of Plato were preserved as an esoteric teaching.

A diametrically opposed attitude to the New Academy was taken up somewhat later, in the mid-second century, by Numenius of Apamea, a Syrian Platonist of extreme Pythagoreanizing tendencies, who wrote an entertainingly satirical work, of which Eusebius has preserved large extracts,[22] entitled *On the Divergence of the Academics from Plato,* in which he traces what he sees as their defection from Arcesilaus down to Philo of Larissa, ending with some unkind words on Antiochus for his Stoicizing innovations. Numenius does not make it clear who pleases him, but since he affected, as I have said, a Pythagorean stance, he may have felt that the true faith was preserved by a Pythagoreanizing underground during the Hellenistic age, which emerged into the light with Eudorus. He also wrote a book entitled *On the Secret Doctrines of Plato,* which may have expressed such views, though the surviving fragment of it[23] is unhelpful.

Plainly the debate about the unity of the Academy, and the true line of succession to Plato, was still a lively one in the second century CE. Efforts to assert unity were also helped by the elaboration of a belief which I have noted above as going back in at least some form to Philo of Larissa, that even the Sceptical Academy had only used scepticism as a weapon against the Stoics, and had preserved the full array of Plato's doctrines as a secret 'mystery' to be imparted to the faithful behind closed doors. Numenius actually knows of, and rejects, this theory, which he attributes to one Diocles of Cnidus, of unknown date,[24] and Sextus Empiricus reports in more detail (perhaps using the same source) about Arcesilaus that:

> he appeared at first glance, they say, to be a Pyrrhonean, but in reality he was a dogmatist; and because he used to test his companions by means of dubitation to see if they were fitted by nature for the reception of the Platonic doctrines, he was thought to be an aporetic philosopher, but he actually passed on to such of his companions as were naturally gifted the dogmas of Plato.[25]

Whatever the accuracy of this belief, it grew in the next centuries to be an accepted truth, reaching Augustine as something generally agreed. The Neoplatonists actually show no interest in the sceptical Academy as such, and the question of unity may have been settled for them definitively by Porphyry in a lost portion of his comprehensive History of Philosophy. A distinction was always made in later times, however, between 'Academics' and

Self-Definition in Later Platonism

'Platonists', the former title referring to the members of the sceptical Academy, the latter to Platonic philosophers of the second century CE and later. Numenius utilizes this distinction (in the work above-mentioned); so do Plutarch (despite his beliefs about the unity of the movement),[26] Lucian,[27] and Aulus Gellius.[28] But the blurring of the self-image of Platonists consequent on the acceptance or rejection of Academic scepticism as part of the tradition ceased in the Neoplatonic era. The only contrast Proclus makes in his commentaries (particularly that on the *Timaeus*, where he is assiduous about quoting previous authorities) is between pre-Plotinian and post-Plotinian Platonists, the former being termed simply *hoi archaioi*, as opposed to *hoi neōteroi hoi apo Plotinou Platōnikoi* (*In Tim.* 2.88. 10–12).

Confrontation with Christianity

By the time we come to the confrontation with Christianity, then, the Platonist tradition knows, if not precisely where it stands, where it might retreat to. This self-consciousness it achieved, as has now been made plain, without the fixed repository of orthodoxy which would be constituted by a physical Academy and a regular succession of scholarchs. What held Platonists together was simply a shared tradition, even a shared mythology. By the third century CE, in addition, they were in the position of being virtually the sole repositories of Hellenic philosophy and culture. The last notable Peripatetic was Alexander of Aphrodisias, at the end of the second century (unless Themistius be counted one, in the fourth century), and the Stoic and Epicurean schools became stagnant at about the same time (though presumably the professorships of the four *haireseis* set up in Athens by Marcus Aurelius in 176 CE continued to function). The Platonists, therefore, from Plotinus and Porphyry on, through Iamblichus (and his devoted admirer, the Emperor Julian) to Proclus in the fifth century and Simplicius and Damascius in the sixth, become the bulwark of defence against the growing challenge of Christianity, 'this delusion that is rushing upon men', as Plotinus terms it in *Ennead* 2.9.6.

The first shots were fired before the end of the second century, by the Platonist Celsus. Unfortunately, even to Origen, who replied to his attack somewhat less than a century later, Celsus's identity was quite obscure. We are at least clear that he is not the Epicurean with whom Origen identified him, but whether he was

69

a Platonist philosopher, or simply a Platonizing sophist, of the type of Maximus of Tyre, is not obvious. His Platonism has affinities with that of Albinus (if the *Didaskalikos* is indeed by him, and not by one Alcinous), but remains on a rather general level. At all events, he understands the conventions of inter-school polemic, and he uses them to good effect on the Christians. In the process, he sounds two notes of particular significance, one of which is echoed by his contemporary Galen, in various passing remarks, and both of which are taken up in the next century by Plotinus (with particular reference to Gnostics) and by Porphyry, in his great treatise *Against the Christians*. These are the charges of anti-intellectualism and irrationality, and of disrespect for tradition. By contrast, Platonism is represented as the supreme defender of Hellenic rationality and the antiquity of Hellenic (and other) wisdom.

To begin with anti-intellectualism, and the blind acceptance of authority: Platonists recognized that this was not peculiar to Christians. Pythagoreans, after all, had long been satirized for their submission to the *autos epha* of Pythagoras. But the characteristic of a philosopher, or even of a rational man (*logikos*), was felt to be the ability to give a *logos* of what he believed. Acceptance of authority as such was not the issue – no Platonist, after all, disputed the correctness of Plato's views; it is rather the disdain of any *logos* in one's beliefs that was offensive. To quote Origen (*Contra Celsum* 1.9):

> After this he [Celsus] urges us to 'follow reason and a rational guide in accepting doctrines', on the ground that 'anyone who believes people without so doing is certain to be deceived'. And he compares those who believe without rational thought to 'the begging priests of Cybele and soothsayers, and to worshippers of Mithras and Sabazius, and whatever else one might meet, apparitions of Hecate or of some other daemon or daemons. For just as among them scoundrels frequently take advantage of the lack of education of gullible people and lead them wherever they wish, so also', he says, 'this happens among the Christians.' He says that 'some do not even want to give or receive a reason for what they believe, and use such expressions as "Do not ask questions; just believe!", and "Thy faith will save thee!" ' And he affirms that they say: 'The wisdom in the world is an evil, and foolishness a good thing.'[29]

This is the voice of the establishment. Galen, who is not being polemical in his remarks, makes very much the same point:

> Those who practise medicine without scientific knowledge may be compared to Moses, who framed laws for . . . the Jews, since it is his

70

Self-Definition in Later Platonism

method in his books to write without offering proofs, saying 'God commanded, God spoke'.[30]

From the other references which Walzer has assembled, it is plain that the impression Galen has of the Jews and Christians is of those who accept dogmas without any attempt at scientific proof – though, as we see, he does not regard them as unique in this.

Celsus's second gibe is that of lack of ancestry. The Jews are peculiar, he says (ap. *CC* 5.25), but at least they have been around for some time. These people cannot even claim that (ibid. 33):

> Now let us take the second chorus. I will ask them where they have come from, or who is the author of their traditional laws. Nobody, they will say. In fact, they themselves originated from Judaism, and they cannot name any other source for their teacher and chorus-leader. Nevertheless they rebelled against the Jews.

A hundred years after Celsus, Plotinus, in *Ennead* 2.9, turns his scornful attention to the Gnostics (specifically Sethians and Valentinians) whose doctrines had affected some members of his own circle. He is not primarily concerned with Christians – indeed, his attack is partly directed against tendencies present in parts of the Platonic tradition itself, such as the school of Numenius – but his accusations are similar to those of Celsus. The Gnostics do not follow the dictates of reason, and they have no respect for truths sanctified by antiquity. In ch. 6, he complains against them that, though anything of any validity in their teachings is in fact borrowed from Plato, they try to disguise this by their abuse of ancient authorities:

> For these doctrines are there in Plato, and when they state them clearly in this way they do well. If they wish to disagree on these points, there is no unfair hostility involved in saying to them that they should not recommend their own opinions to their audience by ridiculing and insulting the Greeks but that they should show the correctness on their own merits of all the points of doctrine which are peculiar to them and differ from the views of the Greeks, stating their real opinions courteously, as befits philosophers, and fairly on the points where they are opposed, looking to the truth and not hunting fame by censuring men who have been judged good from ancient times by men of worth, and saying that they themselves are better than the Greeks.[31]

A good deal of the tractate is devoted to demonstrating the logical incoherences in the Gnostic doctrines of the fall of the soul and the creation of the world, by contrast with the Platonist account. In the same way, a hundred years further on, Julian, in his treatise *Against the Galileans*, sets side by side the cosmogonies of Moses

71

and of Plato (in the *Timaeus*), to show the irrationality of Moses's account.[32]

But I do not wish to get sidetracked into a survey of the conflict between Platonism and Christianity. All that is relevant for my purpose is to show how the polemic against Christians, Jews and Gnostics serves the purpose of self-definition for Platonism, even as had previous struggles with Aristotelians, Stoics or Epicureans. One last feature of this polemic, however, should be adverted to, since it marks an important development in Platonism from Plotinus on, and seems to have been given particular focus as a consequence of Plotinus's ideological struggle with Gnostic tendencies. This is the essentially world-affirming attitude which one finds in *Ennead* 2.9, and in Plotinus's mature thought in general, as opposed to the radically world-negating attitude of the Gnostics, and of a good deal of Middle Platonism, particularly the Pythagoreanizing wing of it, represented by Numenius and Cronius. Plotinus is no friend of the flesh and its pleasures, but it is axiomatic to his system that the physical cosmos is a natural and necessary creation, and as good as it could in the nature of things be. He admits elsewhere, in *Enn.* 4.8.1, that Plato in some places (such as the *Phaedrus*) seems to reject the world as an abèrration – he could have added the *Phaedo* – but he prefers to follow the doctrine of the *Timaeus*, which presents it as necessary and beautiful, though necessarily also inferior to its model. He therefore strongly condemns the Gnostic rejection and abuse of the world, as another example of their insolence and ignorance. In so doing, it seems to me, he adds something to the Platonist world view: Platonism affirms the world as it is. This was not always so clearly the case before Plotinus, but it remains a fixed characteristic after him. This is not to say that one should not fix one's eyes on a better level of existence, to which one hopes to withdraw at the appropriate time; it is just that one does not indulge in vulgar and indiscriminate abuse of what is, after all, a 'moving image of eternal things'. The distinction is made by Plotinus very well in one of his characteristic images, to which one might give the nickname of the Odd Couple.

> But perhaps they will assert that those arguments of theirs make men fly from the body since they hate it from a distance, but ours hold the soul down to it. This would be like two people living in the same fine house, one of whom reviles the structure and the builder, but stays there none the less, while the other does not revile, but says the builder has built it with the utmost skill, and waits for the time to come in

Self-Definition in Later Platonism

which he will go away, when he will not need a house any longer: the first might think he was wiser and readier to depart because he knows how to say that 'the walls are built of soulless stones and timber and are far inferior to the true dwelling place', not knowing that he is only distinguished by not bearing what he must – unless he affirms that he is discontented, while having a secret affection for the beauty of the stones.[33]

Platonism after Plotinus

In the generations after Plotinus, Platonism modified itself further by becoming much more hospitable to magical practice, in the form of theurgy, and by the admission of a wider range of 'inspired' texts, primarily the *Chaldaean Oracles*, a fabrication by one Julian, of the time of Marcus Aurelius, but also of the poems of Orpheus, and even of Homer and Hesiod, viewed allegorically. Plato himself was seen as inspired in a rather stronger sense than heretofore, and every part of those dialogues which were chosen for special comment, such as the *Timaeus* and the *Parmenides*, was taken to be filled with significance, the prefatory portions being interpreted allegorically to lend them suitable dignity and relevance. These developments in the direction of religion were no doubt stimulated by the challenge of Christianity, though this only becomes explicit in the efforts of the Emperor Julian to set up a theurgical Neoplatonism as a substitute for Christianity during his brief reign, in 361–3.

Admirer though I am of the Emperor Julian, I cannot regard his efforts, aided by the philospher-magician Maximus of Ephesus and the philosopher-statesman Sallustius, to set up a form of Platonism as a religion to rival Christianity, as other than an aberration, a bogus attempt at self-definition for Platonism. The experiment was rudely cut short by historical developments, but this combination of Platonic theology and the revival of old cults, together with a good deal of oriental theosophy, was surely too much of a hothouse plant to survive the chill winds of reality for very long.

More important for our purpose are certain significant remarks made by Proclus, with which we may fittingly close this survey. In the preface to his *Platonic Theology*, composed in the latter half of the fifth century CE,[34] Proclus gives an overview of the development of Platonism as he sees it, couched in the language of mystery-cult. Both what he says and how he says it are of interest. I noted earlier that the Neoplatonists do not seem to have concerned themselves with the Sceptical Academy, but they do in fact have a view of the development of this tradition which takes in that period. Since this view reappears in Augustine's treatise *Against the Academics* (3.17.37–19.42), it probably goes back to Porphyry.

Proclus sees theology as having been brought to a peak of perfection by Plato and his immediate successors, 'and then, as it were, after retreating into itself and rendering itself invisible to the great majority of those who professed philosophy, it once again emerged into the light'.[35] This period of darkness, where the truth was either underground (as Augustine presents it as being in the New Academy), or had retired to the heavens, takes in for Proclus not only the period of Scepticism, but also that of Antiochus and his Middle Platonic successors. Only with Plotinus, it seems, does theology emerge again into the light. Numenius's low opinion of Antiochus and his 'new departure' is maintained by the later school. However, in some mystical way the golden chain of true doctrine is not broken, and Plotinus is able to recover it and pass it on.

The other important aspect of Proclus's utterance here is the mystery imagery in which it is couched. Platonism, and philosophy in general, as a mystery into which one may be initiated is a conceit of long ancestry in Platonism. It is, indeed, something more than a conceit, since it embodies a claim by philosophers to uphold the truest form of religion. It thus constitutes an important slogan in the unending contest between religion and philosophy.

Plato himself provides a stimulus for this type of language in such passages as *Meno* 76E, *Symposium* 209E, *Gorgias* 479C, or *Theaetetus* 156A, all of which, however, are tinged, to a greater or lesser extent, with irony. Such irony as there may be vanishes, however, in later Platonic usage. It is actually not in a Platonist, but in the Platonist-influenced Philo of Alexandria that this imagery first reappears (in surviving authors), and then it reappears with a vengeance. So much use does Philo make of it that such a distinguished scholar as E. R. Goodenough was led to postulate Alexandrian-Jewish Mysteries into which Philo might have been initiated. No such hypothesis is necessary or likely. Mystery-imagery occurs in such Platonists as Plutarch,[36] Albinus,[37] and, most elaborately perhaps, in Theon of Smyrna.[38] Theon goes so far as to distinguish five stages in the 'initiation' – purification, communication of the ritual, vision (*epopteia*), 'adornment with garlands', and, finally, 'the joy that comes from unity

74

Self-Definition in Later Platonism

and converse with the gods'. The concept of Platonism as a mystery is thus a commonplace in the Middle Platonic period.

Proclus, in this passage of the *Platonic Theology*, speaks of Plato's teaching as *mystagogia* and *epopteia*, and of Plato himself as 'the leader and hierophant of the truest rites (*teletai*), into which souls are initiated when they are separated from the earthly regions'. The situation is complicated by his time (and at any time after Iamblichus) by the fact that real Chaldaean and other magical rituals were now a part of philosophic practice, and Proclus's references are thus systematically ambiguous; but there is no doubt that he is drawing primarily on this age-old conceit.

Conclusion

Towards the end of antiquity, then, Platonism takes on some of the trappings of a religion, and a greater degree of organization (in the Athenian School after Plutarch of Athens, at least) then it had hitherto possessed, but the fact remains that the Platonic tradition attained self-definition without the aid of any regulating structure or hierarchy of accredited teachers, such as Christianity so quickly built up for itself. Its survival is all the more remarkable for that.

II

Note to page 61

Self-Definition in Later Platonism

1. See on this the chapter *'Platonici, Academici'*, pp. 206–25 of John Glucker's recent book, *Antiochus and the Late Academy*, 1978.

Notes to pages 62–68

2. Glucker, *Antiochus*, esp. pp. 64–88.

3. Cicero, *Luc.* 18; Sextus Empiricus, *Pyrrh.* 1.235.

4. Much later, in the second century CE, the Anonymous Theaetetus Commentary still raises the question as to whether Plato is dogmatizing or not in this work (cf. Hermann Diels, Wilhelm Schubart, *Anonymer Kommentar zu Platons Theatet (papyrus 9782) nebst drei Bruchstücken philosophischen Inhalts*, 1905, cols. 54, 38ff.), though the author feels that he is.

5. Fr. 210, Plasberg (Teubner edition of *Academica*): *Ait enim (Cicero) illis morem fuisse occultandi sententiam suam nec eam cuiquam nisi qui secum ad senectutem usque vixissent aperire consuesse.*

6. Cicero, *Luc.* 139.

7. Glucker, *Antiochus*, pp. 15–17.

8. Slightly revised from H. Rackham, *Cicero: De Finibus bonorum et malorum*, 1914 (repr. 1967), pp. 397–9.

9. See on this Paul Moraux, *Der Aristotelismus bei den Griechen: von Andronikos bis Alexander von Aphrodisias* I, 1973, pp. 3–94.

10. Slightly revised from H. Rackham, *De Finibus*, p. 303.

11. Cf. Moraux, *Der Aristotelismus* I, pp. 181–93.

12. Cf. J. M. Dillon, *The Middle Platonists*, 1977, pp. 124f.

13. See the summary by Arius Didymus of Eudorus's ethical doctrine in Stobaeus, *Ecl.* 2.42.7ff.: *Eklogai Joannis Stobaei anthologium* II (ed. C. Wachsmuth), 1974³, p. 42.7ff.

14. On the murky origins of these documents, see W. Burkert, 'Hellenistische Pseudopythagorica'.

15. Cf. *Middle Platonists*, pp. 114–35.

16. C. G. Zumpt, *Über den Bestand der philosophischen Schulen in Athen und die Succession der Scholarchen*, APAW 1844, pp. 27–119.

17. J. Lynch, *Aristotle's School*, 1972, pp. 54–67, and 177–89.

18. See above, n. 1.

19. See Dillon, *Middle Platonists*, pp. 247–57. The fragments of Atticus, quoted by Eusebius in his *Praeparatio evangelica*, are collected in the Budé ed. of Baudry (Paris 1931), and now in a new edition from Édouard Des Places, in the same series (1980).

20. Plutarch, *An. proc.* 1, 2, *Mor.* 1012B, 1013AB.

21. On Favorinus, see now the excellent discussion of Glucker, *Antiochus*, pp. 280–93. I mention Favorinus only because Phillip De Lacy, in a review of *The Middle Platonists* in the *Southern Journal of Philosophy*, 1980, takes me to task for not recognizing the continuance of the sceptical tradition in Platonism after Antiochus, in such figures as Cicero, Plutarch and Favorinus. I simply do not see these figures adding up to a tradition, nor can I see in the 'scepticism' of Cicero or Plutarch more than an affectation, which does not touch their deepest convictions. The sceptical tradition continued outside Platonism, with Aenesidemus, Agrippa and Sextus Empiricus.

22. Cf. Numenius, frr. 23–8, ed. É. Des Places.

23. Numenius, fr. 23.

24. Numenius, fr. 25, lines 75–83.

25. Sextus Empiricus, *Pyrrh.* 1.234, trs. R. G. Bury, LCL I.

Notes to pages 69–74

26. E.g. Plutarch, *Mor.* 102D, 621F, 791A, 1120C, 1122A.
27. Academics: Lucian, *Pisc.* 43; *Bis Acc.* 15; *VH* 2.18; Platonists, id., *Herm.* 16; *Eun.* 3; *Icar.* 29; *Nigr.* 2.
28. Aulus Gellius, *NA* 11.5.6–8; 15.2.1; 17.15.1; 17.21.48.
29. Origen, *Contra Celsum*, ed. and trs. H. Chadwick, 1953, p. 12.
30. In an Arabic version of his lost work *On Hippocrates' Anatomy*, written between 162 and 166 CE, collected by Richard Walzer in *Galen on Jews and Christians*, 1949, pp. 10f.
31. Plotinus, *Enn..* 2.9.6, trs. Armstrong, LCL II, p. 247.
32. Julian, *Adv. Galil.* 96Cff., LCL III, pp. 328ff.
33. Plotinus, *Enn.* 2.9.18, LCL II, p. 297.
34. The only complete edition of the *Platonic Theology* of Proclus is still that of Aemilius Portus (1618), but this is now being superseded by the excellent Budé text of Saffrey and Westerink, which has so far reached Vol. III (of six). I quote from their edition.
35. Proclus, 1.1. 12–15 (ed. Saffrey and Westerink).
36. Plutarch, *Is. et Os.* 77, *Def. or.* 23, *Quaest. conviv.* 8.2 (*Mor.* 382D, 422E, 718CD).
37. Albinus, *Didask.*, ed. Hermann, p. 182.7ff.
38. Theon of Smyrna, *Expos.*, ed. Hiller, pp. 14.17–16.2.

III
THE ACADEMY IN THE MIDDLE PLATONIC PERIOD

It is the purpose of this paper to enquire into two related questions: first, whether there was, during the period from the capture of Athens by Mithridates of Pontus in 88 B.C. down to the time of Plotinus in the mid-third century A.D., any physical entity that can properly be described as a Platonic Academy, and any succession of figures who can be described as Heads of such an institution; and secondly, if not, what were the conditions of instruction in Platonism during this period?[1]

At least since the exhaustive investigations of Zumpt, published in 1844[2], it has been generally accepted by historians of philosophy that the Platonic Academy maintained a continuous existence from Plato's own time down to late antiquity, until, indeed, Justinian closed the Academy in 529 A.D.[3] John Lynch, in his work mentioned above, has aimed some shrewd blows at this doctrine, but his suggestions deserve further elaboration, and the consequences of them for the nature of instruction and the conditions of succession within the Platonist movement need to be drawn out more fully. I shall here be concerned with the conditions of continuity in a philosophical school. How is authority maintained? How is orthodoxy preserved? How, in the absence of a system of 'certification', is it decided who is a Platonist and who is not? Further, how does one attach oneself to a teacher? How does one live? How does he live? Are there fees? Are there criteria of success or failure in the course? To many of these obvious and basic questions there are, I fear, no answers based upon clear evidence, but at least the asking of them may in itself turn up a few pertinent facts.

---

1. I must acknowledge at the outset my debt to the lucid investigations of John Lynch, in his book *Aristotle's School* (Berkeley and Los Angeles, 1972). Although primarily concerned with the fate of the Peripatos, his remarks on the nature and fate of the Academy (esp. pp. 54-67 and 177-89) first provoked me to consider the present question.
2. "Über den Bestand der philosophischen Schulen in Athen und die Succession der Scholarchen", *Abhandlungen der königlichen Akademie der Wissenschaften zu Berlin* (1844), pp. 27-119.
3. Though even the significance of this sanctified date has been cogently challenged by Alan Cameron, "The Last Days of the Academy at Athens", *Proc. of the Camb. Philol. Soc.* n.s. 15 (1969), pp. 7-29.

III

I am not here concerned with the Academy from the time of
Plato himself to that of Philo of Larissa. That subject has been well
covered by many authorities[4]. During that period there was at
least, without doubt, a formal institution, through which
continuity could be preserved. One thing, however, even in this
period, seems to have been too readily assumed, and that is the
extent of the physical plant that at any time ever accrued to Plato's
foundation. Was there ever, for instance, a marble-porticoed hall,
with or without upon its front the solemn adjuration ΜΗΔΕΙC
ΑΓΕΩΜΕΤΡΗΤΟC ΕΙCΙΤΩ? Most authorities would not accept
the historicity of the inscription, but the existence of some
substantial building housing the Platonic School seems to be a
widely-held, if not always acknowledged, assumption. What the
evidence, such as it is, actually points to is, on the one hand, an
estate owned by Plato in Colonus, bordering on the Academy park
(ὁ Κῆπος ὁ παρά τὸν Κολωνόν mentioned by Alexander
Polyhistor in his *Successions of Philosophers, ap.* Diog. Laert. III 5),
and on the other the public facilities of the Academy, the
gymnasium (where we find Carneades, for instance, still lecturing
in the second century B.C., DL IV 63), the groves, the walks[5]. In all
of these places there were, no doubt, areas understood to be set
aside for the philosophers, but all business was conducted very
much in public. The library of the school presumably found its
home in the house of Plato, which must have passed to the
successive scholarchs[6]. Whether other members, senior or junior,
lived in this house with the scholarch is not known, but it is
unlikely that many could have — perhaps only the scholarch's
chosen successor or favorite (which might give rise to those
recurring rumors of erotic connexions between master and pupil).

I mention these points about the pre-Mithridatic Academy
simply to remind the reader that there was never, even at the best

4. *E.g.* G. C. Field, *Plato and His Contemporaries*, London, 1930; H. I.
Marrou, *A History of Education in Antiquity* (Eng. trans.), London 1956;
Harold Cherniss, *The Riddle of the Early Academy*, Berkeley, 1945. A useful
survey of the evidence in W.K.C. Guthrie, *A History of Greek Philosophy*,
Vol. IV, pp. 19-24.
5. Lacydes used to lecture (ἐσχόλαζεν) in a garden in the Academy which
had been laid out for him by King Attalus of Pergamum, and which came
to be called the *Lacydaeum* (DL IV 60).
6. Though it must be noted that Plato's own will makes no mention of the
estate at Colonus (DL III 41-2), and Arcesilaus in his will left all his
property to his brother Pylades (*ibid.* IV 43). (These are the only Platonic
wills we have preserved to us.) One may deduce from this that the
Platonic School, unlike the Peripatos, was not deemed to be the personal
property of the scholarch.

of times, such a thing as a separate 'Institute of Advanced Studies' in the Academy grove; just the estate at Colonus, and certain familiar haunts in the public park. There was plainly, however, at this time, an organised succession of scholarchs and their associates, making up an official and continuous corporate entity, from at least 347 B.C. (arrangements during Plato's lifetime were probably rather less formal) down to 88 B.C. It is only after this period that the physical nature of the 'Academy' becomes obscure.

II

What happened in 88 B.C. that led to a radical break in the tradition? We learn from Cicero (*Brutus* 306) that "at this time (*sc.* the consulship of Sulla and Gn. Pompeius, 89 B.C.) Philo, the head of the Academy, along with a group of loyal Athenians, had fled from Athens because of the Mithridatic War and had come to Rome." Philo never, it seems, returned to Athens, dying in Rome some years later. As for the Academy grove, it was laid waste by Sulla, who used its trees for timber in his siege of the city in 86 (Plut. *Sulla* 12, 1-3), and, though it was later restored, we do not hear of it being used again as a haunt of philosophers. Whether any faithful followers of Philo returned to Athens we do not know (his follower Heraclitus of Tyre is found in Alexandria in 79 B.C., Cic. *Acad. Pr.* 11), but if they did they seem to have made no impact. The man who became the dominant figure in Platonism in this period was rather Philo's dissident pupil, Antiochus of Ascalon. If we check in with him, in the winter of 79 B.C., when Cicero attended his lectures, we find quite a different arrangement in effect. Antiochus lectured, not any longer in the grove of the Academy, which was deserted, but in the Ptolemaion gymnasium in the centre of the city.[7] Cicero describes himself and his friends at the beginning of Book V of the *De Finibus* as walking out to the Academy one day after the afternoon lecture, and brooding about among the ruins. There were no ruins of buildings, we may note; just seats — "This is where Xenocrates sat", "This was Carneades' seat", and so on. We do not know what Antiochus' procedure was, though he is reported as lecturing with great eloquence (Plut. *Cic.* 4). The remarkable interpretation that he gave of Plato's doctrines

---

7. The site of this has not yet been found, but it is generally agreed to have been not far from the Agora, in the present-day Plaka (Pausanias I 17.2). It was founded, probably, by Ptolemy Philometor in the 150's and almost immediately (about 141/0) attracted the attentions of philosophers (*Index Academicus* col. XXXII, p. 103 Mekler).

and of the development of philosophy since Plato does not primarily concern us now.[8] He felt justified in taking the great bulk of Stoic theory and terminology as a kind of updated version of Platonism, and thus begins, from our perspective, the pattern followed by School Platonism ever afterwards, until a serious attempt was made at the beginning of the last century by German scholars such as Schleiermacher to get back to the doctrine of Plato's dialogues.[9]

After Antiochus' death in about 67 B.C., his school was taken over by his brother Aristus, who seems to have been of no distinction as a philosopher (Plutarch, *Brutus*, 2, 2). He survived until at least 50 B.C. when Cicero visited him on his way back from governing Cilicia. By 44 B.C. Artistus had been succeeded by one Theomnestus of Naucratis, whose lectures Brutus attended in that year, while getting his forces together to face Antony. What happened to the school after this we have no idea. Possibly nothing.[10]

Our next glimpse of Platonist school activity in Athens comes from a century afterwards, when Plutarch records himself as studying under Ammonius, in 66-7 A.D. and later. Plutarch refers to himself once as 'joining the Academy' (ἐν Ακαδημεία γενόμενος, *De E ap. Delph.*, 387 F), but since this is the only possible reference to the Academy as a living institution in this whole period I am inclined to interpret the phrase metaphorically, as meaning simply 'became a Platonist' — or a more orthodox Platonist — as opposed to an enthusiast for Pythagorean number-mysticism, as he portrays himself at this time.[11] If he joined a material Academy, than I suggest it was no more than Ammonius' school, which seems to have been a fairly simple foundation.

The only occasion on which Plutarch mentions formal instruc-

---

8. An attempt to evaluate Antiochus' philosophical position is made in Dillon, *The Middle Platonists*, London/Cornell 1977, Ch. 2.
9. In a most useful survey of this question, E. N. Tigerstedt, *The Decline and Fall of the Neoplatonic Interpretation of Plato*, Helsinki 1974, wishes to remove this distinction from Schleiermacher, and push it back to Jean de Serres (1540-98), *op. cit.* pp. 39-43.
10. The heroic effort of Zumpt (see above, n. 1) to find a 'golden chain' of scholarchs to preside over a putative Academy during these centuries has had a lasting influence, from Zeller and Praechter (in Überweg's *Grundriss*) to Philip Merlan, in his contribution to the *Cambridge History of Later Greek and Early Mediaeval Philosophy* (Ch. 4), but the attempt must founder on lack of evidence.
11. Lamprias' reference at *Def. Or.* 431A to 'recalling the Academy to our minds' is clearly a reference to the Academic tradition (here, of scepticism), rather than to any tangible institution.

The Academy in the Middle Platonic Period   67

tions by Ammonius is in an anecdote recorded in his essay *How to Tell a Flatterer* (70C):

My professor (καφηγητής) Ammonius, at an afternoon lecture (ἐν δειλινῇ διατρίβῃ) perceived that some of his students had lunched rather too elaborately, and so he ordered his freedman to chastise his own servant, remarking by way of explanation that "the boy can't seem to eat his lunch without a tot of wine!" At the same time he glanced towards us, so that the rebuke took hold of the guilty.

It sounds from this, as from other indications, as if Ammonius ran his school in his own house,[12] and what we hear later of Calvenus Taurus confirms this impression. Plutarch is not specific about the circumstances of the *De E*, but it sounds like a *conversazione* of the school, presided over by Ammonius. We get the impression of about a dozen students at a time, at most. Elsewhere, Ammonius appears as presiding over dinner-party discussions which, again, we know from reports of Taurus to be a basic feature of school life. The whole of Book IX of Plutarch's *Table Talk* consists of conversations held over dinner at Ammonius' house during a festival of the Muses (whether a public or a private, Platonist, festival is not clear). At the time, Ammonius was acting as *strategos* of Athens, a most prestigious post which he actually held three times (*Quaest. Conv.* VIII 3, 1) a sign of the political importance of philosophers at this period.

In Ammonius' case, then, we can discern no very elaborate format. We also do not know what form instruction took. Plutarch himself later presided over a group in his native town of Chaeroneia, which he refers to as a *schole*, (e.g. *De E*. 385A) and to which he lectured, or allowed questions to be proposed for discussions, the results of which he records in various dialogues. Texts of a controversial nature were often read aloud, it seems, and then discussed. Such was the case with Colotes' essay "That it is not possible even to Live according to Doctrines of the Other Philosophers" which the group then makes response to (*Adv. Col.* 1107EE). Straight commentaries on Plato are not included, though he frequently brings in Platonic passages to clinch an argument, and one surviving work, the *De Procreatione Animae*, is a

---

12. If Ammonius used a public place to lecture, it may have been the Diogeneion gymnasium, where he is recorded by Plutarch QC IX 1, 736D), as conducting an examination of the ephebes. This, however, was in his capacity as *strategos*, and proves nothing about his normal place of lecturing.

commentary, dedicated to his sons, on the account of the creation of the soul in the *Timaeus*. There is also a collection of comments on problematic passages in Plato. Mainly, however, he is discussing topics such as the nature of God, fate and freewill, and other ethical and metaphysical questions, on which Plato could be quoted as an authority, and here one can see how notions of what Plato taught can suffer strange transformations. We have no evidence that there was actually a handbook of Platonic passages on the various topics going the rounds, but there was certainly a series of set passages always used to illustrate the same themes, and these come to form the basis for a scholastic codification of his doctrine.

III

If we turn to the next generation, in the mid-second century A.D. we are quite well informed by the Roman lawyer Aulus Gellius about the circumstances and habits of his teacher in Platonism, L. Calvenus Taurus. Gellius nowhere speaks of Taurus as being head of an Academy. He refers to him only, rather vaguely (*NA* VII 10), as '*vir memoria nostra in disciplina Platonica celebratus*', implying simply that he was the leading Platonist of his time in Athens. Thanks to his reminiscences, we have a reasonably full picture of the workings of Taurus' school. There were obviously formal sessions, at which the works of Plato were read and commented on, and even, it seems, works of Aristotle (though only, perhaps, the more strictly 'scientific' ones, such as the *Problems*, *NA* XIX 6). At *NA* XVII 20 we find the *Symposium* being read in class. One might alternatively take a set problem in philosophy and discuss that, adducing various authorities. After the formal discourse, Taurus encouraged his pupils to raise questions. We see the process described at *NA* 1 26:

> I once asked Taurus in the *diatriba* whether a wise man got angry. For after his daily lectures he often gave anyone the opportunity of asking whatever questions one wished. On this occasion he first discussed the disease or passion of anger seriously and at length, setting forth what is to be found in the books of the ancients and in his own commentaries.

The great man, then, quoted on occasion from his own works. On this occasion, besides telling an anecdote about Plutarch, he makes reference to Plutarch's essay *On Freedom from Anger*, and the 'ancients' referred to by Gellius would perhaps be those whom Plutarch was relying on in that work.

Taurus was in the habit of inviting certain favoured pupils to his home for dinner (if in fact they were not already there!), and, as Gellius tells us (*NA* VII 13), one was expected on these occasions to bring along (in lieu of a bottle) topics for discussion, which were raised after dinner. We have a number of examples of these, and they closely resemble those presented by Plutarch in his *Table Talk.* The problem raised in VII 13, for instance, 'At what moment can a dying man be said to die?' leads Taurus into an exposition of the notion of 'instant', based on Plato's *Parmenides*, 156D. At XVII 8 the question arises as to why oil congeals, the problem being raised on this occasion by the prank of a slave boy.

Besides dinner parties, there were expeditions to the country. At XVIII 10 some of the school accompany Taurus to visit Herodes Atticus' villa at Cephisia, where Gellius is lying ill, afflicted with a bout of diarrhoea. On this occasion Taurus is recorded as setting an ignorant country doctor right on the difference between veins and arteries. At XII 5 we find an account of a journey to attend the Pythian Games at Delphi, on which Taurus is accompanied again by a group of pupils. We also find him, in II 2, receiving distinguished visitors, namely the Governor of Crete, presumably a former pupil, who had come to Athens expressly to visit the philosopher, accompanied by his father. Here Gellius portrays Taurus as sitting outside the door of his *cubiculum* (which sounds like a small room) after class. When the Governor and his father arrived, there was only one spare chair (on which circumstance the anecdote turns). All this seems to denote a very simple establishment.

These glimpses of academic life are most welcome. What they reveal is, not a full-scale Academy, but rather a one-man show. There is no suggestion of any other professors besides Taurus himself, or of any other property beyond his (modest) personal possessions. If we talk about the Platonic Academy at this period, then, we must bear in mind that it may be no more than what we see described here.

Taurus did write commentaries, of which we have evidence, on Plato's *Gorgias* and *Timaeus*,[13] in the latter of which, among other things, he wrestled with the problem of Plato's meaning at *Tim.* 28 B when he states that the world is created. It is not Taurus, however, but another Platonist of this era, Albinus, who seems to * have taught in Smyrna, in Asia Minor, who gives us a comprehensive survey of Platonism as it was understood in this

---

13. On the *Gorgias*: Gellius *NA* VII 14; on the *Timaeus*: Joh. Philoponus, *De Aeternitate Mundi*, p. 520, 4ff. Rabe.

III

age. There is no reason to suppose that Albinus is any more 'eclectic' than a supposedly 'pure' Athenian school of Platonism. 'Purity' of doctrine in our sense is simply a mirage in this era.

Of Albinus' activity as a teacher we can derive some notion from his brief work, *An Introduction (Eisagoge) to the Dialogues of Plato*.[14] The *Eisagoge* discusses, in six short chapters, first the nature of the dialogue form in general, then the various types of Platonic dialogue, and lastly the order in which the dialogues should be read in order to provide a coherent course in Platonic philosophy. The whole work is of a suitable length and format for an introductory lecture of an hour or so, and indeed is probably a bald record of how Albinus customarily started his course in Platonism.

I wish to draw attention in particular here to the information that one can derive from this source as to the course in Plato practised by Albinus. He divides the dialogues (in ch. 3), along the lines laid down in the previous century by Thrasyllus, Tiberius' court philosopher, into dialogues of instruction and dialogues of enquiry, though he considerably simplifies the elaborate scheme of subdivisions of these which Thrasyllus had laid down. Albinus actually rejects Thrasyllus' order of the dialogues as a useful order for teaching. Thrasyllus' arrangement, by tetralogies, beginning with the *Euthyphro*, *Apology*, *Crito*, *Phaedo* (the order still preserved today) seems to follow, he says, a dramatic principle rather than a pedagogical one. Albinus prefers to begin with *Alcibiades* I, since it concerns knowledge of self, the first requisite for a would-be philosopher. Then one should turn to the *Phaedo*, which teaches the nature of the philosophic life, taking as a premise for this the immortality of the soul. Then the *Republic*, since it sketches a complete educational theory, and lastly the *Timaeus*, since it takes us through the whole range of things natural and divine, leading us to a clear view of divinity (*ta theia*). The *Parmenides*, we may note, has not yet become anything more than a good exercise in logic. Only in certain Pythagorean circles, at this time, it seems, did anyone see any 'higher' metaphysical significance in the hypotheses of the *Parmenides*. All this is less elaborate than the course of ten dialogues laid down in the next century by Iamblichus, with the *Timaeus* and *Parmenides* following as the two summits of philosophy, but it operates on the same educational principle.

In the final section of his work, Albinus adds that before studying positive doctrine one should purge the mind of false notions and exercise the wits by studying the dialogues of enquiry, namely the early Socratic dialogues. What chronological order is to

14. Printed in Vol. 6 of C. F. Hermann's edition of Plato, Leipzig 1921-36.

III

be followed is not made entirely clear, but we derive a picture of an articulated course of instruction in Platonism, which prefigures the more elaborate order of Neoplatonic times.

We get a glimpse then, from the *Eisagoge*, of the nature of instruction in at least one Platonic school of the period. A course in Platonism is also intended to be a course in moral and spiritual development, beginning with knowledge of self, and ending with a complete course in physics and theology, based on the *Timaeus*. Thus the study of the dialogues of Plato is virtually co-extensive with higher education in general. Aristotle's logical works, also were plainly used by Albinus, though not by every Platonist of the period, as an introduction to philosophical study.

IV

The Platonic school of which we know most, however, is that of Plotinus in Rome, in the middle of the third century, A.D. Porphyry's *Life of Plotinus*, from which we derive our information about it, has been subjected to repeated study, but there are nevertheless a number of interesting gaps in his account which have never, I think, been given the attention they deserve.

The first point is a general one, and I think it is of prime importance. Porphyry is neither blind to, nor reticent about, Plotinus' various eccentricities, but at no point does he suggest that the general organisation of the school, or Plotinus' position in it, is noticeably peculiar. This I find significant. Porphyry, after all, had come to Plotinus from Longinus in Athens; he was presumably also familiar with the establishment of the Platonic *diadochos* Eubulus, even if Longinus himself was not part of that establishment; yet he does not note in the *Life* any startling change of structure, such as from a large, organised 'research institute' to a totally personal, informal group of 'friends'. Certainly, he notes that Plotinus' method of commentary was remarkable (ch. 14), but this in itself emphasises that the overall set-up was not a shock to him at all. My conclusion from this is that Plotinus' school was — apart from the personality of the Master himself — not in any essential way different in structure from that of any other teacher of philosophy in these centuries.

What, then, was Plotinus' situation? As far as we can gather from Porphyry's narrative, he lived, when Porphyry knew him, and presumably for long before that, in the house of a wealthy and respectable widow called Gemina (ch. 9). The household included Gemina's daughter, and a number of young boys and girls who had been entrusted to Plotinus' care on the death of their parents.

Whether this was Gemina's only residence, or just a house belonging to her, is not quite clear, but it was obviously a fairly large and elaborate establishment, in which young ladies and middle-aged philosophers could live decently together.

Around Plotinus in this establishment was gathered a circle of 'companions' — Porphyry does not speak of pupils, only of 'companions', *hetairoi*. These companions may be divided into three classes: (1) wealthy patrons, (2) close companions, and (3) more casual auditors. The first category is not exclusive of the other two, but the latter two categories represent, I think, the distinction in the establishments of Ammonius and Taurus in the previous two centuries between young men who attended philosophical lectures to complete their education (as would be the case with Aulus Gellius or Apuleius), and serious students of Platonism, who would go on to become masters themselves, and one or other of whom would, normally, be the master's chosen successor (as Albinus was, presumably, of Gaius).

In Plotinus' case, patrons included the wealthy senators Castricius Firmus, Marcellus Orontius, Sabinillus and Rogatianus (ch. 7), the last of whom in fact went rather overboard, giving away all his possessions and adopting the philosophic life. This did wonders for his gout, it seems, but presumably rather lessened his usefulness as a patron. The others, however, seem to have found philosophy compatible with the *bios praktikos*. Castricius Firmus was a particularly good friend. Plotinus was always welcome, one gathers, at his country estate at Minturnae, and when the philosopher was afflicted by his final illness in 269, it was to an estate adjacent to this in Campania that he retired (ch. 2). This estate belonged to, and was presumably bequeathed to him by, a prosperous doctor of Arabian extraction called Zethus, who had himself been given it by Castricius — interesting patterns of patronage are revealed here. "His Wants",Porphyry tells us, "were provided in part out of Zethus' estate, and for the rest were furnished from Minturnae, where Castricius' property lay." We see in all this Castricius providing very much the same range of services for Plotinus as Herodes Atticus did for Taurus.

Plotinus' patrons actually came to include the Emperor Gallienus himself, and his wife Salonina (ch. 12), which imperial favor led Plotinus to propose a wild project to establish a philosophic city in Campania, to be called Platonopolis and to be run according to Plato's *Laws* (presumably with Plotinus and his circle acting as a kind of Nocturnal Council). This project came to nothing, Porphyry tells us, through opposition at court. Perhaps it is just as well.

The presence on the scene of the lady Gemina and of Castricius explain, perhaps, a question which might bother the modern observer. What were the financial arrangements, in an ancient philosophic school, between master and pupil? Such matters are, after all, never mentioned in our sources. The answer is, I suggest, that they were left quite vague. The pupil was expected to provide for himself (Porphyry, at least, had a house of his own, ch. 11), and perhaps to contribute to such communal meals as were held. The pupil's father, or he himself, if he were mature and rich, might make the philosopher presents of various sorts, but such matters would not be regulated to the extent of constituting any sort of fees. As far as one can see, one simply presented oneself at the house of the master of one's choice and hoped to be allowed to enter his circle.

About attending lectures there was, it seems, no great difficulty. Plotinus' lectures, at least, were open to all (ch. 1). Amelius was once able to bring along a friend of his who was a noted portrait painter, to gather material surreptitiously for a portrait of the Master, and no notice was taken of this. Visitors in town might drop in unexpectedly, as did once, to Plotinus' great confusion, his former fellow-pupil Origenes (ch. 3).

As regards the outer circle of followers, Porphyry gives a comprehensive list of what he calls 'enthusiasts' (ζηλωταί). These included a number of doctors (medicine being, after all, a species of applied philosophy), Paulinus, from Scythopolis, Eustochius of Alexandria, and the aforementioned Zethus, who besides being a doctor had been successful in public life, in what capacity we are not told (ch. 7). There was also the critic and poet Zoticus, and the rhetor Serapion (whom Porphyry dislikes). All of these, I would suggest, were more than able to pay their way, in one form or another.

Of philosophers proper, Porphyry mentions only Amelius and himself. Here an interesting rivalry becomes apparent. Amelius Gentilianus, an Etruscan by origin, had been one of Plotinus' earliest adherents, having joined him only two years after his arrival in Rome in 244. When Porphyry arrived in 262, Amelius had been at Plotinus' right hand for sixteen years. However, in the course of the next six years it is plain that Porphyry gradually supplanted him. "I myself, Porphyry of Tyre", so Porphyry ends his catalogue, "was one of Plotinus' very closest companions, and it was to me that he entrusted the task of revising his writings." This supplanting cannot have taken place without certain tensions, but Porphyry writes always warmly of Amelius, who was dead by the time he wrote the *Life*. Amelius had in fact left Rome in 269, a year before Plotinus' death, to settle in Apamea in Syria, the home town of his greatest hero (after Plotinus), the Neopythagorean philosopher Numenius. What exactly prompted him to leave, other than reverence for Numenius' memory, we are not told. Porphyry himself had retired a year before that to Lilybaeum in Sicily, to recover from a depression which had almost led him to suicide (until Plotinus came round to his house and talked him out of it). In fact, at Plotinus' death, only the faithful doctor Eustochius was present (ch. 2), a rather peculiar situation at which Porphyry betrays some embarrassment.

But to return to the structure of the school: it is plain that it was of the simplest. The main activity was the lecture or seminar:

> At the conferences (συνουσίαι) he (Plotinus) used to have treatises by various authors read aloud. Among the Platonists it might be Severus or Cronius, Numenius, Gaius or Atticus; and among the Peripatetics Aspasius, Alexander, Adrastus or some such writer, at the call of the moment. But it was far from his way to follow any of these authors blindly; he took a personal, original view, applying Ammonius' approach (νοῦς) to the investigation of every problem.

Porphyry expands on this further in ch. 18:

> He was entirely free from all the inflated pomp of the professor. His lectures had the air of conversation, and he never forced upon his hearers the severely logical substratum of his thesis.

One thinks of Wittgenstein, or of Austin.

We may note here — and it is significant, I think, for the growth of the scholastic tradition in Platonism, — that what are being read are not primarily texts of Plato or Aristotle, but rather commentaries upon them, these commentaries depending in turn upon previous commentaries. No doubt the group also read works of these authors which were not explicit commentaries on a dialogue or treatise, such as essays *On the Soul, On the Gods,* or *On Happiness,* but these would also be based on an interpretation of Plato or Aristotle. On these works Plotinus in turn would comment, inviting questions from the group, and pursuing long trains of argument, even to the exasperation of certain auditors — as once when Porphyry kept on at him for three days about the problem of the soul's relation to the body (ch. 13):

> He was always as ready to entertain objections as he was powerful in meeting them. At one time I myself kept interrogating him during three days as to how the soul is associated with the body, and he continued explaining; a man

III

called Thaumasius entered in the midst of our discussions; the
visitor was more interested in the general drift of the system
than in particular points, and said he wished to hear Plotinus
expounding some theory as he would in a set treatise, but that
he could not endure Porphyry's questions and answers.
Plotinus asked, "But if we cannot first solve the difficulties
Porphyry raises, what could go into the treatise?" (MacKenna's
trans.)

In fact, no doubt, these deliberations form the basis of what we
have in *Problems of the Soul* (*Enn*. IV 3-4). Plotinus encouraged
questions — as did Taurus, indeed, and no doubt every
philosopher of this period worthy of the name — and the tractates
which we have, Porphyry tells us (ch. 4), arise out of these
questions and the debates they engendered. Since Plotinus, we are
told (ch. 8), wrote as he thought, in a continuous flow, not
checking over what he had written (his eyesight was bad), we
should in theory be able to discern behind his writings the course
of the discussion and even the content of the treatise upon which
he is basing himself at any particular time. We know, for one thing,
that to the superficial observer his philosophy seemed to be hardly
distinguishable from that of Numenius (ch. 17), which should be a
useful clue. In fact, in the absence of anything more than the
sparsest fragments of his immediate predecessors, all reconstruc-
tions must remain precarious, but at least from the titles of his
tractates one may derive a fair idea of the subjects most often
discussed by the Platonists of previous generations.

Over and above normal participation in the seminar, tasks might
be set to various trusted disciples, some arising out of the seminar,
some not. When Porphyry first arrived, and raised difficulties in
the seminar about the relation of *nous* to the *noeta* (he was still
under the influence of Longinus), Plotinus set Amelius to reply to
him (ch. 18). Later, when Eubulus, the Platonic Successor, wrote
from Athens, sending treatises on some questions in Platonism,
Plotinus turned them over to Porphyry to answer (ch. 15). One
would dearly love to know more about this exchange. Also, before
Porphyry came on the scene, Amelius had been doing the service
for Plotinus that Albinus appears to have done for his master Gaius
(and which, one might add, various pupils have done for
Wittgenstein), that of taking notes of the proceedings in the
seminar, and these he had compiled in something like a hundred
treatises (ch. 3). Whether this Amelian version of Plotinus'
teaching has left any trace in the Neoplatonic tradition is a question
of which there has been a certain amount of inconclusive

discussion among scholars. At any rate, Porphyry informs us that it was he whom Plotinus entrusted with the editing of his writings (ch. 7), and it is Porphyry's edition which has prevailed.

Besides the activities of the seminar, there were other formal activities of the school, as we saw in the case of Taurus. The birthdays of Plato and Socrates were celebrated with a sacrifice and feast, at which every member of the circle who was able was expected to deliver an address (ch. 2), on the model of the *Symposium*. At one feast of Plato, Porphyry tells us that he read a poem 'abounding in mystic doctrine conveyed in veiled words and couched in terms of enthusiasm', called "The Sacred Marriage", which provoked mixed reactions (ch. 15). On another occasion, a nasty fellow called Diophanes, a rhetor, read a defence of Alcibiades' conduct as described in the *Symposium*, greatly to Plotinus' displeasure.

To conclude, then, my contention is that Plotinus' school, despite the remarkable character of its master, was not essentially different in structure from the other philosophical schools of that and the preceding centuries. What sort of establishment Eubulus, the Platonic *diadochos*, maintained in Athens at this time we do not know. If, as I assume, he was the official Professor of Platonic Philosophy, incumbent of the Chair set up in 176 A.D. by Marcus Aurelius (Dio Cassius, LXXII, 31), then he had a salary from the State (the original endowment provided for a salary of 10,000 dr. per annum), and, no doubt, a somewhat more elaborate library than Plotinus, but there is no evidence that he presided over anything comparable to a modern university or institute, or that he was any more than a one-man show (though, like Plotinus, assisted by senior pupils). We must never underestimate the simplicity and informality of the arrangements in any ancient philosophical school.

V

A survey of Platonic school instruction could be carried on for centuries more, down to the time of Proclus and beyond (when, indeed, our information as to what went on is considerably more copious), but my concern at present is particularly with what may be termed the Middle Platonic period.[15] My purpose has been simply to suggest that our image of the Platonic school during this period, and indeed at any stage of its development, is in danger of becoming far too elaborate. After 86 B.C., I do not believe that

---

15. Cf. the recent article by Garth Fowden, "The Platonist Philosopher and His Circle in Late Antiquity", ΦΙΛΟΣΟΦΙΑ[7] (1977), pp. 359-383.

there was any such thing as an official Platonic Academy, until (perhaps) Marcus Aurelius founded his Regius Professorships in 176 A.D. This foundation, then, over a century or so, will have taken on the trappings and the consciousness of a Platonic Academy, until finally, in the fifth century A.D., it came to believe that it had always been there.[16]

As to the conditions of instruction and study, they were, I suggest, oral to a far greater degree than we generally seem to recognise. One learned one's philosophy from one's Master, as he had learned it in his turn from his Master. With this Master one lived in close personal contact, sometimes staying in his house, often dining with him, sometimes marrying his daughter. Only after one's views had been largely formed did one proceed to direct study of the original texts of Platonism. Such a scenario would, I think, go far to explain the remarkable distortions of doctrine which appear in the tradition from Antiochus of Ascalon onwards.

If one goes on to ask how one is to know that a given teacher is an 'official' Platonist, in the absence of any system of examinations, accreditation of schools, or conferral of degrees, I can only suggest that, in what was after all a very small world by modern standards, it simply became generally known that so-and-so had studied under so-and-so (say Albinus under Gaius), was, perhaps, his favorite pupil, and had inherited his library and thus received his official blessing. Students then gather round him, making whatever personal arrangement, financial and otherwise, may be mutually agreeable (I would suggest the possibility of a series of 'gifts' conveyed to the philosopher by the pupil himself, or his parents). But our final admission on all these questions must be, I fear, that we are miserably ill-informed.[17]

---

16. See on this question J. Lynch, *op. cit.* pp. 185-7, emphasising the ambiguous nature of Damascius' evidence.
17. For a study of medical education in antiquity, on parallel lines to the present one, see the excellent article by Vivian Nutton, "Museums and Medical Schools in Classical Antiquity", *History of Education*[4] (1976), pp. 1-15.

IV

Female principles in Platonism*

This is not exactly intended as a feminist tract, but I cannot deny that its theme was prompted to some extent by current debates as to the essence and the role of the female in society and in theology. I am concerned here, however, rather with the role of the female in the cosmos. The point has been made, with some justification in my view, that, in the case of Christianity, the circumstance that the Holy Spirit, the *Hagion Pneuma*, which is functionally and, in Hebrew, grammatically, a female principle, *ruah*, happens to become in Greek a neuter noun (and in Latin a masculine), results in an impoverishment and a distortion in orthodox Christianity in respect of the feminine, a lack for which even the elevation of Mary to the status of a Mother Goddess does not really compensate. In this respect, as we shall see, the Gnostic sects are more imaginative and accommodating.
But I do not really want to involve myself in making controversial judgements on Christianity. My concern is primarily with the Platonist tradition, and secondarily with certain sectors of the «underworld» of Platonism, such as the Gnostic sects and the Chaldaean Oracles. Within that tradition I want to discuss the various roles which have been found for a female principle to play.
Before I begin I would like to make what seems to me a significant distinction between *functional* femininity & merely grammatical femininity.[1] Since

---

*   This originated as a lecture to the Department of Classics of the University of Barcelona, to whose hospitality and friendly criticism I am much indebted.

1.   For some remarks on the origins of the feminine endings in Greek, see P. CHANTRAINE, *Morphologie historique du Grec*, 2nd. ed., París 1964, pp. 29-33, *La formation des noms en grec ancien*, Pa-

nouns in the various languages we are involved with, Greek, Hebrew and Latin, can find themselves in the feminine gender from purely technical causes, a significant term in a philosophical system may find itself in the feminine for no very substantial reason. For instance, it is not clear to me that there is any compelling reason why the word for «soul» in Greek (*psyche*), Latin (*anima*), and Hebrew (*nephesh*), should be feminine, while the word for mind (*nous, animus, lev*) should be masculine. But the fact that this is so does, I think, at least help to create the basic antithesis between reason, or intellect, and the unreasoning life-principle, or even sense-perception (which, of course, is also a feminine, *aisthesis*). To anticipate for a moment our historical account, Philo is following the logic of Greek grammar, as well as being thoroughly Platonic, when, in Book I of the *Allegories of the Laws*, he allegorises Adam as *nous* and Eve as *aisthesis*.[2]

II

But let us begin at the beginning, both chronologically and cosmologically. There is a case to be made for regarding Platonism proper as beginning only with the death of Plato, but I do not propose to be as strict as that.[3] There are three entities in particular which I wish to dwell on in Plato's own philosophy. These are the Indefinite Dyad, the World Soul of the *Timaeus*, the *Statesman*, and *Laws* X, and the Receptacle (ὑποδοχή), or Nurse of Becoming in the *Timaeus* —all feminine entities both grammatical and functional.

The Indefinite Dyad (ἀόριστος δυάς), of course, occurs nowhere as such in Plato's written works, except perhaps in the form of the Unlimited of the

ris 1933. On the origins and significance of gender distinctions in language in general, see the excellent discussion of Götz WIENOLD, *Genus und Semantik*, Meisenheim am Glan 1967. Efforts on the part of comparative philologists to characterise the features of grammatical gender have been frequent, and entertaining. I give, as an example, that of Jakob GRIMM, in his *Deutsche Grammatik* (New ed. Gütersloh 1890), Vol. III, p. 357 (quoted by WIENOLD, *op. cit.*, p. 20):

«Das maskulinum scheint das frühere, grössere, festere, sprödere, raschere, das thätige, bewegliche, zeugende; das femininum, das spätere, kleinere, weichere, stillere, das leidende, empfangende; das neutrum das erzeugte, gewirkte, stoffartige, generelle, unentwickelte, collective.»

This plainly aspires to scientific objectivity, and to some exent attains it, but even as a statement of Grimm's personal views it is valuable, as the content of a well-schooled Indo-European-speaking mind. Those who have speculated on this question are broadly in agreement that the assigning of grammatical gender to objects not distinguished by natural gender is largely due to the personifying tendency of the primitive mind, which assigns sexual roles and characteristics to inanimate objects and even to abstractions, aided in this activity by its power of analogy. Certainly such «primitive» mental activities have left their mark on Greek philosophical speculation.

2. *Leg. All.* II 19-25.

3. I cannot at the moment think of anyone who is, but it could be argued that Platonism, as a system, originates only with Xenocrates.

Philebus (16C) - which also has a feminine form, ἀπειρία - but it is generally accepted, on the testimony of Aristotle, to have been a basic principle of his metaphysics, at least in his later period.[4] At *Metaphysics* I 6 (987b20ff), Aristotle refers to Plato's basic principle opposed to the One as a dyad of the «great and small», performing the role of matter (ὕλη). This is presented by Aristotle, rather tendentiously, as if it were a kind of pair, instead of an undifferentiated indefiniteness, but what Plato probably had in mind is more or less what is derivable from *Philebus* 24A-26D, where Unlimitedness is presented as something which can range indefinitely between opposite poles, the most general of which are the opposites Great and Small. (Aristotle uses the phrase ἀόριστος δυάς later, in Books M, 1081a14, and N, 1088a15, to describe this principle, though it is not quite clear whether this is Plato's own term for it).

At any rate, we have, as one of the two first principles of all things, a feminine entity which serves as «matter», or the womb of all becoming. As such, it is tempting to bring it into some relationship with the receptive principle of the *Timaeus,* described at 48D-53C, as, indeed, Aristotle does, on various occasions, as we know. This entity, however, the «Receptacle» (ὑποδοχή) or «Nurse (τιθήνη) of all becoming» (49A), seems to be something lower on the ontological scale, since it merely receives the copies of the Forms, which have already taken shape in the Paradigm (or, to demythologise all this, in the divine Intellect), without serving as the *material out of which* anything is made,[5] whereas the Indefinite Dyad is the principle out of which the Forms, regarded as Numbers, emerge in the first place. Ne-

4. I say 'generally accepted', but of course there has been fierce controversy on this question, notable protagonists being Harold CHERNISS, in *Aristotle's Criticism of Plato and the Academy,* I, and many trenchant book reviews (against), and the Tübingen School of Konrad Gaiser (*Platons Ungeschriebene Lehre*) and H-J Krämer (in favour). But I think it is fair to say that a consensus exists to the effect that Aristotle is not simply mistaken in his reports of Plato's doctrine of the One and the Great-and-Small.
   One possible explanation of the extraordinary degree of misinterpretation present in such a passage as *Phys.* IV 209b11-16 (on which, see Harold CHERNISS, *Aristotle's Criticism of Plato and the Academy,* pp. 112-24), where Aristotle first declares that in the *Timaeus* Plato says that χώρα is the same as ὕλη, and then that he uses a different terminology for this (presumably the Great-and-Small) ἐν τοῖς λεγομένοις ἀγράφοις δόγμασιν, would be that the 'ἄγραφα δόγματα' were in fact a document put together in the Academy only after Plato's death, perhaps not till the time of Xenocrates, purporting to be what the Master had maintained in conversation, and which would thus involve grave distortions, especially if, as I believe, the Master in fact played his cards pretty close to his chest. If so, this would be paralleled later in what Clitomachus and others did to Carneades' 'doctrines', and Amelius to those of Plotinus. Such a document would then in effect be the Gospel According to Xenocrates, which would help to explain the distortions. Aristotle would know this, of course, but would feel free to take it at its face value for polemical purposes.
5. It is important to specify that the Receptacle in the *Timaeus* is not a material principle in the Aristotelian sense, though later Platonists generally took it as such. The combinations of triangles which form the primary bodies are not formed by the Demiurge *from* the Receptacle, but rather projected onto it, as onto a kind of television screen. The Receptacle is simply their χώρα or ἕδρα (*Tim.* 52A). Only Plotinus, however, among later Platonists, really seems to appreciate the complexities of Plato's position (cfr. *Enn.* II 4).

vertheless, the fact that at *Tim.* 50D Plato is prepared to characterise it as a
«mother», with the realm of Forms (or perhaps Intellect?) as the Father,
and the cosmos as the offspring, seems to give it a status akin in honour to
the Dyad, and this has productive results, I think, in such entities as Xenocrates' Dyad and Philo's Sophia.

So, from the perspective of later Platonism, we find in Plato a female, receptive, formative principle at both the top and the bottom, so to speak, of
the cosmic scale. Whether or not for Plato himself these two entities are in
some way the same is quite obscure, but in the metaphysical schema of his
immediate follower, Speusippus, they seem to have been, as we shall see
presently.

For the moment, however, I wish to turn to the other vitally important female principle in Plato's philosophy, the World Soul. In *Timaeus* 34B-36D
the creation of this entity is presented in terms that are notoriously obscure,[6] but what at least is clear is Plato's intention to present it as an essentially intermediate and mediating entity. The intricate blending of the three
elements of Substance, Sameness, and Otherness is designed to enable the
Soul to commune with both the realm of True Being and that of Becoming, the physical world. It must be noted that the World Soul, thus constituted, is a rational entity; even the Circle of the Other «partakes of reason
and harmony» (36E), as it contemplates every aspect of reality along with
the Circle of the Same. On the other hand, this rationality of the Soul's is
derivative, having been bestowed upon it by its maker, the Demiurge - or,
once again to demythologise the *Timaeus* story, Intellect (*Nous*). The relations of *Nous* and World-Soul, and the degree of rationality accorded the
latter, will be a recurring theme in this account of Platonic doctrine.

The position of the World Soul in relation to the Demiurge has further
light thrown on it in the Myth of the *Statesman* (269C-274D), though a
light that brings with it its own obscurities.[7] Here the soul is much more
closely linked to the body of the cosmos, to the extent that in a number of
passages it is unclear what is being talked of, and some scholars, notably
P-M. Schuhl, have wished to take the motion of the cosmos independent of
the Demiurge as purely mechanical.[8] However, later Platonists saw here

6. I find CORNFORD's interpretation (in which he follows Proclus) still the most convincing (*Plato's Cosmology*, pp. 59-66), though it is a little disturbing that Xenocrates, on the evidence of
   Plutarch (*De Proc. An.* 1013E) does not seem to have grasped the subtleties of it.
7. I treat the *Statesman* after the *Timaeus* διδασκαλίας ἕνεκα, though I regard it as in fact somewhat
   earlier (I am not among those who accept 'Owen's Theory' as to the early dating of the *Timaeus*). However, the relation between Demiurge and World Soul in the *Statesman* is better
   discussed, I think, in the light of the more circumstantial exposition in the *Timaeus*, and I do
   not see that we need to postulate any development or alteration of Plato's doctrine between
   those two fairly contiguous dialogues —if they are correctly interpreted (along the lines laid
   down by Harold CHERNISS, e.g. in «The Sources of Evil according to Plato», *Proc. Amer. Philos. Soc.* 98, 1954, pp. 23-30).
8. There has been much discussion of this question. I refer the reader to the following: P-M.
   SCHUHL, 'Sur le mythe du Politique', *Revue de Metaphysique et de Morale* 39, 1932; Gregory

the workings of a World Soul, and it is the *Statesman* Myth in particular that encourages Plutarch in his distinctive view of the World Soul as essentially irrational, so we cannot neglect the passage.

The Stranger describes the universe (τὸ πᾶν) in 269c7 as «a living thing which has been allotted reason by its framer» (ζῷον ὂν καὶ φρόνησιν εἰληχὸς ἐκ τοῦ συναρμόσαντος), and this would, on Platonic principles, imply the presence in it of soul, though a soul granted rationality by a principle external to it, as is the case in the *Timaeus*. The phrase used to describe its innate motion just below (269d2), ἐξ ἀνάγκης ἔμφυτον, can be taken to refer to this essential irrationality, though it may just as well, I suppose, refer to the purely mechanical tendency of the world body to revolve on its axis when released from constraint. Again, in 270A, when released from the control of the Demiurge, it «proceeds of its own accord» (δι᾽ ἑαυτοῦ αὐτὸν ἰέναι), having built up a momentum which carries it on for many myriads of revolutions, a turn of phrase really more compatible with purely mechanical motion. Later, at 273B-D, we hear of the world being «taught» by the Demiurge, then «forgetting» its teaching, and tending back towards its original state of chaos, presented in very similar terms to that of the «original» state of things in the *Timaeus* (30A) — all of which is at least compatible with a description of the behaviour of inanimate matter. It is, furthermore, a remarkable fact that the word ψυχή is nowhere used in the whole course of the Myth (except to refer to individual souls, at 272el-2).

Plainly, however, *pace* Schuhl, there is a soul of some sort involved here. At 269d8, the universe is said to «partake in body» (κεκοινώνηκέ γε καὶ σώματος) which implies that it is not just body, and at 270a3-4 it receives life and a «contrived immortality» (ἀθανασία ἐπισκευαστή) from the Demiurge, at least the former of which implies the presence of a soul of some sort. Then there is the σύμφυτος ἐπιθυμία of 272e6, which, together with the «learning» and «forgetting» of 273B-D, suggests an irrational soul amenable to rational ordering, but having no innate reason of its own, which is precisely what Plutarch sees here.

So Soul is pretty certainly present in the *Statesman* Myth, but how exactly its activity is to be distinguished from the mechanical motions of the world body remains a disputed question.

The other place in which the doctrine of a World Soul emerges —this time explicitly— is in *Laws* X, and here the complication arises, or appears to

VLASTOS, 'The Disorderly Motion in the Timaeus', *CQ* 33, 1939, pp. 71-83 (repr. in R. E. ALLEN, *Studies in Plato's Metaphysics*, London 1965); Hans HERTER, 'Gott und die Welt bei Platon: Eine Studie zum Mythos des Politikos', *BonnJbb*, 158, 1958, pp. 106-117; id. 'Die Bewegung der Materie bei Platon', *RhM*. 100, 1957, pp. 327-47; T. M. ROBINSON, *Plato's Psychology*, Toronto 1970, ch. 8; J. B. SKEMP, *The Theory of Motion in Plato's Later Dialogues*, Cambridge 1942 (2nd ed. Amsterdam 1967); id., *Plato's Statesman*, London 1952. Intro., pp. 82-112; and, most recently, R. D. MOHR, 'Disorderly Motion in Plato's *Statesman*', *Phoenix* 35, 1981, pp. 199-215.

arise, of two opposing Souls, a beneficent and a maleficent. In a well-known passage, 896DE, the Athenian Stranger reasons as follows:

> «Must we then necessarily agree, in the next place, that Soul is the cause of things good and bad, fair and foul, just and unjust, and all the opposites, if we are to assume it to be the cause of all things?»
>
> *Cleinias:* «Of course we must».
>
> *Athenian:* «And as Soul thus controls and indwells in all things everywhere that are moved, must we not necessarily affirm that it controls the heavens also?»
>
> *Cleinias:* «Yes».
>
> *Athenian:* «One soul, is it, or several? I Will answer for you-«Several». Anyhow, let us assume not less than two —the beneficent soul and that which is capable of effecting results of the opposite kind.»
>
> (trans. Bury).

I am prepared to agree with Harold Cherniss [9] and others that no dualism of Good and Evil World-Souls is, despite appearances, intended by Plato here, but it is more relevant to our theme that, rightly or wrongly, later Platonists generally did assume that an Evil World-Soul is being described in this passage, though subordinate to, rather than coordinate with, the good Soul, which Plato presents as presiding over the heavens, and the regular motions of the heavenly bodies. The implication here is, though it is not stated in this passage, that the irregularities of the sublunar world must be laid as a charge against the evil Soul.

We have here, then, between the *Philebus,* the *Statesman,* the *Timaeus* and *Laws* X, with some reinforcement from reports of Plato's oral teaching, a comprehensive range of female cosmic principles, such as continues to be of basic significance in later Platonism, in one guise or another: first, the Indefinite Dyad; then, a rational World Soul; then (at least in the view of later Platonists), an irrational (either neutral or maleficent) World Soul; and lastly, formless and all-receptive Matter. I wish now to make some attempt to trace the subsequent development of these entities over the five hundred years or so that separate Plato and Plotinus. Of necessity, this survey must be selective, but I will try to pick out the most important, and most interesting, manifestations.

---

9. In 'The Sources of Evil According to Plato's, cfr. above, n. 7.

III

First of all, the Old Academy. Both Speusippus and Xenocrates retained the basic pair of principles, One, or Monad, and Indefinite Dyad,[10] and each of them develops the doctrine in interesting ways. This is particularly true of Speusippus, if we are prepared, as I am,[11] to accept as essentially Speusippan ch. 4 of Iamblichus' *De Communi Mathematica Scientia,* which certainly presents a cosmology highly compatible with what we can gather from Aristotle's rather contemptuous and very allusive accounts of Speusippus' doctrine. In this passage the two primary principles are presented as the One and Multiplicity (πλῆθος). This latter is, admittedly, a neuter noun, but it performs a characteristically female role, being the cause of division, and thus of the generation of all things, and is referred to directly below as «like an entirely fluid and pliable matter (ὑγρᾷ τινι παντάπασι καὶ εὐπλαδεῖ ὕλῃ)». In fact, what Speusippus seems to be doing is to connect the primal Multiplicity (the Unlimited, or «Great-and-Small») with the Receptacle of the *Timaeus,*[11a] by postulating the same «female» creative principle manifesting itself at a series of levels, altering its nature as a receptacle according to the level of formative agent which acts upon it. This is, at any rate, the best sense I can make of Speusippus' scheme (which Aristotle, as we know, satirises as making the universe «episodic», *Met.* XII 10,1076a1). The primal union is that between One and Multiplicity, and this produces numbers. The first principle of number, then —whatever that is— acts upon the matter corresponding to it, which is only the original Multiplicity as modified by the action of the One. This union in turn produces geometricals, both plane figures and solids. This third level of entity produces, out of the first principle of geometricals and its corresponding Matter, the Soul, which sets the geometrical level in motion, and hence acquires the definition «the Idea of the omnidimensionally extended» (Fr. 40 Lang). The identities of the fourth and fifth level are not made clear in the *DCMS* passage, but, if we are to extrapolate logically from what we have seen so far, the fourth level would result from the action of Soul on its corresponding Matter, to produce the level of physical life. The fifth and last level, arising out of the action of immanent Soul upon what is now Matter in the

10. Speusippus, Fr. 34 Lang.= Fr. 48 Taran (the doctrine is here attributed to 'the ancients', but that should not deceive us); Xenocrates, Fr. 15 Heinze.
11. Following the brilliant lead of Philip MERLAN in *From Platonism to Neo-Platonism,* ch. 5. See also the excellent article of Harold TARRANT, 'Speusippus' Ontological Classification', *Phronesis* XIX, 1974; pp. 130-145. The attempt of Leonardo TARÁN in the introduction to his recent edition of the fragments (*Speusippus of Athens,* Brill, Leiden 1981, pp. 86-107), to impugn the identification I do not find decisive. I deal further with this in an article in *Phronesis* XXIX, *
    1984, pp. 325-332.
11a. An identification actually made by Aristotle at *Phys.* 209b35ff., and one for which he has been strongly criticised, e.g. by CHERNISS in *The Riddle of the Early Academy,* p. 17 ff.

114

«vulgar» sense, would be that of the world of inanimate bodies. Since this elaborate process cannot be conceived of as taking place in any sort of chronological succession, how the various levels can be distinguished becomes for me, at least, a deep mystery, as it plainly was for Aristotle. The argument given in *DCMS* IV (p. 16, 18ff) for this process, however, deserves quotation, since it provides a rationale for the whole procedure:

> «If one postulates one single Matter and Receptacle,[12] it would be unreasonable not to expect that, since the Form of the One that imposes itself upon it is totally uniform, we should get a uniform class of thing resulting. The consequence of that would be that all classes of thing would be numbers, for we would not be able to postulate any differentiating cause why at one stage numbers were generated, and then lines, and planes, and solid figures, and not always the same class, since they would be springing from the same principles uniting in the same way.»

The argument, therefore, is that, since different classes of entity do in fact arise in the cosmogonic process, and we cannot postulate a differentiation within the One itself, nor yet within Multiplicity, «pliable» though it is, unless different stimuli are applied to it, one must come up with some such scheme as this to account for the phenomena. Whatever about the validity of this argument, the interest of Speusippus' scheme from our perspective is that it provides a link between all the female principles we have so far been considering, Dyad, Soul and Matter. We do not see any such linkage again till Plotinus, with his doctrines of Intelligible Matter, and of Soul as in a sense the «matter» of Intellect (e. g. *Enn.* II 4, 1-5; V 1, 3, 20-23).

Xenocrates presents no such complexities, but he does present us with a problem —or at least his Fr. 15 does. Since this is a doxographic summary of his doctrine by Aetius, the problem may not in fact go back to Xenocrates himself. From Aetius we learn that Xenocrates

> «held as gods the Monad and Dyad. The former, as the male principle, has the role of Father, ruling in the heavens. This he terms Zeus and "Odd" (*perittos*), and Intellect, and it is for him the supreme God. The Second is, as it were, the female principle, *in the role of Mother of the* Gods (if this is how μητρὸς θεῶν δίκην is to be taken), ruling over the realm beneath the heavens, who is for him the Soul of the All.»

Now either Xenocrates really made his second principle a subcelestial entity, and identified it with the World Soul, or there is a lacuna in the text, or there is no lacuna, but Aetius is misunderstanding Xenocrates. As to the

---

12. Note here the conjunction of ὕλη and ὑποδοχή, indicating that Speusippus (if it is he) had no qualms about presenting the Platonic Receptacle as Matter. I do not, however, see this as an objection to Speusippan authorship of this text, as does TARÁN (*op. cit.*, p. 107). The term ὕλη does not have to be either the invention of Aristotle, or, even if it is, confined to him by copyright.

first possibility, it is difficult to see how Xenocrates could have combined the Indefinite Dyad with a World Soul, especially as we learn from the same Aetius (Fr. 28H) that he called his second principle «the everflowing» (ἀέναος), by which, says Aetius, he means Matter, by reason of its multiplicity (πλῆθος). This reference to πλῆθος may be an intentional reminiscence of Speusippus, and if so, it is possible that Xenocrates could have telescoped all the levels of Speusippus' second principle, and identified it with the World Soul. But that leaves him in the strange position of identifying an essentially negative entity with one which is basically positive, being the principle of order (presumably) in the cosmos, since it rules over it —unless, of course, Xenocrates is taking a distinctly Gnostic view of the ruling principles of this world.

In *The Middle Platonists*,[13] I was inclined to suspect the second alternative, a lacuna in the text of Stobaeus (where the doxographical notice is found), and I am still inclined to that solution. A possible alternative, however, is that Aetius is grossly confused. At any rate, the text cannot be correct. We know, after all, from Plutarch (*Proc. An.* 1012D) that Xenocrates held that the Soul (and we are talking about the World Soul of the *Timaeus*) is a product of the action of the One on the Indefinite Dyad (his definition of the Soul as «number moving itself» gains in meaning, I think, if one sees it as a development of Speusippan doctrine). So the Soul cannot also be the Indefinite Dyad.

Faced with this problem, some scholars, notably Heinze [14] and, more recently, H-J. Krämer,[15] have maintained that the Dyad mentioned in Fr. 15 cannot be the Indefinite Dyad, but must simply be the Soul seen as a dyad. But this will hardly do. As reported by Plutarch (*Proc. An.* 1013E), Xenocrates identified the «undivided essence» of *Tim.* 35A with the One, and «that which is divided about bodies» with Multiplicity (πλῆθος), «which he also calls the Indefinite Dyad», and the Soul is the product of these two. Aetius is purporting to present here a summary of Xenocrates' metaphysics, and if he leaves out the Indefinite Dyad, and calls the Soul a dyad instead, then he is plainly in a state of deep confusion about his subject-matter —a much more probable situation, in my view, than that Xenocrates is involved in self-contradiction.

This does not quite dispose of the problem, though. Xenocrates chooses to theologise his principles, making the Monad Zeus, and the Dyad «the mother of the gods», by whom we must understand Rhea (already identified with the Dyad by Philolaus (Fr. 20a), no doubt on the basis of a supposed connexion with ῥέω —which would also concord with Xenocrates' epithet for it, ἀέναος). The fact that this puts Zeus in an Oedipal relationship with

13. P. 25. There is, incidentally, an embarrassing misprint in my translation of Fr. 15 there. For 'beyond the heavens' read 'beneath the heavens'.
14. *Xenokrates*, p. 35 n. 1.
15. *Der Ursprung der Geistmetaphysik*, pp. 39-41.

his own mother does not seem to disturb him. What disturbs me, though, about the text is the phrase «μητρὸς θεῶν δίχην». «Δίχην» used adverbially is a rather high-flown locution. It actually occurs no less than seven times in the surviving portions of Aetius, but in all other cases it has its correct meaning of «in the manner of», whereas here it would have to mean rather «in the role of», or «representing», which would be something of a solecism, though not, perhaps, impossible for a late Hellenistic writer. It is here, at any rate, that I would conjecture a lacuna, adopting a proposal of Pierre Boyancé [16] that we understand Δίχη with a capital letter, as a personification. Boyancé does not, however, take the obvious next step of postulating a lacuna between θεῶν and Δίχην. But Xenocrates is not a fool. Rhea cannot be Dike, since Dike is known, since Hesiod (*Works and Days*, 256) to be a *daughter* of Zeus, not his mother; and that is a very proper theologising of the World Soul.

If either of my solutions of the problem of Fr. 15 is accepted, we find Xenocrates making use of two female principles, the first, the Indefinite Dyad as a material principle, the second, the World Soul. Neither of these entities can be considered an «evil» principle in any dualistic sense. I was wrong, I think, in *The Middle Platonists* (p. 26), to describe Xenocrates' Dyad, following Heinze,[17] as an «evil and disorderly principle», because of his alleged influence on the metaphysical schema of Plutarch's *Isis and Osiris,* to which I shall turn presently. No entity which is theologised as Rhea, it seems to me, can be regarded as positively evil, as opposed to incidentally introducing into the world effects that seem «evil» to us, as by-products of multiplicity. Certainly, Xenocrates is attested as believing in evil daemons (φαῦλοι δαίμονες Fr. 23-5ff), and the role of Hades as ruler of the realm below the moon is a rather ambiguous one, but it does not follow from that that we can refer back to him the strong dualism represented by Osiris and Seth-Typhon. Plutarch's dualism is picked up elsewhere.

As for the World Soul, the theologising of it as Dike is very apt, I think, as a portrayal of the Soul as presented in the *Timaeus.* Dike, in Hesiod, on the one hand sits by Zeus' side as his *paredros,* or assessor, and on the other roams about in the physical world and reports back her impressions. This seems to characterise very well the circles of the Same and the Other of which the Soul is composed. Xenocrates' World Soul is thus a rational entity, though it possesses reason derivatively, as bestowed upon it by Nous; it also presides over the realm of coming-to-be and passing away, of motion in all its forms. That is what it is to be «a number moving itself».

16. 'Xenocrate et les Orphiques', *REA* 36, 1948, p. 218ff.
17. *Xenokrates,* pp. 30-5.

IV

The legacy of the Old Academy in the matter of female principles is thus a broadly coherent one —Indefinite Dyad, World Soul, Matter, all three creative, receptive of rational influence, «evil», if at all, only incidentally or negatively. Only the possible maleficent Soul of *Laws* X stands out as anomalous, and we cannot be sure what Plato really intended there. What I would like to do in the latter part of this paper is to examine a few of the female entities which occur in the later Platonist tradition, and see how they fit into this Old Academic framework. I will take, in turn, Philo of Alexandria's Sophia, Plutarch's Isis, the Hecate of the Chaldaean Oracles and the Sophia of Valentinian Gnosticism.

Strictly speaking, Philo's monotheism should leave no place for an independent female principle in the universe, but in fact, both the influence of Platonism and the already established Wisdom tradition in Hellenistic Judaism conspire to carve out a place in his system for such a principle. Such a principle is often simply equated with the Logos, and as such is outside the scope of this investigation, but in a number of passages we find the figure of Sophia, God's Wisdom, coming into her own.

In Sect. 109 of *On Flight and Finding (Fug.)*, for example, we find the Logos described as the son of God, and Sophia «through whom the universe came into existence» (δι'ἧς τὰ ὅλα ἦλθεν εἰς γένεσιν). Sophia is here not simply a material cause, since Philo uses the preposition *dia*, which is that proper to the instrumental cause - normally, in fact, the Logos (cfr. *Cher.* 125ff). This representation of Sophia as the instrumental rather than the material cause concords well, in fact, with a piece of allegorising we know of from Varro [18] (who was in philosophy a follower of the Platonism of Antiochus of Ascalon). He is reported as identifying Athena (Minerva) with the cause *secundum quod*, a rendering of *kath'ho*, which is a variant of *di'ho*. It looks very much as if Philo is influenced by the contemporary Stoic and Platonist allegorisation of Athene, springing, as she does, from the brow of Zeus, with the Logos, in his treatment of Sophia here. She is not quite an Indefinite Dyad here (Philo uses the term «dyad», e. g. *Spec. Leg.* III 180; *Somm.* II 70, but always to describe Matter); she is more like a rational World Soul, assisting a divine Nous in his creation —somewhat reminiscent, indeed, of Xenocrates' Dike.

At 116-117 of *The Worse Attacks the Better (Det.)*, however, Sophia is given the epithets τροφός and τιθηνόκομος (reminiscent of the τιθήνη of *Timaeus* 49A), and described as «mother of all things in the world (μήτηρ τῶν ἐν κόσμῳ γενομένη), affording to her offspring, as soon as they are born, the nourishment which they require from her own breasts, a development of

---

18.   *Ap*. Aug. *CD* VII 28.

118

Plato's image which he would certainly not have approved of, as it gives Matter far too benign and positive a role. Indeed, one is now inclined to think rather of Xenocrates'. Rhea, as earth-mother. To complicate the issue further, Philo just below (118) represents Sophia as the manna in the desert, which he etymologises as «ti», the most general category of Stoic logic, but, which he normally identifies with the Logos (cfr. LA III 175), and which he here describes as λόγος θεῖος.

What this indicates is not, I think, complete incoherence in Philo's thought, so much as a tension between the concepts of Sophia and the Logos, which potentially fulfil very much the same cosmogonic role. We can see the same tension between the roles of Demiurge and World-Soul in later Platonists such as Albinus or Numenius. What we have here is a creative and nurturing principle, plainly, in Philo's mind, subordinate to God, but still presented as *mother* to all things (including the Logos), rather than anyone's daughter, and so more a Rhea-figure than a Dike-figure. Sophia certainly owes something to the tradition of Jewish Wisdom literature, but in Philo's thought, in my view, Platonism predominates.[19]

Philo had the problem of fitting a female principle into a strongly monotheist framework. With Plutarch we find the contrasted situation, of a female principle or principles being introduced into a thoroughly dualist framework. I propose to confine my investigations to just one manifestation of femininity, the figure of Isis in the treatise *On Isis and Osiris*.

Plutarch does also recognise the Indefinite Dyad *(Def. Or.* 428F), as «the element underlying all formlessness and disorder», which he identifies not only with the Necessity *(Anagke)* of the *Timaeus* (48A, 56C, 68E), but also with what he sees as the Maleficent Soul of *Laws* X. However, when he theologises this, as he does in the *De Is.* (369E), it is as *male* principle, the Persian Ahriman or the Egyptian Seth-Typhon. It also fills the role of Matter, though it is a more actively evil principle than Matter is traditionally. taken to be. Isis, however, takes on some characteristics of Matter as well, as we shall see.

Isis is presented at *De Is.* 372E as follows:

«Isis is, in fact, the female principle in nature, and that which receives all procreation, and so she is called by Plato *(Tim.* 49A, 51A) the «nurse» and «all-receiving» (πανδεχής), and by the majority of people «myriad-named» since, through being turned this way and that by the Logos (if that is the meaning of ὑπὸ τοῦ λόγου τρεπομένη), she receives into herself all the shapes and Forms (ἰδέας). She has an innate love for the primal and most dominant element of all things, which is identical with the Good, and this she yearns for and pursues; but the portion which comes from evil she tries to avoid and reject,

---

19. For an interesting discussion of the *Wisdom of Solomon*, see David WINSTON, *The Wisdon of Solomon*, trans., with intro. and comm., New York 1979 (Anchor Bible Series), esp. pp. 20-63.

for she acts as place and matter (χώρα καὶ ὕλη) to both, but inclines naturally always towards the better, and offers to it opportunity to create from her and to sow into her effluxes and likenesses, in which she rejoices and is glad that she is made pregnant and filled with these creations. For creation is the image of Being in Matter, and the thing created is the imitation of the existent.»

What we have here is a female principle of the «World Soul» variety, but an irrational World Soul, which Plutarch assimilates to the Receptacle of the *Timaeus*. In fact we find very much such an entity in ch. 10 of Albinus' *Didaskalikos*, a World-Soul essentially irrational, which requires «arousing» by the supreme God, who is the cause of its intellect.[20] It is not positively an evil principle; simply ambivalent, and open to influence from either side, though inclining towards the better.

Isis is, then, poised between a pair of antithetical principles. She is not herself the antithesis of the Good. Yet she is presented by Plutarch a little further on (373EF), rather curiously, as the antithesis of a triad (Osiris - Isis - Horus) into which, he says, «the better and more divine nature» is divided: «the Intelligible (νοητόν), Matter (ὕλη), and the product of these, which the Greeks call the world (κόσμος)». Plutarch goes on to identify these respectively with the Paradigm, the Receptacle and the «offspring» (ἔκγονος) of the *Timaeus* (50 CD). This triadic division must leave out of account the primally evil principle (the Dyad, or Seth-Typhon), and also, I suggest, the primally good one. What we have is a triad of Logos, irrational World-Soul (acting as its matter), and physical world.[21]

Isis is, then, a significantly different figure from Sophia, and more than a step from her in the direction of Gnosticism.[22] Indeed, there is one strange phrase in Plutarch's account (373A), which I now think I made too much of in *The Middle Platonists* (pp. 202-3), but which I still find puzzling. Plutarch speaks of the *logoi* which descend to be «impressed» on the World Soul being seized by «the disorderly and disturbing element which has been driven here from the region above» (τὸ ἄτακτον καὶ ταραχῶδες ἐνταῦθα τῆς ἄνω χώρας ἀπεληλαμένον). If we take ἡ ἄνω χώρα to refer to the intelligible, divine world, as seems indicated, this would imply that the Indefinite Dyad (Seth-Typhon) originated in that realm, and that some sort of Fall occurred

---

20. Cfr. also *Did.* ch. 14, p. 169, 30 ff. Hermann, where the same thing is said, the evocative word κάρος being used for the 'slumber' of the soul.

21. I have been criticised by reviewers (e. g. Harold TARRANT in *Prudentia* X, 1978, p. 111) for speaking so confidently about a *logos* doctrine in Plutarch. There is some justice in this criticism, and I should be more cautious now, but I do not see how Plutarch's presentation of Osiris as the logos here can be dismissed as not 'part of Plutarch's regular system'. What is his regular system?

22. I have not here dealt with the World Soul as presented in the *Proc. An.*, which, as Werner DEUSE has recently shown (*Untersuchungen zur mittelplatonische und neuplatonische Seelenlehre*, Wiesbaden 1983, ch. II) is regarded by Plutarch as essentially non-rational, receiving reason as something external to it. Plutarch is much influenced here by his interpretation of the *Politicus* Myth.

120

which would involve the World-Soul itself (Sophia), but it seems to imply the ultimate origin of the principle antithetical to the One from the One itself. However, perhaps one should not press this too far— ἀπεληλαμένον may only imply that Evil is forever banished from the divine realm. In any case, it does not directly bear on the situation of Isis herself, which seems archetypally median and ambivalent.

V

But let us turn now from Plutarch to a brief and selective survey of the «underworld» of Platonism, where female principles abound and prolifera-te. First let us consider the Sophia of Valentinian Gnosticism, as the Valen-tinian is that one among the Gnostic systems that gives the clearest evidence of Platonist influence, at least in the form in which it is (indig-nantly) relayed to us by the heresiologist Hippolytus.[23]
Sophia is, of course, not the only female principle in Gnosticism, merely the most interesting, in that it is her Fall and repentance that sets the who-le cosmogony going. In Valentinus' system, as presented by Hippolytus, we begin with the supreme God, the Forefather, who procreates by himself[24] an initial pair of entities, one male (Intellect - *Nous*) and one female (Truth - *Aletheia*), and through them, then, a string of paired male and female en-tities, called Aeons, the most junior of which, on the female side, is Sophia. These aeons, twenty-eight (or thirty) in all, together form the Pleroma. I will let Hippolytus take up the tale of Sophia's misadventures (*Ref.* VI 28,6-7):

> «Now when the twelfth of the twelve (sc. Aeons proceeding from the Aeons Anthropos and Ecclesia), the youngest of all the twenty-eight aeons, a female, Sophia by name, observed the quantity and po-wer of the productive aeons, she hastened back into the depth of the Father and perceived that all the other aeons, being begotten, were procreating in pairs, but that the Father alone was procreating wit-hout a partner. She wished to emulate the Father and to produce offs-pring of herself alone, without a partner, in order that she might achieve a work which would not be in any way inferior to that of the Father.»

Sophia is thus the first feminist. Her ambition is not really evil, just radica-lly misguided. (In Irenaeus' account (see n. 24 above), her sin is simply de-sire to know her Father, «to comprehend his greatness»; there is no ques-

---

23. *Refutation of All Heresies*, VI 29, 2-36, 4.
24. In another version, that of Irenaeus (*Adv. Haer.* I 1, 1-8, 6), who seems to be reporting the system of Valentinus' follower Ptolemaeus, the Forefather is paired by a female principle, his Ennoia (Thought), an entity rather reminiscent of Philo's Sophia, on whom he engenders *Nous* and *Aletheia*, and then a total of *thirty* aeons.

tion of emulation, since in that version he has a consort, Ennoia). In any case, the result of Sophia's presumption is a feeble abortion, the Demiurge, Ialdabaoth, who then creates the physical world, and a host of demons to rule it, and ultimately Man himself - although he and his henchmen cannot get Man to work properly. Meanwhile Sophia, full of repentance, sets about correcting her error. This involves inserting a spark of divine pneuma into Man, and ultimately provoking the generation of Christ from the whole Pleroma, as a saviour of the world, after the completion of which salvation the world will dissolve.

Sophia's production of Ialdabaoth finds a curious parallel in Plutarch's *De Iside*, if we may turn our attention back there for a moment. At 373BC, Plutarch gives an allegory of a composite Greco-Egyptian myth about the birth of Apollo (Horus) from Isis and Osiris, «while these gods were still in the womb of Rhea». This means that «before this world was made visible and its rough material (*hyle*) was completely formed by the Logos, it was tested by nature (φύσει ἐλεγχομένην, whatever that really means), and brought forth of itself the first creation imperfect». This «first creation» is termed the elder Horus, and is said to have been born in darkness, a cripple —«a mere image and phantasm of the world that was to be».

So Isis, it seems, produced a sort of foreshadowing of the cosmos on her own, before being filled with logoi by Osiris.[25] For Plutarch, this only indicates her desire for Form and order, but it has a curious resemblance to Valentinus' myth. A possible connexion (apart from direct dependence —Valentinus is a generation or so younger than Plutarch) would be a common dependence on Egyptian mythology. Valentinus was, after all, an Egyptian, and other aspects of his system show the influence of Egyptian religious conceptions.[26]

There is much more that could be said about Sophia in Gnosticism, and about other female principles associated with her. In some versions, for instance, she generates a lower projection of herself, Achamoth (from Hebrew *hokhmah*, wisdom), who serves as an immanent organising principle for the physical world (like Plotinus' concept of *Physis* later), while Sophia remains above. But I want to turn, in the time remaining to us, to consider one further female principle from the Platonic Underworld, the formidable Hecate of the Chaldaean Oracles.

The Oracles date from the last decades of the Second Century,[27] somewhat later than Valentinus, and approximately contemporary with the Neopyt-

25. As is correctly noted by R. M. JONES, in *Classical Journal* 19, 1924, pp. 565-6, who compares the state of the Receptacle and its contents in *Tim.* 53.

26. For instance, the Forefather's production, without a partner, of Nous and Aletheia is reminiscent of Atum's production of Shu and Tefnut. On the question of a possible common source for Plutarch's Isis and Valentinus' Sophia, see TOUSHOUDT, *Ein onbekend gnostisch systeem in Plutarchs De Iside et Osiride*, Louvain 1942.

27. Their author, a certain Julian, served with Marcus Aurelius on his campaign against the Quadi in 173 A.D. as a sort of witchdoctor-in-residence, which provides a date for his *floruit*.

hagorean Numenius, with which they have some points of contact. In Fr. 3,[28] we hear of the «Power» (*dynamis*) of the Father, a female principle more intimately associated with the supreme god than even his Intellect —rather like Philo's Sophia, or the Valentinian Ptolemaeus' Ennoia, except that there is no indication that Power has any role in generating Intellect; it merely «remains with» the Father, while the Intellect «proceeds from» him.

This *dynamis*, however, is distinct from and superior to Hecate,[29] who stands on the border between the intelligible and sensible worlds, acting both as a barrier and as a link between them, very much in the role of World Soul. In Fr. 6 she is presented as an intellectual «diaphragm» or «membrane» (ὑπεζωκώς τις ὑμὴν νοερός) between the two worlds, while in Fr. 30 she is described as «fount of founts, a womb containing all things» (πηγὴ τῶν πηγῶν, μήτρα συνέχουσα τὰ πάντα). She is regularly given the epithet ζωογόνος, «lifegiving» (Fr. 30; Proclus, *In Tim.* I 5,15; 11, 19-20; *In Parm.* 1153,30).

Thus presented, Hecate seems to fill much the same role as Plutarch's Isis, or Xenocrates' Dike (if we knew more about her). Some of her epithets, such as *metra*, «womb», connect her, like Isis, with the Receptacle of the *Timaeus*, but she is also analogous to the World Soul, in that she perfoms an active role in transmitting *logoi* to the physical world. Why the author of the *Oracles* chose Hecate for this central mediating figure, rather than, say, Athene or Isis, is not quite clear to me, but perhaps her role in magical ritual was significant in this connexion, since the Oracles are, after all, a handbook of theurgy, and Hecate, as a chthonic deity, is easier to summon up than Athene might be.

A complication in Hecate's status in that she is presented (in Fr. 50) as having «her centre established in the midst of the Fathers» and Psellus confirms this (*Expos.* 1152a), by saying that she is in the middle of the «source-fathers» (πηγαῖοι πατέρες), flanked by the ἅπαξ ἐπέκεινα (whom we might term «Transcendental I») above her, and the δὶς ἐπέκεινα (Transcendental II) below her.[30] Hecate is thus the median element in a triad, fulfilling the same role, that of *dynamis*, that the highest female principle performs. It is possible, I suppose, that Psellus' account of Chaldaean theology reflects Neoplatonic elaboration, and that in the Oracles themselves this basic triad is all there ever was. Des Places is of this opinion, but I am not so sure. Either way, though, Hecate takes on some of the character of the *Hagion Pneuma*, the Second Person of the Christian Trinity. It is with that figure that we began, so it is suitable to end our survey at this point.

28. I use the Budé edition of E. DES PLACES, Paris 1971.

29. DES PLACES tries to identify them (*Intro.* p. 13), but Psellus' *Exposition of Chaldaean Doctrine* (1152a, p. 189 Des Places) makes it clear that they exist on different levels.

30. These curious titles seem to result from an interpretation of the Chaldaean deities Ad and Adad ('Adad' being 'Ad' doubled).

VI

The entities surveyed in the second part of the paper demonstrate, I think, in interesting ways, that the relationship set up by Plato in the *Timaeus* between Demiurge, World Soul, and Receptacle is philosophically a most uncomfortable one. I cannot believe that he intends us to take it literally, and I am continually astonished at those scholars, some very distinguished, who wish to take it so. The lesson to be derived, I think, from the way in which the creative divine Intellect, the World Soul and the Dyad, or Matter, are presented in the Old Academy and in Middle Platonism is that those philosophers found it in all cases necessary to rearrange the relationship. Either the Demiurge becomes the supreme Intellect, repository of the Forms, and the World Soul his active principle or *logos*, while Matter takes on the features of an irrational World Soul, or the Demiurge is preserved as a secondary, creator god, while the World Soul takes on the role of a material principle, with or without a further material principle, either positively or just negatively evil, in the background.

At any rate, be that as it may, what I hope I have shown is that functional, as opposed to purely grammatical femininity has an integral place in the Platonic world-view —not the highest, certainly, but an honourable place nonetheless. «The female» has been given such a negative connotation, ever since the promulgation of the Pythagorean Table of Opposites, that it is right to remind ourselves of the considerable spread of roles which female principles in fact take on. *Chercher la femme* can be a rewarding activity for the Platonic philosopher.

V

TAMPERING WITH THE *TIMAEUS:* IDEOLOGICAL EMENDATIONS IN PLATO, WITH SPECIAL REFERENCE TO THE *TIMAEUS**

Ancient scholars, as we know, did not neglect the emendation of texts, but the principles on which they worked, as we also know, were by modern standards eccentric.[1] The work of Aristophanes of Byzantium on Homer, and of Aristophanes and Didymus Chalcenterus on Euripides, to mention but two conspicuous instances, are well attested in the respective scholia, and we can see from them how what one might term "hard" scholarship was mixed with subjective judgements on what was "proper" to the author concerned which surpass the excesses of any nineteenth-century German philologist.

Of course, like nineteenth-century German scholars, the Alexandrians had ample excuse for their obelising and athetising in the perilous state of the manuscripts which confronted them in the library. Centuries of rhapsodes and actors had made their contributions to the texts of epics and tragedies, and the Alexandrian scholars knew this well, even as modern scholars, at the dawn of scientific textual criticism, came to realise what could happen to mediaeval manuscripts at the hands of monkish scribes and scholars. This knowledge, in either case, led to excesses, but they were the excesses of scholarly expertise, not of ignorance.

All this by way of a general introduction to my particular theme. Apart from interpolations and emendations due to artistic vanity or misplaced literary ambition, I would like to argue for a class of textual disturbances which is due rather to what one may term "ideological" considerations. A famous example of this in Homer is the line about Ajax's contingent from Salamis in the Catalogue of Ships (2.558), which became a political weapon in sixth-century struggles for control of Salamis between Athens and Megara.

Here, however, we are dealing with interpolation rather than emendation. My concern, in relation to the works of Plato, and the

---

* This article was composed in the delightful surroundings of the Institute of Advanced Studies in Princeton, to whose hospitality I am much indebted.

[1] On this subject, I have derived benefit from the following works: Denys Page, *Actors' Interpolations in Greek Tragedy* (Oxford 1934) and H. Alline, *Histoire du texte de Platon* (Paris 1915).

Timaeus in particular, is strictly with emendation. There has not, to my knowledge, been a collection and study of this class of emendations in Plato,[2] and this study of the *Timaeus* is intended simply as a tentative preliminary contribution. One reason for this lack, perhaps, is the problem of deciding what counts as an *ideological* emendation. There are two sorts of difficulties, as we shall see: first, we would have to decide in each case what Plato actually wrote, before deciding what the nature and purpose of the emendation was; and secondly, it is not always clear what constitutes a deliberate alteration, and what could be the result of carelessness or the illegibility of the text. Nevertheless, despite the inevitable uncertainties, I think that a significant body of relevant instances remains.

Let me illustrate what I have in mind with a number of famous instances from other dialogues, which point up the difficulties rather well:[3]

1. First of all, *R.* 6.509d6:

ὥσπερ τοίνυν γραμμὴν δίχα τετμημένην λαβὼν ἄνισα τμήματα, . . .

ἄνισα ADM Proclus; ἄν, ισα F.

---

[2] The present investigation was actually provoked originally by two stimulating notes of John Whittaker, "*Timaeus* 27D5ff," *Phoenix* 23 (1969) 181–185 and "Textual Comments on *Timaeus* 27C-D," *Phoenix* 27 (1973) 387–91 (both now reproduced in his collection of essays, *Studies in Platonism and Patristic Thought* [London 1984]), in the latter of which he makes the following remark (p. 389): "The extent to which already in antiquity the text of Plato was deliberately tampered with in matters of detail but of nonetheless crucial concern is a topic which calls for detailed investigation." This challenge has not yet, I think, been taken up.

As far as I can observe, the only ancient author to comment on this phenomenon in general terms is the fifth-century Neoplatonist Hierocles of Alexandria, who in Book 6 of his *De Providentia* (as reported by Photius, *Bibl.* cod. 251. p. 461 a 24ff. Bekker, 7, p. 191 Henry), says: "Numerous Platonists and Aristotelians have put themselves to great trouble to produce contradictions between their respective masters in relation to their principal doctrines. Indeed, they have carried their love of disputation and their audacity to such a pitch that they have even tampered with the texts of their own masters, in order the better to prove that they were not in agreement." Hierocles is referring here to Middle Platonists, since he claims that Ammonius Saccas put an end to this tendency.

[3] I use the Oxford Text as a starting point, without wishing to grant it uniquely authoritative status.

V

52

If we accept the reading of the majority of Mss., including the *Parisinus* along with the evidence of Proclus (*In Remp.* 1.288. 20ff. Kroll), then we must take the tradition presented by Ms. F (*Vindobonensis* 55) to be tampering with the text. But can such tampering be assumed to be "ideological"? Certainly, some modern editors, such as Ast and Stallbaum, have preferred *isa* or *an' isa,* dividing the line into two parts, because they could see no point in the detail that the parts were *unequal* (and indeed, without further specification—*sc,* as to which segment is intended to the larger—there *is* something a little peculiar about the text). But it is possible that the scribe of F, or its ancestor, simply divided the words wrongly, without making any judgment as to whether the line was to be equally or unequally divided, so some doubt must remain as to the status of this passage.

2. Turning from the *Republic* to the *Meno,* there is a curious little problem about the transmission of 98a4, concerning the 'tying down' of true opinions so as to make them into pieces of knowledge:

πόλυν δὲ χρόνον οὐκ ἐθέλουσι παραμένειν, ἀλλὰ δραπετεύουσιν ἐκ τῆς ψυχῆς τοῦ ἀνθρώπου ὥστε οὐ πολλοῦ ἄξιαί εἰσιν, ἕως ἄν τις αὐτὰς δήσῃ αἰτίας λογισμῷ

There are here no textual variants in the direct tradition, and this is the text that makes the best sense. It is by the working out *(logismos)* of a causal explanation *(aitia)* that opinion is transformed into knowledge, and so 'tied down'.

Nevertheless, somewhere in the Middle Platonic period, if not earlier, an alternative reading *aitiāi logismou,* found favour, and it is interesting to speculate how this may have arisen. The reading is attested only in the *Anonymous Theaetetus Commentary* (col. 15.23),[4] in the context of a distinction which the author is making between 'simple' *(haplē)* and 'compound' *(synthetos)* knowledge (i.e., individual theorems of a science as opposed to the whole science as a complex of theorems).

---

[4] In *Berliner Klassikertexte,* Heft 2, ed. H. Diels and W. Schubart (Berlin 1905). The only variant reading I observe in the direct tradition is λογισμῶν for λογισμῷ in F, which may betoken a similar misreading by a scribe. It should be noted that the actual text of *Anon.* reads αἰτίαν, which Diels and Schubart have corrected, reasonably enough, to αἰτίᾳ.

ἡ τοίνυν ἁπλῆ προτέρα ἐστὶν τῆς συνθέτου καὶ ταύτην αὐτὸς μὲν ὡρίσατο ἐν τῷ Μένωνι δόξαν ὀρθὴν δεθεῖσαν αἰτίᾳ λογισμοῦ.

'The simple is prior to the compound, and this latter he himself has defined in the *Meno* as 'true opinion tied down by causality (instrumentality?) of reasoning'.

This is perhaps quoted from memory, and there may not seem at first sight to be much ideological significance in the misquotation; it could be the result of a mere tendency to regularise the word order. But it is possible that a greater emphasis is here being placed on *logismos*, as a variant of *logos,* as the means of attaining scientific knowledge, a formulation more proper to the Middle Platonic period than to that of Plato himself, though it could, admittedly, be influenced by the formula proposed at *Tht.* 201c ff. for knowledge, "true belief with an account *(logos).*"

We may be dealing here, then, with a misquotation rather than a variant reading, but one stimulated by "ideological" considerations, and interference from other Platonic passages (of also *logon didonai* in *R.* 7.534b).

As a third example, I choose *Phaedrus* 247c6–7:

ἡ γὰρ ἀχρώματός τε καὶ ἀσχημάτιστος καὶ ἀναφὴς οὐσία, ψυχῆς[5]
κυβερνήτῃ μόνῳ *θεατὴ νῷ* . . .
θεατῇ νῷ Β; θεατῇ νῷ χρῆται ΤW

Here the whole manuscript tradition of Plato reads *theatēi* in the dative, adding *nōi* or *nōi chrētai,* the verb being a palpable effort to provide some grammatical underpinning for this string of datives. However, we find in the later Neoplatonists, from Iamblichus on,[6] a series of quotations of the passage which read *theatē* without any *nōi* following.[7] Of these, the quotation by Iamblichus is the most signifi-

---

[5] There are variants at this point in the text also, but I will not concern myself with them in the present context.

[6] Plotinus does not actually quote this phrase, though he makes use of the first part of the sentence on a number of occasions.

[7] Iambl. *ap.* Hermeias, *In Phaedr.* 159.23 Couvreur; Hermeias, *In Phaedr.* 152.2 and 8; Proclus, *In Alc.* 77.10 Creuzer; *In Parm.* 6.1128, 1 Cousin, *Theol. Plat.* 4.13, p. 43, 1 Saffrey-Westerink; Simpl. *In Phys.* 546.3 Diels; Damasc. *De Princ.* 1.293, 15 Ruelle. Burnet in the Oxford Text is misleading to quote Proclus as an authority for θεατὴ νῷ. Nowhere does Proclus seem to *read* νῷ, though he certainly *understands* it in each case.

cant. He makes it clear from his exegesis of the passage that he cannot have read *nōi*, since he takes the 'helmsman' of the soul to mean precisely *not* the intellect, but the 'One' of the soul, its mystical faculty. In this he is followed by Hermeias, but Proclus, Simplicius, and Damascius seem to understand the helmsman as referring to intellect—as indeed is Plato's plain intention—without however, including *nōi* in their quotations of the passage. It seems probable to me that *nōi*, and then *nōi chrētai*, was added to our manuscript tradition at some stage in antiquity to clarify just what Plato *was* referring to, thus heading off such an interpretation as that of Iamblichus. Its inclusion acutally rather spoils the style of the passage, as being prosaically explicit.

But when would such an addition have taken place? One might assume late antiquity, but for the fact that the passage is quoted with *nōi* already in the second century A.D. by Celsus in his *Alethes Logos* (Frag. 6 19b). Celsus makes a further small but significant change in the text just following this, reading *peri hon* (referring back to *nōi*), instead of the otherwise universal reading *peri hēn* (referring back to *ousia*). Celsus may be quoting from memory, but one cannot dismiss him on that possibility. I would suggest that he represents one strand, perhaps a "popular" one, in the Mss. tradition, which only entered the "school" tradition much later.

II

Pickings, therefore, from the rest of the Platonic corpus are rather thin, so far as I can see. Turning now to the *Timaeus* itself, I begin with two textual variants from the prefatory section (17a–27b), which deserve mention, I think, though they have no strictly "ideological" content, since they share some characteristics with the ideological class, and thus serve to set them off more clearly from the others. The first occurs at 25d5, in connection with the final disappearance of Atlantis beneath the waves:

διὸ καὶ νῦν ἄπορον καὶ ἀδιερεύνητον γέγονεν τοὐκεῖ πέλαγος, πηλοῦ κατὰ βραχέος ἐμποδὼν ὄντος, ὃν ἡ νῆσος ἱζομένη παρέσχετο.

Here the *Parisinus* (A) reads κάρτα βαθέος,[8] but the letters ρταβ and θ have been partially erased, and we find κατὰ βραχέος written in the margin. (The scholiast, however, read κάρτα[9], since he glosses it with σφόδρα.) All this shows uneasiness on the part of a reader, who presumably had access to a Ms. of the family of F (which reads καταβραχέος as one word) or Y (which reads κατὰ βραχέος). Proclus, as is often the case, sides with F, taking καταβραχέος as a single word, understood as an adjective agreeing with πηλοῦ.

Now why all this fuss? No philosophical problem is at issue here: simply a problem of interpretation. What is meant by κατὰ βραχέος (or καταβραχέος) in this context? Cornford has a good note on this in an appendix to his edition (pp. 366–7), where he argues persuasively that Plato wrote κατὰ βραχέος, intending it as an adverbial phrase on the lines of κατὰ γῆς, 'beneath the earth', or, more closely, κατὰ βάθους, 'at a depth'; κατὰ βραχέος will then mean 'at a little depth', 'a little way down', which is the meaning required to describe the phenomenon of shallows due to mud below the surface beyond the Pillars of Hercules as described by Aristotle in *Meteorologica* 354a22 (who uses the expression βραχέα διὰ τὸν πηλόν). Misunderstanding of this idiom, and an attempt to make βραχέος agree with πηλοῦ, will then have led progressively to the various distortions in the Mss.

If we were, however, to seek some quasi-ideological rationale behind the variant κάρτα βαθέος, it could be that, as a result of greater geographical knowledge of the area outside the Pillars of Hercules in the Hellenistic (or Roman) era, it was thought desirable to save Plato's credibility by altering the text to fit the observed facts. There is, after all, no shallow, muddy area in the Atlantic off Gibraltar.[10]

The second interesting variant is at 26c3—interesting not really because of an ideological aspect to it, but because it is a relatively rare instance of a variant noticed by an ancient commentator. Critias is recollecting how he was taught the Atlantis poem by his grandfather,

---

[8] As, it would seem, did Calcidius, if we can deduce this from his translation *crasso dihiscentis insulce limo*—unless, as E. R. Bevan suggests (*ap* Taylor, *Comm. ad loc.*), he is actually reading κάρτα παχέος.

[9] The κάρτα βραχέος presented in the Oxford Text is a reading from no manuscript, but found only in the Basle edition.

[10] We may note, by the way, that if κάρτα were the reading here, it would be the only surviving instance of the use of this Ionic adverb in classical Attic prose.

56

and that it became fixed in his memory because of repetition induced by his frequent requests: ὥστε οἷον ἐγκαύματα ἀνεκπλύτου γραφῆς ἔμμονά μοι γέγονε, 'so that the story remained fixed in my mind like those encaustic paintings with ineffaceable characters'.

This makes perfectly good sense. What is being referred to is a technique of encaustic painting (described much later by Pliny in Book 35, 149, of his *Natural History*), and it seems clear that γραφῆς is the correct reading. However, one manuscript, *Vat. 228* (generally a twin of F, but not in this case), reads βαφῆς, 'dyeing', and Proclus in his Commentary ad loc. notes that this is an alternative reading, though without making anything of it. What is interesting is that Proclus usually follows the readings of F, and here, where we have a variation in that tradition, he notes a variant reading.[11]

If we may speculate, the variant probably arose simply from a scribe, consciously or unconsciously, recalling *R.* 4.430a, where Socrates is describing how good citizenship should be instilled into the soldier class ὥσπερ βαφήν, and care should be taken μὴ ἐκπλύναι τὴν βαφὴν τὰ ῥύμματα ταῦτα. If it is a conscious recollection of this passage, then we come near once again to an "ideological" emendation, striving to preserve consistency in Plato's imagery, but one cannot be sure that the scribe is not just being careless. βαφῆς, after all, could be described as the *lectio facilior*.[12]

III

Let us pass on, however, to more serious matters. It is really only after 27b, after all, that serious questions of doctrine begin to arise, on which some manipulation of the text might be thought advantageous. At this point we should remind ourselves what the overriding issue was in the interpretation of the *Timaeus*. Aristotle had (perhaps mischievously, perhaps genuinely) presented Plato as describing in the *Timaeus* the creation of the world in time, and had criticised him for that (*De Cael.* 1.10.280a28ff.; 1.12.283a4ff.; 3.2.300b17ff.). Speusippus

---

[11] Calcidius, for what it is worth, seems to read γραφῆς (*inobsoletam . . .notam*).

[12] A curious confirmation that the *Timaeus* and *Republic* passages might be associated occurs in the Pseudo-Pythogorean letter of Lysis to Hipparchus (112, 9 Thesleff), where the author, although doubtless thinking primarily of *R.* 4.430a, uses the phrase ὅπως ἀνέκπλυτον τὰν βαφὰν ἀναπίωντι.

and Xenocrates responded to this by denying that the *Timaeus* account was to be taken literally. Plato had presented it in this form merely 'for didactic purposes' (διδασκαλίας χάριν, Xenocr. Frag. 54 Heinze). Most of the emendations we shall be considering are designed to support this position. In fact, we find such a passage straight away, and it is a particularly interesting one.

27C 4–5: ἡμᾶς δὲ τοὺς περὶ τοῦ παντὸς λόγους ποιεῖσθαι πῃ μέλλοντας, ἦ γέγονεν ἦ καὶ ἀγενές ἐστιν, ... ἀνάγκη θεούς τε καὶ θεὰς ἐπικαλουμένους εὔχεσθαι

ᾖ . . . ἦ A: ᾖ . . .ἦ FY: ᾖ . . . ἦ (or εἰ) Albinus: εἰ . . . εἰ Taurus: ἦ . . . ἦ Porphyry Iamblichus, Proclus: εἰ . . . ἦ Philoponus; om. Calcidius

This is a fine mare's nest. To add to the complexities, Proclus in fact follows Porphyry and Iamblichus (whom he reports) and F and Y, in reading ἦ . . . ἦ but one of the Proclus Mss., C, manages to read ᾖ . . . εἰ in the lemma; two, C and P, read ᾖ . . . ἦ in the text at 1.219.29 Diehl ("correcting" their text, presumably, from the A tradition); and *all* the Mss. read εἰ . . . ἦ, when Proclus returns to the text later, at 1.275.8ff.

The modern consensus (OCT, Budé, Teubner) seems to be to read ᾖ . . . ἦ, so we may start from that as a base.[13] Such a reading, and indeed the accepted Neoplatonic reading ἦ . . . ἦ, may be regarded, I think, as ideologically neutral, though in fact the Neoplatonists all held that the description of the temporal creation of the world was not to be taken literally. The other readings, however, were thought to contain various nuances, to support one position or another on this vexed question.

Let us begin by quoting Proclus on the problem (1.218.28ff. Diehl):

Let us turn now to the phrase η γέγονεν η καὶ ἀγενές ἐστιν. Some have interpreted this by taking the first *ē* as aspirated and the second as non-aspirated—all those who regard Timaeus as proposing to treat of the uni-

[13] John Whittaker, however, in his article "Textual Comments" (389), notes that in fact Burnet (OCT) and Rivaud (Budé) misrepresent the situation in the Parisinus (A): πῃ and ᾖ are indeed written there, but πῃ and the iota subscript of ᾖ are then elided with dots, showing that the scribe, on reconsideration (after consulting another exemplar?), wished to excise πῃ and change ᾖ to ἦ. Nothing is simple in the tradition of this passage!

58

verse *in so far as* (καθ᾽ ὅσον) it has come to be from a causal principle, *even though* (εἰ καὶ)[14] it is ungenerated. They use such terminology in order that, by comprehending the sense in which it is created, we may properly discern its nature. That is the opinion, at least, of the Platonist Albinus, who considers that according to Plato, the world, while uncreated (in time), nevertheless contains a principle of createdness (ἀρχὴ γενέσεως).[15] In his view, the cosmos has by that very fact something in excess of real Being, because that is only eternal, while the cosmos, as well as being eternal, possesses also a first principle of generation, so that it is at the same time eternally existent and coming into being (γενητός), not, of course, in the sense of temporal creation—that would exclude its being eternally existent—but in the sense that it has a principle of createdness[16] by virtue of being compounded of a multiplicity of disparate elements, which makes it necessary to refer its substantiation back to a causal principle prior to itself, through the prior existence of which it itself is also in a way (πῃ) eternally existent, and not only generated but also ungenerated.

Albinus' exegesis, then, involves not only giving a special significance to ἢ . . . ἢ (whether or not he introduced the emendation himself), but also giving a special weight to the adverb πῃ in the previous line, to mean 'in some way'.

Albinus was equalled in emending zeal by his near-contemporary L. Calvenus Taurus, whose elaborate list of senses of *genētos* I have mentioned (n. 15).

John Philoponus[17] tells us that Taurus read 27c5 as εἰ γέγονεν, εἰ

[14] This poses a problem. Proclus seems to be listing Albinus as reading ἢ . . . ἢ but in the text he gives ἢ . . . εἰ (though one late Ms., *Monac. gr.* 382 (A) "corrects" that to ἢ). It may be, as Whittaker suggests ("Textual Comments" 390), that Proclus is not distinguishing between ἢ and εἰ. I would accept this, as it lends more sense to Albinus' position.

[15] This differs interestingly in detail from the views expressed in the *Didaskalikos*, Ch. 14 (p. 169, 26ff. Hermann), whether the author of that be Alcinous or Albinus. In the *Did.*, the senses of *genētos* given are 'always in process of generation' and 'dependent for its existence on an outside cause', which are the third and fourth respectively in the list of four senses of *genetos* worked out by the Platonist Taurus in his *Timaeus Commentary* (see my *Middle Platonists*, p. 243), whereas Albinus here favours Taurus' *second* sense, 'that which is in theory composite, even if it has never been compounded' (though Albinus also sees this as involving an outside cause).

[16] If this is a reasonable rendering of λόγος γενέσεως.

[17] *De Aeternitate Mundi*, p. 186, 17ff. Rabe.

καὶ ἀγενές ἐστιν, meaning 'whether it was created, *even if* it is uncreated', and actually quoted Homer, *Iliad* 3.215: εἰ καὶ γένει ὕστερος ἦεν as a parallel.[18] (Philoponus himself, a believer in the temporal creation of the world, read εἰ . . . ἤ.) That Taurus felt it desirable to quote a parallel seems to indicate that, at least in the case of the second εἰ, he was not choosing between variants, but actually emending; in which case Albinus may (if indeed *he* read εἰ) have been following him in this.

All this fiddling around with the text by Platonists attracted the indignant attention, in the next generation, of the great Peripatetic Alexander of Aphrodisias. In his *Commentary on the De Caelo*,[19] Alexander pours scorn on those who "make themselves ridiculous by trying to change the (second) *e* into *ei*, and read εἰ γέγονεν, εἰ καὶ ἀγενές ἐστιν for apart from the absurdity of changing the given text into something else (τὸ μεταγράφειν τὰ μὴ οὕτως ἔχοντα), they have not thought through the consequences: their text is quite out of tune with what follows." And he then proceeds to quote *Ti.* 28b.[20]

The Platonists who annoyed Alexander (presumably including Taurus) put forward, it seemed, the sense of *genētos* as 'having its existence in a state of becoming' (τὸ ἐν γενέσει τὸ εἶναι ἔχειν),[21] Taurus' *third* meaning, which comes nearest, interestingly enough, not to Albinus as reported by Proclus, nor yet to Taurus (if indeed he is favouring, as he seems to be, his own *fourth* meaning, 'dependent for its existence on an outside cause'), but to the meaning given in the *Didaskalikos*. But all these Platonists are at one in attempting to doctor the text to facilitate their interpretation.

The Neoplatonists (Porphyry, Iamblichus, and Proclus), by contrast, though they too held that the creation account in the *Timaeus* was mythical, did not feel it necessary to adopt the controversial second *ei,* plumping for the more neutral ἤ . . . ἤ, in agreement with our Mss. F and Y (and it seems, on reconsideration, even to A). Proclus' report of their position (*In Tim.* 1.219.21ff.) indicates that they were prepared to understand the passage as presenting a completely open

---

[18] Where, we may note, many Mss. of Homer actually read ἤ for εἰ!

[19] Lost, but quoted in this connexion by John Philoponus, *Aet.* p. 214, 10ff. Rabe.

[20] We may note, by the way, that when Alexander quotes 27c4–5 (at 214, 7–9), he omits πῃ, which would seem to indicate that it was not in his text, and so perhaps another addition of the second-century Platonists.

[21] *Ap.* Philop. *Aet.* p. 213, 24–5 Rabe.

question ('Has the cosmos come to be, or is it uncreated?'), and thus giving no clue one way or another to Plato's true intentions.

I have dwelt on this passage at what is perhaps inordinate length, because it seems to provide a particularly good example, both because of the complexity of the positions taken up, and because of the publicity they attracted, of the sort of manouevres that could go on, as Plato's faithful followers picked over the texts that he had bequeathed to them.

But this is only one such passage in the *Timaeus*. Let us look now at a few others.

We turn next to 27d5, another passage on which John Whittaker has made a useful contribution. In the generally accepted text it runs:

τί τὸ ὂν ἀεί, γένεσιν δὲ οὐκ ἔχον, καὶ τί τὸ γιγνόμενον μὲν ἀεί, ὂν δὲ οὐδέποτε;

giving the meaning: 'What is it that always exists, having no generation, and what is it that is always coming to be, never having existence?' Here the problem centres round the second *aei*. The manuscripts are divided. F, W, and Y omit it, as does the whole Neoplatonic tradition,[22] as well as both Cicero and Calcidius in their translations. In the second century A.D., Nicomachus of Gerasa (*Intro. Arith.* 1.2.2), Numenius (Frag. 7 *Des Places*), Alexander of Aphrodisias (*ap.* Philop. *Aet.* 214. 3–4), and Sextus Empiricus (*AM* 7.142) omit it. In fact the problem is, not who omits it, but who includes it. There is a probable reading in Pseudo-Justin, *Cohort.,*[23] a definite one in Eusebius, *P.E.* 11.9, two occasions in Philoponus (*in de An.* 76.23f.; *in Phys.* 56.2ff.), and a doubtful allusion in Plutarch (*Def. Or.* 433E).[24]

---

[22] Whittaker quotes Syrianus, Proclus, Simplicius, Olympiodorus, Asclepius and Lydus, and one instance from John Philoponus (*Aet.* p. 205, 17), where however, John may be under the influence of a source work, since on two other occasions (see below) he puts in the *aei*.

[23] That is to say, *aei* is read in all Mss. save one (D). Pseudo-Justin is generally considered to be third-century A.D.

[24] Ἔκγονον ἐκείνου καὶ τόκου ὄντος ἀεὶ γιγνόμενον ἀεὶ τοῦτον ἀποφάινοντες, referring to the Sun as the offspring of Apollo. I must say the most natural assumption would be that he is alluding to the text of the *Timaeus* as known to him, so I would count Plutarch in.

We have here to do with an impressive plurality against the second *aei*.[25] What is strange here is that, although there should be an ideological issue here—the inclusion of *aei* with *gignomenon* should strengthen the hand of those who wish to argue for an eternal generation of the world (that is to say, if anything, Taurus' third meaning of *genētos*)—this reading was precisely *not* adopted, or even, it seems, known to[26] the great majority of Platonists who were partisans of the non-literal interpretation of the *Timaeus,* whereas it was apparently known to, and adopted by, such men as Plutarch, who maintained the temporal creation of the world, and Christians like Eusebius and John Philoponus, who held the same view. It would seem that neither side was inclined to draw the conclusions from the text that seem obvious to us.

However, things may not be quite as they seem. First of all, as John Whittaker himself points out, the author of the *Didaskalikos,* in Ch. 14 (p. 169 Hermann), when discussing the question of Plato's description of the world as "created," after first asserting that it is not to be taken as denoting temporal creation, says that what it means is that it is 'always in process of generation' (ἀεὶ ἐν γενέσει ἐστί),[27] which seems to suggest (though not perhaps necessarily that he read *aei* with *gignomenon.* Furthermore, there are at least two passages in the *Corpus Hermeticum,* which largely reflects contemporary (i.e., second century) Platonism, which are fairly plainly drawing on this passage of the

---

[25] The situation is even more lopsided than Burnet and Rivaud in their editions allow. As Whittaker reveals in his second article (n. 2 above), ἀεί is actually not present in the *Vaticanus Palatinus gr.* 173 (P), and in the *Parisinus* (A), though present, it has been cancelled by dots (as was the case with πῃ and ῇ in the last passage). We may perhaps assume that it was present in the original Ms. available to the scribe of A, but cancelled on correction from another ms.

[26] Here I would differ with John Whittaker as to the interpretation of a remark of Proclus, (*In Tim.* 1.233, 18ff.), where he says, "Why, they say, did Plato not add ἀεί to γιγνόμενον also, as he did to ὄν, or ποτέ ('at one time or another'), so that he could have a thorough going antithesis to ἀεὶ ὄν?" Proclus' suggested answer is that neither ἀεί nor ποτέ would apply to all aspects of the physical world, ἀεί being appropriate to 'totalities' (by which he perhaps means genera and species), and ποτέ to 'parts' (presumably individuals). Whittaker suggests that this indicates that Proclus *knows* such a reading. It seems to me rather to indicate just the opposite, although it does show that there was some speculation on the matter, which may precisely have led to the inclusion of the ἀεί.

[27] Cf. n. 14 above.

Timaeus, and reading *aei*. In *Tractate* 10.10, we find the physical cosmos referred to as αὐτός ποτε μὲν γενόμενος, ἀεὶ δὲ ὤν, ὢν δὲ ἐν γενέσει. Here the Hermetist seems to assert that the universe did have a beginning in time, but continues always in generation. There is a problem here, however, since the other passage (11.3) seems directly to contradict this, when it says ἔργον τοῦ αἰῶνος ὁ κόσμος, γενόμενος οὔποτε, καὶ ἀεὶ γινόμενος ὑπὸ τοῦ αἰῶνος. It may well be, as Reitzenstein has proposed,[28] that we ought to read οὐδέποτε in 10.10, but the Hermetists do on occasion contradict each other, and this could be one of the cases. At any rate, both Hermetists do seem to be familiar with the second *aei*, and, if we may preserve the text of each passage, they show an interesting variety of interpretations of it.

The second complication I would note is Plotinus, whom Whittaker does not mention, simply because Plotinus does not quote the passage verbatim. However, Plotinus does in fact use the passage indirectly on occasion. At the end of *Enn.* 3.3, for instance, in the course of an image comparing the universe to a great tree, he contrasts the root (which is the noetic world) and the branches, fruit and leaves (the physical world) as follows:

καὶ τὰ μὲν ἔμενεν ἀεί, τὰ δὲ ἐγίνετο ἀεί, οἱ καρποὶ καὶ τὰ φύλλα. καὶ τὰ γινόμενα ἀεὶ εἶχε τοὺς ἐπάνω λόγους ἐν αὑτοῖς οἷον μικρὰ δένδρα βουληθέντα εἶναι (3.3.16-19)

Ἔμενεν here, I should say, has the same connotation as ἦν, permanence being the characteristic of true Being. This seems to me unmistakably to indicate that Plotinus knows the passage as containing the second *aei*. He deliberately plays on the variation of meaning which the two uses of *aei* must involve—something like the distinction in English between "continuously" and "continually" (except that, for Plotinus, eternity is not *continuous,* but rather transcends time altogether).

Another significant passage occurs at 5.7.3.5-6, where the argument turns on the fact that Plato has added ἀεὶ to γιγνόμενον, signifying (for Plotinus) that the process of creation was eternal, and thus there was no deliberating about it on the part of the Demiurge.[29]

---

[28] *Poimandres* (40, n. 1).

[29] A possible counter-example has been pointed out to me by Prof. Steven Strange, from *Enn.* 6.2.1.20, where Plotinus quotes 28a3-4, but then (28-30) alludes to the fact

So Whittaker cannot dispose of the second *aei* as easily as that, although I would agree with him that it is possibly not Plato's own contribution. If that is so, then we have a case of tampering with the text, though the philosophical implications of either reading do not seem to be clearly established. It may well be, in fact, that the addition was originally made for stylistic rather than ideological purposes, and so does not properly concern us at all—except in so far as beautifying Plato's style has ideological implications! If, as I do not believe, the second *aei* was cut out of some texts, then the ideological implications (in favour of the literal interpretation) would be clearer, though we have seen that the second *aei* did not bother John Philoponus. It can easily be interpreted to refer to the Universe's present state of constant generation, without any implications for its creation or eternity.

I pass over now a number of small variants of no clear ideological content,[30] to notice a detail at 30a5, which may be significant. Here Mss. A, P, and Y, followed by Simplicius (*In Phys.* 704. 14ff., and 1122. 1ff. Diels) and Stobaeus (*Anth* 1.128.28 Wachsmuth), say that the Demiurge εἰς τάξιν αὐτὸ (*sc.* the physical universe) ἤγαγεν ἐκ τῆς ἀταξίας, where the aorist would seem to suggest a definite temporal act. This, I believe, is probably what Plato wrote, but Ms. F, followed by Porphyry, Iamblichus, and Proclus (as one would expect), and, in the middle Platonic period by the author of the Pseudo-Plutarchan *De Fato* (573 E),[31] reads the imperfect ἦγεν, which *could* be interpreted as denoting a continuous activity of the Demiurge. Of course all the Greek imperfect *need* denote is that an action begun at a certain time has consequences that carry on for a period (or that the action itself carries on for a period).

For Proclus however, the imperfect does seem to bear some ideological weight. Apart from the lemma, he quotes the passage at one

---

that Plato has added ἀεί to ὄν at 27d5 to emphasise that time being eternal never belies its nature. This is troublesome, certainly, but I would submit that Plotinus' emphasis on the ἀεί with ὄν does not exclude there being an ἀεί with γιγνόμενον also. It would in any case have a different meaning.

[30] 29b9: ἀνικήτοις A, Procl., Cic., Calc.; ἀκινήτοις FY (ἀκινήτους, P, A²); 30a2: φλαῦρον, APY, Simpl., Stob., φαῦλον F, Plut., utrumque Procl.

[31] Pseudo-Plutarch's use of ἦγεν (*De Fato* 573B) must mean that it was embedded in the tradition available to him, since it was not in his interest to alter the text in this direction. Ps. Plu. does not in fact make clear where he stands on the createdness of the world.

64

point in the text (1.371.6) in a context where other imperfects are being used to emphasise the continuous, sempiternal nature of the Demiurge's activity:

εἰ γὰρ ἀγαθὸς ἦν, ἠβούλετο πάντα ἀγαθὰ ποιεῖν, εἰ δὲ *ἠβούλετο,* καὶ *ἐποίει* καὶ εἰς τάξιν 'ἦγε τὸ πᾶν; ἐξήρτηται γὰρ ἡ μὲν πρόνοια τῆς βουλήσεως, ἡ δὲ βούλησις τῆς ἀγαθότητος.

That is to say, his Providence (which involves bringing all to order) is eternally dependent on his Will, which in turn is dependent upon his Goodness. Proclus makes nothing explicit of the imperfect other than this, but it plainly suits his interpretation, in a way in which the aorist would not.

On the other hand, as I have said, the imperfect *need* not be seen as loaded in favour or either interpretation, and how far is has an ideological origin one cannot be sure. It is plainly a reading that goes back beyond the second century A.D., but it is probably not what Plato wrote. More one cannot say, I think, except that it is part of the F tradition which was available to the Neoplatonists.

Another little detail is perhaps worth noting *en passant,* though I am not sure that much can be made of it. That is 33a5, where Plato very probably says: "for he reflected that when hot things and cold and all such as have strong powers gather round a composite body from without, and fall unseasonably upon it, they *dissolve* it (λύει), and bringing upon it sickness and age cause its decay."

If we can assume that he did use the rather strong expression λύει (though probably with an *inceptive* meaning, 'tend to dissolve'), we can see here, I think, some slight record of someone's attempt to modify this into the less violent λυπεῖ. We find this in the *Parisinus* (A), in a slightly garbled form (λύπας, with dots over the πας), though λύει is written in the margin. All other Mss., and Proclus,[32] have λύει, but λυπεῖ is used by Philo Judaeus, who quotes the passage in the *De Aeter-*

---

[32] It is strange, though, that at *In Tim.* 2.59.7 Proclus, in commenting on this passage, says εἰ γὰρ εἴη τι (*sc.* ἔξω) προσβάλλον αὐτῷ *λυπήσει* καὶ διαλύσει τὸ πᾶν. But not only in the lemma (which, as we know, is always subject to "correction" by scribes), but also twice elsewhere in the text (2.63.2; 64.31) he uses parts of λύω so λύει must be his reading.

nitate Mundi, 26, and Jakob Bernays,[33] actually wanted to incorporate it into Plato's text.

There is not much at issue here doctrinally. It seems rather to indicate a concern that Plato should not seem loose or immoderate in his language. But such a concern, as I have suggested before, is after all quasi-ideological.

Of somewhat more substance is a variation found at 37b5, in the midst of the description of the way in which the soul cognises both the intelligible and the sensible realms: "This verdict (λόγος) of hers is true alike, whether it deals with Same or with Other, produced without voice or sound in the self-moved (ἐν τῷ κινουμένῳ ὑφ' αὑτοῦ)." Here ὑφ' αὑτοῦ is the reading of all the Mss. and of Stobaeus (*Anth.* 1.49.28[p. 359, 9 Wachs.]), but Proclus (*In Tim.* 1.307.30–309.2) wishes to read ὑπ' αὐτοῦ, by *it* (*sc.* the *logos*), which he takes not as 'utterance' or 'verdict', but rather as the intellectual element in the soul, represented by the "charioteer" of the *Phaedrus* myth, which directs the two "circles" of the soul, and receives their reports.

Proclus starts from this reading, but notes, interestingly, that the reading in "the more accurate, corrected manuscripts' (ἐν τοῖς ἀκριβεστέροις, τοῖς κεκολασμένοις), which in this case would seem to indicate the Mss. of the F tradition which he normally follows, is ὑφ' αὑτοῦ. Proclus is prepared to accept this reading, in fact, but he feels that it still refers to the *logos,* though taking it as the whole soul in a sort of "whole for part" construction (308.28ff.): "What Plato then means to say is that the *Logos,* established in the soul (for that is what is referred to by 'that which is moved by itself') takes cognisance of the Same and the Different, now in the intelligible realm, and now in the sensible." So the basic meaning that Proclus wants is preserved.

It is plain from Proclus' reports on Porphyry's and Iamblichus' views in this lemma (306.1–5) and the next 309.7–310,11) that they both propounded this view of the passage, relating the *logos* mentioned here to the Charioteer of the *Phaedrus* myth.[34] What we seem

---

[33] In his essay on the inauthenticity of Philo's *De Aeternitate Mundi* in *Abh. d. Berl. Akad. d. Wiss.* Phil.-Hist. Kl. III (1882).

[34] There are complications, though. Porphyry (306, 2) makes the connection between the *Logos* here and the Charioteer of the *Phaedrus* myth. Iamblichus seems to reject this, and refers it to ἡ ὅλη ψυχή, by which he means the All-Soul, but in fact we see from p. 309, 25ff. that he accepts the image of the charioteer and horses, so he prob-

to have to do with here, then, is a Neoplatonic ideological emendation (perhaps initiated by Porphyry), accepted with some misgiving by Proclus, whose scholarly instinct is bothered by the lack of manuscript support, but who assents to the meaning being sought from the text.

The ideological question at issue is not insignificant, at least for a Neoplatonist. As far as we can discern from Proclus' report, the *logos* in Prophyry's view describes that highest element even in the human soul which Plotinus is famous for declaring always to remain "above".[35] Iamblichus rejected that doctrine, as did Syrianus and Proclus, so, while accepting Porphyry's reading of the text, he wishes to confine its application to the structure of the World Soul, not extending it to the individual soul. That seems to be the point of the controversy reported by Proclus at *In Tim.* 1.309.7ff.

The next notable passage is an old chestnut, and I am not sure how far it really counts as an ideological *emendation,* but I think that it is worth discussing. This is 40b8–c1.

γῆν δὲ τρόφον μέν ἡμετέραν, ἰλλομένην δέ (τὴν) περὶ τὸν
διὰ πάντος πόλον τεταμένον . . .

b8 ἰλλομένην F Aristotle, Plut, Procl; εἰλλομένην P, Galen;
εἰλλομένην A
c 1 τὴν AP; om; FY, Ar, Plut, Galen, Procl.

'And the earth our foster-mother, winding (or compressed) about the axis stretched throughout all (or, the All).' Here the crux is the variant interpretations, and spellings, of ἰλλομένην. Ἰλλομένην is read by F, and by Aristotle (whereby hangs the tale), Plutarch and Proclus (though a compromise variant εἰλλομένην is read by the Ms. P), and εἰλλομένην is the reading of A. The problem arises from the ambiguity inherent in the meaning of the verb, however it is spelled. Εἴλω, or εἰλέω, or εἴλλω, or ἴλλω may very well be a conflation of various different roots, but if so they have become by historical times inextricably confused. Three meanings can be distinguished: (1) 'to shut in' (or

---

ably accepted the same reading as Porphyry. I would thus like to retract my comments in *Iamblichi Fragmenta,* Comm. at *In Tim.* Frag. 59, p. 340, where I decided that Iamblichus must have read ὑφ' αὑτοῦ. This does not now seem to me necessary, and I think that Proclus would remark on it had it been the case.

[35] Cf., e.g., *Enn.* 4.8.8; 3.4.3.22–26; 2.9.2.9. For a significant Plotinian exegesis of the image of the charioteer and horses, cf. *Enn.* 3.8.5.34–39.

V

sometimes, 'to shut out') which is not relevant here; (2) 'to press' (as of olives or grapes); and (3) 'to wind, turn around' (which is probably to be connected with the verb εἰλύω, 'to enwrap, enfold', cf. Lat. *volvo*).

The issue is, of course, whether Plato is declaring that the earth is revolving on its axis, or is merely compressed about its axis. The former alternative had been thought to involve Plato in incoherence, since he has already stated in 39c that the universe as a whole revolves in a day and a night, and if the earth also had a revolution of its own, that would seem to conflict with the cosmic circuit. So loyal Platonists, such as Plutarch (*Quaest. Plat.* 8. 1006C), Alcinous (*Didasc.,* Ch. 15), and, most copiously, Proclus (*In Tim.* 3.136.29–138.11), maintained stoutly that Plato can only have meant that the earth is "compressed about" its axis.[36]

However, we have the awkward fact that Aristotle, in *De Caelo* 2.13 and 14 (293b30–32 and 296a26–27), presents Plato as postulating the *rotation* of the earth on its axis in the *Timaeus,* glossing the ἴλλεσθαι as κινεῖσθαι. I do not intend to enter into any protracted discussion on the present occasion as to whether Aristotle was correct or not in this assumption. I am prepared to accept Cornford's argument (*Plato's Cosmology,* pp. 120–134) that he was right. What really concerns me in the present context is what the reaction to this interpretation was.

The reaction from the Old Academy was defensive, very much of a piece with their general defensive reaction to Aristotle's interpretation of the *Timaeus.* No one, it seems, thought of Cornford's explanation, that the earth's rotation is taken into account in calculating the movement of the whole universe. It is precisely if the earth did *not* rotate on its axis that there would be no day or night. In any case, the earth is a living divinity with a soul, and circular motion is thus nat-

---

[36] Also Theon of Smyrna (reproducing Adrastus and Dercyllides), p. 200, 7 Hiller; and Calcidius, *In Tim.* (122, 166, 3ff. Wasz) *constrictam limitibus per omnia vadentis et cuncta continentis poli.* Calc. is particularly interesting here. He renders ἰλλομένην by *constrictam,* but then declares that it is *dupliciter intelligendum,* either in a "Pythagorean" sense, of an *ignem vertentem se circum axem,* or, "rather more probably," *medietati mundi adhaerentem quiescere.* This made sense in his Greek original (no doubt Adrastus—he adduces Hestia from the *Phaedrus* (247a), just as Theon does (loc. cit.), indicating a common source), but he no longer makes sense once he has adopted the translation *constrictam.* What we have here, then, is the exegesis of the judicious Peripatetic Adrastus. The source of Diogenes Laertius (3.75), on the other hand, plumps unequivocally for motion (κινεῖσθαι περὶ τὸ μέσον).

V

68

ural, even necessary, for it. But the Platonists were embarrassed, it seems, by Aristotle's interpretation, and put forward the *other* possible meaning of ἴλλω/εἴλω, 'to compress'.

At what point, though, if at all, does ideological *emendation* enter in? I would suggest that it may have consisted in the slight alteration of ἰλλομένην to εἰλλομένην, or better, εἰλουμένην (which does not, however, seem to be attested in surviving testimonia). Admittedly, both forms of the verb seem to be able to bear both meanings,[37] but Aristotle apparently read ἰλλομένην, and the use of the form in the famous chorus of Sophocles' *Antigone* (340: ἰλλομένων ἀρότρων) might seem to strengthen the supposition that it would have the sense of 'winding' here, whereas such Homeric usages as ἀνδρῶν εἰλομένων (*Iliad* 5.203; 8.215) might be seen as giving support to the other meaning. The only problem with this suggestion is that it does not fit the evidence very well. Both Plutarch (*Mor.* 1006C) and Proclus (*In Tim.* 3.138.7), in discussing the passage, read ἰλλομένην,[38] and gloss it respectively by ἀνειλουμένην and εἰλουμένην (or εἰλουμένην, D). The insertion of τὴν (*sc.* ὁδόν) after ἰλλομένην δὲ given in A and P (but absent from all ancient testimonia) would of course weight the evidence strongly in favour of the meaning of motion, but it may be a much later addition, since it would have suited Aristotle very well to include it, had it been in the text before him.[39]

That the counter-attack on Aristotle goes back to the Old Academy (which is probable enough anyhow) seems indicated by the fact that Cicero (*Acad. Pr.* 2.123) is aware that the word can be taken in two ways.[40] By Plutarch's time, the issue is still alive, but he misun-

---

[37] Indeed, in the *Cratylus* (409a), we find περὶ τὴν γῆν ἀεὶ εἰλεῖν presented as an etymology of ἥλιος.

[38] Though we must note that in the case of both authors there are textual variants. For Plutarch, the corrector of B reads εἰλλουμένην, and εἰλουμένην is read by the *codex Vossianus* and *Escorial* T-11-5, while in Proclus' case εἰλλομένην is read by Q, and εἰλλομένην/εἰλουμένην by the *recensio vulgata*.

[39] Plotinus' interpretation of the passage is not easy to determine, but in one place where he makes use of it (*Enn.* 4.4.22.25ff.), he answers an objection to the earth's being ensouled that it is δυσκίνητον, by saying that this only relates to *spatial* motion (πρὸς τὸ μὴ κινεῖσθαι ἐκ τόπου λέγοι τις ἄν) which leaves open the possibility that it revolves *in place*—an activity proper, after all, to an ensouled body, especially a divine one.

[40] *Atque hoc* (*sc.* that the earth rotates on its axis) *etiam Platonem in Timaeo dicere quidam arbitrantur, sed paullo obscurius.* I take it that such questions did not much concern the New Academy, so that we can refer this back to the Old Academic period.

derstands the alternatives (in *Quaest. Plat.* 8.1006CD) as being either motionless position at the centre of the universe (which he favours), or *planetary* revolution around a central fire—ignoring the possibility of axial rotation. As for Proclus, he takes nearly two pages (*In Tim.* 3.136.29–138, 17) to argue the case against the earth's rotation, and makes some forceful points in the process. One linguistic point is of particular interest. Later in the dialogue, he points out, at 76c1, Plato uses the verb unequivocally to mean 'compacted', of the hair on the head. The problem is, though, that the phrase there, ὑπὸ τὸ δέρμα εἰλλόμενον κατερριζοῦτο (where, by the way, there is no recorded variant ἰλλόμενον, though there is some vacillation about the rough breathing), *could* mean 'coiling around under the skin'.

Another argument he uses also fails to establish its point satisfactorily. He appeals to *Timaeus Locrus,* who, at 97D, uses the expression γᾶ δ' ἐν μέσῳ ἰδρυμένα. This certainly conveys the meaning 'established at the centre', but seems to leave it open (as indeed "Timaeus" may have intended) whether the earth is rotating or not. I admit, though, that the balance of probability is with Proclus, but this only shows that "Timaeus" is part of the Academic reaction.

One could, I think, compose a substantial monograph on the history of the interpretation of this passage alone, in both ancient and modern times.[41] All I wish to derive from the whole mess on the present occasion is the suggestion that there is some evidence (though perhaps hopelessly confused) that certain parties to the controversy thought that a shift from ἰλλομένην to εἰλλομένην or εἰλουμένην would slant the interpretation in favour of compacting as opposed to rotating, while whoever inserted τὴν before περὶ (if that is indeed what has happened, rather than the opposite!) was certainly trying to settle the question in favour of rotation (or perhaps even planetary motion), for reasons either friendly or hostile to Plato. Why, one might ask, does Plato choose to use such a palpably ambiguous verb to express his

---

[41] The course of modern interpretation, from August Boeckh's *Über das kosmische System des Platon,* in 1852, through Martin, Grote, Archer-Hind, Taylor, Cornford, Cherniss, and beyond, is quite a saga in itself. In going along with Cornford, the only thing that I find troubling is the fact of the complete failure of ancient Platonists to see the truth. But one may reflect that, if Cornford is right about the interpretation of the account of the composition of the World-Soul at *Ti.* 35a, as, again, I think he is, then we must recognise that this completely escaped no less a man than Xenocrates (*ap.* Plu., *Proc. An.* 1012E = Frag. 68 Heinze). But then Xenocrates also understands Plato to be postulating *five* basic elements in *Ti.* 55a–c, taking the dodecahedron, as forming aether (Frag. 53 Heinze). Somewhere here, I feel, we must postulate a failure in communication.

meaning? Surely, στρεφομένην would have done, if that is what he meant? Is he trying to tease his disciples, or hedge his bets? I would suggest the possibility that, sensitive as he is to the nuances of the Greek language, he precisely chose a verb which seemed to combine the two meanings of 'press round' and 'wind round', since he conceived the earth to be doing *both* of those things in relation to its axis. But, if that is what was in his mind, it would appear that he did not make himself clear.

One more passage, and I will have done. That is the troublesome opening sentence of the Demiurge's address to the Young Gods (41a7–8):

Θεοὶ θεῶν, ὧν ἐγὼ δημιουργὸς πατήρ τε ἔργων, δι' ἐμοῦ γενόμενα ἄλυτα ἐμοῦ γε (μὴ) ἐθέλοντος

a7 δι' F: ἃ δι' APY: τάδε in marg. A. (ἃ) δι' ἐμοῦ γενόμενα AFPY, Philop., Stob., Ps. Themist.; om. Cicero, Philo, Eus., Athenag., Hippol., Cyrill., Julianus, Procl., Simpl.

a8 γε μὴ ἐθέλοντος A, Cicero, Philo, Eus., Athenag., γε ἐθέλοντος FP (et μὴ punct. not, A²), Procl., Philop., Themist., Hippol., Cyrill., γε θέλοντος Y, Procl., Stob.

As to the mysterious invocation 'Gods of Gods', textual emendation in antiquity has nothing to offer, though many suggestions as to its interpretation were made. Down to ἔργων, however, all is unanimous as to the text. I will therefore thankfully leave the meaning of the first phrase aside in the present context. The ancient Platonists worried over the meaning of θεοὶ θεῶν, as we can see from Proclus' discussion in the *Timaeus Commentary,* ad loc., but they did not try to emend it.[42] The latter part of the sentence, however, ran into difficulties, one aspect of which at least seems to me to harbour an ideological dimension.

Apart from the ἃ, which is introduced for syntactical reasons, the first problem concerns δι' ἐμοῦ γενόμενα. This is the reading of all the Mss., but a significant part of the indirect tradition, beginning with Cicero in his translation (*Tim.* 11: *haec sunt indissoluta me invito*), and continuing through Philo (*Aet.* 13: ἄλυτα ἐμοῦ γε μὴ θέλοντος)

---

[42] They did, however, try to alter the punctuation, as Proclus tells us (3.202.28ff.), taking θεῶν with the clause following, and understanding, "of which gods I am the creator . . .". But since there probably was no form of punctuation mark involved, this does not count as an emendation.

and various Church Fathers, down to the Emperor Julian (*c. Gal.* 58B) and Proclus—and so therefore, in all probability, the Neoplatonic tradition in general[43]—is ignorant of it, only John Philoponus (*Aet.,* p. 128, 2 Rabe), Stobaeus (*Anth.* 1, p.181, 8), and Pseudo-Themistius (who is actually the twelfth-century Byzantine commentator Sophonias) include it.[44] There is an interesting variation in both the Mss. and the indirect tradition between ἐμοῦ μὴ ἐθέλοντος and ἐμοῦ γε ἐθέλοντος, but I can discern no clear ideological issue here, so I leave it aside.

Once again, one may ask "Cui bono?" If we could presume that Plato wrote the phrase, one can discern a reason for suppressing it on the part of opponents of the literal interpretation. Jakob Bernays, however, in commenting on Philo (*op. cit.,* n. 33 above), condemned it as gloss, and he may be right. It must be admitted that its pedigree is not good. Even the Church Fathers know nothing of it. Its earliest witness is actually John Philoponus (since the reference to Themistius in the app. crit. is actually, as we have seen, to Sophonias, *In Parv. Nat.* p. 13), apart from its possible recognition by Calcidius in the fourth century. If the phrase was in fact interpolated, it may just have been a gloss on ἔργων. There was no need to reinforce the literal interpretation, after all. I am surprised, I must say, that it has been allowed to stand in all modern texts. If one desires to preserve it, then Cornford's suggestion, to emend the ἅ of APY to τὰ seems more or less necessary, but the ἅ itself seems to be an effort to provide some secure syntax for the phrase.

This is not the end of the story of tampering with the text of this supremely important dialogue. In the later part of the work, there are in particular some interesting alterations due to Galen, or at least preserved by him, designed to make Plato's anatomical speculations sound a little more sensible in the light of advances made in medicine

---

[43] Calcidius is rather troublesome. He produces: *Dii deorum, quorum opifex idem paterque ego, opera siquidem vos mea, dissolubilia natura, me tamen ita volente indissolubilia.* The *dissolubilia natura* seems to be stylistic elaboration, not a representation of δι' ἐμοῦ γενόμενα, but on the other hand *opera siquidem vos mea* may well conceal the phrase, ἔργων being taken with it rather than with the previous clause. We may observe, at any rate, that he records no μή before ἐθέλοντος.

[44] In the case of Proclus, we have the interesting circumstance that the lemma has been "corrected" (as often happens), and includes ἃ δι' ἐμοῦ γενόμενα, and from Proclus' comments ad loc. (3.208, 5ff.) it is not clear whether he is reading it or not. But on the one occasion where he actually quotes the passage in full, back in 1. 265, 29–30, he omits the tell-tale phrase.

in Hellenistic and Roman times,[45] but I think that enough has been presented here to make my point. Though many instances of emendation are ambiguous, there seems to me to be a hard core left of instances where the text is being altered to suit one doctrinal position or another. Broadly speaking, as we have seen, the battle in the case of the *Timaeus* is between the supporters of a literal interpretation of the Demiurge's creation of the world and those who wish to take it as a mythical representation of reality. Efforts to slant the text in one direction or another may seem to us to be superfluous, since, if, as I believe, the *Timaeus* account *is* a myth, then even the most literal-sounding descriptions should not disturb us at all, since they are simply reinforcing the verisimilitude of the mythical description, but it is plain that many Platonists, initially under the goad of Aristotle's provocatively literal interpretation, were concerned to leave as few handles as possible for such an interpretation. What is disturbingly plain, arising out of all this frantic activity, is that the Master himself managed to avoid giving any definitive account of what he meant to his immediate followers. How he managed to avoid this I do not know, but I see no other explanation of the phenomena.

What is true for the *Timaeus* should hold, though doubtless to a lesser degree, for the rest of the Platonic corpus, but I am not aware that anyone has gone through the direct and indirect textual traditions of the dialogues, or even of the most utilised passages of the dialogues, with this possibility in mind. It would be a formidable task, but it might turn out to be rewarding. Let this, anyhow, be a start.

---

[45] E.g., 77c4; 83b2; 85e4; 86c4; 86d1; 86d5. Not all of them are of much interest, but a study of them would be worthwhile. At the very end of the work, in 92c, there are a cluster of interesting variants as well which seem to have some ideological content, the most interesting of which is νοητοῦ/ποιητοῦ at 92c7 (on which see the comments of Archer-Hind and Taylor). A reading ποιητοῦ (as genitive of ποιητής), supported by half the Mss. (including the Parisinus) and Stobaeus (*Anth.* 1.300, 23ff.) would be a strong indication, right at the end of the work, that Plato intended the demiurgic creation as a myth, but such a twist would undeniably be rather abrupt. It is more likely, I think, to be the "ideological" emendation.

Apart from these passages, all through the work there is discernible a tendency to vary the spelling of parts of γίγνομαι (including γενητός) and γεννάω, which seems to me to have some ideological content, forms with two *n*'s having, I think, a more *literal* emphasis.

VI

Speusippus in Iamblichus*

Philip Merlan, in chapter V of that most stimulating book *From Platonism to Neoplatonism*, first published in 1954,[1] presented powerful arguments for identifying the substance, at least, of ch. IV of Iamblichus' work *De Communi Mathematica Scientia*[2] as taken directly from a work of Speusippus', and as presenting a fuller and more accurate account of his doctrine of first principles than that relayed to us by Aristotle.

Merlan's arguments convinced many, including myself, but have recently come under attack from Leonardo Tarán, in his edition of the 'fragments' of Speusippus.[3] Judging, correctly, that it is a matter of some consequence whether or not Merlan was justified in his attribution, he devotes a separate chapter of his Introduction (ch. V, pp. 86-107) to this question.

It is indeed a matter of consequence, since ch. IV of *DCMS*, if really Speusippean, yields a relatively coherent metaphysical schema which would provide us with a most useful control to Speusippus' doctrine on the allusive and polemical references of Aristotle. This Tarán rejects, on the grounds of what he sees as a series of irreconcilable contradictions between it and what we know, or think we know, of Speusippus' doctrine from other sources, particularly Aristotle. It is my purpose in this article to argue that these differences are not irreconcilable, and that there is nothing in *DCMS* IV that is not attributable, at least in substance, to Speusippus — and, indeed attributable to no other philosopher of whom we have knowledge.

---

[1] The Hague. Merlan brought out a second edition in 1960, in which he replied to various criticisms of his views, and yet a third one in 1968.

[2] Ed. N. Festa, Teubner, Leipzig, 1891 (hereafter cited as *DCMS*). Refs. are to Festa's pages.

[3] *Speusippus of Athens: A Critical Study with a Collection of the Related Texts and a Commentary* (Leiden, 1983).

II

I will take Tarán's objections in order, without dwelling on the various points of similarity, which he admits (p. 104). The first significant doctrine of *DCMS IV* is that the One, which, with Multiplicity (πλῆθος), is one of the two highest principles (of mathematical numbers in the text, p. 15, 6-7 Festa, but necessarily of all other things as well), "should not yet be described as 'being'" (ὅπερ οὐδὲ ὄν πω δεῖ καλεῖν, 15, 8). Merlan naturally picked on this statement, comparing it with the well-known testimony of Aristotle at *Met.* N, 1092 a 11-17 (fr. 43 Tarán):

> Nor is someone correct who compares the principles of the universe to that of living things and plants, on the grounds that the more complete always comes from what is indefinite and incomplete (this being his reason for saying that this applies to the primary principles too, *so that the One itself would not even be an existing thing*). For even in this case the principles from which these things come *are* complete; it is a man that produces a man, and it is not true that the sperm is primary. (tr. Julia Annas, modified).

The contentious phrase here is that italicised above, ὥστε μηδὲ ὄν τι εἶναι τὸ ἓν αὐτό. As Tarán correctly reminds us (p. 104, and in his commentary *ad loc.*) this is a clause of *natural* or intended result, not one of *actual* result. Annas in her translation — "so that the One is not even an existent thing" — distorts this, though in her notes she recognises, as do most other commentators, including Merlan (*op. cit.* p. 104), that it is presented as Aristotle's own inference. Tarán's argument is that the ὥστε-with-infinitive construction implies that this is Aristotle's inference (a reduction ad absurdum), *and not Speusippus' conclusion*.

I in turn beg to differ with Tarán on this. One may grant that Aristotle is presenting this as the natural, and *absurd*, conclusion of Speusippus' position (the τι is, I think, a touch of sarcasm), but the natural result construction does not seem to me to exclude this being Speusippus' *actual conclusion*. As in the case of his other objections also, Tarán, in my view, is being excessively 'legalistic' in his interpretation of the text. Aristotle is certainly laying emphasis on the *natural* conclusion of Speusippus' theories, and Speusippus himself may have shrunk from presenting his conclusion in just these terms (the expression in *DCMS* IV, οὐδὲ ὄν πω, implies not so much something baldly non-existent as something which may not properly be said yet to exist), but I do not see that the 'natural result' construction *contradicts* the supposition that Speusippus himself advanced this theory.

The line of reasoning presented in *DCMS* IV (p. 15, 9-10) is that 'a first-principle (ἀρχή) is not yet such as are those things of which it is the principle', so that if something is an *arche* of all existent things, it cannot itself have existence in the sense that they have (though it may be thought to subsist in some higher way: one does not see it being described as simply μὴ ὄν). Plainly something that Speusippus said allows Aristotle to allege at *Met.* 1092a11ff. (= Fr. 43), and 1072b30ff. (= Fr. 42) that he compares the First Principle to the seed of animals or plants. In Aristotelian terms this makes it imperfect (ἀτελής), since the seed has not attained it proper τέλος, as the animal and plant concerned. It also conflicts with Aristotle's doctrine that actuality precedes potentiality. But even if Speusippus did compare the First Principle to a seed, he need not for that reason have declared it to be imperfect, in the Aristotelian sense. We do not, I think, have to assume development either upwards or downwards in the Speusippean universe.

III

This is relevant to the next alleged point of conflict between *DCMS* and Aristotle's testimony, the relation of Beauty and Goodness to the First Principles. *DCMS* IV (p. 16, 10ff.) says that "it is not proper to apply the terms 'beautiful' or 'good' to the One, because it is superior to (ὑπεράνω) both the beautiful and the good." The author goes on to distinguish the levels at which the beautiful and the good arise: "for as Nature proceeds further from the primary level (τὰ ἐν ἀρχῇ), *first* the Beautiful makes its appearance (sc. at the level of mathematics and geometricals), and *secondly*, when the elements are at a still further remove, the Good". Tarán seizes on this as contradicting Aristotle, *Met.* 1072b30 ff., and particularly 1091a29ff. (= Fr. 44), where Aristotle gives Speusippus' position as being: "after the nature of things proceeds, both the good and the beautiful make their appearance." "The Aristotelian testimony", says Tarán, "shows that Speusippus did not distinguish between beauty and goodness in this sense, and clearly implies that there is neither goodness nor beauty in mathematicals."

I submit, with much respect, that it shows nothing of the sort. All it shows is that Aristotle was not much concerned with whether Good appeared before or after Beauty in Speusippus' system, since he regarded each alternative as equally absurd. The main focus of his scorn is the notion that the First Principle is neither good nor beautiful. That Speusippus in fact only postulated good as arising 'at the mid-point' of his system, which may be identified with the level of Soul, is attested by the rather satirical remark of Theophrastus in his *Metaphysics* (11a18 ff. = Fr. 83 Tarán) that

Speusippus σπάνιόν τι τὸ τίμιον ποιεῖ τὸ περὶ τὴν μέσην χώραν, τὰ δ'ἄκρα καὶ ἑκατέρωθεν.

Theophrastus makes it sound as if Speusippus postulated good only in the middle, and evil (by implication) at either extreme, which is absurd, and is presumably a consequence of confusing (probably deliberately) his ethical doctrine with his metaphysics. (Speusippus does, after all, hold that the good is a mean between the two evils of pleasure and pain, cf. Fr. 80-1 Tarán). The valuable thing about Theophrastus' testimony is that it would make no sense had not Speusippus notoriously argued for good only arising 'at the mid-point' on the metaphysical level as well. This does not, of course, mean that good ceases to operate at the fourth or fifth stages of his universe (embodied soul and inanimate matter) — that is a distortion introduced by Theophrastus — but it is asserted that it is meaningless to apply the epithet 'good' to anything 'above', or prior to, the level of Soul. And that is the doctrine we have in *DCMS* IV.

A further troublesome point raised by Tarán (pp. 95, 105) is whether or not Speusippus regarded his One as a number, or, if not, whether he postulated a number One besides the One, or, alternatively, regarded the sequence of numbers as beginning with Two. Tarán further denies that Speusippus can have regarded numbers as in any sense 'derived', since he postulated them as external and immutable entities (Ar. *Met.* 1083a20ff. = Fr. 34). But in this very passage Aristotle also presents Speusippus as regarding the One as their *archē*, and Tarán is forced to argue that Aristotle is mistaken here (p. 38). I do not see Tarán's problem. All it is necessary to postulate, surely, is that Speusippus did not regard this derivation as being a temporal process, but rather a logical one (in line with his views on the creation of the world in the *Timaeus*, cf. Fr. 61), and it can been seen that Aristotle's testimony is in accord with the text of *DCMS* IV, where the One and Multiplicity are stated to be the *archai* of mathematical numbers. The evidence does not permit certainty as to whether Speusippus began mathematical numbers with One or Two, but I would interpret Ar. *Met.* 1075b37ff. (= Fr. 30 Tarán) as attributing to Speusippus a monad as the first principle of numbers, even as the point is the first principle of geometricals (cf. *DCMS* IV p. 17, 13ff).

V

A final discrepancy that Tarán discerns (*op. cit.* p. 107) is the doctrine of evil expressed in *DCMS* IV (p. 18, 9-12). In Tarán's words (p. 102), "evil appears only towards the extreme (sc. of the spheres of being), in the fourth and fifth kinds of entities, which come from the last elements. Evil, however, does not appear as a direct result of the elements, but because of something in nature that falls out and is not able to rule. This implies the doctrine of evil as the incomplete information of the material."

This is a fair interpretation, I think, of the text, which runs as follows: ἐπὶ ἐσχάτῳ δὲ ἐν τοῖς τετάρτοις καὶ πέμπτοις τοῖς συντιθεμένοις ἀπὸ τῶν στοιχείων τῶν τελευταίων κακίαν γενέσθαι οὐ προηγουμένως, ἐκ δὲ τοῦ ἐκπίπτειν καὶ μὴ κατακρατεῖν τινα τοῦ κατὰ φύσιν.

First of all, as has been noted by Merlan (with whom I agree), this last section of ch. V has the air of being summarised to a far greater extent than what precedes it, where Iamblichus, as in most of the rest of the work, seems to be quoting some source virtually verbatim.[4] The doctrine here, therefore, would be presented in summary form. Nevertheless, the point the author wants to make is clear enough. Evil is not a primary entity (οὐ προηγουμένως[5]), but rather an incidental result of the imperfect mastering of matter by the principles of the fourth and fifth stages (presumably the first principles of animate and inanimate physical objects respectively, though we get no clear guidance on this from Iamblichus' summary). Matter itself, as Tarán points out (*loc. cit.*), is not itself evil.

Tarán maintains (p. 107) that this doctrine of 'negative evil' conflicts with the testimony of Theophrastus in Fr. 83, quoted above. But once again one must protest that Tarán is reading more into Theophrastus' rather satirical and free-swinging comments than is reasonable. First of all, Theophrastus, to accentuate the absurdity of Speusippus' position, presents him as postulating just a small patch of Good at the mid-point of his universe, so to speak, and great stretches of Evil on either side of it (ἑκατέρωθεν). The ἑκατέρωθεν is plainly absurd, and I have explained, I think, how Theophrastus could have come to make such a statement. As for whether Evil in general is primary or incidental, Theophrastus is not in the least concerned, any more than was Aristotle at *Met.* 1091a29ff. (Fr. 44 Tarán), as to whether the Beautiful appeared before the Good. Once again, therefore, I see no contradiction, merely inconcinnity.

[4] H. Dörrie, indeed, in his review of Merlan (*Philos. Rundschau* 3, 1955, pp. 15-16 = *Platonica Minora*, pp. 276-7) argues against this last passage being Speusippean, but his arguments only throw doubt on its being a verbatim quotation.
[5] This term also occurs in a summary of Speusippus' doctrine given by Sextus Empiricus (*M* VII 146 = Fr. 75 Tarán). Tarán would deny that it is Speusippean, but it is attested for Theophrastus (*De Igne*, 14).

VI

Finally, there are some details of vocabulary which Tarán sees as incompatible with Speusippus (p. 107). When examined, however, they come to very little. Neither the use of ὕλη to mean 'matter', nor the use of ὑφίσταται to mean 'subsist' (both p. 18, 4), seems to me impossibly un-Speusippean — ὕλη is Aristotelian, and ὑφίσταμαι in this sense at least Epicurean, which brings it within a generation of Speusippus. In any case, both the locutions complained of come from the final section, where, as I have said, Iamblichus is probably summarising his source. The most remarkable word in the whole chapter, εὐπλαδής (used of ὕλη in a rather less technical sense than above, p. 15, 13) is unique and so proves nothing. As for the lively compound συμμολύνω (as in τὸ συνεχὲς καὶ τὸ συμμεμο-λυσμένον, p. 17, 20), the fact that it is not otherwise attested until the Septuagint and Philodemus does not disturb me greatly. Any fool can add σύν to μολύνω, which is securely attested for Plato (*Rep.* VII, 535e5), if only once. In general, the argument from vocabulary is a shaky one (except in extreme cases, which do not occur here), precisely because so much Greek literature is lost.

VII

Where, then, does all this leave us? I hope that it leaves us with access reopened, and indeed widened, to a potentially most valuable source for our knowledge of Speusippus' doctrine. Tarán has undoubtedly done a service in setting out most lucidly the points of alleged conflict, but I do not think he has proved his case.

It is actually rather curious that the identification of the source of this section of the *DCMS* as Speusippus should arouse such a degree of opposition. No one, after all, complains about the Anonymus Iamblichi (who is, admittedly, anonymous, but securely located in the 5th-4th century B.C.), and only a few eccentrics doubt that Iamblichus is making liberal use of Aristotle's *Protrepticus* in his *Protrepticus*. It seems reasonable to ask why it is so offensive to suppose than *DCMS* IV should be (at least in substance)[6] Speusippus. There are, I think two main reasons, and they both merit some discussion.

---

[6] I say 'at least in substance' simply because we can see from Iamblichus' use of Plato that he is quite prepared to abridge his source somewhat, and alter particles and sentence structure; but in the case of Plato he is adapting dialogue, so we need not assume even so much here.

First, there is the circumstance that in the whole stretch of time between Speusippus himself and Iamblichus we have no verbatim quotation from any work of Speusippus[7], nor do his peculiar doctrines appear to have had any influence on any later Platonist. This does certainly make his appearance in Iamblichus remarkable, but we have to concede, from the fact of his access to Aristotle's *Protrepticus* and to the work of an otherwise lost 5th-century Sophist (as well as to many Pythagorean pseudepigrapha), that Iamblichus had access to a good library. The only other verbatim quotation we have of Speusippus, from his work *On Pythagorean Numbers*, comes from a work which Iamblichus at least had something to do with, the *Theologumena Arithmeticae* (Fr. 28 Tarán). It is from this treatise, *On Pythagorean Numbers*, indeed, that *DCMS* IV could be plausibly taken to come. Since it admitted by all who know anything about Iamblichus' methods of composition in this sequence of Pythagorean works that the bulk of *DCMS* IV must be a quotation from somebody, the anti-Speusippean faction must propose an unknown Neopythagorean source (e.g. Tarán, p. 107, "a Neopythagorean or Neoplatonic sympathiser") as a surrogate. But a) such of these as Iamblichus quotes employ invariably a bastard Doric dialect, and b) if there are no longer serious grounds for disputing that the passage contains Speusippean doctrine, it multiplies entities needlessly to propose a later, unknown imitator. Even the sugges-tion, by a friendly critic of Merlan such as Kohnke, in his review of the book[8], of Posidonius as a 'Mittelquelle' (pp. 160-1) seems to be super-fluous.

The other, more serious, objection to accepting the doctrine of *DCMS* IV is the fear of importing what are seen as Neoplatonic mystical tendencies back into the Old Academy, particularly the doctrine of a One above Being. The fear is, I believe, misguided. Speusippus may indeed have been as much of a mystic as his uncle, but there is nothing necessarily mystical about his doctrine of the One, any more than there is about that of Plotinus. In both cases, they arrived at their conclusions for logical reasons. Speusippus' point surely is that, even as that which is for all other things the cause of beauty and (for most other things) of goodness will not be itself beautiful or good, at least in the same sense that other things are, so that which is for all things the cause of their existence must itself not yet exist, at

---

[7] Athenaeus reports extensively from Speusippus' *Homoia* his distinctions of types of sea creatures, and Sextus, at *M* VII 145-6, gives a valuable summary of his theory of knowledge, but in neither case verbatim. Otherwise, all we have are doxographical tags.
[8] *Gnomon* 27 (1955), 157ff.

least in the sense that they do. This argument may or may not be cogent, but there is certainly nothing specifically mystical about it. (Something such, indeed, must be the reasoning behind Plato's famous dictum οὐκ οὐσίας ὄντος τοῦ ἀγαθοῦ, ἀλλ' ἐπέκεινα τῆς οὐσίας πρεσβείᾳ καὶ δυνάμει ὑπερέχοντος of *Rep.* VI 508B). If modern critics want to attach 'mystical' overtones to this doctrine, that is not Speusippus' fault. It is even possible that he was trying to make a logical point about what it is proper to attribute to a perfectly unitary First Principle, and he seems to have presented it, if anything, rather tentatively than dogmatically.

If I am right in my defence of Merlan's position, then we must resolve to accept the fact that we do have a source which contains a coherent, if compressed, account of Speusippus' doctrine, which gives us a salutary control on the tendentious and allusive references of Aristotle and Theophrastus. It certainly does not solve all the problems attendant on Speusippus' metaphysics (what really is the process which leads one level of being to develop the next one, for instance?)[9], but it makes him appear considerably less idiotic than Aristotle would have us believe. And that is surely a step in the direction of the truth.

[9] I have essayed a solution in *The Middle Platonists* (London, 1977) pp. 12-18, but I have no great confidence that it is correct.

VII

Xenocrates' Metaphysics: Fr. 15 (Heinze) Re-examined

Xenocrates has actually been receiving a modest share of attention in recent years. Hans-Joachim Krämer featured him prominently both in *Der Ursprung der Geistmetaphysik* of 1964 and in *Platonismus und hellenistische Philosophie* in 1971. Heinrich Dörrie contributed an excellent *RE* article on him in 1967 (ix A2 1511-1528) and W.K.C. Guthrie, a useful survey of current opinion at the end of volume 5 of his *History of Greek Philosophy* in 1978 (469-483). Margherita Isnardi Parente has crowned a series of books and articles related to the Old Academy and Xenocrates (1977, 1979, 1980, 1981) with a magisterial collection of his fragments (1982), thus finally providing an alternative to Heinze's collection of 1892. Most recently, Matthias Baltes has specifically addressed the problems of Fr. 15 (Heinze) in a contribution, shortly to be published (1987), to a Symposium held in Utrecht in May, 1986 on the topic of *The Knowledge of God from Alexander the Great to Constantine*.

All this activity has clarified much, though nothing can really compensate us for the lack of any more than a few lines[1] of the many works with which our sources credit Xenocrates. However, there is one document of central importance for the understanding of his metaphysical system which has not, I believe, hitherto been correctly interpreted, and it is on that that I wish to concentrate in the present article.

In chapter 1 of his *Anthology* (i 36 [Wachsmuth]), John of Stobi preserves for us a doxographical account of Xenocrates' metaphysical system, lifted virtually verbatim, as all are agreed, from Aetius' *Placita*. Owing to the unsatisfactory state of our information on Xenocrates' doctrines, this rather miserable document takes on a not inconsiderable importance. It is a pity, therefore, that, despite the attention that has been given to it, particularly by Krämer and more recently by Isnardi Parente, its anomalies have not been properly faced. As it stands, I would submit, it puts great difficulties in the way of reconstructing Xenocrates' system; properly emended and elucidated, however, it could throw considerable light upon it. One complication that has distracted commentators is that it is presented, not as a straight description of Xenocrates' metaphysics, but rather as a series of identifications with traditional deities. It has thus been regarded as 'theology' rather than metaphysics and is so denominated in both Heinze's and Isnardi Parente's collections. However, this cannot exempt it from having to cohere with Xenocrates' known philosophical positions.

I will first give the text of the passage as it stands, followed by a translation of the first section, which is all that I am concerned with in the present instance.

Ξενοκράτης 'Αγαθήνορος Καλχηδόντος τὴν μονάδα καὶ δυάδα θεούς, τὴν μὲν ὡς ἄρρενα πατρὸς ἔχουσαν τάξιν ἐν οὐρανῷ βασιλεύουσαν, ἥντινα προσαγορεύει καὶ Ζῆνα καὶ περιττὸν καὶ νοῦν, ὅστις ἐστὶν αὐτῷ πρῶτος θεός· τὴν δὲ ὡς θήλειαν, μητρὸς θεῶν δίκην, τῆς ὑπὸ τὸν οὐρανὸν λήξεως ἡγουμένην, ἥτις ἐστὶν αὐτῷ ψυχὴ τοῦ παντός. θεὸν δ' εἶναι καὶ τὸν οὐρανὸν καὶ τοὺς ἀστέρας πυρώδεις 'Ολυμπίους θεούς, καὶ ἑτέρους ὑποσελήνους δαίμονας ἀοράτους. ἀρέσκαι δὲ καὶ αὐτῷ < θείας τινὰς δυνάμεις > καὶ ἐνδιήκειν τοῖς ὑλικοῖς στοιχείοις. τούτων δὲ τὴν μὲν < διὰ τοῦ ἀέρος "Αιδην ὡς > ἀειδῆ προσαγορεύει, τὴν δὲ διὰ τοῦ ὑγροῦ Ποσειδῶνα, τὴν δὲ διὰ τῆς γῆς φυτοσπόρον Δήμητρα. ταῦτα δὲ χορηγήσας τοῖς Στωικοῖς τὰ πρότερα παρὰ τοῦ Πλάτωνος μεταπέφρακεν.

Xenocrates, son of Agathenor, of Chalcedon, (holds) as gods the Monad and the Dyad, the former as male, having the role of father reigning in the heavens, which he terms 'Zeus' and 'odd' and 'intellect', which is for him the primary god, the other, as female, in the manner of the Mother of the Gods, ruling over the realm below the heavens, who is for him the soul of the universe.

I am on record in *The Middle Platonists* (1977, 26) as protesting that there has to be something badly wrong here. The Monad is readily identifiable as what we know from other evidence to be Xenocrates' first principle,[2] but the Dyad in the form here presented to us I find profoundly disturbing. I am not alone in this feeling. Heinze (1892, 35ff.), Krämer (1964, 39-41), Dörrie (1967, col. 1520), Isnardi Parente (1982, 404-405) and now Baltes (1987) are all uncomfortable in varying degrees about the identifying of the second principle, the Dyad, with the World Soul. They agree, however, in a solution to the problem which I find unconvincing. Heinze would argue that the Dyad mentioned here cannot be regarded as identical with the Indefinite Dyad, which we know to be Xenocrates' second principle proper, but must be taken simply as a term for the World Soul,[3] though he recognises at the same time that the identification with the Mother of the Gods fits well with the attested identification of the Pythagorean Indefinite Dyad with Rhea by Philolaus,[4] who is etymologising here on the basis of a derivation of Rhea from ῥέω, which in turn fits well with Xenocrates' characterisation of his second principle as ἀέναος, 'everflowing' (Fr. 28 [Heinze]/101 [Isnardi Parente]).[5] Krämer also feels that such an identifcation is impossible, though I do not agree entirely with his reasons. He regards Xenocrates' second principle as evil ('*das κακόν schlechthin und also solche widergöttlich*' [1964, 39]), whereas the World Soul is plainly a positive and ordering principle. I am no longer convinced that the Indefinite Dyad is an *evil* principle for Xenocrates. It is certainly the principle of Matter (Fr. 28 [Heinze]/101 [Isnardi Parente]) and would rank in the συστοιχία of evil in Pythagorean terms, but to see it as being the inspiration for such entities as Plutarch's Typhon in the *Isis and Osiris* or the disorderly World Soul of the *De proc. an.* (Heinze 1892, 35; Krämer 1964, 40) is, I think, not justified. Plutarch himself in the *De proc. an.* 1012d ff. (= Fr. 68 [Heinze]/188 [Isnardi Parente]) presents Xenocrates' interpretation of the components of the Soul in *Tim.* 35a as being an identification of 'the undivided and unchanging substance' as the One, and 'that which is divided about bodies' as 'multiplicity' (the Speusippan term) or as the Indefinite Dyad. There is no suggestion here that this latter entity is evil, except perhaps in the sense that one may formally term κακόν the source of multiplicity and extension and materiality.[6]

An any event, it is true to say that this Dyad cannot be identified with the World Soul, since it is one of the elements out of which the Soul is formed. But neither, I would maintain, is it plausible to suggest that an entity presented as a basic principle over against the Monad and further characterised as 'Mother of the Gods' can also be described by Xenocrates as a World Soul. Nor can it reasonably be maintained that Aetius is not purporting to give an account of Xenocrates' metaphysical system as a whole, but only of the subcelestial world or some other such partial account, as Isnardi Parente would wish to claim (1982, 405).[7] Aetius plainly thinks he is starting with Xenocrates' first principle and going on from there.

So there has to be something wrong with the text. The only question is, What is the nature of the defect? I see two possibilities: either we must postulate a lacuna in the text of Aetius (due to a misreading either by Stobaeus himself or some other intermediary source) or we must assume that Aetius has misunderstood his source (which may or may not be an actual text of Xenocrates—we cannot be sure that Aetius himself is not excerpting some previous doxographer). Let us consider these possibilities in turn.

(1) If we are to suppose a lacuna, I would pick on the phrase μητρὸς θεῶν δίκην as being most likely to conceal it. The adverbial δίκην is actually used no less than seven times by Aetius[8] but is nevertheless a distinctly high-flown, not to say poetical, term;[9] so in each instance he could be alleged to be borrowing from his source.[10] We know nothing of Xenocrates' style, except that he did not 'sacrifice to the Muses' (Diogenes Laertius, iv 6); but he was not writing hexameter verse or even (with a few possible exceptions) Platonic dialogues, so that his use of a locution such as this is improbable.

In fact, δίκην has attracted some attention. Pierre Boyancé (1948, 218-231) has proposed to read Δίκην with a capital letter and to understand it as a personification of Dike, taking μητρὸς θεῶν as depending on ἔχουσαν τάξιν (understood). I think that this is a very sound proposal, but I am surprised that Boyancé did not go a step further and ask himself what mythological connexion there can be between Rhea (for it is surely she who is mother of the Gods) and Dike? They certainly can not be identified. Rhea is Zeus' mother, whereas Dike is, if anything, his daughter. Xenocrates may take some liberties with the Greek pantheon, but he will not be entirely indiscriminate in his identifications.[11] Dike's ancestry and role are securely fixed by Hesiod—ἡ δέ τε πάρθενος ἔστι Δίκη, Διὸς ἐκγεγαυῖα/ κυδρή τ' αἰδοίη τε θεῶν, οἵ Ὄλυμπον ἔχουσιν. (Op. 256-257) She sits beside her father and tells him of men's wickedness. Translated into philosophic terms, Dike both contemplates the noetic realm, represented by Zeus, and cognises also the sense-world. This is precisely the mediating role assigned in the Timaeus to the Soul (37a-c), a role which Soul is enabled to perform by reason of its composition from the two classes of substance, which Xenocrates understands as the Monad and the Indefinite Dyad.[12]

Dike, then, is a very suitable mythological equivalent of the World Soul, but in no way suitable to the Indefinite Dyad. If there is a lacuna in our text, it is here that it must be.

I have toyed with the possibility of inserting something like μητρὸς θεῶν < τάξιν ἔχουσαν, ἥντινα προσαγορεύει καὶ Ῥέαν καὶ ἄρτιον καὶ ὕλην. ὡς δὲ ἔκγονον τούτων ὑποτίθεται >

VII

50

Δίκην. Some supplement such as this would, on the one hand, give us a series of three epithets for the Dyad to balance the three accorded to the Monad and, on the other, give Dike the ancestry proper to her as World Soul. However, one cannot deny that there are difficulties. First of all, a union between Zeus and his mother to produce Dike has no sanction in traditional mythology. However, there is in non-traditional mythology a source on which Xenocrates could draw. As we know, he was much interested in Orphism[13] as well as in Pythagoreanism and there is, in Orphic tradition, the belief that Zeus mated with his mother to produce a female offspring, identified as Kore/Persephone, who is in a way a reincarnation of the mother (and with whom he also mated).[14] Such a conjunction, then, would not be entirely without mythological precedent.

Secondly, though, there is the stylistic consideration emphasised by Baltes (1987),[15] that a contrast could be seen to be made between ἐν οὐράνῳ βασιλεύουσαν, referring to the Monad, and τῆς ὑπὸ τὸν οὐρανὸν λήξεως ἡγουμένην, referring to the Dyad (as well as ὅστις ἐστιν αὐτῷ . . . and ἥτις ἐστιν αὐτῷ . . .). The idea that the Dyad in its capacity as Matter is immanent in the cosmos and indeed is to be identified with ὁ ὁρατὸς κόσμος, is reported in the doxographical tradition as a doctrine of Pythagoras,[16] as is the idea that the Dyad is a δαίμων and τὸ κακόν,[17] which at least attests to such a doctrine in the Neopythagorean tradition. Xenocrates is occasionally paired with Pythagoras in the doxographic tradition[18]—though not in this instance—and this leads Krämer (1964, 54-59) to attribute this doctrine to him also. I agree that Xenocrates is probably somewhere in the background of this tradition; but I do not see that we need attribute this type or degree of dualism to him, despite his attested belief and interest in evil daemons (Frs. 24-25 [Heinze]/226-230 [Isnardi Parente]). However, even if one does take these reports to represent his doctrine, that still does not resolve the contradiction between Dyad and World Soul.

(2) This consideration of the stylistic balance of the text as it stands does, however, seem to me to carry some weight. Aetius is, after all, making reasonable sense and doing it with some artistic balancing of *clausulae*. This leads me to my second alternative. It may be the case that there is no lacuna in our text,[19] but that Aetius has carelessly surveyed and excerpted his source, which may ultimately, but not immediately, be Xenocrates' two books Περὶ θεῶν (Diogenes Laertius, iv 13). There Xenocrates' descriptions of the functions of Rhea and Dike may have exhibited sufficient overlapping to confuse a doxographer of little brain. He may, indeed, have attributed some form of soul (a disorderly soul, derived from both the *Timaeus* and the myth of the *Politicus*?) to the Dyad; and he probably presented both entities as, albeit in diverse ways, immanent in the cosmos. Indeed, if, as the evidence of Philodemus suggests (above, n14), Xenocrates made use of the Orphic belief that Rhea is both mother and daughter of Zeus, rather than introducing the figure of Dike (if, that is to say, the δίκην of the text does not after all conceal Dike),[20] then the possibilities of confusion on the part of a doxographer greatly increase.

These, then, are the two possibilities which I would offer for rehabilitating this text. I am unwilling to choose between them, though I incline towards the latter.

Of one thing only am I certain, *pace* all previous commentators, and that is that the confusion between Indefinite Dyad and World Soul does not go back to Xenocrates. Indeed, I would suggest that the contradictions in this passage should not have been allowed to stand without serious challenge. Had Xenocrates been a Presocratic philosopher, for instance, instead of a member of the sadly-undervalued Old Academy, I believe that all this would have been thrashed out effectively long since, even at the cost of radical surgery on the text. The matter is not trivial. Fr. 15 [Heinze]/213 [Isnardi Parente], properly evaluated, is a most useful confirmation, admittedly in the theological mode, of Theophrastus' commendation in *Metaphysics* (6b6-9) of Xenocrates for being the only member of the Old Academy who gave a properly comprehensive account of the universe, whereas the others get no further than the outer rim of the heavens. We can see in the latter part of the present passage something of what that involved and what influence it had on the theologising of the Stoics; but that is not my concern at present.

NOTES

¹ Even those are of rather doubtful status and in any case unremarkable—chiefly a short quotation from his *Life of Plato*, quoted by Simplicius on a number of occasions (Frs. 53 [Heinze]/264-266 [Isnardi Parente]).

² The fact that the Monad is described as ἐν οὐρανῷ βασιλεύουσαν should not deceive us into supposing that Xenocrates conceives of his first principle as being immanent in the cosmos. This is to be understood as simply a poetical manner of speaking, based probably on the description of Zeus in the *Phaedrus* (246e4) as μέγας ἡγεμὼν ἐν οὐρανῷ. We know from Plutarch (*Quaest. plat.* ix 1.1007b = Fr. 18 [Heinze]/216 [Isnardi Parente]) that Xenocrates placed his 'upper Zeus' (Ζεὺς ὕπατος) ἐν τοῖς κατὰ τὰ αὐτὰ καὶ ὡσαύτως ἔχουσιν, a clear designation of the intelligible realm.

³ 'Dass diese Δυάς ganz verschieden ist von der ἀόριστος δυάς, bedarf wohl keines Beweises' (1892, 35n1). In this he is followed by Dörrie (1967, col. 1520): 'wichtig ist aber, dass die ἀόριστος δυάς aus der man gern τόπος κενὸν ἄπειρον ableitete, aus dieser Konzeption verschwinden ist'.

⁴ DK 44 B20a: ὁ Φιλόλαος τὴν δυάδα Κρόνου σύνευνον εἶναι λέγει.

⁵ Though Isnardi Parente seems to want to challenge the accepted meaning of ἀέναος (1982, 336-337), suggesting simply the general meaning 'sempiternal' ('*perenni*'). I do not see that this is justified on the evidence.

⁶ I would wish therefore to retract my characterisation of the Indefinite Dyad in *The Middle Platonists* (1977, 26), where I was simply following Heinze and Krämer.

⁷ She is inclined to reject my solution (put forward in 1977, 26, on which see further below) by suggesting that 'Xenocrates could have made a distinction between the formation of the soul in general and that of the cosmic function of the universal soul, in its opposing itself to the higher nature of the heavens, as an inferior and subordinate nature, and he could in this way have restructured previously-existing cosmological religious schemes.' I find this a rather desperate speculation.

⁸ Diels, 1879, 300a14, ἐργάτου δίκην καὶ τέκτονος (in a rather rhetorical part of the 'Plutarchan' recension); 304b8 (our passage); 332b21 τρόπεως δίκην (giving doctrine of Philolaus); 335a12b9, τείχους δίκην (Parmenidean doctrine); 367a11b10, σπινθήρων δίκην (Anaxagorean doctrine); 378a13, τροχοῦ δίκην (doctrine of Heraclides of Pontus and Ecphantus the Pythagorean); 406a19b19, κώδωνος δίκην (Empedoclean doctrine). Note that all examples, except the first two, involve inanimate objects.

⁹ Among classical prose authors, only Plato seems to use it (e.g., *Phaedr.* 235d, 249d; *Theaet.* 164c; *Rep.* ix 586a). Otherwise it is poetical (much favoured by Aeschylus) and late prose.

¹⁰ One cannot insist on such an argument. If Aetius is to be identified, as Diels would argue (1879, 49) with the dedicatee of a funeral epigram by Philip of Thessalonica, he was a ῥῆτωρ of the Augustan Age and thus capable of anything in the linguistic line. In the other six cases, however, the word is used, correctly, to signify 'in the manner of', whereas in our passage it would have to mean rather 'in the role of' or 'corresponding to'.

¹¹ Even the Oedipal situation in which he places Zeus with regard to Rhea can be justified in terms of Orphic theology, as we shall see in a moment.

¹² To this extent it is possible, as Krämer repeatedly points out (1964, 40, 79-81), to describe the World Soul as 'dyadic' but not, I would maintain, as 'the Dyad' without qualification.

[13] Cf. Frs. 18-20 [Heinze]/217-219 [Isnardi Parente], and Boyancé (1948).
[14] See on this West 1983, 93-98. We now have, in the last line of the Derveni papyrus (contemporary with Xenocrates), the significant statement (referring to Zeus): ἤθελε μητρὸς ἑᾶς μιχθήμεναι ἐν φιλότητι. The mother is presented as Rhea but also as Demeter. For Xenocrates she is plainly the former. Dike for Kore is presumably his own idea. The notion is also attested as Orphic by Philodemus, De pietate, 80 (Gomperz), where Rhea is stated to be both mother and daughter to Zeus.
[15] But even he concedes that a balancing epithet for περιττός (i.e., ἀρτιά) might have been expected and he supposes this to have fallen out in the transmission.
[16] Aetius ap. Plutarch, Epit. i 3, and Stobaeus Ecl. i 10 (quoted in Krämer 1964, 56).
[17] Aetius ap. Plutarch Epit. i 7 and Stobaeus Ecl. i 1 (also quoted in Krämer 1964, 57). This can hardly be related too closely to Xenocrates' doctrine here, as Krämer would wish to do, since he has stated at the outset that the Dyad is θεός on the same footing as the Monad, not a δαίμων.
[18] In, e.g., Fr. 60 [Heinze]/169-170 [Isnardi Parente], the definition of the Soul; and Fr. 69 [Heinze]/205 [Isnardi Parente], on separate nature of νοῦς.
[19] Not too much can be made of the two lacunae further down, since their presence is clearly indicated in the mss. and since they cause incoherences in the syntax.
[20] I am not absolutely wedded to the postulation of Dike as part of the original text, and it is not necessary to the main point I am making, which is that Xenocrates must have distinguished the Indefinite Dyad from the World-Soul.

BIBLIOGRAPHY

Baltes, M. 1987. 'Zur Theologie des Xenokrates' in The Knowledge of God from Alexander the Great to Constantine. R. van den Broek, ed. Leiden: Brill.

Boyancé, P. 1948. 'Xénocrate et les Orphiques' Revue des études anciennes 50 218-231.

Diels, H. 1879. Doxographi Graeci. Berlin.

Dillon, J. 1977. The Middle Platonists. London and Ithaca, NY: Cornell University Press.

Dörrie, H. 1967. Xenokrates in RE ix A 2 cols 1511-1528.

Guthrie, W.K.C. 1978. History of Greek Philosophy. v. Cambridge: Cambridge University Press.

Heinze, R. 1892. Xenokrates: Darstellung der Lehre und Sammlung der Fragmenten. Leipzig.

Isnardi Parente, M. 1977. 'Dottrina delle idee e dottrina dei principi nell'Academia antica' Annali della Scuola Norm. Sup. di Pisa ser. III 7 1017-1128.

Isnardi Parente, M. Studi sull'Academia platonica antica. Firenze: L.S. Olschki.

Isnardi Parente, M. 1980. Speusippo: Frammenti. Napoli: Bibliopolis.

Isnardi Parente, M. 1981. 'Per la biografia di Senocrate' Rivista di Filologia e di Istruzione Classica 109 129-162.

Isnardi Parente, M. 1982. Senocrate-Hermodoro: Frammenti. Napoli: Bibliopolis.

Krämer, H.-J. 1964. Der Ursprung der Geistmetaphysik. Amsterdam: Schippers.

Krämer, H.-J. 1971. Platonismus und Hellenistische Philosophie. Berlin and New York: De Gruyter.

West, M.L. 1983. The Orphic Poems. Oxford: Oxford University Press.

VIII

Metriopatheia and *Apatheia*:
Some Reflections on a Controversy
in Later Greek Ethics

I

LATER Platonic theory on the passions faced considerable problems, largely inherited from Plato himself. The master had in various places in his dialogues given occasion for rather different doctrines, or at least varieties of emphasis, in this area. From a dialogue such as the *Phaedo* one could derive the doctrine that the passions were to be extirpated root and branch from the soul of the wise man. The passage of the *Theaetetus* (176A ff.) advocating *likeness to god* as the purpose of life could be taken as implying the same view. On the other hand, in the *Republic* and the *Timaeus* all three parts of the soul are accorded their due place, and there is no question of abolishing the passionate element, simply of controlling it. In such a passage as *Polit.* 284E ff., Plato actually seems to propound the doctrine of *virtue as a mean* in the Aristotelian sense, implying that passions are bad only as excesses that require moderating, or "measuring," by logos. Again, in *Laws* I, 631B ff. the distinction between *divine* and *human* goods (goods of the soul as opposed to goods of the body and external goods) finds a definite place for such lower goods, if only an inferior one, and these goods are inseparable from the passions.[1]

Let us first briefly recall the positions which form the basis for the controversy, as propounded by their originators. In the *Nicomachean Ethics* Book II, as we know, Aristotle puts forward a theory of virtue as a mean, which involves it in being, as set out in Chapter 5 (1105b19 ff.), a *hexis* imposing a correct measure upon *pathe*, which, left to themselves, would tend to irrational excess. On the other hand, for Zeno of Cition and his immediate successors (*SVF* I 205 ff.), all pathos was an irrational movement of the

This paper was presented at the 1978 Vancouver meeting of the Society for Ancient Greek Philosophy and has not previously been published.

soul , a *hormē pleonazousa*, an "excessive impulse," which must simply be removed from the soul of the wise man. The passions in question are chiefly four: desire, fear, grief, and pleasure.

The question necessarily arises as to what is left to the soul, and it has been variously answered. There are, after all, two possibilities. Either the wise man is to be seen as a sort of yogi, totally impervious to normal human impulses, or we must redefine what it is to be *rationally* affected by events. The former alternative does seem to have been attractive to certain Stoic "heretics" such as Ariston, but orthodox Stoicism, as represented by Chrysippus, and—it seems probable to me—by Zeno himself, did not intend to impose upon the Wise Man total impassivity.

This involves us with the theory of the *eupatheiai*,[2] and thus brings us to the point at which the Stoic and Aristotelian positions require considerable powers of discrimination to distinguish, powers not granted, it seems, to many of the Platonist writers who have come down to us. The theory of *eupatheiai* in its explicit form seems to be the creation of Chrysippus, but Zeno is on record as making the remark (*ap.* Seneca, *De Ira* I 16, 7) that "in the soul of the Wise Man, even when the wound (of the passions) is healed, a scar remains. He will feel therefore certain suggestions and shadows of passions, though he will be free of the passions themselves." Whether or not the latter remark is that of Zeno or of Seneca himself, the point is clear enough. The wise man will experience *something*, and it is not a passion.[3] Whether or not Zeno conceived a name for it, he stated the position. The only respect in which Chrysippus is reported as differing with him on this question (Galen, *De Hipp.* V 429, p. 405 Mu. = *SVF* III 461) is that Chrysippus held the passions to be actually "judgments" (*kriseis*), while Zeno held that they were disturbances in the soul that arise after (some) judgments.

We see here, I think, Chrysippus pressing the Stoic position to its logical conclusion. Zeno is trying to separate off the purely intellectual element in, say, a decision in the mind of the wise man arising from righteous indignation, from any trace of emotion that might supervene upon that. Chrysippus sees this as illogical; there is only one element operating in the soul (the *hēgemonikon*); it is illegitimate to break down certain of its *kriseis* into two operations. Some *kriseis* of the wise man cannot be performed without some emotion, however rational. Such an emotion cannot be a *pathos*, since that is essentially irrational, and thus unworthy of the wise man. Let us therefore propound a new term, *eupatheia,* for this inevitable accompaniment of certain judgments. There will be *eupatheiai* answering at least to three of the four *pathē*—"joy" (*chara*) to pleasure, "willing" (*boulēsis*) to desire, and "caution" (*eulabeia*) to fear (*SVF* III 431, 437, 438). Only to Grief was Chrysippus unwilling to allow any rational equivalent, though later Stoics seem to have recognized a permissible "nibbling" or "gnawing" at the soul (*dēgmos*, e.g., Cic. *Tusc. Disp.* III 83), to match *lypē*.   *

II

With the development of the doctrine of *eupatheiai* in its full form, the positions of the two schools seem to come, on the practical level at least, dangerously close.[4] The Stoic sage is not, after all, a totally passionless yogi. He begins to appear very much like the well-moderated Aristotelian gentleman. What then does this great controversy amount to, and, in particular, what did the Platonists make of it? That is the proper subject of this paper. Let us take a few significant passages, and analyse them.

I begin with Antiochus of Ascalon, as reported by Cicero.[5] Antiochus was a thoroughgoing Stoic sympathizer both in physics and in ethics (though he felt that Zeno and his followers had rather gone out on a limb in denying all place in rational life to the "lower" goods, sc. the goods of the body and external goods.[6]) Here is how Cicero makes Antiochus' mouthpiece, Varro, present Zeno's position in the *Academica Posteriora* (I 38):

> Also, whereas they (sc. the Old Academy, with Aristotle and Theophrastus) did not remove emotion out of humanity altogether, and said that sorrow and desire and fear and pleasure were natural, but curbed them and narrowed their range, Zeno held that the wise man was devoid of what he termed "these diseases"; and whereas the Ancients said that these emotions were natural and non-rational, and placed desire and reason in different parts of the soul, he did not agree with these doctrines either, for he thought that even the emotions were voluntary and were experienced owing to a judgement of opinion, and he held that the mother of all the emotions was a sort of immoderate intemperance (a rendering, no doubt, of *hormē pleonazousa*).

Antiochus here presents a strong antithesis between the two doctrines, ignoring the subtlety introduced by the doctrine of *eupatheiai*. He himself, on Cicero's evidence, seems to have been in sympathy with the Stoic position. In an admittedly polemical passage of the *Acad. Pr.* (II 135–36), Cicero presents Antiochus as adhering to the Stoic line on extirpation of the passions, and reproaches him for importing into the "Old Academy" an *atrocitas* foreign to it. But Antiochus was, as we know, wedded to the doctrine that there was no essential difference between the Old Academy (including the Peripatos), and the Stoics (except in this matter of the self-sufficiency of virtue), so that he must in fact have made some satisfactory equation in his own mind between Aristotelian moderation of the passions and the Stoic *eupatheiai*. This equation, if indeed he made it, may be regarded as the beginning of a long-standing confusion in later Platonism as to what the opposition to the Stoic ideal was about. The main element in the opposition, plainly, is the contrast between the Stoic belief in a unitary soul, which should be dominated by logos, and in which anything irrational must be a perversion (*diastrophē*) of logos (cf. *SVF* I 208), and the Platonic-Aristotelian bipartite or tripartite soul. If one does not postulate an irrational part of the soul, as the Platonists did (and as, later, Posidonius, among the Stoics, came to do[7]), then the phenomenon of *pathos* becomes extremely troublesome. There can be no "moderate" form of it. One cannot be partly or moderately irrational, rather as one cannot be half pregnant. The logos is the guiding principle within the soul, and it is the only principle, since the soul is unitary; either it is perverted, or it is not. It cannot be in full or partial control of some other "irrational" element within the soul.

The issue, then, would seem to turn on how one views the structure of the soul. The Stoic position derives with rigid logic, as did all their positions, even the most paradoxical, from their basic premises, in this case the unitary nature of the soul. The Platonists recognized this in theory, as we see Antiochus doing here, but the traditions of ancient polemic, even in the philosophical schools, were such that in practice the Peripateticisers among them are frequently to be found attacking the Stoic position without any apparent regard for its theoretical underpinnings—simply appealing to the "facts" of human nature. Here is a passage from Plutarch's *Consolation to Apollonius* (102CD)—admittedly a rhetorical rather than a strictly philosophical work—which serves to state the Peripatetic polemical position well enough:

> The pain and pang felt at the death of a son has in itself good cause to awaken grief, which is only natural, and over which we have no control. For I, for my part, cannot concur with those who extol that harsh and callous indifference (*apatheia*), which is both impossible and unprofitable. For this will rob us of the kindly feeling which comes from mutual affection and which above all else we must conserve. But to be carried beyond all bounds and to help in exaggerating our griefs I say is contrary to nature and results from a perverted opinion (*phaulē doxa*) within us. Therefore this also must be dismissed as injurious and depraved and most unbecoming to rightminded men, but a moderate experiencing (*metriopatheia*) of grief is not to be disapproved.[8]

Plutarch here provides us with a useful contrast between *apatheia* and *metriopatheia*, borrowing the Stoic doctrine of passion as a perverted opinion to characterize *excess* in passion, rather than passion as a whole, and concentrating on the one passion, grief, of which the Stoics admitted no rational equivalent. The important question of the structure of the soul, however, is something that he does not touch upon.

Perhaps the most important surviving document in this controversy, on the other hand, is another work of Plutarch's, this time a philosophical treatise, his essay *On Moral Virtue*. This constitutes the best defense of the Platonist-Peripatetic position against Chrysippus that has come down to us, and I propose to concentrate on it in my examination of the nature of the controversy.

Plutarch begins by defining the subject matter of moral virtue (*ēthikē aretē*) as having as its 'matter' (*hylē*), the passions, and as its form (*eidos*) the reason (*logos*), thus presenting to us forcibly the image of form being imposed on a matter external to it, and even antithetical to it. He recognises as a possible question whether the passionate part itself has a *logos* (440D), but he takes as a basic premise that there can be no talk of *ēthikē*, as opposed to *theorētikē, aretē* without the postulation of some such passionate part of the soul distinct from the rational part. He thus rejects at the outset the premises on which the Stoics base their doctrine.

In his doxography of previous opinions, however, he does state clearly the Stoic position (441C):

> Yet all these men agree in supposing virtue to be a certain disposition of the governing portion (*hēgemonikon*) of the soul and a faculty engendered by reason, or rather to be itself reason which is in accord with virtue and is firm and unshaken. They also think that the passionate and irrational part of the soul is not distinguished from the rational by any difference or by its nature, but is the same part, which, indeed, they term intelligence and the governing part; it is, they say, wholly transformed and changes both during its emotional states and in the alterations brought about in accordance with an acquired disposition or condition (*hexis* or *diathesis*) and thus becomes both vice and virtue; it contains nothing irrational within itself, but is called irrational whenever, by the over-mastering power of our impulses, which have become strong and prevail, it is hurried on to something outrageous which contravenes the convictions of reason. Passion, in fact, according to them, is a vicious and intemperate reason, formed from an evil and perverse judgment which has acquired additional violence and strength.

This position seems to Plutarch repugnant to common sense. Is not one of the basic facts of our psychic life the struggle between what one should do and what one would? His most effective argument invokes the difference between moderation and continence (445B ff.), which, he claims, could not be made unless there were in fact two opposed elements within our souls, which are now overcome the one by the other, now locked in combat. The whole essence of *enkrateia* and *akrasia* is surely the imperfect domination of one of these elements by the other. Chrysippus is in fact involved in maintaining very much the position of Socrates before him and is open to the same kind of criticisms.

Plutarch here appeals to the fact of human existence. How is Chrysippus to answer him? His position must be, surely, that no action, in the sense of conscious or purposive action, could take place without a decision to act, and the only element in us that can make a decision is the "ruling part," the *hēgemonikon*. The *hēgemonikon* may act as a result of extensive, rational deliberation, or in accordance with an impulse of some sort or other, and the impulse may well prove stronger in moving the *hēgemonikon* then the set tled attitude resulting from previous deliberations—as in the case where one decides to have another drink, though one "knows," on the basis of previous experience, that this action is dangerous or will have unpleasant consequences. To say here that desire is overcoming reason is superficially plausible, but in fact it misdescribes what takes place and merely shifts the difficulty to another quarter. In fact one makes a *decision* to have another drink, and this is essentially the same sort of mental act as would be the decision not to have another drink. The mind, or soul, directs the limbs (by activating the *pneuma*) either to reach out for a glass, or to get up, excuse oneself, and leave the room. Those who have emancipated themselves from the idea of a mind at all can rephrase this in suitably Rylean terms, but the essential similarity of the two actions is not altered.[9]

And further, Chrysippus might say, what if we do postulate this other element, warring against the reason, and all too frequently winning? How does that solve our problems? We must then explain how *it* acts, and what its relation is (abandoning Platonic imagery of spatially distinct parts of the soul as poetic fancy) to the so-called rational part of the soul.

Well, says Plutarch in reply, what then do we envisage happening in a state of *akrasia*, this being the most difficult situation to explain? Here above all we have a sensation of two warring principles. If there is after all only one principle, what is it that is warring?

> For those who assume that the *hēgemonikon* becomes now desire, and now that reason (*logismos*) which is opposed to desire, are in the same position as those who assume the hunter and the beast to be not two, but one and the same body, which, by a change, is now the beast and now becomes the hunter. (447C)

Eloquently put, Chrysippus might say, but not really compelling. In talking of the hunter and the beast, you are already assuming two antithetical elements in the soul, which is just what I am concerned to deny. Is there after all anything stranger about *akrasia* than about the purely rational process of changing one's mind on a question of science or philosophy, on a reconsideration of the evidence, or on the acquisition of new evidence?

Yes indeed, says Plutarch (447D). In the latter case, the intellectual part of the soul is not opposing itself, but on receiving new impulses, in the form of new evidence, or new views of the evidence, assents to the new impulses.

In the former case, on the other hand, the evidence remains the same, and the intellect assents to it, but yet the individual acts contrary to this assent.

> In such cases the senses make the decision, since they have contact with both (sc. reason and passion); and if, in fact, one gains the mastery, it does not destroy the other, but forces it to comply and drags it along resisting. For the lover who admonishes himself uses reason against his passion, since they both exist at the same time in his soul, as it were pressing with his hand the other member, which is inflamed, and clearly perceiving that there are two distinct forces and that they are at variance. (448B)

But this, replies Chrysippus, is surely rubbish. First of all, purely intellectual changes of mind are not as unequivocally dispassionate as all that. Life would be rather less troublesome than it is if that were so. In fact, one often clings tenaciously to settled convictions long after the evidence has made them rationally untenable. Secondly you are disregarding the fact that even the lover, in throwing prudence to the winds and climbing up the drainpipe, is making a *decision*, and a decision is a rational activity. The senses do not make decisions; the senses only *sense*. What is this other decision-making entity? No, there is only one mind. Sometimes, through bad conditioning, it assents to impressions that it should not assent to, and this is what we have to try to prevent by philosophical argument and training. It is not a question of taming a beast; it is a question of preventing the dislocation (*diastrophē*) of the mind as a whole.

The fact is that Plutarch, despite the lucidity and eloquence of his presentation, does not really come to grips with this problem. He cannot seem to take the notion of a unitary soul seriously. When he turns to discuss the doctrine of *eupatheiai* (449A ff.), he can only view this as a piece of Stoic casuistry, inventing high-sounding terms to disguise the fact that they recognize the passions after all. At 450C, he triumphantly quotes Chrysippus against himself:

> In his work *Peri Anomologias*, Chrysippus has said: "Anger is a blind thing: often it prevents our seeing obvious matters, and often it obscures matters which are already apprehended (*katalambanomena*)"; and, a little further on, he says, "For the passions, when once raised, drive out the processes of reasoning and all things that appear otherwise than they would have them be, and push forward with violence to actions contrary to reason. . . ."
>
> And again, Chrysippus proceeds to say that every rational creature is so disposed by nature as to use reason in all things and to be governed by it; yet often reason is rejected when we are under the influence of some other more violent force. Thus in this passage he plainly acknowledges what conclusion is to be drawn from the difference which exists between passion and reason. (450CD)

We are glad to have these extracts from Chrysippus' work, but beg leave to dispute that they prove what Plutarch wants them to prove. Of course Chrysippus recognizes the existence of what are commonly known as passions, and that all too frequently what is commonly known as passion overcomes reason. Plutarch is surely missing the point. All Chrysippus wishes to maintain is that whatever impulse is dominant, it is the *hēgemonikon* that must assent if an action is to result. This is precisely why the passions are so dangerous. They cannot be confined in a dungeon below stairs, and chastised repeatedly to keep them moderate. If they are around in the soul at all, they are necessarily right in the center of things, twisting the ruling element in their direction. Nor does Chrysippus wish to deny that even the wise man will be affected. Some sense-perceptions, and the assents to them, are inseparable from such affections (*propatheiai*), and there is nothing wrong with that, so long as the reason is in command of them. Plutarch reports Stoic doctrine as follows (449B): "*Eupatheia* arises when reason does not destroy the emotion, but composes and sets it in order in the souls of temperate persons." He states it, however, in such a tendentious way as to suggest that the Stoics in fact recognize a passionate element in the soul. What he might more properly have said was, e.g., "*Eupatheia* arises (in the soul of the wise man) when reason deliberates about some thing which has value relative to us" (cf. *SVF* III 118–21).

What we find, then, in Plutarch (and in other Platonists of the period, such as Taurus, Albinus, and Apuleius, and in such a Platonist-influenced thinker as Philo of Alexandria) is a remarkable unwillingness or inability to comprehend what the Stoic position was. Only so can Plutarch alternately represent Chrysippus as advocating total insensibility, *and* think that he is convicting him out of his own mouth when he catches him talking of anger overcoming reason. Only so can Taurus (*ap.* Gellius *NA* I 26) contrast Stoic "insensibility" (*analgēsia*) with Platonic-Peripatetic "moderation" in the matter of the control of anger. Only so can Philo comfortably make a distinction between *metriopatheia* as being proper to the man of median virtue, who is still improving (the *prokoptōn*, symbolized by Aaron), and *apatheia,* which is proper to the achieved sage (symbolized by Moses, *Leg. All.* III 129–32), as if the two concepts could be accommodated on a sliding scale. Plainly Philo is here taking *apatheia* as being a truly yogic ideal and is quite missing the significance of the great debate.[10]

To return to our starting point, then: the controversy about *metriopatheia* and *apatheia,* which generated such heat in later Greek philosophy, is properly one between the concept of a bipartite or tripartite soul, in which the lower part of parts can never be eradicated—at least while the soul is in the body—but must constantly be chastised, and that of a unitary one. Of course, a Stoic *eupatheia* comes out in practice as being very similar to a properly moderated Platonic-Aristotelian pathos, but that, as we have seen, is irrelevant to the main point.

The incomprehension on the part of Platonists as to what the argument was really about is remarkably analogous to a similar incomprehension in ancient sources, drawn attention to not long ago in an excellent article by Michael Frede,[11] about the true difference between Stoic and Aristotelian logic. Platonists such as Albinus, Apuleius, or Galen[12] are quite prepared to use both side by side, entering into discussion as to which was the more basic, but not seeming to be much concerned about the difference between a logic of propositions and a logic of terms. In each case, one is tempted to wonder if something was obvious to them that we are missing, but on the face of it one can only wonder at these blind spots.

NOTES

[1] Plotinus draws attention to this apparent tension in Plato's thought in a somewhat different context, at *Enn.* IV 8, 2.

[2] For good discussions of the Stoic doctrine of the passions and, of *eupatheiai*, see J. M. Rist, *Stoic Philosophy* (Cambridge, 1969), ch. 2, pp. 25–36, A. A. Long, *Hellenistic Philosophy* (New York, 1974), pp. 175–78, and F. H. Sandbach, *The Stoics* (New York, 1975), pp. 59–68.

[3] There is another thing that the wise man may experience, with which we are not now concerned but which should be noted. That is what were later, at least, termed *propatheiai*. These are the instinctive feelings, preliminary to a passion proper, which result automatically from certain *phantasiai*. Seneca, *De Ira* II 1–4 has a good discussion of these, which he terms *nec adfectus, sed principia proludentia affectibus* (II 2). Cf. also Aulus Gellius *NA* XIX 1, 14 ff., where the doctrine is traced back to Chrysippus from Epictetus. This, however, does not seem to be what Zeno is talking of here, but rather of something "remaining."

[4] I quote Sandbach, *The Stoics*, p. 63: "The distinction (sc. between *apatheia* and *metriopatheia*), although justified, can be exaggerated. The Stoic passion is an excessive uncontrolled drive, due to an overestimation of indifferent things, but there is also a correct drive towards these same things. The moderate passion of the Peripatetic is a correct feeling and so could perhaps not be regarded by a Stoic as a passion at all."

[5] On Antiochus, see further J. M. Dillon, *The Middle Platonists* (Ithaca, N.Y., 1977), ch. 2.

[6] E.g., Cicero *De Finibus* IV, 20 ff.

[7] Cf. I. G. Kidd, "Posidonius on Emotions," in *Problems in Stoicism*, ed. A. A. Long (London, 1971), pp. 200–15.

[8] The translations of Plutarch here are borrowed from the Loeb translators, Babbitt (for *Cons. ad Apoll.*) and Helmbold (for *Virt. Mor.*), though with modifications where they do not attain the required degree of accuracy.

[9] Cf. J. M. Rist, *Stoic Philosophy*, ch. 14: "The Unity of the Person"—a most useful discussion.

[10] Elsewhere, we may note, Philo is prepared to commend *metriopatheia* as opposed to *apatheia* as an ideal even for the sage. At *Abr*. 256–57, for example, he praises Abraham, on the loss of his wife Sarah, for "neither fretting beyond measure, nor showing a complete lack of emotion (*apatheia*), but choosing the mean rather than the extremes, and trying to moderate his passions (*metriopathein*)," a position concordant with that of Plutarch.

[11] "Stoic vs. Aristotelian Syllogistic," *Archiv f. Gesch. d. Philos.* 56 (1974): 1–32.

[12] E.g., Galen, *Inst. Log.* p. 17, 13 f. Kalbfleisch; Apuleius, *Peri Herm.* cf. 13. (I accept this work as genuine, regarding the arguments against this as less than cogent, but its authenticity does not greatly affect the point I am making.)

IX

THE TRANSCENDENCE OF GOD IN PHILO: SOME POSSIBLE SOURCES

I wish in this paper to trace the history of a certain conception of
God, or the supreme principle, that is, its absolute transcendence and superiority to all qualification, which has a distinct influence on Philo's theology.
I will confine myself to what seem to me to be two main stages of its development, first in Speusippus, the successor of Plato as head of the Old Academy,
and then as one strand of the Neopythagorean tradition, which I believe to owe
its inspiration to Speusippus. Finally, I will review the relevant passages of
Philo. None of this is very new, perhaps, but the conjunction seems worth
making, for purposes of debate.

I

Speusippus accepted from Plato the doctrine of two opposite principles,
the Monad and the Indefinite Dyad, but he altered it in an interesting direction,
by laying particular emphasis on their status as "seeds" or "potencies" of all
things. He argued that what is itself the cause of some quality in other things
cannot have that quality itself in the same way, so that if the One is the cause
of goodness and being for all other things, then it cannot itself properly be
termed good or even existent (Fr. 34 Lang), any more than an acorn is itself an
oak tree. This led him to an interpretation of Plato's One which placed it at an
extreme of transcendence. In an important passage preserved in Proclus' *Commentary on the Parmenides*, only recently brought to light by Raymond Klibansky,[1]
Speusippus makes his position clear (although he affects to attribute it to
certain "ancients," presumably Pythagoreans, of whom he was an even greater par-
tisan than Plato):

> "Holding the One to be superior to Being, and the source from which
> Being springs, they freed it even from the status of a principle. And
> so, considering that if one took the One in itself, thought of as
> separate and alone, adding no other element to it, nothing else at all
> would come into being, they introduced the Indefinite Dyad as first
> principle of Beings."

The Indefinite Dyad is thus brought in as the cause of all differentiation and
individuation, which is what is involved in being the cause of the existence of
things. But the Dyad is not an evil principle, any more than the One is a good
one (Fr. 35 Lang). Speusippus, reasonably, denied that "good" or "evil" in an
ethical sense could have any meaning at this level. Good and evil only arise
at the level of actualised Being, perhaps only at the level of Soul. In a way
this is a question of semantics. Plato only termed his supreme principle The

---

[1]*Procli Commentarius in Parmenidem*, ed. Klibansky, Labowsky, Anscombe
(London 1953) pp. 38, 31ff.

2

Good as being (a) the object of all striving, and (b) the source of goodness
and existence to all things, but Speusippus is plainly trying to remove the
notion of the One (and simultaneously from that of the Dyad) any ethical colour-
ing at all.

Aristotle denounced this thesis of Speusippus' at *Met.* XII 7 (1072b30
ff.):

> "Those then have a wrong opinion who suppose, as do the Pythagoreans
> and Speusippus, that supreme beauty and goodness are not at the
> beginning, because the beginnings of both plants and animals are
> causes, whereas beauty and completeness are in what proceeds from
> those beginnings. For the seed comes from other individuals which are
> prior and complete, and the first is not a seed but a complete being;
> for example, we must admit that a man is prior to his seed, not the
> man generated from the seed, but he by whom the seed was generated."

Aristotle thus puts the chicken before the egg, and his objection to Speusippus'
position seems to have prevailed in the Academy, beginning with Speusippus'
successor Xenocrates. Aristotle's Prime Mover, an actualisation rather than a
potentiality, a mind thinking itself, became the concept of God dominant in
orthodox Platonism up to Plotinus. What I wish to consider here, however, is
whether Speusippus' conception of the Supreme Principle may not have had some
influence in less orthodox circles, specifically in certain strands of Neopythagoreanism.

II

The dating of the various Pseudo-Pythagorean documents is a well-nigh
hopeless activity. Two eminent authorities in recent years, Holger Thesleff
and Walter Burkert, have given much attention to this question,[2] but without
arriving at any very satisfactory results. In the case of such documents as
"Archytas," *On the Categories* and "Timaeus Locrus," *On Nature and the World,*
two young scholars editing these texts in recent years[3] have made good cases
for dating them after the first generation or so of Aristotelian and Platonist
scholarship in Alexandria in the first century B.C., but the great majority of
the texts resist even such loose dating as this.

One of these texts is a short passage of "Archytas," *On First
Principles,* preserved by Stobaeus (*Anth.* I 278-9 Wachs. = p. 19 *Pyth. Texts*).
"Archytas" produces a metaphysical scheme which postulates, above the two

---

[2]Thesleff, *An Introduction to the Pythagorean Writings of the Hellenistic Period,* 1961; *The Pythagorean Texts of the Hellenistic Period,* 1965;
Burkert, "Hellenistische Pseudopythagorica," *Philologus* 105 (1961); *Weisheit
und Wissenschaft* (1962; Eng. trans. 1972). Both Thesleff and Burkert made useful contributions to the 1972 Entretiens of the Fondation Hardt, *Pseudopythagorica* I, modifying their previous views, but still finding no firm solutions.

[3]T.A. Szlezak, *Pseudo-Archytas über die Kategorien* (Berlin 1972); M.
Baltes, *Timaios Lokros: über die Natur des Kosmos und der Seele* (Leiden 1972).

principles of Form (μορφώ) and Matter (ὡσία), corresponding to the traditional Pythagorean Monad and Dyad, a third principle superior to both, which brings them together:

> "It is not·possible for Matter to partake of Form of its own volition, nor for Form to come together with Matter, but it is necessary for there to be some other cause which will move the substance of things (ἁ ἐστὼ τῶν πραγμάτων) towards Form; and this must be primal in power and the supreme principle of all. This it is proper to call God. So there are now three principles, God and the substance of things and Form. And God is the craftsman (τεχνίτας) and the mover, Substance is the matter and the thing moved, and Form is the art (τέχνα) and that towards which substance is moved by the Mover."

So far we have nothing very remarkable--just the three principles of Middle Platonic metaphysics, God, Matter and Idea. But a little further on the supreme, self-moving principle is characterised as follows: "Such an entity should not be simply Intellect, but something superior to Intellect; and it is clear that what is superior to Intellect is what we call God (τὸ δὲ τοιοῦτον οὐ νόον μόνον εἶμεν δεῖ, ἀλλὰ καὶ νόω τι κρέσσον· νόω δὲ κρέσσον ἐστὶν ὅπερ ὀνομάζομεν θεόν, φανερόν)."

Here we have a suggestion, at least, of a supranoetic First Principle above a pair of causes, corresponding to the Monad and the Dyad. Such a doctrine is also found in a report by the Neoplatonist Syrianus, in his *Commentary on the Metaphysics* (P. 165, 33ff. Kroll), of the views of Philolaus, Archaenetus (perhaps an error for Archytas), Brotinus, and finally Plato:

> "And in general these men (sc. the Pythagoreans) did not trace the beginning of things from any pair of opposites, but knew also of something above and beyond the two columns of co-ordinates (συστοιχίαι), as witness Philolaus declaring that God brings into being Limit and Unlimitedness, by the term 'Limit' denoting the whole συστοιχία more akin to the One, by 'Unlimitedness' the one inferior to this; and further they postulated the unitary causal principle (ἡ ἑνιαία αἰτία) above these two causes and transcending everything (ἐξῃρημένη πάντων), which Archaenetus calls 'the cause above cause,' where Philolaus asserts that it is the first principle of all things, and Brotinus says that it surpasses all Intellect and Substance in power and dignity (δυνάμει καὶ πρεσβείᾳ); and taking his start from these authorities the divine Plato also utters the same sentiments about these same entities in the *Letters* and the *Republic* and the *Philebus* and the *Parmenides*."

Syrianus, of course, accepted these *Pseudopythagorica* as genuine, and so got his lines of derivation exactly backwards. But he has put his finger on certain important passages, to wit, *Ep.* II 312E, *Rep.* VI 508Bff., *Phil.* 26Eff., and *Parm.* 137Cff. and 141E. From these passages a doctrine of a first principle which transcends all qualities whatever can indeed be derived, and was, it seems, derived by certain Neopythagoreans, probably through the intermediacy of Speusippus.

4

III

But it was not only in the underworld of the *Pseudopythagorica* that such a doctrine was propounded. There is one figure rather nearer the region of Platonic orthodoxy (though with pronounced Pythagorean sympathies) who adopts the theory of a supreme principle above a pair of opposites. This is the philosopher Eudorus, who flourished in Alexandria about 25 B.C., just a generation or so before Philo was active.

The Neoplatonist commentator Simplicius (*In Phys.* p. 181, 10ff. Diels) gives us an account by Eudorus of the "pythagorean" doctrine of first principles. The Pythagoreans, says Eudorus, postulated first a supreme principle which they called The One, and below that a pair of opposites, a Monad and a Dyad, the Monad representing Form, the Dyad Matter:

> "It must be said that the Pythagoreans postulated on the highest level the One as a First Principle, and then on a secondary level two principles of existent things, the One and the nature opposed to this. And there are ranked below these all those things that are thought of as opposites, the good under the One, the bad under the nature opposed to it. For this reason these two are not regarded as absolute first principles by this school; for if the one is the first principle of one set of opposites and the other of the other, then they cannot be common principles of both, as is the (supreme) One."

Eudorus reports this doctrine as Pythagorean. This does not mean that he does not accept it himself—quite the contrary—but it does seem to indicate that he had access to *Pseudopythagorica* such as that of Archytas or Philolaus on which to draw, since normal Pythagoreanism, as I have said, gives no indication of a One above a pair of opposites.

He goes on here to make this supreme One the causal principle of Matter as well as of all created things, and to call it the Supreme God (ὁ ὑπεράνω θεός). Further on again, he gives the title of "Unlimited Dyad" to the principle opposed to the second One, and finally calls the second One the Monad.

Now Eudorus here may merely be combining elements which were readily available to him from Plato. From the *Philebus* (26E - 30E) he could have gleaned the elements of this theory, since the Monad and the Dyad there are inevitably also Limit and Unlimitedness, and the Cause above them, though not called the One, has a unifying purpose, and is identified with Mind or God (or at least with Zeus). It is possible also that he was influenced by the language of the first hypothesis of the *Parmenides*.[4] At any rate, this theory of a supreme First Principle seems to be derived rather from a certain interpretation of Plato than directly from Old Pythagoreanism. The conviction that Plato himself was a follower of Pythagoras (a view shared by Philo) facilitated such a development.

---

[4]See on this the important article of E.R. Dodds, "The *Parmenides* of Plato and the Origin of the Neoplatonic One," *CQ* 22 (1928).

IV

After these preliminaries, let us turn to an examination of Philo's
views on God. To anticipate at least one line of criticism, I must make it
clear that I am not trying to give a complete explanation of Philo's theology.
I merely want to draw attention to a doctrine of God's absolute transcendence
within the Hellenic tradition to which he almost certainly had access (he
certainly knew some *Pseudopythagorica*, such as Ocellus Lucanus, and a work of
Philolaus on Numbers), and on which he could well have drawn.

Philo follows a system in which the Supreme Principle is the One,
though for him it is also, of course, the personal God of Judaism. He calls
it frequently the One, the Monad, or "the really existent" (τὸ ὄντως ὄν), for
example at *Deus* 11 and *Heres* 187. At *Spec.* II 176 the Monad is said to be
"the incorporeal image of God," whom it resembles because it also stands
alone.[5] Among other normal epithets of God, such as "eternal," "unchanging,"
and "imperishable," Philo produces others for which he is our earliest
authority. At *Somn.* I 67, for example, God is described as "unnameable"
(ἀκατονόμαστος) and "unutterable" (ἄρρητος) and incomprehensible under any
form (κατὰ πάσας ἰδέας·ἀκατάληπτος), none of which terms are applied to God
before his time in any surviving source. The question thus arises as to
whether Philo is responsible for introducing the notion of an "unknowable" God
into Greek thought. I find it difficult to credit, however, that a man like
Albinus (in ch. 10 of his *Didaskalikos*) is influenced in his terminology by
Philo. There is no indication that any of the school Platonists ever read
Philo. The alternative is that the influence of the first hypothesis of the
Parmenides, which is behind Albinus' negative theology, was already at work in
Alexandrian Platonism in Philo's time. I have suggested above that Eudorus'
Supreme God is a suitable recipient for such epithets as these, being as he is
above Limit and Limitlessness, but the nature of the evidence does not admit of
certainty.

Philo is not always content, however, to refer to God even as a One or
a Monad. On occasion he goes further, indulging in flights of negative theology. In the essay *On the Contemplative Life* (*Cont.* 2), he speaks of the
Therapeutae as worshipping "the Existent, which is better than the Good, purer
than the One, and more primordial than the Monad (τὸ ὄν, δ καὶ ἀγαθοῦ κρεῖττόν
ἐστι καὶ ἑνὸς εἰλικρινέστερον καὶ μονάδος ἀρχεγονώτερον). At *Praem.* 39-40, we
find the following:

"The Father and Saviour, perceiving the sincerity of his yearning, in
pity gave power to the penetration of his eyesight and did not grudge
to grant him the vision of Himself in so far as it was possible for
mortal and created nature to contain it. Yet the vision only showed
that He is, not *what* He is. For this which is better than the Good,
more venerable than the Monad, purer than the One, cannot be discerned
by anyone else; to God alone it is permitted to apprehend God."

[5]Philo in fact often varies the Platonic title τὸ ὄν with a more personal form derived from the LXX, ὁ ὤν (He Who Is). This may be accepted as an
influence from Judaism, and so is of no concern to us at present.

6

All this goes even further than Eudorus, for whom the Good and the One are epithets of the Supreme Principle, though both are more primordial than the Monad. But then one must not treat what is perhaps an essentially rhetorical flourish as if it were a strictly philosophical statement. Philo is quite content on other occasions to use any of these terms to designate God. Nevertheless, he is undeniably acquainted with the formulae of negative theology. His conclusion is that a kind of mystical vision is the only faculty that will connect us with God, since reason is inadequate. This is made clear in a passage at the beginning of *The Embassy to Gaius* (*Leg.* 6):

> "For reason (λόγος) cannot ascend to God, who is totally untouchable and unattainable, but it subsides and ebbs away, unable to find the proper words to use as a basis to reveal, I do not say Him Who Is (ὁ ὤν), for even if the whole heaven should become an articulate voice, it would lack the apt and appropriate terms needed for this, but even God's attendant Powers."

Only the kind of "seeing" (ὅρασις) that is proper to the visionary Israel-soul can attain to a comprehension of Him (*ibid.* 4-5).

V

We have, then, in Philo statements about the ineffability of God which go beyond anything which we can produce from the surviving remains of Speusippus or of the Neopythagoreans. And yet the conditions for such a theology are certainly there. Perhaps we need after all look no further as a basic inspiration for all this talk to the famous passage of *Republic* VI (508Eff.) which certainly formed the basis for such God-talk in later Platonism, bearing in mind that it comes to Philo having already been interpreted both by Speusippus and by the Neopythagoreans:

> τοῦτο τοίνυν τὸ τὴν ἀλήθειαν παρέχον τοῖς γιγνωσκομένοις καὶ τῷ γιγνώσκοντι τὴν δύναμιν ἀποδιδόν τὴν τοῦ ἀγαθοῦ ἰδέαν φάθι εἶναι· αἰτίαν δ' ἐπιστήμης οὖσαν καὶ ἀληθείας, ὡς γιγνωσκομένης μὲν διανοοῦ, οὕτω δὲ καλῶν ἀμφοτέρων ὄντων, γνώσεώς τε καὶ ἀληθείας, ἄλλο καὶ κάλλιον ἔτι τούτων ἡγούμενος αὐτὸ ὀρθῶς ἡγήσῃ ... καὶ τοῖς γιγνωσκο- μένοις τοίνυν μὴ μόνον τὸ γιγνώσκεσθαι φάναι ὑπὸ τοῦ ἀγαθοῦ παρεῖναι, ἀλλὰ καὶ τὸ εἶναί τε καὶ τὴν οὐσίαν ὑπ' ἐκείνου αὐτοῖς προσεῖναι, οὐκ οὐσίας ὄντος τοῦ ἀγαθοῦ, ἀλλ' ἔτι ἐπέκεινα τῆς οὐσίας πρεσβείᾳ καὶ δυνάμει ὑπερέχοντος.

Here the Supreme Principle is still The Good, but Speusippus had deprived it of that title also by using the same argument that here places it above Being, that the source cannot itself be given the characteristic that it is bestowing upon others. We are left then with a principle superior to all qualification whatsoever, and superior also to all (rational) knowledge. It is such a principle that is picked up by Speusippus, by certain Pythagoreans, and, I think, by Philo, but not by orthodox Platonism before Plotinus.

7

APPENDIX

It is, no doubt, somewhat irregular to contribute comments on one's own paper, but I am in the position of having received from Professor Michael Frede a number of most acute criticisms, which he has no time to put into writing. I felt therefore that rather than lose the benefit of them, I should record them myself, together with such reply as I can make to them. In the process of replying, I shall adduce further texts which may be of interest.

(1) *Speusippus is surely not claiming, nor is he accused by Aristotle of claiming, the proposition "that what is itself the cause of some quality in other things cannot have that quality in the same way."*

At Fr. 34 Lang (*Met.* XII 7, 1072b30ff.), Aristotle simply says that the Pythagoreans and Speusippus postulate that what is most beautiful and best does not reside in the first principle, on the analogy of plants and animals, where the most beautiful and perfect form appears not in the seeds but in the complete forms. The first principle, or One, is analogous to a seed, having no beauty or perfection in itself, but being the "cause" of it in its products.

I must admit that there is stated here no such formal principle as I have enunciated. .That was simply my interpretation of what, it seemed to me, Speusippus must have been arguing. However, my interpretation is not based on Aristotle alone, whose accounts of Old Academic doctrines are, as is generally agreed, partial and tendentious, but upon a certain chapter of Iamblichus' *De Communi Mathematica Scientia* (ch. 4), which has been shown (in my view) by Philip Merlan[6] to be either a verbatim extract or a verbally accurate summary of part of a work by Speusippus. To appreciate the likelihood of this apparently bizarre suggestion one must be acquainted with the method of work of Iamblichus in this treatise and others of the same sort. He is essentially stringing together a cento of previous authorities, Plato, Aristotle, Pythagoreans, and some unidentified authors, to make an anthology of views on the subject under discussion. He elsewhere (in the *Theol. Arithm.*) uses a work of Speusippus on the Decad, so that at least one work of Speusippus was available to him.

Chiefly, however, it is the doctrine that marks this passage as Speusippean. It is in accord with what we know of his doctrine, and with that of no one else in the history of Platonism. I wished to spare the colloquium this long story, but I see now that it is not possible to do so. I will quote certain relevant passages, in my translation:

"Of mathematical numbers one must postulate two primary and highest principles, the One (which one should not even call Being [ὄν], by reason of its simplicity and its position as principle [ἀρχή] of everything else, *a principle being properly not yet that which those are of which it is the principle* [τὴν δ' ἀρχὴν μηδέπω εἶναι τοιαύτην οἷα ἐκεῖνα ὧν ἐστιν ἀρχή]); and another principle, that of Multiplicity (πλῆθος),..." (p. 15, 6-11 Festa)

It is not suitable, he goes on to say (11.23ff.), to attribute evil or ugliness to this second principle simply because it causes multiplicity. Similarly, the One is not to be termed either beautiful or good, since it is

---

[6]Philip Merlan, *From Platonism to Neoplatonism* (The Hague, 1960) chapter 5.

8

superior to both these attributes (τὸ δὲ ἓν οὔτε καλὸν οὔτε ἀγαθὸν ἄξιον
καλεῖν, διὰ τὸ καὶ τοῦ καλοῦ καὶ τοῦ ἀγαθοῦ ὑπεράνω εἶναι). One might,
however, describe it as the cause of certain beauties in numbers (καλῶν
τινων ἐν τοῖς ἀριθμοῖς αἴτιον εἶναι).

All this falls short of a formal enunciation of this principle, I
must admit, but it seems to me inevitable that this was Speusippus' point.
If something is the cause of beauty or goodness in other things, it seemed
to him to introduce confusion into language to grant those same attributes
to the causative principle. Admittedly, fire introduces heat to other
things, and we would describe it as itself hot. I do not know what
Speusippus would say to that, but he might, if he had command of modern
terminology, have suggested a distinction between, say, hot$_1$ and hot$_2$, or
good$_1$ and good$_2$, the former term in each case denoting "cause of..."
However, he did not have such terminology, and it seemed to him less evocative of confusion simply to deny the epithets "beautiful" and "good" to the
supreme principle. In doing that, it seems to me that he provided a stimulus to later negative theology.

This brings us to Professor Frede's second point.

(2) *Speusippus is surely concerned, not with the via negativa, as followed
by later theologians, but rather with a logical question, as to what is
properly predicable of the supreme principle.*

I quite agree. It was clear in my mind, though it may not have
emerged clearly in the paper, that Speusippus is not concerned with hymning
the excellences of the One, but rather with working out what can properly
be predicated of it. This he finds to be strictly speaking nothing, except
possibly Unity. However, it seems to me possible--and that is my thesis in
the paper--that Speusippus' doctrine provoked certain Neo-pythagorean writers,
who were in a much more pious frame of mind, to the postulation of a
supreme principle above all attributes such as Intellect, Goodness or
Beauty. Of course they could also derive inspiration from certain passages
of Plato such as *Rep.* VI 508Eff. and the First Hypothesis of the *Parmenides*
(137Cff.), but they needed, it seems to me, to be stimulated to this
interpretation of those passages of Plato by some tendency in the Old
Academy. We, after all, are not at all sure that we see this sort of significance in these passages.

(3) *From the passages of Philo that I quote (Praem. 39-40; Leg. 6), it is
not clear whether Philo believes that God is superior to all attributes, or
simply that his attributes, whatever they may be, are not such that our
human intellect can comprehend, or speech utter, them.*

This latter position would, as Professor Frede reminds me, be
true of such later writers as Dionysius the Areopagite. Philo is somewhat
ambiguous in its utterances, I admit, but I do not think that this complication had occurred to him. I think that he simply means God to be above all
attributes whatever. A further good passage, which I commend to all
interested hermeneuts, is *Mut.* 7-8, where the ambiguity is also present.
I give the following reference to what sounds like a useful article, to
which I do not have access: Didier Baer, "Incompréhensibilité de Dieu et
théologie négative chez Philon d'Alexandrie," *Présence Orthodoxe* 8 (1969),
pp. 38-46. I would be grateful if someone could produce it.

X

PHILO AND THE STOIC DOCTRINE OF ΕΥΠΑΘΕΙΑΙ

A Note on Quaes Gen 2.57

That Philo of Alexandria both knew and made use of
the Stoic contrast between the passions (πάθη) and the so-
called "proper emotions" (εὐπάθειαι, the "rational" equivalents of the passions in the psyche of the Stoic sage),
is not disputed.[1] Philo's fullest account of the εὐπάθειαι, however, at Quaes Gen 2.57, which should be of considerable doxographical interest, has come down to us in
such a state that it is virtually incomprehensible as it
stands. It is the concern of this note to straighten it
out for the record.

In the case of the *Quaestiones in Genesin*, as with a
number of other works of Philo, we are in a less than
satisfactory position of having only a medieval (late 6th
century C.E.) Armenian translation. The Latin translation
of Aucher and the English translation of Marcus[2] are often
inadequate for making detailed judgements, and in this
case they both fail us when faced with the technical Stoic
distinction between πάθη and εὐπάθειαι.[3] At various
points in his notes Marcus confesses his uncertainty as to
the true meaning, but at no stage does his translation of
the passage in question give any indication that he understood the underlying philosophy.

Émile Bréhier[4] was the first to draw attention to the
passage and to discern its correct form, but he did not
pause long enough over it to present a fully corrected
version with further comments. It seems worth doing this
since the passage, properly rendered and rightly

X

18

understood, not only merits inclusion in *SVF* (between
3.432 and 433), but also reveals a significant modification in basic Stoic doctrine.

The crucial part of the Armenian text reads as
follows:

> . . . *իսկ ի միտս, սողնոց նմանեալ լինին պղծոցն
> ափտր. իսկ մարբրոգն՝* բերկրութիւն. *բանգի առ Ճեշտ գան-
> կութեան աիտ՝ լինի* բերկրութիւն, ՝ընդութիւն. *իսկ առ
> ցանկութեանն՝ կամբ, խորՃուրդ. իսկ առ տրտմութեան՝* խայ-
> թումն ՝եւ գկձումն. *իսկ առ* փափարման՝ *երկեղաձնութիւն:*

To retranslate this passage into Greek, we need to
give special consideration to the underlined words.[5]

բերկրութիւն, which occurs twice here and again, in
plural form, in the last part of the passage (here omitted),
occurs nowhere else in the Armenian version of Philo. That
this word is a rendition of both εὐπάθεια and χαρά may be
shown from the following examples: εὐπάθεια καὶ χαρά in
Abr 201 and Leg All 1.45 is rendered as *խրախութիւնն եւ
՝ընդութիւնն* and *փափկութիւն եւ խրախութիւն* respectively. It
is noteworthy that *խրախութիւն,* which is a synonym of
բերկրութիւն, is the equivalent of εὐπάθεια in the first
instance and of χαρά in the second. It would also appear
that *բերկրութիւն, ՝ընդութիւն* is a rendition of one word,
namely, χαρά. Very often, the Armenian translator of
Philo rendered a Greek word with two or more words.[6]

կամբ, խորՃուրդ also appears to be a rendition of one
word, namely, βούλημα or βούλησις; e.g., τὰ βουλήματα in
Provid 2.29 is rendered as *գխորՃուրդս կամացն,* and τῶν
βουλημάτων in Spec Leg 1.333, *խորՃրդոյ կամաց.*

խայթումն եւ գկձումն also appears to be a rendition of
one word. δηγμός in Leg All 2.84 is rendered as *խածումն,*
which is a compound of parts of the two words.

The Greek equivalent of the last underlined word,
փափարման, is πόθον, as in Vita Cont 35, 48, 68, etc. A
corruption of the word φόβον may be suspected in the Greek
exemplar. It may also be possible that the Armenian translator deliberately departed from the text to avoid doubling,

since the Armenian equivalents of φόβος and εὐλάβεια have
the same root and are sometimes interchangeably used (cf.
Abr 14; Spec Leg 1.330; Provid 2.26; etc.).

All the other words have one-to-one equivalents in
Philonic works extant in both languages and need no special consideration.

In the light of the preceding observations, a rough
version of the original Greek of this passage would be:

> ...τὸ δὲ πρὸς διάνοιαν οὕτως· τὰ πάθη ἔοικεν τοῖς
> ἀκαθάρτοις ἑρπετοῖς, τοῖς δὲ καθαροῖς ἡ εὐπάθεια·
> παρὰ γὰρ τὸ πάθος τῆς ἡδονῆς ἐστιν ἡ χαρά. παρὰ δὲ
> τὴν ἐπιθυμίαν ἡ βούλησις· παρὰ δὲ τὴν λύπην ὁ
> δηγμός· παρὰ δὲ τὸν φόβον ἡ εὐλάβεια.

The section then may be most accurately translated as
follows:

> Why does (Scripture) say, "Every reptile that
> lives shall be to you for food" (Gen 9:3)?
>
> The nature of reptiles is two-fold. One is poi-
> sonous, and the other is tame. Poisonous are
> those serpents which in place of feet use the
> belly and breast to crawl along; and tame are
> those which have legs above their feet. This
> is the literal meaning. *But as for the deeper*
> *meaning, the passions resemble unclean reptiles,*
> *while proper emotions (resemble) clean (reptiles).*
> *For alongside the passion of Pleasure there is*
> *Joy. And alongside Desire there is Will. And*
> *alongside Grief there is Compunction. And*
> *alongside Fear there is Caution.* Thus these
> passions threaten souls with death and murder,
> whereas proper emotions are truly living, as He
> Himself has shown in allegorizing, and are the
> causes of life for those who possess them.

It will be recalled that the Stoics, while rejecting
the passions root and branch, were prepared to recognize
certain "rational" equivalents of them (*SVF* 3.431). In
place of ἡδονή there was χαρά; in place of φόβος, εὐλάβεια;
in place of ἐπιθυμία, βούλησις. Only for Grief, λύπη, was
there declared to be no rational equivalent (ibid., 437).
In this passage, however, as we have seen, there is an
equivalent for λύπη, namely, δηγμός.

Although this modification is first encountered in
Philo, a passage in Plutarch, *Moralia* 449A (*SVF* 3.439),
would suggest that some such equivalent for λύπη was
floating about. In the cited passage Plutarch gives examples of the shifty euphemisms which the Stoics employ
to recognize the passions in fact, while seeking to banish
them in theory. It is best to give the passage in full:

> ...ὅταν δὲ δακρύοις ἐλεγχόμενοι καὶ τρόμοις καὶ
> χρόας μεταβολαῖς <u>ἀντὶ λύπης καὶ φόβου δηγμούς
> τινας καὶ συνθροήσεις</u> λέγωσι καὶ προθυμίας τὰς
> ἐπιθυμίας ὑποκορίζωνται, σοφιστικὰς δοκοῦσιν οὐ
> φιλοσόφους διακρούσεις καὶ ἀποδράσεις ἐκ τῶν
> πραγμάτων μηχανᾶσθαι διὰ τῶν ὀνομάτων. (Emphasis
> supplied.)[7]

Here we might seem to have, on the face of it, a term
provided by Plutarch as the εὐπάθεια corresponding to λύπη.
He throws doubt on this, however, by having συνθροήσεις
instead of εὐλάβεια in conjunction with φόβος and by following this in 449B (*SVF* 3.439) with a list of Stoic εὐπάθειαι which comprise only the usual three (χαρά, βούλησις, εὐλάβεια). It is obvious that he recognizes neither
δηγμός nor συνθρόησις as official εὐπάθειαι. The pairing
of δηγμός with λύπη, however, cannot be accidental.

The recognition of this fourth εὐπάθεια could be due
to the speculations of Stoicizing Platonists, i.e., Platonists who, while in general siding with the Stoa on
ethical questions against Aristotle, were moved, in this
case, to soften the rough, edges of the Stoic ideal by
allowing for a rational form of Grief. Since Philo reflects this position, we may reasonably place these Platonists in Alexandria in the last few decades B.C.E. It
happens that this position agrees very well with that of
Eudorus, a Platonist of Alexandria who flourished at about
this time, and of whose Pythagorean and Stoic tendencies
we know a certain amount.[8] Whether or not this modification in basic Stoic doctrine be due to Eudorus or another,
it is encountered only in Philo, and that on the basis of
a correct rendition of Quaes Gen 2.57. An echo of this
formula, carried perhaps from its developmental stage, is
found in the above quoted lines of Plutarch.

APPENDIX

Professor David Winston, of the Graduate Theological Union in Berkeley, has kindly brought to my notice a passage of Cicero (*Tusculanae Disputationes* 3.83) which I had overlooked, and which puts a new complexion on the question of the origin of δηγμός as an equivalent of some sort, on the rational level, for λύπη. Cicero, in outlining the various types of consolatory discourse put out by (Stoic) philosophers, makes the point that they all involve the purging of *Aegritudo* (λύπη) from the soul. The passage runs as follows:

> "Hoc detracto, quod totum est voluntarium, aegritudo erit sublata illa maerens, *morsus* tamen et *contractiunculae* quaedam animi relinquentur."

> "By the removal of this, which is totally a product of will, that mournful distress will be done away with; though there will be left behind a 'bite' and certain contractions of soul."

Morsus is, plainly, a translation of δηγμός, even as *contractiunculae quaedam* is a cautious rendering of συστολή (translated as *contractio*, e.g. *Tusculanae Disputationes* 1.90; 4.14). This passage indicates that Stoic philosophers known to Cicero (no doubt in the first instance Posidonius, but probably earlier ones also) were prepared to speak of δηγμός, not as an official rational equivalent to λύπη, but rather as a term for the insignificant physical symptoms that even a fully operative Stoic sage might feel. The evidence of Plutarch quoted in the article confirms this impression.

On consideration of this, I think that I would withdraw my suggestion that the passage in Quaes Gen 2.57 implies any formal elevation of δηγμός to the status of a fourth εὐπάθεια, among, say, Stoicizing Platonists in Alexandria. It may very well be simply an *ad hoc* development by Philo to produce symmetry in this passage. Philo is loose enough elsewhere in his use of technical

terminology to be open to suspicion here. The passage
nonetheless remains interesting, I think, and the translation of the Armenian needed cleaning up.

NOTES

[1]Note especially the observations made and the passages cited by E. Bréhier, *Les idées philosophiques et religieuses de Philon d'Alexandrie*, Études de philosophie médiévale 8, 3d ed. (Paris: Librairie Philosophique J. Vrin, 1950), 254-255, 276. On the influence of Stoic πάθη on Philo, see M. Pohlenz, "Philon von Alexandreia," *Nachrichten von der Akademie der Wissenschaften in Göttingen*, Phil.-hist. Klasse 5 (1942) 409-487. For a good discussion of the Stoic doctrine of εὐπάθειαι, see J. M. Rist, *Stoic Philosophy* (London: Cambridge University Press, 1969) 22-36, 49-53.

[2]J. B. Aucher, *Philonis Judaei paralipomena Armena* (Venice: Typis Coenobii PP. Armenorum in Insula S. Lazari, 1826); R. Marcus, *PLCL Supplement* 1.

[3]The Latin and English translations from the above cited works (n. 2) are given for comparison:
Aucher renders, "Ad mentem vero, reptilia imitantur foeda, vitia; munda autem, gaudium: apud enim affectum concupiscentiae erunt gaudium et laetitia; apud desiderium voluntas et consilium; apud tristitiam punctio et compunctio; et apud aviditatem timor" (p. 140).
Marcus, relying on Aucher, renders, "But as for the deeper meaning, the passions resemble unclean reptiles, while joy (resembles) clean (reptiles). For alongside sensual pleasures there is the passion of joy. And alongside the desire for sensual pleasure there is reflection. And alongside grief there is remorse and constraint. And alongside desire there is caution" (p. 143).

[4]Bréhier, *Les idées philosophiques*, 254, n. 7.

[5]It has been rightly observed that the Armenian translation of Philo maintains the word order of the Greek and that it can be reliably retranslated. Aucher in his preface ("Ad lectores Armenios") to *Philonis Judaei sermones tres hactenus inediti* (Venice: Typis Coenobii PP. Armenorum in Insula S. Lazari, 1822) n.p.; F. C. Conybeare, *De Vita Contemplativa: Philo on the Contemplative Life* (Oxford: Clarendon, 1895) 155; R. Marcus, "The Armenian Translation of Philo's *Quaestiones in Genesim et Exodum*," *JBL* 49 (1930) 63; and H. Lewy, *The Pseudo-Philonic De Jona*, Part 1, Studies and Documents 7, ed. Kirsopp and Silva Lake (London: Christophers, 1936) 2-3.

[6]R. Marcus, "An Armenian-Greek Index to Philo's *Quaestiones* and *De Vita Contemplativa*," *Journal of the American Oriental Society* 53 (1933) 252. Such occurrences are more frequent than Marcus seems to realize.

[7]The following is W. Helmbold's translation: "But when, convicted by their tears and tremblings and changes of colour, in place of grief and fear they call these emotions 'compunctions' and 'perplexities' and gloss over the desires with the term 'eagerness,' they seem to be devising casuistic, not philosophic, shifts and escapes from reality through the medium of fancy names" (LCL 6, 65).

[8]H. Dörrie, "Der Platoniker Eudoros von Alexandria," *He* 79 (1944) 25-39; W. Theiler, "Philo von Alexandria und der Beginn des kaiserzeitlichen Platonismus," *Parusia: Festgabe für J. Hirschberger*, ed. K. Flasch (Frankfurt/M.: Minerva, 1965) 199-218.

XI

GANYMEDE AS THE LOGOS: TRACES OF A FORGOTTEN ALLEGORIZATION IN PHILO?

Philo's attitude to the mythologizing activities of the Greeks is well known.[1] In many passages he contrasts the practices of Greek writers unfavourably with that of Moses.[2] In one passage (*Conf.* 2 ff.), for example, he condemns those who see the Tower of Babel story as a reflection of that of Otus and Ephialtes' assault on Olympus; the truth, he asserts, is quite the contrary – the Greeks have borrowed the story from Moses.

On the other hand, Philo is himself prepared on occasion to allegorize figures of Greek mythology, though never explicitly on a subject of central doctrinal importance. For instance, he appears to be acquainted with the allegorization of various parts of the *Odyssey*. In his treatise *On Mating with the Preliminary Studies* (*Congr.*), he makes use of the allegorization of the Suitors' mating with the handmaidens because they cannot gain Penelope, first employed, it seems, by the Cynic Bion of Borysthenes, but no doubt of wide currency by Philo's time, as a figure of those who cannot attain to Philosophy consoling themselves with *ta enkyklia* (e.g. *Congr.* 14–19). Again, the use here and there in his writings of compounds of the verb νήχω, 'swim', particularly ἀνανήχομαι,[3] in connection with descriptions of our struggle through the storms and shipwreck of material existence, suggests his acquaintance with the allegorizing of Odysseus' shipwreck off Phaeacia in *Odyssey* V, where Homer employs this verb repeatedly.[4] Other, more specific allegories include Scylla as ἀφροσύνη, a 'deathless evil' (*Od.* 12. 118), at *Det.* 178; Odysseus' escape from Charybdis (ibid. 219) at *Somn.* 2. 70, to symbolize our escape from the cares of mortal existence; and Castor and Pollux (*Od.* 11. 303) at *Somn.* 1. 150, as an image of the life of the *askêtês* or *prokoptôn*. He is familiar also with the equating of the Olympian Gods with the various elements, e.g. Zeus, *Aet.* 81; Hera, Demeter, Poseidon, Hephaestus, Hades, *Dec.* 54; Hades, *Heres* 45.

All this, as I say, is well enough known. One detail, however, which has not, I think, received notice is his apparent acquaintance with, and use of, an allegorization of Ganymede as the Stoic Logos. It is on the face of it strange that Ganymede should be pressed into service in this role, since Hermes normally fills it quite adequately in later Stoicism and Platonism.[5] For Philo, however, Hermes represents only the planet Mercury (e.g. *Dec.* 54), never the Logos. The epithets which he favours in connection with the Logos are rather, if anything, those of Athena, sprung as she is from the head of Zeus. Her in turn he associates with the number Seven, which, following the Pythagoreans, he terms 'the motherless and ever-virgin maiden' (*Leg. All.* 1. 15) and 'motherless Victory and Virgin' (*Opif.* 100).[6]

---

[1] See especially the useful discussion of J. Pépin, *Mythe et Allégorie* (2nd ed. Paris, 1976), pp. 231–44.

[2] For example *Opif.* 1–2, 157, 170; *Leg. All.* 2. 19; *Det.* 125; *Gig.* 58; *Deus* 59; *De Prov.* 2. 109.

[3] *Det.* 100; *Post.* 178; *Gig.* 13; *Conf.* 66, etc. Also ἐπινήχομαι, *Sacr.* 13; *Migr.* 125, etc. Cf. further *Virt.* 14, where (κατακλύζεσθαι) ὑποβρύχιον is reminiscent of *Od.* 5. 319, ὑπόβρυχα, though *Phaedr.* 248A is also an influence.   [4] *Od.* 5. 364, 375, 399, 439.

[5] Cornutus, *ND* 16, p. 23, 16–22 Lang; Heraclitus, *Alleg. Hom.* 72. 4–19; Plotinus, *Enn.* 3. 6, 19.

[6] cf. also *Ebr.* 61, where Sarah, as Sophia, is described as ἀμήτωρ, being sprung from a father, but no mother – θήλεος γενεᾶς ἀμέτοχος, a probable reminiscence of Athena's famous speech in Aeschylus' *Eumenides* (734–41): μήτηρ γὰρ οὔτις ἐστιν ἥ μ' ἐγείνατο, κ.τ.λ.

184

However, there is an aspect of Ganymede's activity which qualifies him well for this role, and that is his position as Zeus' wine-steward (οἰνοχόος). The image of the divine Logos as an outpouring from God, a continuous flow which brings constant order to all creation, may seem to call for some figure other than Hermes or Athena, neither of whom has traditionally anything to do with pouring.

There are three passages in particular in which Philo seems to make use of this allegory. In each case he does so allusively, as one would expect, but yet with sufficient specificity, as I hope to show, to make the allusion clear. First, at *Quod Deus sit Immutabilis*, 155–8, God's grace is compared favourably with the nectar and ambrosia of the Olympians, as he rains it down upon us:

Are we, upon whom God pours down like snow or rain, from above, the founts of his blessings, going to drink from a cistern, and seek out fiddling springs of water from beneath the earth, when the heavens unceasingly rain down upon us a food superior to the nectar and ambrosia of the myths?... (158) He is not, then, going to drink from a cistern, to whom God has granted unmixed draughts of intoxication, either from the hand of one of his servants among the angels, whom he has designated to be his wine-steward (οἰνοχοεῖν), or even from his own hand, without the mediation of anyone between the donor and receiver.[7]

Here we have not only the picture of God's grace raining down from above in the form of an intoxicating draught (designed to produce, no doubt, 'sober drunkenness'),[8] but an angelic figure designated to pour it.

This figure reappears in a passage of the *De Somniis*, Book II, in the course of an exegesis of the dream of Pharaoh's chief wine-steward (ἀρχιοινοχόος, Gen. 40: 9–11). This figure has, of course, negative connotations for Philo, and his wine is evil. At *Somn.* 2. 183, however, Philo opposes to the wine-steward of Pharaoh, who stands for sensual existence, the wine-steward of God.

'Who, then,' he asks, 'is God's wine-steward? It is he who pours the libation of peace, the truly great High Priest who first receives the loving-cups of God's perennial bounties, then pays them back when he pours a libation of that potent undiluted draught, himself (ἑαυτόν).' For Philo, the figure of the High Priest (of whom the ideal example is Moses himself) is a mediator between God and man, a representation of the Logos immanent in the world.[9] In 188 he is described as μεθόριός τις θεοῦ ⟨καὶ ἀνθρώπου⟩ φύσις, τοῦ μὲν ἐλάττων, ἀνθρώπου δὲ κρείττων; in fact, a μεσίτης between God and man (*Mos.* 2. 166) – an epithet, we may note, accorded by the Persians to Mithra, as Plutarch tells us in *De Iside et Osiride*, 369 E.[10] A curious feature here, to which I shall return a little lower down, is that the draught which the wine-steward pours is specified to be nothing other than *himself*.

In a third passage, *Somn.* 2. 249, the imagery is more vivid yet. The Logos is here described as ὁ οἰνοχόος τοῦ θεοῦ καὶ συμποσίαρχος, pouring cupfuls of true gladness into the intellect of the righteous man, and then, as at 183, himself actually becoming the drink that he pours (οὐ διαφέρων τοῦ πόματος, ἀλλ' αὐτὸς ἄκρατος ὤν), this drink being described as, among other things, τὸ γάνωμα[11] and τὸ χαρᾶς, τὸ

---

[7] This translation, and that which follows, are Colson's, from his Loeb edition, with minor alterations.

[8] For the concept of νηφάλιος μέθη, cf. *Opif.* 71; *Leg. All.* 3. 82; *Mos.* 1. 187; *Prob.* 13; always in the context of feasting and the dispensation of ἄκρατος. See H. Lewy, *Sobria Ebrietas* (Giessen, 1929).

[9] For example *Fug.* 108–12; *Mos.* 2. 66–75. Cf. H. A. Wolfson, *Philo* I, pp. 359–60.

[10] διὸ καὶ Μίθρην Πέρσαι τὸν μεσίτην ὀνομάζουσιν. Plutarch portrays Mithra in this passage, in fact, as exercising priestly functions. Cf. R. Turcan, *Mithras Platonicus* (Leiden, 1975), pp. 14–22.

[11] γάνωμα occurs also at *Plant.* 39, as 'the draught of unmixed wine' (γάνωμα ἄκρατον) which the follower of Moses may drain off at the banquet of God.

εὐφροσύνης ἀμβρόσιον. Without actually naming Ganymede, a thing which, as I have said, one cannot expect Philo to do, he could hardly make clearer the source of his imagery.

But if we grant that we have here an employment by Philo of an allegorization of Ganymede, two aspects of the situation are notable, if not troublesome. The first is that there is, so far as I know, no other surviving testimony to this allegory. The second is that the Ganymede myth is, after all, a rather disreputable one, such as one would think Philo would hesitate to attribute, even by suggestion, to the relationship between God and his Logos.

On the first question there is not much to be said. If Philo is the only surviving source for this allegory, then one can only recall that it is by no means the only instance in which he is our sole repository for a piece of Hellenistic lore. As to the second, it is possible that the allegorization was made palatable for Philo because it had actually been made some time before, and was by his time relatively well accepted, establishing thus a sanitizing filter between him and the original myth. One sign, perhaps, of such allegorizing is the circumstance that Ganymede had, by Hellenistic times at least, been identified by astronomers with the zodiacal sign of the water-carrier, and had thus assumed a role as cosmic pourer.[12]

But there is also a more exotic possibility which, however, I hesitate to mention, since the question of Iranian influences on Philo – and on Greek thought in general – is such treacherous ground. It is, nevertheless, a fact that in Avestan tradition the divine being Haoma is both an intoxicating liquor and the spirit which presides over and inhabits the liquor. Like the High Priest of *Somn.* 2. 185–9, this being seems to perform a demiurgic and mediating function in the universe, as indicated by his discourse with Zarathustra in the *Homa-Yasht*, where most of the blessings of human existence are attributed to him.[13]

In the unravelling of the sources of Philo's thought, nothing is simple. He is plainly in this case able to draw on imagery derived from the Old Testament, such as Pharaoh's chief wine-steward, and perhaps the banquet organized by Sophia for her followers at *Proverbs* 9:5 (though he never actually quotes the passage), but it is hard to deny, I think, that other influences are at work here as well – influences, however, which he would not wish to acknowledge explicitly. Whatever about Haoma or Mithra – identifications which I shall leave to bolder spirits than myself – Ganymede seems to stand before us, in the pages of Philo, as the Logos of God. If he has an advantage over Hermes or any other rival, it is, I have suggested, in his role as *pourer*, since this enables the Logos to be presented by Philo as a fountain. At *Spec. Leg.* 1. 303, for example, we find the Logos described as ἀέναος τῶν καλῶν πηγή, from which God rains down the virtues, 'a drink more immortalising than nectar'.[14] Whether the allegorizing of Ganymede actually provoked the fountain-imagery so beloved of Philo – and later of the Neoplatonists – or vice versa, is not clear, but it is plain that, in Philo's case at least, they are closely connected.

---

[12] *Homil. Clement.* 5. 17; Ampelius 2. 11; Ps.-Eratosth. *Catast.* 26, 30.

[13] See R. C. Zaehner, *The Teachings of the Magi* (London, 1956), pp. 126–30.

[14] cf. also *Sacr.* 64: ἡ πηγὴ τῆς σοφίας, ὁ θεός; *Cher.* 86; *Fug.* 198, commenting on *Gen.* 14:7, and *Jer.* 2:13. As the passage from Jeremiah serves to remind us, though, fountain-imagery as such is readily derivable from the OT.

XII

THE DESCENT OF THE SOUL IN MIDDLE PLATONIC AND GNOSTIC THEORY

PERHAPS the chief problem that faces any religious or philosophical system which postulates, as does the Platonic, a primary state or entity of pure and unitary perfection, is that of explaining how from such a first principle anything further could have arisen. Any further development, after all, from a perfect principle must necessarily be a declination of some sort, and it is not easy to see why the supreme principle, if omnipotent, should want this to occur.

The solution resorted to in Platonism, and generally in Gnosticism as well, is the postulation of a female principle, either generated by or somehow arising beside the primal entity (which is invariably male). This is a principle of negativity, boundlessness and lack, and provokes the generation of the multiplicity of creation.

Arising out of this solution, however, is a further problem. Accepting that a world or universe of some sort is thus brought into being, how can we further explain the imperfect and disorderly nature of *our* world as it now exists? Something, surely, has gone wrong somewhere. There must at some stage, over and above the basic creation, have been a declination, a Fall.

Not necessarily, one may say. Plotinus, for instance, though he does give us in one tractate (4.8; and cf. 5.1.1) a rather vivid portrayal of the fall of the soul, also argues both elsewhere and in the same tractate, that the world has developed to its present state by a natural progression. There is nothing actually *wrong*. Since the first principle, the One, is supremely perfect, anything it produces must, since it must be different from it, necessarily be 'worse' than it, and the process of creation, once begun (though not of course at any point in time), must proceed through all possible stages of inferiority to the ultimate depth of nonbeing, which is unformed Matter. No specific *fall* is required. Such an attitude seems to Plotinus himself to derive its authority from Plato's *Timaeus* (4.8,1).

Yet Plotinus, as we know, entertained the idea of a fall of the soul, and sees this belief also justified in Plato, particularly in the myth of the *Phaedrus*. What I wish to do in the present paper is to examine the various forms which this concept takes on in Middle Platonic thinkers, and then to direct a rather cursory glance at some Gnostic thinkers, such as Valentinus, who were more or less their contemporaries.

I will take as my point of reference the treatise *On the Soul* of the Neoplatonist Iamblichus,[1] composed around 300 A.D., as Iamblichus here sets out in a usefully scholastic form the heads under which the question of the descent of souls was normally discussed in later Platonism. He divides the question into various topics (p. 377.11ff.): (1) the varieties of the descent of souls; (2) the varieties of the manners and purposes of descent; (3) the relation of the soul to the body, once descended; (4) times and modes of incorporation; (5) how the soul uses the body, (6) how the soul can be united with the Gods. Iamblichus refers to the views of a good many of his predecessors under these various heads, and I shall base myself on his account, confining myself, however, for the present purpose, to the first two subjects, namely, whence do souls descend, and why.

I would like to start with one Middle Platonic predecessor whom Iamblichus does not mention by name in this connexion, though he recognises the doctrine concerned (p. 378), namely Plutarch, and specifically the doctrine which Plutarch puts into the mouth of the Stranger whom his friend Sextius Sulla met in Carthage, in the dialogue *On the Face in the Moon*. Whether or not Plutarch himself stands over this account it is not essential for our purpose to decide; but I see no reason to doubt his basic endorsement of it. For the Stranger, the Moon is the repository of souls (943 f.). After describing how souls reach the Moon, and what befalls them there, he describes the various ways in which and reasons why they descend thence (944cd). The first stage is for the *daimones*, as these disembodied, purified souls are termed, to come down as incorporeal administrators of the sublunar realm; but then it is envisaged that some, through the influence of some passion or other, will not perform their duties properly, and

---

[1] Preserved, in large fragments, in Stobaeus, *Anthologia* 49, p. 362ff. of Wachsmuth's edition (and, in short passages, elsewhere in the same work). There is a useful translation, with notes, by A.-J. Festugière, as Appendix 1 to vol. 3 of *La Révélation d'Hermès Trismégiste* (Paris: Lecoffre, 1953). I use Wachsmuth's pagination as a basis for reference.

these are condemned to be confined once again in mortal bodies. This
is a notion which goes back at least to Empedocles, but which is still
a live theory in Middle Platonism. Here the Moon is the point of
origin, not any supercelestial realm, and the real fall takes place only
after the descent, and not in all cases.

Other possibilities which Iamblichus considers are descent from the
Milky Way (the view of Heraclides of Pontus, as he recognises), and
descent from all the celestial spheres, a view for which he quotes no
specific authorities. This probably refers to a belief that some souls
descend from, and are in the 'chain' (*seira*) of, one planet, and some
of another, but Iamblichus's reference is too brief and allusive for
certainty to be possible.

However, we are not primarily concerned here with where the souls
come from, but rather why. In the next section of his work (pp. 378-79),
Iamblichus presents two bases of distinction as to the reason for the
soul's descent, the first of which he attributes to 'the Platonists of the
school of Taurus', the second of which he favours himself.

> The Platonists of the school of Taurus [he says] say that souls are sent
> down by the Gods to earth—some of them, following the *Timaeus*, de-
> claring it to be for the completion of the universe [*eis teleiôsin tou pantos*],
> so that there should be as many living things in the cosmos as there are
> in the noetic realm, *others* describing the purpose of the descent as being
> the manifestation of divine life [*theias zoês epideixis*]. For this, they say,
> is the will of the Gods, to make their divinity manifest through the
> medium of souls; for the Gods advance to a visible state and reveal them-
> selves through the pure and uncontaminated life of souls.

Taurus and his followers thus represent what one might term the
'optimistic' wing of Platonism on the question of the descent of the
soul, a tradition, as Plotinus notes, taking its inspiration from the
Timaeus. The second reason given, indeed, is curiously similar to what
I take to be the Christian belief—certainly the belief I was brought up
on—that God made us for his own honour and glory. Presumably
the idea is that, although most souls, in their lives, will not reflect
much glory on the Gods, yet enough will do so to make the effort
worth while. No omelette without breaking eggs, after all.

Iamblichus's account here of Middle Platonic opinion needs some
filling out, however. All Platonist tradition was not so 'world-affirming'.
In Albinus's *Didaskalikos*, more or less contemporary with Taurus
(mid-second century), we find a list of possible reasons why souls
should descend into bodies, complementary to those attributed to
Taurus and his followers (*Didasc.* 25).

1. *'arithmous menousai'*. I used to think I knew what this meant, but now I am not so sure. I would take it to mean 'waiting for their numbers', in the sense of 'answering the call when their number comes up', with a view to keeping up the number of souls in the universe; but I am not confident about this. At any rate, it sounds like a reason involving cosmic necessity rather than individual delinquency. Albinus unfortunately does not explain any of his very summary reasons, except to some extent the last.

2. *The will of the Gods (boulêsis theôn)*. Again, this needs amplification, and for this we can turn, I think, to Taurus. For him, we recall, the Gods wish to make themselves manifest through souls. Presumably that is what Albinus has in mind here. At any rate, once again no individual delinquency is envisaged.

3. *Wantonness (akolasia)*—that is, presumably, sinful wilfulness on the part of the individual soul. Here we are presented with a Fall, and it would seem from Iamblichus's evidence that we are close to Albinus's own view. Slightly earlier in the *De anima* (p. 375.2ff.) Iamblichus gives quite a doxography of reasons for the descent of the soul. As that of the Gnostics he gives 'derangement or deviation' (*paranoia ê parekbasis*), and, immediately following this, that of Albinus as 'the mistaken judgement of a free will' (*hê tou autexousiou diêmartêmenê krisis*). This seems to place Albinus pretty squarely in what one may term the 'world-negating' tradition within Platonism, which is that which accords with the Gnostic vision of the world.

4. *Love of the body (philosômatia)*. This final reason does not sound very different from the previous one, and is also, at first sight, world-negating. But here Albinus adds a curious rider, suggesting that in fact some natural tendency is being envisaged. 'Body and soul', explains Albinus, 'have a kind of affinity (*oikeiôsis*) towards each other, like fire and asphalt'. If we press this simile, it would imply that when soul, in the course of its peregrinations through the universe, comes into a certain degree of proximity to a body, it must spring towards it and ensoul it, and this would happen without any forethought on the part of the soul in question. Embodiment would, thus, once again be a necessary consequence of the arrangement of the universe, and not a fault to be imputed to soul. It is not quite clear, however, whether Albinus wishes to exclude the notion of a Fall here.

Albinus presents all these possibilities as disjunctions, but he may after all have recognised them as joint possibilities, or as true of different classes of souls. We do not know. Iamblichus himself (p. 379) wishes to make a distinction between two types of descent, one voluntary, 'the soul itself choosing to administer the terrestrial realm', the other involuntary, 'the soul being forcibly drawn to what is worse than it'. Iamblichus does not make clear here why this second class should be forcibly drawn down, but we can conclude from what follows that some element of previous sin is envisaged. What I am interested in here, though, is the distinction of two main types of descent, as this is a notion which seems to go back quite far in Platonism, drawing its ultimate inspiration, it would seem, from Plato's distinction in the *Phaedrus* myth between the fate of the philosophic soul and that of the others. Plato himself, though, it must be noted, does not make any distinction between modes or purposes of descent, such as we find later. Iamblichus goes on to distinguish two different ways of relating to the body practised by these two classes of soul.

> The pure and perfect souls come to settle in bodies in a pure manner, without being subject to passions and without being deprived of the power of intellection; for souls of a contrary character, the opposite is the case.

A little further on, Iamblichus makes the distinction clearer, though he now envisages not two, but three possible classes of embodied soul.

> Furthermore, in my opinion, the variety of purposes creates differences in the modes of descent of souls. For the soul that comes down for the purpose of salvation and purification and perfection of the material realm is immaculate in its descent; that soul, on the other hand, which has turned to bodies for the exercise and correction of its moral life will not be entirely free of passions, nor will it be left free [*apolytos*] on its own; while that soul which has come down here by way of punishment and judgement seems, as it were, to be dragged and driven along [p. 380].

Iamblichus goes on to criticise his predecessors for ignoring such distinctions, and maintaining that all entries of souls into bodies are evil, but mentions only Numenius, Cronius, and Harpocration as holding this view. In turning to Numenius and the Neopythagorean tradition, he has fixed on the most world-negating and Gnostic wing of Middle Platonism, and he is not being quite fair to the whole Platonic movement. Plutarch, for instance, in the myth of the *De Facie* mentioned above, makes a clear distinction (591d) between some souls which 'sink entirely into the body' and others which 'only mingle in part, leaving outside what is purest in them'. It is these latter whose intellects are seen in the vision riding quietly in the heaven above their souls, 'like the corks we observe riding on the sea to mark nets'.

But the figure I would like to dwell on, in conclusion, since he gives evidence of a still earlier date for these distinctions, is Philo of Alexandria, who seems to recognise already most of the ideas we have been discussing. Philo has certain difficulties with the concept of re-incarnation, which is an essential part of Platonic doctrine, but this does not prevent him from having quite developed notions about the soul's descent into body. At *Heres* 240, for example, he produces the doctrine of the soul's Fall as a result of 'satiety' (*koros*) with its happy state—not quite the same sin as the *tolma* envisaged by Plotinus, or as the restlessness and inquisitiveness of Sophia in Valentinianism, but analogous.[2]

> Surely then we must suppose that misery wholesale and all-pervading must be the lot of those souls which, reared in air and ether at its purest, have left that home for earth, the region of things mortal and evil, through not being able to overcome a satiety with divine blessings.

Once fallen, these souls become prey to innumerable 'notions' (*ennoiai*) some voluntary, some arising out of ignorance (*kat' agnoian*). Such as become possessed by 'upward-flying' thoughts are lucky, and may win their way back to the heavenly and divine region, but those who are occupied by thoughts which tend downwards are doomed to wallow around down here forever.

Philo in this passage distinguishes two types of descended soul, but only on the basis of how they make use of their unfortunate lot once in the body. There is nothing here that cannot be derived from Plato, whether the *Phaedrus*, the *Republic* or the *Timaeus*. However, Philo does also make a distinction between different purposes of descent. I quote from *Conf.* 77-78:

> That is why all whom Moses calls wise are represented as 'sojourners' [*paroikountes*]. Their souls never set out as colonists to leave heaven for a new home, but rather their way is to visit earthly nature as men who travel abroad to see and learn. So when they have stayed a while in their bodies, and beheld through them all that sense and mortality has to show, they make their way back to the place from which they set out at first, regarding as their fatherland the heavenly region where they exercise their

---

[2] Cf. Hans Jonas, *The Gnostic Religion* (Boston: Beacon, 1963), 62-65, and the references there given.

XII

363   THE DESCENT OF THE SOUL

citizenship, and as a foreign land the earthly region in which they have
become sojourners [tr. Colson (LCL), slightly emended].

Philo does here make a strong distinction between two types of descent, prefiguring the distinctions made by Iamblichus in the passage quoted earlier. The notion of a distinction between the wise and the others is not entirely new, perhaps. It can dimly be discerned behind the theology of the *Somnium Scipionis*, for example, whether that be Posidonian Stoicism or Antiochian Platonism. There, in section 13, we find the view that only the souls of the great attain a definite place among the stars; the rest are presumably ploughed back into the world-soul. There, however, there is admittedly no suggestion that souls descended on different terms in the first place. One could perhaps conclude from the myth of *Republic* 10 that the choosing of different lots constitutes a distinction in conditions of descent, but no very clear distinction of classes is there made by Plato. Philo seems to me to be the first to suggest that souls may be going about in bodies for quite different reasons, and this suggestion is one which is certainly picked up in Gnosticism. Philo even comes to Iamblichus's distinction of three classes of embodied soul in an interesting three-way distinction which he makes at *Gig.* 60 between the sons of earth, the sons of heaven, and the sons of God, but he does not there suggest that these three classes descended originally on different terms.[3]

In conclusion, we have, I think, within the Platonism of the first few centuries A.D. a fairly wide spectrum of doctrines concerning the descent of the soul into body. Broadly speaking, either the soul is guilty of some transgression, or it is not. If it is not, it is still possible for it to acquire guilt (or merit) by its behaviour when in the body. As for the Gnostics, at least in Valentinianism, it is clear that Sophia, the transcendent world-soul, is guilty of a transgression in seeking to know more about her Father, and this inquisitiveness leads to the creation of the material world, and ultimately to our incarceration in it. The probably Valentinian *Exegesis on the Soul*, with rather prurient enthusiasm, represents the soul as falling among ruffians, who rape her repeatedly, and then as repenting and calling upon her father,

---

[3] Three classes of embodied soul are of course attested also in Valentinianism, e.g., in Theodotus's system (Clement, *Exc. Thdot.* 56.2), where the distinction is made between hylics, psychics, and pneumatics, these descending from Cain, Abel, and Seth respectively. Here, however, there is the suggestion that there are three types of soul, deriving their distinctions from their descent from these three archetypal souls.

but does not make it clear what leads to the original transgression.[4] The individual soul is often allowed to reproach God with having thrust it into such a foul prison, but this is the rhetoric of repentance and salvation, not the higher theology. There does, however, seem to me to be in Gnostic theory, as in Platonism—represented most clearly by Plotinus—a tension between two views of the soul's lot, a conviction that a conscious transgression of some sort has taken place, and an equally strong conviction that somehow God willed all this, and that thus it is all, if not for the best, at least an inevitable consequence of there being a universe at all.

---

[4] W. Foerster, *Gnosis* (tr. R. McL. Wilson; Oxford: Clarendon, 1974) 2. 102-9. Here it is only stated that the soul 'fell into a body and came into this life'. We do not hear why.

XIII

Plutarch and Second Century Platonism

I T IS SUITABLE, perhaps, to begin such an essay as this, as Plutarch himself would have wished, with a Plutarchan profession of faith and of humility in the face of the divine. By way of preface to his reply to certain objections to divine providence presented in his essay *On the Delays in the Divine Vengeance* 549E, Plutarch says the following:

> The fact is that we really have no part or parcel in Being, but everything of a mortal nature is at some stage between coming into existence and passing away, and presents only a dim and uncertain semblance and appearance of itself; and if you apply the whole force of your mind in your desire to apprehend it, it is like the violent grasping of water, which by squeezing and compression, loses the handful enclosed, as it spurts through the fingers. (Trans. Babbitt)

In a way, these are banalities (though the imagery of taking a handful of water is lively), but they appear also to be deeply felt. When one is approaching the question of the living faith of a man like Plutarch, who is both a Platonic philosopher in an age of scholasticism, and a scholar and an antiquarian in an age of profound conservatism and reverence for the past, it is no easy matter to disentangle the genuine beliefs from the formalities. This goes also for the other figures with whom we shall be dealing: Taurus, Atticus, Albinus, Apuleius, Maximus of Tyre, and Numenius, all second-century men enmeshed in traditional attitudes, but each with personal challenges to face. To adopt Plutarch's image, one must handle the evidence gently, lest the truth spurt out like water through our fingers.

Plutarch

What, then, were the guiding principles of Plutarch's spirituality? I would identify them as devotion to Apollo as god of Delphi and to Delphic worship and ceremony; a cosmic dualism; and, in ethics, a civilized moderation—Peripatetic *metriopatheia* as opposed to Stoic *apatheia*. Let us discuss each of these features in turn.

The Delphic Divinity

To begin with Apollo, it is plain that for Plutarch it is not the son of Zeus and Leto who is to be worshiped nor yet the Sun (see his strictures in *De Pythiae oraculis* 400D), but rather the supreme God of Platonism, the Good of the *Republic*, the Demiurge of the *Timaeus*, who reveals himself preeminently as the god of Delphi. Apollo is to be etymologized, following the Pythagoreans, as 'Not-Many', and, therefore, the Unitary and Simple (*De E apud Delphos* 393BC):

> In fact the Deity is not Many, as is each of us who is compounded of hundreds of different factors which arise in the course of our experience, a heterogeneous collection combined in a haphazard way. But Being must have Unity, even as Unity must have Being. Now divergence from Unity, because of its differing from Being, deviates into the creation of that which has no Being. Whereafter the first of the god's names is excellently well adapted to him. . . . He is "Apollo," that is to say, denying the Many and abjuring multiplicity. (Trans. Babbitt)

Such a god may be symbolized in this world by the sun (as in the *Republic*), but he is by no means to be identified with the sun (393DE). As to his nature, Plutarch accepts, both here and elsewhere, the Platonic norms, enunciated in *Republic* 2, concerning how God should be spoken of: he is unitary, as we have seen, unchanging, beneficent, not subject to passions. Any untoward supernatural manifestations must be attributed not to the Supreme God but to an inferior deity, about whom we will have more to say later, in connection with Plutarch's dualism and demonology. In chap. 39 of his *Life of Pericles*, he takes the opportunity to remark that Pericles was called "Olympian" because "his pure and undefiled exercise of power was an image of the immortal gods," and he criticizes the poets for attributing anything else than this to the gods.

In a passage like this, and in numerous others, Plutarch speaks of "the gods" but it is not clear that in this he is paying much more than lip-service to polytheism. If we are to talk of "gods," they can be seen at most as manifestations of the supreme deity in various roles; Plutarch is happier with the more indefinite term *to theion*, "divinity."

Such divinity, of course, is not to be thought of as having human (or any other) form, or human personality. In another passage from the *Lives*, the *Life of Numa*, chap. 8, Plutarch, in discussing Numa's alleged Pythagoreanism, notes that he followed Pythagoras (and, it is implied, right reason) in banning images of God in either human or bestial form:

> For that philosopher maintained that the first principle of Being was beyond sense or feeling, was invisible and free from mixture, and discernible only by the intellect.

But to a God so devoid of personal characteristics what personal devotion can there be? A good vantage point from which to discern Plutarch's attitude to the divinity is the prefatory portion of his essay *On Isis and Osiris*, addressed to his good friend, the Delphic priestess Clea. The whole passage (351C–352A) constitutes a useful statement of what one might term Plutarch's "philosophical *gnōsis*."

He begins by stating that what one asks first and foremost of the gods is a knowledge of themselves—with the Platonic caveat "so far as such a thing is attainable by men" (see *Theaetetus* 176A). God, he explains, gives human beings the other things that they request, but of *nous* and *phronēsis* he gives them only a share (*metadidōsin*), since these are properties peculiar to himself. The excellence of God lies not in his power and strength but in his wisdom, both his acquaintance with Real Being and his providential care of our realm of Becoming.

So the striving after the truth, and especially the truth of the divine things, is a fulfillment of the injunction to become like unto God. It becomes plain, however, that 'knowledge of God' does not consist merely in fashioning true propositions about the godhead, but in the performance of approved rituals and religious observances. The end of these, he says (*On Isis and Osiris* 352A), is "the knowledge (*gnōsis*) of him who is the first, the Lord of All, the object of intellection." Isis constitutes a proper symbol and vehicle of this *gnōsis*, as her very name indicates (Plutarch etymologizes it as deriving from *eidenai to on*, "knowledge of Being").

One might feel here that he is saying much of this as a compliment to Clea, but in fact he did not have to embark on the enterprise of praising Isis at all, if all this did not reflect his deeper convictions; and there is no reason to suppose that it does not. To call Plutarch a "gnostic," then, is, I think, meaningful, if the term is carefully qualified (the usefulness of the term in its "traditional" sense, after all, is being seriously questioned by scholars these days). Plutarch plainly holds that knowledge of God is not simply a matter of philosophizing in the modern sense, but rather of training and disciplining the mind through ascetic practices and the observance of ritual. Of course, intellectual philosophizing—the practice of dialectic and other Platonic methods—is necessary also, but it will not achieve knowledge of God without the observance of a certain way of life. This position can, I think, be characterized as "gnostic."

This, however, addresses only the summit, so to speak, of Plutarch's system of belief. Like Philo in relation to the observances of Judaism, Plutarch held that possession of the higher gnosis did not exempt one from the observances of one's religion. He took great pride in being a priest of Apollo at Delphi and served actively as such for many years, even into old age, as he testifies in his essay *Whether an Old Man should Engage in Public Affairs* (792F):

> Now surely you know that I have been serving the Pythian Apollo for many Pythiads, but you would not say: "Plutarch, you have done enough sacrificing, marching in processions, and dancing in choruses, and now that you are older it is time to put off the garland and to desert the oracle on account of your age." (Trans. H. N. Fowler)

As the elderly Plutarch danced in his choruses, in whose honor did he consider that he was dancing? One does not dance, I think, in honor of the Good, or of the One. Possibly Plutarch felt, as did later Platonists such as Porphyry, Iamblichus, or Proclus (though not, I think, Plotinus), that the correct way to honor the deity was through the forms of ritual traditional to one's culture, but one may detect also in Plutarch, as later in Proclus, a delight in ritual for its own sake, which is only, after all, to put Plutarch in the mainstream of traditional Greek piety, as emphasized by A. H. Armstrong in the introduction to this volume.

Cosmic Dualism

Plutarch is notable, within the Platonic spectrum, for his dualist tendencies. It is the general consensus of modern scholars, as it was of ancient ones, that Plato was not a dualist, in the strong sense. He recognizes the disorderly influence of matter, certainly in the *Timaeus*, but even in *Laws* 10, despite appearances, there is no need to assume any such entity as an evil world soul. However, Plato does lay himself open to such an interpretation for those who want to find such an entity, and his description of the creation of the world in the *Timaeus* is ambiguous enough to persuade some distinguished modern scholars, such as Gregory Vlastos, that he envisages a precosmic state of disorderly motion, upon which order is then imposed.

Plutarch was certainly of this opinion, which he presents in his treatise *On the Creation of the Soul in the Timaeus*—recognizing, however, that in this he is going against the views of his predecessors. It is his contention, carefully argued particularly in chaps. 6–7, that the cause of evil in the world cannot be matter, which has no qualities or propensities whatever, but an irrational, 'evil' soul and that this is Plato's doctrine in the *Timaeus*, *Philebus*, *Politicus*, and *Laws* (see particularly *On the Creation* 1014B).

I have suggested elsewhere that Plutarch may owe his dualism to his teacher Ammonius, whom he portrays in the *De E* (394A) as holding that the sublunar world is in the grip of a secondary god whose characteristics are antithetical to those of Apollo.[1] But wherever he derived it from, it seems to be part of his world view. It emerges strongly in the *Isis and Osiris*, where its Persian origin is also made evident (see 369A–E). It is worth quoting from this passage what is a definitive statement of Plutarch's dualism:

> There has, therefore, come down from the theologians and lawgivers to both poets and philosophers [he has quoted Heraclitus and Euripides] this ancient belief, which is of anonymous origin, but is given strong and tenacious evidence—that the universe is not kept on high of itself without mind and reason and guidance, nor is it only one principle that rules and directs it as it were by rudders and curbing reins, but that many powers do so who are a mixture of evil and good. Rather since Nature, to be plain, contains nothing that is unmixed, it is not one steward that dispenses our affairs for us, as though mixing drinks from two jars in an hotel. Life and the cosmos, on the contrary—if not the whole of the cosmos, at least the earthly one below the moon, which is heterogeneous, variegated and subject to all manner of changes—are compounded of two opposite principles (*archai*) and of two antithetic powers (*dynameis*), one of which leads by a straight path and to the right, while the other reverses and bends back. For if nothing comes into being without a cause, and if good could not provide the cause of evil, then Nature must contain in itself the creation and origin of evil as well as of good.

For Plutarch, the tensions within the cosmos center on the figure of the World Soul, symbolized in the myth of Isis and Osiris by Isis, who is not itself an evil entity but irrational and subject to the evil influence of the Indefinite Dyad, symbolized by Typhon, or Ahriman. This World Soul, however, strives blindly toward the light of order, represented by the One and its Logos, and accepts ordering from that source, which leads to the creation of the physical cosmos (see *Isis and Osiris* 372E; *On the Creation* 1026E–1027A). The same tension must be seen as present in the human soul, and thus Plutarch's spirituality may be seen as containing a more pronounced notion of 'original sin' than is usual for a Platonist.

On the other hand, Plutarch is no 'world-negater' in a gnostic sense, or even to the extent that this might be said of the Neopythagorean Numenius, whom we shall consider presently. He simply sees this world as a theater in which a cosmic drama is played out, resulting from the tension between opposing forces, but where the Good triumphs. His position in ethics bears this out.

Ethics

In the area of ethical theory, a Platonist of Plutarch's time had in effect a choice between adhering to the Peripatetic doctrines of moderation of the passions (*metriopatheia*) and of virtue as a mean, and the more austere Stoic doctrines of extirpation of the passions (*apatheia*) and of the almost unattainable level of virtue of the Stoic sage, the great majority even of philosophers being mere 'improvers' (*prokoptontes*), not yet possessing true virtue. Antiochus of Ascalon, in the previous century, despite his Stoic tendencies in physics, was Peripatetic in his ethics, as were Taurus and Albinus later, in the mid-second century, whereas Eudorus of Alexandria and Atticus (who was Plutarch's follower in other respects) favored the Stoic ethical system. This is not, of course, the way they would have seen it: Plato could be quoted in support of either position, and Aristotle's *Nicomachean Ethics*, in particular, seems to have been taken by Platonists to represent Academic teaching.

Plutarch himself, despite frequently striking Stoic attitudes in his popular essays, was firmly on the side of *metriopatheia* and the mean. The essay *On Moral Virtue* gives a definitive statement of his ethical theory. Here Aristotle's doctrine in *Nicomachean Ethics* 2.5–7 forms the basis of his position, though tinged with the Pythagorean conception of the mean as a quasi-musical harmonizing of the irrational soul by the rational (see *On Moral Virtue* 444EF). For Plutarch, the individual soul is a battlefield of opposing forces, even as is the cosmos. In the course of criticizing the Stoic conception of a unitary soul, he has the following to say (445B):

> In this last instance [the case of temperance], indeed, the irrational seems, with particular clearness, to allow us to observe the difference between itself and the rational, and to show that passion is essentially quite a different thing from reason. For self-control (*enkrateia*) would not differ from temperance (*sōphrosynē*), nor incontinence (*akrasia*) from intemperance (*akolasia*), as regards the pleasures or desires, if it were the same part of the soul that we naturally use for desiring as for forming judgments. But the fact is that temperance belongs to the sphere where reason guides and manages the passionate element like a gentle animal obedient to the reins, making it yielding in its desires and willingly receptive of moderation and propriety; but the self-controlled man, while he does indeed direct his desire by the strength and mastery of reason, yet does so not without pain, nor by persuasion, but as it plunges sideways and resists, as though with blow and curb, he forcibly subdues it and holds it in, being the while himself full of internal struggle and turmoil. (Trans. Helmbold)

He here invokes the Platonic image of the charioteer and horses, from the *Phaedrus* myth, as constituting a particularly striking image of the soul's true nature. Plutarch's moral stance is in fact no less stern than that of any Stoic; it is just that his vision of the world, and of the human soul, is different.

Daemons

I have not, so far, alluded to a popular topic in discussions of Plutarch, his views on daemons. This aspect of his belief structure should not be neglected, but it is wrong to single him out as unusual in this respect. Everyone in Plutarch's world, not least the Christians, believed in daemons, in the sense of intermediate beings between God and humans, beneficent or maleficent, to whom a great many phenomena affecting one's daily life could be attributed. It has been well remarked that daemons in the ancient world filled many of the roles taken on by germs today. They were responsible for diseases of both mind and body, as well as for many infelicities of the weather. But on a more philosophically significant level, they provided a bridge between a divinity who (or *which*) was not subject to change or passions nor even possessed a personality and suffering and hoping humanity.

Plutarch's views on daemons are not, I think, entirely consistent, but they are nonetheless interesting for that.[2] One can discern in his thought both a 'static' and a 'dynamic' doctrine of daemons. On the one hand, we have passages (e.g., *On the Obsolescence of Oracles* 416C–F) in which what seems to be envisaged is a permanent class of intermediate beings, relieving god of too intimate connection with the concerns of earthly existence; on the other, we have a remarkable doctrine of the apparently endless cycle of changes upward and downward on the scale of being, which souls may undergo as they pass from human to daemon to god and, it seems, back again (e.g., *On the Face in the Moon* 944 CD; *De defectu oraculorum* 415B).

It is not relevant to our present purpose to discuss Plutarch's theory of daemons as such. All that concerns us is to note that daemons serve, on the one hand, to exempt god from any imputation of malevolent behavior or of taking pleasure in bloody or cruel sacrifices, and on the other, to buttress Plutarch's belief in the immortality of the soul and reincarnation, which, though traditionally Platonic, has some distinctive aspects.

Soul and Intellect

Plutarch derives from somewhere a strong contrast between soul and intellect (*nous*) (e.g., *On the Daemon of Socrates* 591 DE) and, together with that, a belief in what he calls a "double" or two-stage death, set out in the myth of the dialogue *On the Face in the Moon* (945BC). Soul and intellect depart from the body at what we call death and ascend to the region of the moon, but then intellect leaves soul behind and ascends to the region of the sun. The reverse process also takes place, the sun sowing intellects in the moon, and the moon sowing the new intelligized souls into bodies.

In another myth, that of the dialogue *On the Daemon of Socrates* (591DE), we learn more. Relations between intellects and the soul–body complexes they manage will differ widely; normally the intellect is separate, floating above the body "like a fisherman's buoy," and it is this that may be seen as our personal daemon, but sometimes, it seems, it is dragged down into body as well.

Such a belief in a separable intellect is reminiscent of a doctrine that turns up in the Hermetic Corpus (*Tractate* 10, esp. sections. 19–21), where we learn that not all individuals have a *nous* and that in some cases the relationship with the *nous* becomes so unsatisfactory that it constitutes an avenging daemon. Whether Plutarch derives any influence from that quarter is doubtful, but certainly this doctrine, like his basic dualism, is an accretion of his Platonism brought in from outside.

Basically, however, Plutarch's religion is that of a Platonist, and such is his resounding affirmation of the immortality of the soul, delivered in the course of an attack on the Epicureans, toward the end of his treatise *That Epicurus Actually Makes a Pleasant Life Impossible* (1105CD):

Hence in abolishing belief in immortality, they also abolish the pleasantest and greatest hope of ordinary men.

What, then, do we suppose they do to the pleasures of the good, whose lives have been just and holy, who look forward to nothing evil in that other world but instead to all that is most glorious and divine? For in the first place, just as athletes receive the crown not while they are engaged in the contest but when it is over and victory is won, so men who believe that life is done are inspired by their virtue to a most wonderful confidence when they fix their eyes on these hopes, which include that of seeing at last the condign punishment of those who in their wealth and power are injurious and insolent now and who in their folly laugh all higher powers to scorn. In the next place no one impassioned for the truth and the vision of reality has ever been fully satisfied in this world, since the light of reason, veiled by the body as by a mist or cloud, is wavering and indistinct; but like a bird that gazes upward, they are ready to take wing from the body to some luminous expanse, and thus they lighten and disburden the soul of the gear of mortality, taking philosophy as an exercise in death. (Trans. Einarson and De Lacy)

This, inspired as it is by Plato's *Phaedo*, gives no hint of the complexities arising out of one's relationship with one's *nous* or problems of identity resulting from reincarnation. What Plutarch really believed in that area is not clear, but certainly he held, with Socrates at the end of the *Apology*, that

223   PLUTARCH AND SECOND CENTURY PLATONISM

"nothing bad can happen to a good man."

We began with God, and let us end with God. The purpose of life, for Plutarch as a Platonist, is "becoming like to God," *homoiōsis theō*. We have seen this expressed in this passage from the dialogue *On the Divine Vengeance* (550DE):

> Consider that God, as Plato says (*Theaetus* 176E), offers himself to all as a pattern of every excellence, thus rendering human virtue, which is in some sort an assimilation to himself (*exhomoiōsin . . . pros hauton*), accessible to all who can "follow God." Indeed this was the origin of the change whereby universal nature, disordered before, became a "cosmos": it came to resemble after a fashion and participate in the form and excellence of God. The same philosopher says further that Nature kindled vision in us so that the soul, beholding the heavenly motions and wondering at the sight, should grow to accept and cherish all that moves in stateliness and order, and thus come to hate discordant and errant passions and to shun the aimless and haphazard as the source of all vice and jarring error; for man is fitted to derive from God no greater blessing than to become settled in virtue through copying and aspiring to the beauty and the goodness that are his. (Trans. Einarson and De Lacy)

Plutarch's spirituality, then, is basically optimistic and world-affirming. He recognizes a tension in the world between good and evil, but without falling into nihilistic, world-abhoring gloom. In that, at least, he is more akin to Plotinus after him than to many of his contemporaries, products of that "age of anxiety" which E. R. Dodds so acutely identified in his well-known book of that title.[3]

Other Platonists of the Second Century

It would be desirable, I think, to set Plutarch in the context of other second-century Platonists and Pythagoreans to see how representative or otherwise he is of Platonism in this era, but unfortunately the material for making such an assessment is very largely lacking. We know the names and something of the views of fully half a dozen figures of this period in Platonism, but we do not have much that tells us what religious beliefs they held.

What we know of L. Calvenus Taurus is derived primarily from the reminiscences of Aulus Gellius in his *Noctes Atticae*, and these reveal an urbane and donnish figure, not subject to mystical or ascetic excesses. However, we do learn, not from Gellius but from Iamblichus, in his *De Anima* (ap. Stobaeus *Anthologium* 1.378, Wachsmuth), that Taurus "and his followers" put forward two views as to why souls are sent by the gods into bodies—*either* "for the completion of the universe, that there may be as many living things in the cosmos as there are in the intelligible realm" (a doctrine derived from Plato's *Timaeus*) or (what is more interesting) "that the gods may reveal themselves through souls; for the gods come out into the open and manifest themselves through the pure and unsullied life of souls." This latter notion has, it seems to me, a distinctly religious content. We are placed on this earth as projections of the divinity, and it is up to us to live up to this high calling, necessarily by 'likening' ourselves to God, in the accepted Platonic manner. This is perhaps derivable in part from such Platonic passages as *Phaedo* 62B (we are here on guard duty, as it were, for the gods) and *Laws* 644DE (we are puppets of the gods), but the tone of it is rather different. However, on a doxographic notice such as this one should not build too much.

We are no better served with such figures as Atticus and Albinus. From the former we have a polemical tract directed against those who try to interpret Plato through Aristotle[4]—and thus against Aristotelianism. This includes a spirited defense of God's providence against Aristotle's effective abolition of it, which takes on distinctly theological overtones. Atticus was doubtless a man of exemplary Platonic piety, but one cannot, I think, derive a true idea of his personal spirituality from this rhetorical polemic. From Albinus, on the other hand, what we have is a dry scholastic handbook of Platonic doctrine, from which nothing that could be regarded as a personal spiritual stance can be extracted.[5]

The situation is not much different with the interesting figure of Apuleius, who also, in his self-styled capacity as a Platonic philosopher (he may more properly be regarded as a lawyer and rhetorician), writes a treatise on Platonic philosophy, as well as an essay *On the Daemon of Socrates*. These, however, are products of scholasticism and rhetoric respectively and reveal little about Apuleius's personal views, except that he was a Platonist. The personal devotion to Isis shown by Lucius in *Metamorphoses* 11 is possibly much nearer the views of the real Apuleius, but that is more relevant to the beliefs of "ordinary men" than of Platonists as such.

Another quasi-Platonist figure of whom we have evidence is the sophist Maximus of Tyre, a number of whose orations concern topics that could come under the head of "spirituality." Particularly interesting are Oration 2 (Hobein), *Who Is God according to Plato?*, which complements the descriptions of the divinity given by Albinus and Apuleius in the handbooks; Orations 8 and 9, *On the Daemon of Socrates*, which gives a comprehensive theory of daemons analogous to that of Apuleius; Oration 5, *Whether One Should Pray*; and Oration 13, *Whether, If Divination Exists, There Is Free Will*. It is in these last two orations, which concern the problem of providence and free will, that we may most possibly discover something of Maximus's own views, and indeed this topic may serve to unite our discussion of all the previous figures, since the conflict between the doctrines of God's providence and human free will is perhaps the most burning philosophical and spiritual issue in second-century Platonism.

For the Stoics, being materialists and determinists, there is no theological problem (though some logical ones remain), nor is there for the Epicureans, who allow a different sort of determinism to hold sway; but for Platonists (and Aristotelians) the contradiction between the all-foreseeing and all-directing providence of God and the urge to preserve initiative and free choice on the part of the individual was a very grave problem, over which much ink was spilled in this period and later. If all is foreordained, how can there be praise and blame for human actions, and what is the use of praying to the gods? If human beings are free agents, how can their actions be foreseen by God, and in what sense, therefore, is God omniscient?

Besides Maximus's rather superficial contributions, we have a whole essay *On Fate* falsely attributed to Plutarch,[6] another treatise of the same title by the Peripatetic Alexander of Aphrodisias,[7] and chapters in the handbooks of both Albinus (chap. 26) and Apuleius (chap. 12). There is no need in the present instance to go into the complexities of the scholastic solutions offered in particular by Pseudo-Plutarch. Suffice it to say that, although the problem can hardly be said to have been solved in this period, much progress was made toward defining its parameters. Somehow the concepts of providence, free will, fate, and chance have to be fitted harmoniously into an overall world view.

For a Platonist, it is axiomatic, first of all, that God cares for the world, has set the course of events in it in motion, and knows, at least in general, what will happen to it. But it is also axiomatic that the human will is autonomous (this guaranteed for later Platonists by the famous phrase in *Republic* 10.617: "The blame is with the chooser; God is blameless"). It was also generally accepted that, below the Moon at least, *heimarmenē* or Fate, in the sense of a chain of necessary causes, held sway in the physical world and had considerable effect on our lives. But it was held to be somehow subsumed into, or comprehended by, God's providence, and it still left room for *to eph' hēmin*, "what is in our power," or individual discretion. It is in trying to accommodate these two concepts to each other that most ingenuity is expended. Here is Albinus's attempt:

All things are within the sphere of [lit. "in"] Fate, but not all things are fated.
(*Didaskalikos* 26)

Fate has the status of a law. It does not say, as it were, "Because so-and-so has done this, he will suffer this," for that would result in an infinity of possibilities, since the actions that take place are infinite, and the results of them are also infinite.

> [If all things are fated], then what is in our power (*to eph' hēmin*) will disappear, and therefore praise and blame and everything like this.

> [The chain of causality begins] because, if a soul chooses such and such in life, it will then also perform such and such actions, and such and such results will follow for it. The soul is thus autonomous, and it is in its power to act or not, and this is not forced upon it, but what follows upon its action will be brought about in accordance with Fate.

Whether we find this satisfactory or not is beside the point. The important thing is that the preservation of a role for individual free will is a basic condition of Platonic spirituality. Only on this basis do prayer, self-discipline, and the practice of the virtues have any meaning.

It remains to round out our survey by considering at least one important representative of the Pythagorean "wing" of Platonism in this era. I use this form of words, since I do not see Neopythagoreanism as an independent philosophical movement in this era, so much as an attitude that might be taken up within Platonism. Admittedly, there is a tension between devotion to Pythagoras and to Plato as founding fathers, since a Pythagorean will attribute all that is good in Platonism to Pythagoras and his immediate followers and regard Plato as one (admittedly brilliant) follower. One may even become quite belligerent, as does Moderatus of Gades,[8] against the alleged tendency of Platonists to appropriate all that is best in Pythagoreanism for themselves and leave Pythagoreans with the dross. But generally, Pythagoreanism simply means, besides a personal devotion to Pythagoras and particular enthusiasm for number mysticism and a mathematical model for the universe, a more austere stance in ethics and the observance of a certain *bios*, or way of life, involving abstention from meat and beans and the adoption of the other Pythagorean rules, or *symbola*.

Leaving aside the remarkable figure of Apollonius of Tyana, whom I do not see as a philosopher in the strict sense and who may in any case be largely a literary creation of Philostratus, the only Pythagorean of whose spirituality we can form much idea is Numenius of Apamea, and even with him the situation is not very satisfactory, since we have only fragments of his works (once again, as in the case of Atticus, in Eusebius's *Praeparatio evangelica*) and doxographic reports.[9]

One first aspect of Numenius's spirituality to note is his omnivorous hospitality to the great religions of the world. In fragment 1a, we learn from Eusebius of his great respect for the teachings of the Brahmins, the Jews, the Magi, and the Egyptians (only the Druids, it seems, escaped his benevolent attentions). Of course, respect for ancient wisdom is very much a part of Platonism from the time of Plato himself, but Numenius seems to have carried his interest rather further than others, especially in respect to Judaism. Origen tells us (fr. 1b and c) that he discoursed much about the God of the Jews in his dialogue *On the Good* and that he gave allegorical interpretations of the works of Moses and the prophets. There is the intriguing possibility that he was acquainted with the works of Philo, but this cannot be proved. At any rate, from our point of view, what is important is his sense of the unity of religious experience and its concordance with the teaching of Plato and Pythagoras.

Other features of his philosophy connect him in an intriguing way with an extraordinary production of the second century A.D., the so-called *Chaldaean Oracles*,[10] the composition (possibly through a series of mediumistic trances) of a certain Julian in the reign of Marcus Aurelius. Both Numenius and the *Oracles* make a strong distinction between a First God, whom both claim is generally unknown to mortals,[11] and a secondary, demiurgic god, who is immediately responsible for the creation and guidance of the world. This is not a distinction made by Plutarch, though some such distinction appears in chap. 10 of Albinus's *Didaskalikos*. The relations between these two in Numenius's philosophy are of great interest, but not immediately relevant to our purpose. More to our purpose is to observe the mode of approach that Numenius recommends to his supreme principle, since it anticipates to some extent that of Plotinus to the One and may well be in its turn influenced by the doctrine of the *Chaldaean Oracles* that the Father may only be known by the "flower of the intellect," the mystical element in each of us (fr. 1). Fragment 2 of Numenius's *On the Good* provides a striking image of the watcher on the shore catching glimpses of a tiny fishing boat between the waves:

> We can acquire the notion of any material object from the comparison of similar objects and by the distinguishing characteristics of objects available to our sense: the Good, on the other hand, it is quite impossible to grasp on the basis of anything present to us or similar to it, but like someone seated in a lookout post, who, straining his eyes, catches sight for one moment of one of those little fishing vessels, a one-man skiff all on its own, bobbing amid the waves, even so must one remove oneself far from the things of sense, and consort solitarily with the Good in its solitude, where there is neither man nor any other living thing, nor any body great or small, but some unspeakable and truly indescribable wondrous solitude, there where are the accustomed places, the haunts and pleasances of the Good, and it itself in peace, in benevolence, in its tranquillity, in its sovereignty, riding gently upon the surface of Being.

Numenius's view of the world is more starkly dualist than that of Plutarch. Not only does he believe in an evil principle at work in the world,
which he identifies with the Indefinite Dyad of Pythagoreanism (fr. 52), but
he feels a dualism within the individual soul, to the extent of postulating
two souls within each individual (fr. 43), a rational and an irrational. The
descent of the rational soul into body he sees as an unqualified misfortune
(fr. 48), and no reconciliation, only constant struggle, can come about
between these two souls. This "gnostic" view he shares with the *Chaldaean
Oracles* (fr. 102–4, 107, 112), and it adds up to a distinctly world-negating
attitude, in distinction to that of Plutarch.

The spirituality of the second-century Platonists is not, therefore, a
uniform thing, but embraces a fairly broad spectrum of attitudes, particularly toward the physical world and our place in it. The full extent of the
diversity of the views of these thinkers is obscured for us, however, by the
nature of the surviving evidence. Especially in the case of Numenius, we
may regret the loss of a full text of his dialogue *On the Good,* and a man
like Atticus, when not incensed by Peripatetic pretensions, might have
revealed spiritual depths. On the other hand, it was not the fashion among
Platonists of this period, as far as one can see, to compose personal testaments; there is no Platonist equivalent of the *Meditations* of Marcus
Aurelius. Plutarch comes nearest to such self-revelation, but his utterances
are generally given the protective filter of dialogue. Nevertheless, in the case
of Plutarch, at least, one can feel, in reading his works, that one is touching
a man.

Notes

1. Dillon, *Middle Platonists,* 191.
2. See Guy Soury, *La démonologie de Plutarque* (Paris: Les Belles Lettres, 1942); F. E.
Brenk, *In Mist Apparelled,* esp. chaps. 6, 7; and Dillon, *Middle Platonists,* 216–21.
3. Dodds, *Pagan and Christian in an Age of Anxiety.*
4. Fragments are preserved by Eusebius in his *Praeparatio evangelica,* but the material is most conveniently available in the Budé edition of É. des Places (Paris: Les Belles
Lettres, 1977).
5. If indeed Albinus it is. The *Didaskalikos* is attributed in the manuscript to
"Alkinoos." It has long been held that this was a scribal error for "Albinos," but John
Whittaker (whose new Budé edition of the *Didaskalikos* may be expected shortly) has
made a spirited effort to reestablish the name of "Alkinoos." The existing edition is that
of P. Louis (Budé; Paris: Les Belles Lettres, 1945). *Didaskalikos* 19.10 contains interesting doctrine on the nature of God, but it cannot be claimed as personal to Albinus.
6. There is an edition by E. Valgiglio, *Ps.-Plutarco, De Fato* (Rome: A. Signorelli,
1964). See also vol. 6 of the Loeb edition of Plutarch, and Dillon, *Middle Platonists,*
320–26.

7. Now in a good edition by R. W. Sharples, *Alexander of Aphrodisias: On Fate* (London: Duckworth, 1983).

8. See Dillon, *Middle Platonists*, 346.

9. A collection of fragments and good introduction and notes are in the Budé edition of É. des Places, *Numénius* (Paris: Les Belles Lettres, 1973). See also Dillon, *Middle Platonists*, 361-79.

10. Fragments edited by É. des Places (Budé; Paris: Les Belles Lettres, 1971).

11. Numenius fr. 17; des Places; *Chaldaean Oracles*, fr. 7, des Places.

Bibliography

For the translations of Plutarch, I have used those by the various editors of his works in the Loeb Classical Library series, making such minor alterations as seemed desirable: *Plutarch's Moralia* (15 vols.; Cambridge, MA: Harvard University Press, 1949-). All other translations are my own. The relevant literature is not very extensive, but the following works may be helpful:

Babut, Daniel. *Plutarch et le Stoicisme.* Paris: Presses universitaires de France, 1969.

Barrow, Reginald Haynes. *Plutarch and His Times.* Bloomington: Indiana University Press, 1967.

Brenk, Frederick E. *In Mist Apparelled: Religious Themes in Plutarch's Moralia and Lives.* Leiden: Brill, 1977.

Dillon, John. *The Middle Platonists.* Ithaca, NY: Cornell University Press, 1977.

Dodds, E. R. *Pagan and Christian in an Age of Anxiety.* Cambridge: University Press, 1965.

Dörrie, Heinrich. *Platonica Minora.* Munich: W. Fink, 1976. (Collected essays on Middle Platonism).

Krämer, Hans Joachim. *Der Ursprung der Geistmetaphysik.* Amsterdam: B. R. Güner, 1967.

Merlan, Philip. *From Platonism to Neoplatonism.* 2nd rev. ed. The Hague: Nijhoff, 1960.

———. "The Later Academy and Platonism" and "The Pythagoreans." Chaps. 4 and 5 of *The Cambridge History of Later Greek and Early Medieval Philosophy.* Edited by A. H. Armstrong. Cambridge: University Press, 1970.

———. *Monopsychism, Mysticism, Metaconsciousness: Problems of the Soul in the Neo-aristotelian and Neoplatonic Tradition.* The Hague: Nijhoff, 1963.

Theiler, Willy. *Die Vorbereitung des Neuplatonismus.* Berlin: Weidmann, 1930.

"Plutarch and Second Century Platonism" originally published in CLASSICAL MEDITERRANEAN SPIRITUALITY: Egyptian, Greek, Roman edited by A.H. Armstrong (World Spirituality Vol. 16). Copyright © 1986 by the Crossroad Publishing Company. Reprinted by permission of the publisher.

NOTE: P.221, with a plate of no relevance to this study, has been omitted.

XIV

Harpocration's *Commentary on Plato*: Fragments of a Middle Platonic Commentary

I.

Our evidence for the form and content of pre-Neoplatonic (pre-Porphyrian) commentaries on Plato is not great. Apart from one valuable fragment of a commentary on the *Theaetetus*, we have only a number of essays on particular subjects—Plutarch on *The Immortality of the Soul in the Timaeus*, and Theo of Smyrna's work "*An Exposition of Mathematical Matters Useful for the Reading of Plato*"—and the evidence derivable from the doxographies of the Neoplatonists. Calcidius' *Commentary on the Timaeus* I believe also to be essentially Middle Platonic, but his status is still controversial.[1]

In reading the commentaries of Proclus, Hermeias, and Olympiodorus one is driven again and again to the conclusion, from the form in which pre-Porphyrian references are given, that normally it is to the vast researches of Porphyry that his successors are indebted for their references to earlier opinions. This is especially clear in Proclus'

[1] J. H. Waszink, in his *Studien zum Timaioskommentar des Calcidius* (*Philosophia Antiqua*, vol. 12, Brill 1964), and in his great edition of Calcidius' *Commentary on the Timaeus* (*Corpus Platonicum Medii Aevi*, vol. IV, 1962) has argued for a dependence of Calcidius on the work of Porphyry. I am unable to see that the possible dependences on Porphyry, all of which I feel can equally well be taken to be a common Middle Platonic heritage, can outweigh the total lack in Calcidius of the characteristic Neoplatonic metaphysics and form of commentary, both of which appear to be largely the work of Porphyry.

Commentary on the Timaeus, where we often find Porphyry's views following immediately on those of his predecessors.[2]

One derives from the evidence the impression that the Middle Platonist commentators are direct forerunners of the Neoplatonists in all respects except in the elaboration of their metaphysics, and in the symbolical interpretation of the characters, and the introductory portions of the dialogues (the *prooemia*), which are such notable characteristics of the Neoplatonist commentaries. Like their successors, the Middle Platonists discussed matters of antiquarian, historical or philological interest, gave an "ethical" interpretation of the text, and carefully distinguished the formal logical steps, the syllogisms, both categorical and hypothetical, which they discerned latent in Plato's argumentation. Their determination in unveiling these is well illustrated in Albinus' *Didascalicus.* The form of their commentaries, to judge from the *Theaetetus* Commentary, consisted of almost continuous exegesis of the text, sometimes with sections of the text forming *lemmata* for separate sections, sometimes with the text integrated into the commentary. Calcidius exhibits the latter format. This is less formally structured than the Procline commentary, but we cannot be sure that Porphyry's or Iamblichus' method was not nearer to that of the Middle Platonists than that of Proclus or Olympiodorus.

The commentaries of the Middle Platonists in general reveal the combination of Plato's metaphysics, Stoic-Academic ethics and Peripatetic-Stoic logic for which Middle Platonism is well known. My aim in the present investigation is to try to reconstruct something of the form and content of one commentary by a neglected Middle Platonist, the *Commentary on Plato* of Harpocration of Argos.

Harpocration was a pupil of Atticus (Procl. *In Tim.* 1.305.6),[3] who was head of the Platonic Academy in the mid-second

---

[2] E.g., Procl. *In Tim.* 1.77.6ff on Atlantis; 1.219.21ff; 1.306.31ff, on the identity of the Demiurge; 3.234.18ff, etc. The doxographic pattern "Anonymi (Plutarch, Atticus, Numenius, etc.) Porphyry (and/or Iamblichus, who seems to have largely copied him)" is a common one in Proclus' *In Timaeum,* which is by far our most comprehensive source.

[3] Von Arnim in *P-W* s.v. *Harpokration* (2), and Zeller, *Phil. d. Gr.* III[2]: 2, p. 200 summarize Harpocration's philosophical position. The Suda describes him as συμβιωτὴς Καίσαρος, but one cannot safely infer from this his identity with the Harpocration who is listed by Julius Capitolinus (*Script. Hist. Aug. Verus* II 5) as a tutor of the future emperor Verus. This Harpocration is serving as a *grammaticus,* while Verus' tutors in philosophy are listed as the Stoic Apollonius, and Plutarch's nephew Sextus of Chaeroneia, both teachers of Marcus Aurelius. It is always possible, of course, that Harpocration accepted the humbler position of *grammaticus,* for want of anything better. He may have been young at the time.

century A.D. It seems implied by Proclus in the passage above-mentioned (*ibid.* 304.24) that Harpocration is referring to Numenius in his commentary at this point, so that he may be placed after Numenius in time and also in influence.[4] Suidas (*s.v.* Ἁρποκρατίων, Ἀργεῖος) credits him with: ὑπόμνημα εἰς Πλάτωνα ἐν βιβλίοις κδ', Λέξεις Πλάτωνος ἐν βιβλίοις β'. Of these works it is obviously the former with which we have to do. Suidas plainly envisages one continuous work, of twenty-four books, containing a commentary on Plato's dialogues, presumably dialogue by dialogue. We have no indications on this point, but we have comments by Harpocration preserved on the following dialogues: Alcibiades I, Phaedo, Phaedrus, Timaeus, and Republic.

I feel that it is worthwhile dealing individually with every reference to this commentary, in order to gain as extensive a notion as possible of the range of it. I will accordingly examine in turn all Harpocration's comments on the dialogues listed above, including also the references to Harpocration in Iamblichus' *De Anima*, where the connection with a particular dialogue is not so clear. (I number the fragments consecutively for convenience in later reference.)

II. ALCIBIADES I

1. Ad *Alcibiadem* 104 E. (*ap.* Ol. *In Alc.* 48.26ff).

Olympiodorus quotes Harpocration on the lemma πάλαι ἂν ἀπηλλάγμην in what for Olympiodorus is the *lexis* as opposed to the *theoria*, the detailed commentary on the text, as opposed to the general discussion of the philosophical content. Socrates is saying that if he had felt that Alcibiades was satisfied with his present situation, he would long since have abandoned his love for him:

ἐνταῦθα γενόμενος ὁ Ἁρποκρατίων καὶ καλῶς
προσεσχηκὼς τῷ ῥητῷ, γραμμικαῖς ἀνάγκαις ἔδειξε τὸν
Σωκράτην ἔνθεον ἐράστην· εἴ φησιν ἐνταῦθα ὅτι 'πάλαι ἂν

---

4 Proclus gives, at *In Remp.* 2.96 Kroll, the following list of Middle Platonists who commented on the Myth of the *Republic*: "Numenius, Albinus, Gaius, Maximus of Nicaea, Harpocration, Eucleides." Neither Maximus of Nicaea nor Eucleides are otherwise known, except that they must be prior to Porphyry, as Proclus ends his list "καὶ ἐπὶ πᾶσιν Πορφύριος." Ancient doxographies are notoriously loose about chronological order, but this one may, I think, be taken, in conjunction with *In Tim.* 1.305.6, to indicate that Harpocration is later than Numenius, and thus later also than Gaius and Albinus, who are more or less contemporary with Numenius (ca. A.D. 150).

128

ἀπηλλάγμην᾽, ὁ δὲ φορτικὸς ἐραστὴς οὐχ ὅτε θέλει ἀπαλλάττεται
ἅτε ἐκ πάθους τοιοῦτος ὤν, τῶν δὲ παθῶν οὐχ ὅτε θέλομεν
ἀπαλλαττόμεθα, καθάπερ οὔτε ἀρχόμεθα, δῆλον ὅτι ἔνθεός
ἐστιν ἐραστής. οὗτος γὰρ ὅτε θέλει ἄρχεται, θέλει δὲ ὅτε
ἀξιέραστα εἴη τὰ παιδικά· οὐκοῦν καὶ ὅτε θέλει παύεται,
καθάπερ καὶ ἐνταῦθά φησιν ὅτι 'εἰ ἑώρων σε ἀληθῶς τῶν
φαινομένων ἀγαθῶν ἐφιέμενον, πάλαι ἂν ἀπηλλαττόμην τοῦ
ἔρωτος᾽.

What were these γραμμικαὶ ἀνάγκαί that Harpocration is
employing here? A statement of proportion, perhaps, which attains
geometrical rigor.[5] Proclus does not mention Harpocration in the
corresponding passage in his commentary (*In Alc.* 134.11ff), but he
refers to οἱ γεωμέτραι (*ibid.* 15). The question is, by what proportion
does the ἔνθεος ἐραστής surpass the φορτικός? As Proclus sets it out
there are φυσικὰ πλεονεκτήματα and ψυχικὰ κινήματα; the latter are
superior to the former. The divine lover is capable of resisting not only
"physical allurements" but also "spiritual impulses"; the vulgar lover
is ensnared not only by spiritual impulses but also by physical allurements. At the risk of indulging in a scholastic romp (which nevertheless
may represent good Middle Platonic procedure), we may express the
proportion, e.g., ὁ φορτικὸς ἐραστής < φυσικὰ πλεονεκτήματα < ψυχικὰ
κινήματα < ὁ ἔνθεος ἐραστής (< signifying "is inferior to" or "subject
to").

The divinely-inspired lover is thus superior to the vulgar
lover in the following proportion: if the "divine" lover is A, and the
vulgar B, the physical allurements X, and the "activities of the soul"
Y; then B < (is subject to) X, X < (are of less value or power than)
Y, and A > (is superior to, in control of) Y (or Y < A). Therefore
B ≪ A. Or something such. At all events, a properly Middle Platonic
pastime.

We may note in passing Olympiodorus' apparent independent knowledge of Harpocration. Proclus certainly knows him also,
but in the *Alcibiades* Commentary he is sparing of doxography. This is,
however, Olympiodorus' only reference to Harpocration in the
Alcibiades Commentary.

[5] Olympiodorus uses the phrase also at *In Gorg.* 92.6 Norvin: δείξει τοίνυν ὁ
Σωκράτης γραμμικαῖς ἀνάγκαις, ὅτι ὁ δίκαιός ἐστιν εὐδαίμων καὶ ὁ μὴ ἔχων δικαιοσύνην οὐκ ἐστιν
εὐδαίμων. There it refers to strict logical proof.

III. Phaedo

2. Ad *Phaedonem* 63 E (*ap.* Ol. *In Phaed.* 20.4ff *Norv.*) ἀνὴρ
τῷ ὄντι ἐν φιλοσοφίᾳ διατρίψας τὸν βίον.

τῷ ὄντι φιλόσοφον λέγει οὐ πρὸς ἀντιδιαστολὴν
τοῦ σοφιστοῦ ὑποδυομένου τὸν φιλόσοφον, ὡς οἱ περὶ
Ἁρποκρατίωνα ἠξίωσαν ἀκούειν· τοῦτο γὰρ πόρρω τῆς
Πλάτωνος μεγαλονοίας· ἀλλὰ πρὸς ἀντιδιαστολὴν τοῦ πολιτικοῦ.
καθαρτικὸς γὰρ ὁ διάλογος.

We would surely agree with Harpocration as against
Olympiodorus, who represents the Iamblichean "higher criticism,"
according to which the *skopos* of this dialogue is the "purificatory
virtues"; these follow upon the "political virtues," which are the subject
of the *Gorgias*, which preceded the *Phaedo* in Iamblichus' pedagogic
scheme.[6] Harpocration had no such scheme, so that nothing hindered
him from giving the more natural interpretation to the text.

The phrase "οἱ περὶ Ἁρποκρατίωνα" could, but need not,
signify the existence of a school of followers of Harpocration. This
expression is used loosely by Neoplatonic commentators, and seems often
merely a stylistic variation of the writer's simple name, e.g., οἱ περὶ
Νουμήνιον, Procl. *In Tim.* 3.196.18; οἱ περὶ Πορφύριον *ibid.* 234,18;
οἱ περὶ Ἀττικόν, *ibid.* 37.12. All these men had followers—indeed
among those of Atticus we might include Harpocration—but the chance
of the phrase referring to independent commentaries is slight.

3. Ad *Phaedonem* 66 C (*ap.* "Ol." *In Phaed.* B ρθ′ 106.11)
διὰ γὰρ τὴν τῶν χρημάτων κτῆσιν πάντες οἱ πόλεμοι γίνονται.

Πῶς διὰ τὰ χρήματα πάντες οἱ πόλεμοι γίνονται;
πολλοὶ γὰρ καὶ δι' ἄλλας αἰτίας ἐγένοντο. ῥητέον οὖν, ὡς μὲν
Ἁρποκρατίων, ἢ ὅτι ἐπὶ τὸ πλεῖστον, ἢ ὅτι καὶ ἡ τῶν λαφύρων
ἐλπὶς ἐπιτείνει τὸν πόλεμον·

Harpocration here is quoted not by Olympiodorus himself, but by one of the anonymous commentaries (*B*) attached to his

6 See further on this subject A–J. Festugiere, "L'ordre de lecture des
dialogues de Platon aux Vᵉ/VIᵉ siecles," *Mus. Helv.* 26 (1969) 281ff.

* commentary, which are suspected by Westerink,[7] with considerable plausibility, of being records of the lectures of Damascius. Olympiodorus himself discusses the point raised, in 6.8, p. 36, 25ff, and refers to Harpocration at p. 37, 1ff:

> ἄλλοι φασίν, ὅτι πάντες οἱ πόλεμοι διὰ χρήματα γίνονται, τουτέστι διὰ λάφυρα· ἀλλὰ γίνονται πόλεμοι καὶ διὰ φιλοτιμίαν, εἰ ἄρα τις καὶ ταύτην ἐθέλει λέγειν λάφυρον.

Obviously this was an *aporia*, of the class which I would term eristic *aporiai*, many examples of which are dealt with, e.g., in Proclus' *Commentary on the Timaeus*. These are always anonymous, but must stem from non-Platonist critics who were giving Plato the same sort of treatment as, for instance, Nicostratus gave Aristotle's *Categories*. Harpocration doubtless dealt explicitly with the *aporia*, making two suggestions. The first utilizes the old argument that a thing may be named from its predominant element—in this case, war is said to arise from concern for material goods, because it *generally* arises from this. He then contributes a second, somewhat less impressive suggestion, that it is because of the fact that hope of booty incites war. Olympiodorus amalgamates the two suggestions, and criticizes the second one. The problem exercised the later commentators also, Longinus and οἱ Ἀττικοὶ ἐξηγηταί being also mentioned by *B*, who gives a solution of his own.

The answering of *aporiai*, real or invented, should also be reckoned as a regular component of the Middle Platonic commentary.

4. Ad *Phaedonem*, 68BC (*ap*. Ol. *In Phaed*. 41.17f): Οὐκοῦν ἱκανόν σοι τεκμήριον, ἔφη, τοῦτο ἀνδρός, ὃν ἂν ἴδῃς ἀγανακτοῦντα μέλλοντα ἀποθανεῖσθαι, ὅτι οὐκ ἄρ᾽ ἦν φιλόσοφος ἀλλά τις φιλοσώματος; ὁ αὐτὸς δέ που οὗτος τυγχάνει ὢν καὶ φιλοχρήματος καὶ φιλότιμος, ἤτοι τὰ ἔτερα τούτων ἢ ἀμφότερα.

καὶ διὰ τί τὸ φιλήδονον παρῆκεν; ὁ μὲν Ἀρποκρατίων ἀπορήσας οὐκ ἐπελύσατο......
This bald statement is amplified by *B*, p. 113, 1ff:

> Διὰ τί παρέλειπεν τὸ φιλήδονον; ὁ γὰρ φιλοσώμ- ατος εἴη ἂν καὶ φιλήδονος. ἢ ὅτι ὁ φιλοσώματος οὗτός ἐστι·

---

[7] Damascius, *Lectures on the Philebus*, ed. L. G. Westerink. Intro. pp. xv–xx.

προστίθενται δὲ καὶ οἱ ἄλλοι. ἢ ἐν τοῖς πρόσθεν τοῦτον
ἀπεσκευάσατο, νῦν δὲ παρατίθεται τοὺς τότε παραλειφθέντας.
οὕτως μὲν Ἁρποκρατίων ἐξηγεῖται.

It sounds from Olympiodorus' words as if Harpocration
had introduced this *aporia* himself. As it turns out, Olympiodorus
oversimplifies in saying merely that Harpocration "did not solve the
problem." He in fact offers two solutions, though he adopts neither. (1)
The "lover of pleasure" does not need to be further mentioned since
he is implied in the "lover of body" in the first sentence. (2) Plato has
already mentioned and rejected the love of pleasure in 64D, and only
needs now to mention what he left out then. Somebody is confused here,
since Olympiodorus (*loc. cit.*) attributes this second solution to Proclus:
ὁ δέ γε Πρόκλος φησίν, ὅτι φιλήδονον οὐκ ἐμνημόνευσεν, διότι ἀνωτέρω
εἶπεν, ὅτι δεῖ φεύγειν τὰς ἡδονάς. There is no difficulty, perhaps, in
assuming merely that Proclus adopted Harpocration's second suggestion, but it shows an interesting independence of sources on the part
of *B*.

5. Ad *Phaed.* 69AC. Ὦ μακάριε Σιμμία, . . . μὴ καθαρμός
τις ᾖ.

This is the passage in which Socrates speaks of φρόνησις as
the proper ethical unit of exchange, and deprecates the balancing of
pleasures and pains and fears against each other, without making use of
this one valid element. With φρόνησις the virtues are true virtues,
without it they are shadows of virtue. To describe these latter, later
Platonists, if the present passage may be trusted, seem to have fathered
upon Plato the term ψευδώνυμοι. Plato himself calls such ἀρετή
'σκιαγραφία τις' (67B7). The pseudo-virtues are such courage and
self-control and justice as result from a nice calculation of advantage;
the real virtues are these same virtues practiced now only with reference
to "wisdom," which for Plato here was perhaps a covert, or half-
formulated, reference to the Good.

This being the situation given, the question was raised as
to what virtues Plato wished to distinguish from what, and which
virtues the purified sage (ὁ κεκαθαρμένος τε καὶ τετελεσμένος of 69C)
should retain.

Let us now consider Harpocration's position ("Ol." B p.
115, 8ff N):

"Ὅτι σκοπὸς αὐτῷ ἀποδιακρῖναι καὶ ὡς ἀληθῶς
καθᾶραι τὰς καθαρτικὰς ἀρετὰς τῶν καταδεεστέρων πασῶν
ἀρετῶν, οὐ μόνον τῶν ψευδωνύμων, ὡς Ἁρποκρατίων, ἀλλὰ
καὶ τῶν ἐσκιαγραφημένων, οἷον τῶν φυσικῶν τε καὶ ἠθικῶν,
οὐδὲ τούτων μόνον, ἀλλὰ καὶ τῶν τελείων πολιτικῶν. ἀποκρίνας
γὰρ τὰς κακίας εἰκότως νῦν καὶ τὰς χείρους ἀρετὰς ἀποκαθαίρει.

*   This seems to me a profoundly confused note, perhaps the
fault of the student who copied it down. The true contrast to be made is
between the ψευδώνυμοι or ἐσκιαγραφημέναι virtues, that is, the physical
and ethical, which Harpocration (surely correctly) believes are here
being distinguished from the purificatory virtues, and on the other hand
the political virtues, which the Neoplatonic commentators also considered to be here rejected. I would excise the first ἀλλὰ καὶ, before
τῶν ἐσκιαγραφημένων, if I did not suspect the corruption of being
basic to the text. The translation should run as follows:

> Plato's aim here is to distinguish off and in
> truth purify the purificatory virtues from all the inferior
> virtues, *not only* the " pseudonymous " ones, as Harpocration
> declares—the "shadow-virtues," such as the physical and
> ethical—not only these, *but also* the strictly political ones;
> for having separated off the vices, it is reasonable for
> him now to purge away the inferior virtues.

The basis of the quarrel of the later commentators with
Harpocration here, as in Fr. 2 above, is simply their dependence on the
Iamblichean table of the virtues, together with Iamblichus' order of the
dialogues, which was based on this table. Iamblichus laid down, in all,
seven grades of virtue, which the *B* commentary sets out at 113.14–
114.25 (Βρλς'–ρμβ'). Iamblichus' fullest statement of his arrangement
seems to have come in the lost Περὶ Ἀρετῶν which is referred to at
113.21, and is doubtless being summarized here.

The levels of virtues are as follows:

(1) φυσικαί, such as are common to us and the beasts, e.g.,
lions are courageous, oxen prudent, storks just, and cranes wise (cf. Ol.
In Phaed. 45.19ff). These are closely involved with one's physical makeup,
and may be mutually opposed to one another. They are discussed in the
Statesman (306A) and in the *Laws* (VII 807C, XII 963E).

(2) ἠθικαί. These are acquired by practice (ἐθισμός) and correct belief (ὀρθοδοξία), and are proper to well brought-up children and also to some animals. They also are dependent on one's physical make-up and may conflict with one another. They are a joint product of the reason and the unreasoning element of the soul (λόγος and ἀλογία). These are also discussed in the *Laws* (Books VII to VIII 842A).

(3) πολιτικαί. These are products of the reason alone, for they involve knowledge (ἐπιστήμη), but of reason as administering the unreasoning element as its instrument, i.e., using wisdom to bring order to the knowledge-acquiring element, courage to the spirited element, self-control to the libido, and justice to all of them. The political virtues do not oppose, but complement each other. They are discussed in the *Republic* (e.g., 4.441A), and are the subject of the *Gorgias*.

(4) καθαρτικαί. These are virtues proper to the Reason alone. They are the virtues of one who has turned towards himself and cast aside all material instruments and the activities connected with them. These are primarily discussed in the *Phaedo*.

(5) θεωρητικαί. These are the virtues of a soul which has already abandoned itself and turned to what is above itself. These are the converse of the "political" virtues, inasmuch as the latter concern the Reason insofar as it directs itself towards what is inferior to it, whereas the former are concerned with the Reason's striving towards what is superior to it. These are the subject of the *Theaetetus* (172C–176E).

(6) παραδειγματικαί. These are virtues of the soul when it is no longer contemplating the Intellect (for this implies separation). These virtues are properly those of the Intellect. It is not clear in which dialogue these virtues are discussed, but I suspect the *Phaedrus* (247Eff), with the account of the ὑπερουράνιος τόπος.

(7) ἱερατικαί. These come into being in the godlike (θεοειδές) element of the soul, surpassing all the aforementioned virtues, as being proper to the One (ἐνιαῖαι), whereas they are proper to Being (οὐσιώδεις). It seems probable that these were thought to have been discussed in the *Philebus*.

This digression may perhaps seem excessive, but it serves to reveal a range of complexities of which Harpocration could have no notion, and which make Neoplatonic criticism of his interpretation so irrelevant. In general, for the post-Iamblichean commentators, the

134

Phaedo, being next "above" the *Gorgias*, must be referring to, and distinguishing itself from, the subject matter of the Gorgias, that is to say, ὁ πολιτικός and the "political" virtues.

Harpocration, then, made a simple distinction between the pseudonymous or "shadow" virtues, and the true "pure" virtues of the philosopher, surely the distinction which Plato is in fact making.

He also, it seems, answered an *aporia* posed by the Peripatetics (p. 115, 19ff):

> Ὅτι ἀποροῦσιν οἱ Περιπατητικοί πῶς ἂν τῷ στελλομένῳ πρὸς θεωρίαν ἁρμόζοιεν αἱ ἄλλαι τρεῖς (sc. ἀρεταί) οὔτε ἀταξίας τῶν παθῶν ἐκεῖ ὑποκειμένης οὔτε ὅλως ἀλογίας παθῶν, ἀλλ' οὐδὲ ἐνεργειῶν τοῦ λόγου τῶν πρὸς ταῦτα κατιουσῶν καὶ δεομένων διὰ τοῦτο, καθάπερ ὅπλων, τῶν ἀρετῶν εἰς τὸν τῆς γενέσεως πόλεμον. διὸ μηδὲ τοῖς θεοῖς αὐτὰς ἐνεῖναι, ἄτε μηδὲν αὐτῶν δεομένοις.
>
> ὁ μὲν οὖν Ἁρποκρατίων εἴξας καὶ ἐνταῦθα τὰς ἐν Πολιτείᾳ φησὶ παραδίδοσθαι· . . .

Why does the Sage require these other virtues, ἀνδρεία, σωφροσύνη, δικαιοσύνη, any more than the gods will, if he is to have no contact with the physical world? Harpocration's reply is interesting, though not satisfactory to the *B* commentator, since it seems to make the virtues as set out in the *Republic* pure forms of the virtues such as are suitable to a sage (or a philosopher-king). Harpocration would thus, presumably, accept the formula for the political virtues as set out in the table above that they are virtues of the *logos* in its administration of what is below it. While in the body, the sage cannot divest himself of the lower parts of himself; he can only bring them under proper control. The difficulty raised by the Peripatetics is thus without force. Whether the gods (or the disembodied souls) have need of these three virtues, is another question, and we do not have Harpocration's verdict on it. The Neoplatonists did ascribe all the virtues to the gods as well, but exercised in a mode proper to gods, a piece of metaphysical double-talk to which Harpocration was not equal.

The matter is raised again at B ρξβ´, p. 120, 1ff, where we are told that οἱ Ἀττικοὶ ἐξηγηταί (the Athenian School) ranked the perfect virtues exercisable on earth as "purificatory," while Harpocration ranked them all as "political"—in other words, the virtues as described in the *Republic*.

6. *Ad Phaed.* 70B: ἢ περὶ αὐτῶν τούτων βούλει διαμυθο-
λογῶμεν, εἴτε εἰκὸς οὕτως ἔχειν εἴτε μή;

An aporia arose, it seems, as to why Plato used the term
εἰκός here, instead, presumably, of "ἀληθὲς τοῦτ᾽ ἐστιν" or something
such. The point of the *aporia* may have been to establish Plato's, or
Socrates', essential nondogmatism.

Harpocration's reply (*Βρπ᾽*, p. 126, 1f) was 'ὅτι ἀπὸ
τεκμηρίου', i.e., he uses the term "likely" simply to mean "the natural
conclusion from a syllogistical proof." This is a reasonably common
Socratic expression, and the aporia is mischievous. Harpocration deals
with it reasonably. The matter was not left at that, however. The whole
passage runs as follows:

> Διὰ τί εἰκός ἔφη; ἢ ὡς πρὸς τὴν ἐκεῖ ἀλήθειαν.
> ἢ ὅτι ἀπὸ τεκμηρίου, ὡς Ἁρποκρατίων, ἢ, ὡς ἔφη, ὅτι ἐνδέξεται
> εἶναι ἐν Ἅιδου· οὐ γὰρ πάντως· εἰ γὰρ ἄπειροι αἱ ψυχαί, μένει ἡ
> γένεσις. βέλτιον δὲ τὸ μὴ ἀεὶ τοῦ εἰκότος αἰτιᾶσθαι· οὐ γάρ, εἴ
> ποτε διαμένειν ἐνδέχεται, ἤδη καὶ ἀεὶ διαμένει.

Why does he use the word "likely"? Perhaps
in relation to the truth of the other realm. Or perhaps
because it is a conclusion from evidence, as Harpocration
suggests. Or perhaps, *as he said*, because it is contingent
whether or not one may be in Hades; for this is not
necessarily the case; for if souls are infinite in number,
generation will continue. It is better, however, to explain
the word "likely" as implying that this is not *eternally*
true; for it is not the case that, if a soul may continue to
exist for a while, that it is already proved by this that it
exists eternally.

The last opinion is presumably that of Damascius, or *B*.
To whom, then, does ὡς ἔφη refer? It may, of course, be a reference
to Plato's own argument, as understood by *B*. It is possible, again, that
it is an elliptical report, by *B*, of what *Proclus* may have said (he is thus
referred to from time to time in the *Philebus* Commentary, e.g., φησίν,
22.4 West.; 70.3 etc.) but I am inclined to refer it to Harpocration,
although I find the phraseology in that case rather odd. If we may
assume, however, that Harpocration is being here referred to, we can
credit him with a further, most interesting suggestion. It is possible, he

136

suggests, that there is a continuous creation of souls, *ad infinitum*. The process of generation could then continue, even though souls dissolved upon death. This was a most heretical notion from the Platonic point of view (though an orthodox *Christian* one), and Harpocration is not proposing it, except as a possibility, but it is, after all, only an extension of the heretical view of Plutarch and Atticus that the world was created in Time. Where there is one creation *ex nihilo*, a presumption is created that there may be more.[8]

We may introduce at this point an interesting testimony from Aeneas of Gaza, very possibly reflecting Harpocration's comments on *Phaedo* 81.d9–82.b8:

7. Aen. Gaz. *Theophr.* 12.1ff Colonna:

> Οἱ μὲν παλαιοὶ μυσταγωγοὶ τῶν λεγομένων
> μετεκίνησαν οὐδέν, εὖ εἰδότες ὅτι τῶν Αἰγυπτίων ὁ Πλάτων τὴν
> παιδείαν δεδιδαχὼς καὶ παρ' ἐκείνων διατεθρυλλημένος τὰ
> ὦτα, ὡς ἡ τῶν ἀνθρώπων ψυχὴ πάντα τὰ ζῷα μεταβαίνει,
> πανταχοῦ τῶν λόγων διασπείρει τὸ δόγμα. Πλωτῖνος γοῦν καὶ
> Ἁρποκρατίων, ἀμέλει καὶ Βοηθὸς καὶ Νουμήνιος τὸν τοῦ
> Πλάτωνος ἰκτῖνον παραλαβόντες, ἰκτῖνον παραδιδόασι καὶ τὸν
> λύκον λύκον καὶ ὄνον τὸν ὄνον· καὶ ὁ πίθηκος αὐτοῖς οὐκ ἄλλο ἢ
> τοῦτο καὶ ὁ κύκνος οὐκ ἄλλο ἢ κύκνος νομίζεται καὶ πρὸ τοῦ
> σώματος κακίας ἐμπίπλασθαι τὴν ψυχὴν δυνατὸν εἶναι λέγουσι
> καὶ τοῖς ἀλόγοις ἐξεικάζεσθαι· ᾧ γοῦν ὡμοιώθη, κατὰ τοῦτο
> φέρεται, ἄλλη ἄλλο ζῷον ὑποδῦσα.

Most of the animals mentioned here—the kite, the wolf, the ass—are mentioned in *Phaedo* 81d8ff, along with wasps, bees, and ants, which are probably reflected in the "ants and flies" which Harpocration is accused by Hermeias of immortalising in Fr. 10 below. The swan and the ape are taken, of course, from the Myth of the *Republic* (620Aff), where Orpheus and Thersites are seen in the forms of swan and ape respectively.

This question of metempsychosis into animals was a hotly debated one in later Platonism. Aeneas goes on to say (12.11ff)

---

[8] We know in fact that Harpocration followed his master Atticus in holding that the world was created in Time. (*Schol. Cod. Vat. in* Procl. *In Remp.* 20.377.15f. Kroll = Frag. 13 below.)

that both Porphyry and Iamblichus later rose above this literal interpretation, and declared that Plato was referring in fact only to different styles of human life. Nemesius of Emesa (*De Nat. Hom.* ss. 50–52, p. 115, 4ff Matth.) discussing the same point, gives a somewhat different doxography. He does not mention Harpocration or Boethus or Numenius or Plotinus for the literal interpretation, but he refers instead (p. 117, 1 Matth.) to an essay by Cronius Περὶ παλιγγενεσίας, as well as to Porphyry and Theodorus of Asine, as all supporting the literal interpretation. He then represents Iamblichus (117.5ff) as opposing all these, and drawing a strict division between human and animal souls.

The *C* commentator on the *Phaedo* discusses the controversy *ad loc.* (p. 166, 24ff N.), but without mentioning names:

> Ὅτι τὴν εἰς τὰ ἄλλα εἴδη μετεμψύχωσιν οἱ μὲν παλαιότεροι Πλατωνικοὶ κατὰ συμπλήρωσιν ἐξηγοῦνται, οἷς πολλὰ μὲν οἱ ἀκριβέστεροι ἀντιλέγουσιν, ἐκεῖνο δὲ μέγιστον τεκμήριον ὅτι μὴ οὕτως εἴρηται, τὸ εἰς θεῶν γένος ἀφικνεῖσθαί τινας· ὡς οὖν οὗτοι οὐ συμπληροῦσι θεούς, οὐδὲ ἐκεῖνοι τὰ ἄλλα ζῷα.

The argument from συμπλήρωσις needs elucidation, which it receives from what follows. The earlier Platonists argued that there must be metempsychosis into animals from the necessity of filling up the quota for each species. They must have derived this notion from *Timaeus* 42BC, where one might assume that at first only souls for male humans are created, then souls for women, and then those for irrational animals. The argument against this, by "the more accurate," is that we agree that certain men become gods, but that does not imply that the quota of *divine* souls needed filling up.

C next mentions those who give a metaphorical, or "ethical" explanation, to which he appends a refutation by his master. He then brings forward a third group of literal interpreters, of whom he seems to approve (p. 167, 5ff):

> τρίτοι δὲ οἱ κατὰ ἐπακολούθησιν τὴν σὺν τοῖς ἀλόγοις ζῴοις ἔξωθεν γιγνομένην, ὧν τὴν δόξαν βεβαιοῖ τό τε ὅμοιον τῷ ὁμοίῳ συντεῖναι βουλόμενον καὶ τὸ οὕτω σαφῶς εἰς θεοὺς ἀπιέναι καὶ συνδιατρίβειν θεοῖς οὕτως εἰρημένον πρότερον,

καὶ εἰ περὶ τὰ μνήματα ἀναγκάζονται πλανᾶσθαι ὑπὸ τῆς δίκης,
διὰ τί οὐχὶ καὶ περὶ τὰ ἄλογα ζῶα, εἰ καὶ ἀλλότρια ὄντα, ὅμως
καλλίω τῶν νεκρῶν σωμάτων.

An argument from the "natural consequence," κατ᾽
ἐπακολούθησιν, is here proposed, which may also be termed an argument from ὁμοίωσις. Like tends to like, so why may not the soul of a
human "ass" tend towards the body of a real ass? It is no stranger,
after all, than the fact of impure souls frequenting graveyards.

Somewhere within these two types of literal interpreter,
almost certainly, lurks Harpocration. I would tend to place him in the
second group, on the basis of the phraseology of Aeneas, who is admittedly speaking generally of the whole group Boethus-Numenius-
Harpocration-Plotinus, but who does say "δυνατὸν εἶναι λέγουσι καὶ τοῖς
ἀλόγοις ἐξεικάζεσθαι· ᾧ γοῦν ὡμοιώθη, κατὰ τοῦτο φέρεται, ἄλλη ἄλλο ζῷον
ὑποδῦσα."

There is one further recorded comment by Harpocration
on the *Phaedo*.

8. Ad *Phaed.* 108C: εἰσὶ δὲ πολλοὶ καὶ θαυμαστοὶ τῆς γῆς
τόποι, κ.τ.λ.

There was much confusion as to what Plato could have
meant here by "the earth." Nobody, it seems, before Damascius
assumed that he simply meant the earth. I quote the whole section
(C III λή, p. 193, 27ff):

> Ὅτι τὴν γῆν οἱ μὲν ἀσώματόν φασι τὴν
> ἐνταῦθα λεγομένην, οἱ δὲ σωματικὴν, καὶ τούτων ὅλον μὲν τὸν
> κόσμον Ἁρποκρατίων, τὸν δὲ ὑπὸ σελήνην Θεόδωρος· τῶν δὲ
> ἀσώματον τὴν μὲν ἰδέαν Δημόκριτος, τὴν δὲ φύσιν Πλούταρχος.

"Plutarch" here is almost certainly Plutarch of Athens,
so that, apart from the shadowy Democritus, probably a third-century
Platonist, Harpocration's is the only Middle Platonic exegesis recorded. He assumed that Plato was referring to something material, and
suggested the whole cosmos. Presumably the greater expansion of
geographical knowledge since Plato's day had made it seem incredible
that Socrates could be referring here to our earth. Hence the elaborate
explanations. Damascius (*C*) pours cold water very properly on all these

suggestions in the next sentence: "πρὸς πάντας ἑνὶ λόγῳ ἀντιρρητέον, ὡς περὶ τῆς αὐτῆς τοῖς γεωγράφοις διαλέγεται ὁ Σωκράτης."

That is the extent of Harpocration's recorded comments on the *Phaedo*. We can see, I think, even from this meager collection, something of the nature of his commentary, chiefly concerned with the interpretation of words and phrases, usually in the form of *aporiai* and *luseis*, often defending Plato from hostile criticism. The more general substance of his commentary, the explanation of Plato's teaching, was, I suggest, largely absorbed without acknowledgement into the general stream of later commentary, with only an occasional "τὶς," "τινές" or "οἱ μὲν" showing through, where the Neoplatonists themselves had evolved a more elaborate interpretation of the same passage.

IV. PHAEDRUS

This said, let us turn to the Phaedrus. Our source now is Hermeias, the pupil of Syrianus, who quotes Harpocration in his *Commentary on the Phaedrus*.

9. Ad *Phaedrum* 230BC: (*ap.* Herm. *In Phaedr.* 32.1ff. Couvreur): Socrates embarks on a praise of the spot beneath the plane tree which Phaedrus has chosen. Harpocration remarked that Socrates is here seeking to outdo Phaedrus's original praise of the place in 229B:

> Ποιεῖται δὲ τὸν ἔπαινον τοῦ τόπου οὐκ ἀντιφι-
> λοτιμούμενος τῷ Φαιδρῷ, ὥς φησιν ὁ Ἁρποκρατίων, ἀλλὰ τοῖς
> ἀληθέσιν ἐπαίνοις χρώμενος·

All that Hermeias seems to be denying was any intention on the part of Socrates to outdo Phaedrus, and since I cannot imagine that Harpocration used the word ἀντιφιλοτιμούμενος, if he used it, to express any malicious intent by Socrates, it is hard to see what the substance of Hermeias' objection is, except perhaps that Socrates' praise is quite spontaneous and without any relation to Phaedrus' previous remarks.

10. The second quotation concerns the famous statement ψυχὴ πᾶσα ἀθάνατος, 245C. Hermeias begins his comment as follows (p. 102, 10ff. Couvreur):

Πρῶτον περὶ ποίας ψυχῆς ὁ λόγος ζητητέον. οἱ
μὲν γὰρ περὶ τῆς τοῦ κόσμου μόνης ᾠήθησαν εἶναι τὸν λόγον διὰ
τὸ εἰρηκέναι αὐτὸν 'πᾶσα' καὶ μετ' ὀλίγα ἐπάγειν 'ἢ πάντα τε
οὐρανὸν πᾶσαν τε γένεσιν ξυμπεσοῦσαν στῆναι· ὧν ἐστι
Ποσειδώνιος ὁ Στωικός. οἳ δὲ περὶ πάσης ἁπλῶς καὶ τῆς τοῦ
μύρμηκος καὶ μυίας, ὧν ἐστιν Ἁρποκρατίων· τὸ γὰρ 'πᾶσα' ἐπὶ
πάσης ψυχῆς ἀκούει.

Posidonius and Harpocration are here quoted as representatives of two extreme interpretations. Hermeias, no doubt simply
representing Syrianus, takes "soul" here to refer only to the rational
soul, but would agree with Harpocration that the meaning is "every
soul is immortal," rather than "soul as a whole is immortal," which is
Posidonius' rather strained interpretation.

Harpocration must, then, have extended immortality even
to souls of "ants and flies," as Hermeias disparagingly suggests. In doing
so he was taking sides in an age-old debate among Platonists. The *B*
Commentator on the *Phaedo* gives a good survey of the range of views
(*In Phaed.* p. 124, 13ff. Norviŋ):

"Ὅτι οἱ μὲν ἀπὸ τῆς λογικῆς ψυχῆς ἄχρι τῆς
ἐμψύχου ἕξεως ἀπαθανατίζουσιν, ὡς Νουμήνιος· οἱ δὲ μέχρι
τῆς φύσεως, ὡς Πλωτῖνος ἔνι ὅπου· οἳ δὲ μέχρι τῆς ἀλογίας, ὡς
τῶν μὲν παλαιῶν Ξενοκράτης καὶ Σπεύσιππος, τῶν δὲ
νεωτέρων Ἰάμβλιχος καὶ Πλούταρχος· οἳ δὲ μέχρι μόνου τοῦ
νοῦ, φθείρουσι γὰρ τὴν δόξαν, ὡς πολλοὶ τῶν Περιπατητικῶν·
οἳ δὲ μέχρι τῆς ὅλης ψυχῆς. φθείρουσι γὰρ τὰς μερικὰς εἰς τὴν
ὅλην.

Posidonius would fit into the last category, but where
should we fit Harpocration? It depends, I think, on what is to be
understood by ἡ ἔμψυχος ἕξις. For the Stoics, ἕξις was the lowest
principle of coherence of a compound body, proper to sticks and stones,
below φύσις, ἄλογος ψυχή and λογικὴ ψυχή. (Plut. *Quod Deus sit immut.*
35, S.E. *Adv. Math.* 9.81–85). The ἔμψυχος ἕξις will be the existential
determination of a living being while inhabited by soul. The material
element itself cannot be immortal, but, for Numenius, it seems, the
part of the life-principle which inhabits it was. I do not think that one is
justified on the evidence for taking it that Harpocration extended

immortality any further than ἡ ἀλογία, at least if Hermeias' reference to ants and flies is a technically accurate reflection of Harpocration's views. Yet we know from Iamblichus' *De Anima* that in respect at least to the origin of evil in the soul, Harpocration largely agreed with Numenius and his student Cronius. We have two references to this:

11. *ap*. Stob. *Anth*. I p. 373, 12ff. Wachsmuth:

> τῶν δ' αὖ διισταμένων πρὸς τούτους καὶ ἀπὸ τῶν
> ἔξωθεν προσφυομένων προστιθέντων ὁπωσοῦν τῇ ψυχῇ τὸ
> κακόν, ἀπὸ μὲν τῆς ὕλης Νουμηνίου καὶ Κρονίου πολλάκις, ἀπο
> δὲ τῶν σωμάτων αὐτῶν τούτων ἔστιν ὅτε καὶ Ἁρποκρατίωνος.

> While of those who are at variance with these thinkers (Plutarch and Atticus, and some others) and who would attach evil to the soul in some way from elements which have accrued to it from outside, Numenius and Cronius in many places derive it from Matter, Harpocration also on occasion from the very nature of these bodies of ours.

Iamblichus has been saying that there has long been a controversy in the Platonic school as to whether there are or are not irreconcilable elements in the soul. Plotinus and Numenius he singles out (374.22ff) as protagonists in this debate. Certain others, such as Plutarch and Atticus, recognise a struggle of warring elements, but postulate a reconciliation of them. All these, and Albinus as well, it seems (375.10) must assume a flaw in judgement, a "sin," within the soul itself; the group to which Harpocration belongs imagine evil as external to the soul, and thus consider the world a totally evil place. It is indeed an important problem in Platonism, and Harpocration is here placed in the ranks of the world-negaters. His position seems to be even more extreme than that of Numenius and Cronius, if he regards the body itself as the source of evil, instead of matter in general. It is thus not likely that he followed Numenius in extending immortality to the ἔμψυχος ἕξις. It is surprising, indeed, that he extended immortality to the souls of irrational animals, but perhaps he felt that in all animate beings there was a spark of immortal soul-stuff that could be salvaged.

He is linked again with Numenius and Cronius in the view that *all* incarnation is evil, in a passage where Iamblichus is dealing

142

with the varieties of union which the soul may have with the body. Harpocration, it seems, felt that there were no significant varieties.

12. *ap.* Stob. 1.380.14ff. Wachs:

⟨Τινὲς δὲ τῶν νεωτέρων οὐχ οὕτως⟩⁹ διακρί-
νουσιν, οὐκ ἔχοντες δὲ σκοπὸν τῆς διαφορότητος εἰς ταὐτὸ
συγχέουσι τὰς ἐνσωματώσεις τῶν ὅλων, κακάς τε εἶναι πάσας
διισχυρίζονται, καὶ διαφερόντως οἱ περὶ Κρόνιόν τε καὶ
Νουμήνιον καὶ Ἁρποκρατίωνα.

Some of the more recent philosophers, however, do not make this division, but, without taking into consideration the differences, they mix up together the entries into body of all souls, and maintain that all such entries are evil. Notable representatives of this view are Cronius, Numenius and Harpocration.

Although Harpocration seems to have agreed with Plutarch and Atticus on the creation of the world (and, presumably, of the rational soul) in Time, he is ranked with Numenius and Cronius against them in the matter of the essential evil of incarnation and of the world.

V. TIMAEUS

We have record of Harpocration's views on two important and contiguous passages of the Timaeus.

Ad *Timaeum* 28BC: γέγονεν· ὁρατὸς γὰρ ἁπτός τέ ἐστι καὶ σῶμα ἔχων, κ.τ.λ.

The great question among Platonists was, in what sense can the cosmos be said to have "come to be"? The orthodox explanation, accepted by the Neoplatonists, was that it "came to be" only in the sense that it depended upon a higher cause, not in the sense that it came into existence in Time. Plutarch of Chaeroneia, however, followed by Atticus and Harpocration, returned to the interpretation of Aristotle (and which Aristotle criticises), that Plato meant that the cosmos, in the sense of an ordered universe, was indeed created in Time, and indestructible only by special dispensation of the Demiurge. Taurus, Atticus' predecessor as head of the Academy, did not accept this view, and Numenius and Cronius are not recorded as taking sides,

⁹ Supplied, reasonably, by Heeren.

while the Platonist Severus, probably contemporary with Harpocration (ca. A.D. 200), produced a Stoic-influenced solution (*ap.* Procl. *In Tim.* I.289.6ff), holding that the cosmos in general was eternal, but that the system in which we presently exist had come into being. He appealed to the ἀνακυκλήσεις described in the *Politicus* (270B), and argued that each alternate cycle could be said to "come to be," and that that is what Plato must mean here.

We have the evidence for Harpocration's view preserved in a scholion on Proclus' *In Rempublicam* 2.10.6 Kroll, where Proclus is criticising τινές for asserting that the cosmos is destructible by nature but indestructible by decree of God. The scholiast explains that reference (*In Remp.* 2.377.15ff Kroll):

13. Ὁ Ἀρποκρατίων καὶ ὁ Ἀττικὸς οἱ τὸ γενητὸν λέγεσθαι τὸν κόσμον ἐν Τιμαίῳ ὑπὸ τοῦ Πλάτωνος κατὰ χρόνον ἀκούοντες, ἐπειδὴ ὁ Ἀριστοτέλης ἐγκαλεῖ τῷ θείῳ Πλάτωνι ἐν τῇ Περὶ οὐρανοῦ, διότι λέγων κατὰ χρόνον τὸν κόσμον γενητόν, ὡς ἐκεῖνος οἴεται, λέγει αὐτὸν ἄφθαρτον εἶναι, ἀπολογίαν οἴονται εὑρίσκειν πρὸς αὐτὸν λέγοντες, ὅτι φθαρτὸς μέν ἐστι διὰ τὴν ἑαυτοῦ φύσιν, ἄφθαρτος δὲ διαμένει διὰ τὴν τοῦ θεοῦ βούλησιν.

The Aristotle reference is to *De Caelo* I 10, p. 280a 28ff. Harpocration is here firmly linked with his master Atticus in this controversy. Proclus mentions, and criticises, Atticus explicitly in the *In Timaeum, ad* 28BC, (I.283.27ff), and *ad* 30A, on a kindred matter, (1.391.4ff). Since the second criticism of Atticus is expressly lifted from Porphyry, we may conjecture that the former was also. The mention of οἱ περὶ Ἀττικόν at 391.7 might be taken to include Harpocration, but one cannot be certain. Harpocration no doubt on this subject repeated and summarized Atticus' position.

He is ranked with Numenius, however, and against Atticus, in his view of the nature of the Demiurge, which may or may not be a comment on *Tim.* 28C: τὸν μὲν οὖν ποιητὴν καὶ πατέρα τοῦδε τοῦ παντὸς εὑρεῖν τε ἔργον καὶ εὑρόντα εἰς ἅπαντας ἀδύνατον λέγειν. Proclus (*In Tim.* I.303.27ff) quotes the views of Numenius, Harpocration and then Atticus in the course of his exegesis of this lemma, but not necessarily from comments of theirs on this particular place.[10]

[10] After these Middle Platonists, he refers to Plotinus (*Enn.* 3.9.1), and then to Amelius, Porphyry, Iamblichus, Theodorus of Asine, and finally to Syrianus, presumably in these cases quoting from formal commentaries. It is a most comprehensive doxography.

144

Numenius' view is as follows. He distinguishes three gods, of whom he calls the first "Father," the second "Creator," and the third "Creation," by which he means the cosmos. He thus, says Proclus, postulates two demiurges. Whether this is a fair description of Numenius' first god, who was in fact freed by Numenius from active service, is another matter. What is interesting is that Numenius took ποιητὴν and πατέρα as referring to two different beings. In this he was followed by Harpocration (I.304.22ff):

14. Ἁρποκρατίων δὲ θαυμάσαιμ᾽ ἄν, εἰ καὶ αὐτὸς ἑαυτόν γε ἀρέσκοι τοιαῦτα περὶ τοῦ δημιουργοῦ διαταττόμενος· ἕπεται μὲν γὰρ τῷδε τῷ ἀνδρὶ (sc. Numenius) κατὰ τὴν τῶν τριῶν θεῶν παράδοσιν καὶ καθόσον διττὸν ποιεῖ τὸν δημιουργόν, ἀποκαλεῖ δὲ τὸν μὲν πρῶτον θεὸν Οὐρανὸν καὶ Κρόνον, τὸν δὲ δεύτερον Δία καὶ Ζῆνα, τὸν δὲ τρίτον οὐρανὸν καὶ κόσμον. πάλιν δ᾽ αὖ μεταβαλὼν τὸν πρῶτον Δία προσαγορεύει καὶ βασιλέα τοῦ νοητοῦ, τὸν δὲ δεύτερον ἄρχοντα, καὶ ὁ αὐτὸς αὐτῷ γίγνεται Ζεὺς καὶ Κρόνος καὶ Οὐρανός.

This is an interesting piece of testimony. Where it came in Harpocration's *Commentary* is not certain, though some presumption is created that it concerned *Tim.* 28C. (Numenius' theory is obviously explicitly related to this passage.) It is interesting, though, that Harpocration is portrayed as contradicting himself. He calls his first god now Uranos and Cronos, and his second Zeus and Zēn, says Proclus, and then again, changing his ground, he calls his first god Zeus and "the King of the intellectual realm," and the second "the Ruler." It is hardly credible that Harpocration contradicted himself in the same passage. What I think we have here is a conflation made either by Proclus, or already by Porphyry. The places in Plato which spring to mind are *Cratylus* 396A–C, for the first identification, and *Phaedrus* 246Eff, for the second. It may indeed be that we have a garbled record of three different comments by Harpocration, if we assume that he commented on *Timaeus* 28C as well, adopting Numenius' interpretation, and perhaps relating it to the first of the identifications mentioned above. Numenius does not seem to have made any identifications here with the traditional gods, but invented names of his own, of which Proclus disapproves (304.3ff), "πάππος" for his first god, "ἔγγονος" for his second, and "ἀπόγονος" for his third.

If I am right in assuming that Harpocration also dealt with the *Phaedrus* passage, then he took the Zeus there described as representing his first god, and a being which he denominates "Archon" as his second, the Demiurge proper. Whence he derived this term is obscure to me (at *Phaedr.* 247a3 the Olympians are termed θεοὶ ἄρχοντες, but this plural does not help us much); it has a Gnostic ring. The Gnostic Basilides (ca. A.D. 130) called the Demiurge ὁ μέγας ἄρχων, ἡ κεφαλὴ τοῦ κόσμου (Hipp. *Ref.* X 14,6). We may recall also that Satan is repeatedly termed ὁ ἄρχων τοῦ κόσμου τούτου in St. John's Gospel (12.31; 14.30; 16.11). Harpocration's view of this world tends in other respects towards Gnosticism, as we have seen (frr. 10 and 11), though we cannot conclude on the evidence that he considered his second god to be a malevolent force, since he is prepared to identify him with the Zeus of the *Cratylus*.

VI. Republic

We have had occasion to mention above (n. 3) a list of commentators on the Myth of Er which Proclus gives *In Remp.* 2.96. 10ff, which includes Harpocration. I give it again here, as a testimony.

> 15. καὶ μάλισθ᾽ ὅτι πολλοὶ τῆς περὶ αὐτὸν ἐφήψαντο κατα-νοήσεως καὶ τῶν Πλατωνικῶν οἱ κορυφαῖοι, Νουμήνιος, Ἀλβῖνος, Γαῖος, Μάξιμος ὁ Νικαεύς, Ἁρποκρατίων, Εὐκλείδης, καὶ ἐπὶ πᾶσιν Πορφύριος, ὃν ἐγὼ πάντων μάλιστα τῶν ἐν τῷ μύθῳ κεκρυμμένων γενέσθαι φημὶ τέλεον ἐξηγητήν.

From this we derive the bald fact that Harpocration commented on the myth. We may also suspect that, for Proclus, Porphyry is the immediate source for his knowledge of all the Middle Platonic commentators. We may note further that Numenius is here recorded as having written on the myth, and a little further on (p. 110.4) we find Cronius quoted on a question pertaining to it, whereas Atticus is not mentioned by Proclus in this connection. We might conclude from this that Harpocration is here following Numenius and Cronius, rather than his master. We do have a record of Numenius' interpreta-tion of the τόπος τις δαιμόνιος of *Rep.* 614C1 (Procl. *In Remp.* 2.128.26), which Harpocration may have followed. However, since there is no necessity that he did, I leave the matter there.

VII.

We have now set out all that survives of the work of Harpocration. There is no reason not to assume that all the references preserved are to his voluminous *Commentary on Plato*. I suspect this work

146

to have been primarily a repository for all of the scholarly activity concerning Plato's dialogues that had taken place up to that time, along with some original comments by Harpocration himself, which are, not surprisingly, all that has been preserved to us. The rest, I suggest, being regarded as *gemeingut*, was plundered without acknowledgement by the Neoplatonic commentators, primarily, perhaps, Porphyry. How the twenty-four books of this commentary were divided up, or why there were twenty-four books, is of course not clear. Possibly, Harpocration ran to twenty-four books with the Iliad and the Odyssey in mind. Certainly a compendium of Platonic scholarship up to A.D. 200 or so could be extended to twenty-four books without much difficulty.

 Harpocration's own philosophical position turns out to be interesting, as constituting a link between the Athenian Academy, in the person of his teacher, Atticus, and the Syrian school of Numenius, who offered a much more exotic Platonism. Harpocration subscribes to the "heresy" of Plutarch and Atticus, as to the creation of the world in time, but on the subjects of the soul, the nature of the world, and the identity of the Demiurge he sided rather with Numenius and Cronius, revealing world-negating tendencies.

 As to how long his work survived, or to whom it was available, the evidence is inconclusive. The latest writer to quote him is Aeneas of Gaza, but it hardly sounds as if Aeneas had direct access to his work. Nor in fact can one be certain about Olympiodorus, Damascius, Proclus, Hermeias, or even Iamblichus. All our references to Harpocration are doxographical in nature, and sound second-hand. Inevitably one thinks of the industrious Porphyry as middle-man. The fact that Harpocration is quoted at second hand by later commentators does not, of course, mean that his work was not available to them, but merely that they did not take the trouble to take it down from the shelf, being satisfied with the second-hand evidence of what they considered to be a reliable witness. I suggest that after a full set of Neoplatonic commentaries on Plato had emerged, by the middle of fifth century A.D., or even earlier, the work of Harpocration ceased to be recopied and crumbled to dust.[11]

---

[11] I am indebted to Dr. Michael Frede for many helpful criticisms.

XV

A DATE FOR THE DEATH OF NICOMACHUS OF GERASA?

MARINUS, in his Life of Proclus (ch. 28), notes of his master: ὅτι τῆς Ἑρμαϊκῆς εἴη σειρᾶς σαφῶς ἐθεάσατο, καὶ ὅτι τὴν Νικομάχου τοῦ Πυθαγορείου ψυχὴν ἔχοι ὄναρ ποτὲ ἐπίστευσεν. Proclus, then, on the basis of a dream, believed himself to be a re-incarnation of Nicomachus, the Pythagorean mathematician of Gerasa. We *may* believe the dream, but we may also credit Proclus with carrying out certain calculations, the nature of which has not, I think, hitherto been noticed in this connection.

In the *Theologumena Arithmeticae* (p. 40 Ast, 52. 8 ff. De Falco), *apropos* the number Six, we find a report of the Pythagorean belief that the metempsychoses of Pythagoras took place at intervals of 216 years—from the death of one incarnation, presumably, to the birth of the next. I give the relevant passage:

ἐπεὶ δὲ ὁ ἀπὸ τοῦ ϛ΄ κύβος σιϛ΄ γίνεται, ὁ ἐπὶ ἑπταμήνων γονίμων χρόνος συναριθμουμένων τοῖς ἑπτὰ τῶν ἐξ ἡμερῶν, ἐν αἷς ἀφροῦται καὶ

διαφύσεις σπέρματος λαμβάνει τὸ σπέρμα, Ἀνδροκύδης τε ὁ Πυθαγορικὸς ὁ περὶ τῶν συμβόλων γράψας καὶ Εὐβουλίδης ὁ Πυθαγορικὸς καὶ Ἀριστόξενος καὶ Ἱππόβοτος καὶ Νεάνθης οἱ τὰ κατὰ τὸν ἄνδρα ἀναγράψαντες σιϛ΄ ἔτεσι τὰς μετεμψυχώσεις τὰς αὐτῷ συμβεβηκυίας ἔφασαν γεγονέναι. μετὰ τοσαῦτα γοῦν ἔτη εἰς παλιγγενεσίαν ἐλθεῖν Πυθαγόραν καὶ ἀναζῆσαι ὡσανεὶ μετὰ τὴν πρώτην ἀνακύκλησιν καὶ ἐπάνοδον τοῦ ἀπὸ ἐξ ψυχογονικοῦ κύβου, τοῦ δ᾽ αὐτοῦ καὶ ἀποκαταστατικοῦ διὰ τὸ σφαιρικόν, ὡς δὲ καὶ ἄλλοτε διὰ τούτων ἀνάζησιν ἔσχεν·

'Since the cube of 6 comes to 216, (which is) the time of birth for seven-month babies, if one counts in with the seven months the six days during which the sperm is in the form of foam and is undergoing germination, Androcydes the Pythagorean, the author of the work On Symbols, and Eubulides the Pythagorean, and Aristoxenus, and Hippobotus, and Neanthes, who have written on

XV

275

the subject of Pythagoras, have declared that the reincarnations which befell him happened at intervals of 216 years. They say, at any rate, that after this number of years Pythagoras came to re-birth, and lived again, as it were after the first circuit and return of the soul-creating cube of six, it being recurring because of its spherical circuit, and that on other occasions he came to new life through this same process.'

This sounds like a piece of Nicomachus himself (perhaps relayed by Iamblichus), embedded in the *Theol. Ar.*, since Nicomachus quotes the above authorities, as we may conjecture from Porphyry's *Life* of Pythagoras,[1] Nicomachus being Porphyry's chief source.

It is plain from the above passage that the figure of two hundred and sixteen years was arrived at by extrapolation from the two hundred and sixteen days in which the embryo comes to birth. A closer examination of this, however, is matter for another treatise. What concerns us is that this figure must have been common knowledge among those of Pythagorean persuasion, and hence I suggest that it profoundly influenced Proclus' dream-revelation. Proclus was born on 8 February A.D. 412, as we can gather from his horoscope, furnished by Marinus (*Vita*, ch. 35). It is simple to calculate back from this to arrive at a date for Nicomachus' death—A.D. 196. If we can so calculate, we can congratulate ourselves on adding one more definite date to the very meagre collection of these, that we have to guide us through the maze which constitutes the second-century philosophical scene.

We must consider, though, what difficulties, if any, arise. Nicomachus is, after all, normally dated 'c. A.D. 100' (Sir Thomas Heath in *O.C.D.*) up to 'um 150 n. Chr.' (Schmid–Stählin, ii. 2, p. 905): Robbins, in the Michigan University translation of Nicomachus' *Introductio Arithmetica*,[2] p. 72, concludes that Nicomachus' life-span fell between 'the middle of the first century and the middle of the second century after Christ'. Hoche (Intro. to Teubner edn., p. iv) gives a good account of the evidence.

We know that Apuleius translated him into Latin,[3] but this in no way conflicts with our new date. It merely makes Nicomachus more or less a contemporary of his translator (Apuleius' own dates being in fact uncertain, c. A.D. 125–200). Robbins (op. cit. 76) notes that in his work on Harmony, Nicomachus' datable astronomical observation is fixed at A.D. 151. Our new date, however, does not compel us to date the composition of the *Enchiridion Harmonikēs* any later than 151, especially since he promises therein a fuller treatment of the same subject (von Jan p. 238. 6 ff.), a promise more suitable to a youngish man.

It is surely reasonable to assume that Proclus was aware of this basic piece of lore about Pythagoras. What I suspect to have happened is that, armed with the number 216, Proclus checked back to see what great man might qualify as his last incarnation, and Nicomachus of Gerasa was what he came up with. Robbins regards this as evidence of Nicomachus' great fame in later antiquity. Certainly Nicomachus was famous, but as opposed to Plotinus, or Iamblichus, or Julian the Theurgist, or even Numenius, he was hardly *the* man of whom to be a reincarnation. No, he was simply the only one who fitted.

If we can make the above assumption, Nicomachus is in effect moved about a generation and a half forward in time, and made a contemporary of Numenius and Julian the Theurgist rather than of Plutarch or Moderatus of Gades. A life-span of c. A.D. 120–196 seems a reasonable postulate. The consequences for the history of philosophy are not, perhaps, earth-shaking, but for those interested in second-century Platonism and Pythagoreanism such a datum is not insignificant.

[1] Aristoxenus *passim* (see Nauck's edn. of Porphyry, *Opuscula Selecta*); Hippobotus and Neanthes, p. 52. 7 Nauck. Androcydes Nicomachus quotes in the *Introduction to Arithmetic*, p. 6. 11 ff. Hoche.

[2] *Nicomachus of Gerasa*, by M. L. D'Ooge, F. E. Robbins, and L. C. Karpinski, University of Michigan Studies, vol. xvi (1926).

[3] Cassiodorus, *De Artibus ac Disciplina Liberalium Litterarum*, ch. 4, p. 1208b Migne.

XVI

The concept of two intellects:
A Footnote to the History of Platonism

I

In the *Adversus Nationes* of Arnobius (II 25), we have the following reference to Chaldaean doctrine:

> "Haecine est anima docta illa quam dicitis, immortalis perfecta divina, post deum principem rerum et *post mentes geminas* locum optinens quartum et afluens ex crateribus vivis?"

> "Is this that 'educated' soul that you talk about, immortal, perfect and divine, occupying the fourth rank, after God the first principle of the Universe and the two intellects, and flowing out from the living mixing-bowls?"

This whole passage is filled with useful evidence on Chaldaean doctrine, but I wish to confine myself to the discussion of the phrase *mentes geminas*[1], as it contains, I think, if rightly elucidated, much that is of interest for the history of Platonism in the third and fourth centuries A.D.

First of all, we have here four entities, in descending order of dignity: (1) *Deus, princeps rerum*, (2) and (3), a pair of intellects, (4) a soul. This soul, in addition to its other honorific epithets, is described as 'flowing out from the living mixing-bowls'. Arnobius is criticising the Platonic theory of *anamnesis*, with its doctrine of the 'education' of the soul in the intelligible world before entry into the body (he has just referred to the *Meno*), so his introduction of distinctively Chaldaean terminology here is most interesting. We must remember, however, that the term 'mixing-bowls', while being a Chaldaean concept, (cf. *Or. Ch.* Fr. 42 *Des Places*), also goes back to Plato's *Timaeus* 35 A and 41 B, where the 'mixing' of the soul is described.

But now to the *mentes geminae*. The phrase by itself does not permit us to conclude that one of these minds is in any way senior to the other, but it does not on the other hand compel us to hold that they are really 'twins'. Arnobius' *geminae* need mean no more than *duae*; he is being somewhat rhetorical and sarcastic in this passage.

[1] Efforts to emend this to *post mentes genuinas* (Marchesi) or even to *post daemones et genios* (! Klussman) are entirely misguided.

In fact we shall see that these two intellects have differentiated functions and that one may be regarded as senior to the other, though they subsist on what one might term the same hypostatic level.

What do the *Chaldaean Oracles* reveal about a pair of intellects? A certain amount, but the evidence is problematic. In *Or. Ch.* Frr. 7 and 8 *Des Places*, we have the following:

> Fr. 7: Πάντα γὰρ ἐξετέλεσσε πατὴρ καὶ νῷ παρέδωκε
> δευτέρῳ. ὃν πρῶτον κληίζετε πᾶν γένος ἀνδρῶν.
> Fr. 8: δυὰς παρὰ τῷδε κάθηται.
> ἀμφότερον γὰρ ἔχει, νῷ μὲν κατέχειν τὰ νοητά,
> αἴσθησιν δ'ἐπάγειν κόσμοις.

These two fragments should be considered together, and may well come, as Lewy suggested,[2] from the same Oracle. In Fr. 7 there is a problem of interpretation. The mention of a 'second intellect' could imply that the Father himself was the first, but it could also mean that, of two Intellects, the Father handed the administration of 'all things' to the second rather than the first. There will then be two intellects (νόες) of which the human race only know the second.[3]

It is this latter interpretation which I would prefer, for reasons that will become plain directly.

> Fr. 8 we may translate as follows:
> "By this a Dyad sits; for it has two tasks, both by Intellect to contain the objects of intellection, and to bring (sense) perception to bear upon the worlds."

That by which the Dyad sits we may assume to be the 'second intellect' of Fr. 7 (cf. Procl. *In Crat.* p. 51, 26-30). The Dyad itself seems necessarily to be the double intellect, the subject of our enquiry. On the evidence of Michael Psellus (*Hypotyposis* p. 74 Kroll, p. 199 *Des Places*) this Dyad is the δὶς ἐπέκεινα, or the Demiurge, though this latter identification may be merely a Neoplatonic interpretation.

This (demiurgic) intellect has two functions, by reason of which it may be seen as a dyad. One function, or one *nous*, contemplates, and contains within itself, the realm of Ideas, the νοητὸς κόσμος, while the other directs itself in some way to the realm of sense-percep-

---

[2] *Chaldaean Oracles and Theurgy*, p. 112, n. 181.
[3] Psellus, in his commentary *ad. loc.*, sees only two entities, the Father and Nous (*Exegesis* PG 1140 d, p. 178 Des Places): ὁ τῆς τριάδος πρῶτος πατὴρ παρέδωκε τῷ νῷ, ὅντινα νοῦν τὸ σύμπαν γένος τῶν ἀνδρῶν, ἀγνοοῦντες τὴν πατρικὴν ὑπεροχήν, θεὸν πρῶτον καλοῦσιν. But Psellus is dependent upon Neoplatonic interpretation, which did not recognise two Intellects, and saw the Father as the first element in the noetic triad.

tion, of physical objects. What is involved in 'bringing perception to the worlds' is not quite clear, but must refer to a demiurgic activity. The κόσμοι may best be understood as the planetary spheres, which would presumably pass the αἴσθησις on to the sublunar world.

So then, what we have here is not exactly two Intellects, but at least an intellectual dyad, with two distinct functions, one introspective, meditating upon its own contents, the other directed outwards and downwards upon the κόσμοι.

The evidence of the Anonymus Taurinensis *Commentary on the Parmenides* is valuable here. At IX 1-5 we find the following description of the supreme entities of Chaldaean theology:

Οἱ δὲ (sc. the Chaldaeans) ἁρπάσαι ἑαυτὸν ἐκ πάντων τῶν ἑαυτοῦ εἰπόντες δύναμίν τε αὐτῷ διδόασι καὶ νοῦν ἐν τῇ ἁπλότητι αὐτοῦ συνηνῶσθαι καὶ ἄλλον πάλιν <ν>οῦν, καὶ τῆς τριάδος αὐτὸν οὐκ ἐξελόντες ἀναιρεῖν ἀριθμὸν ἀξιοῦσιν, ὡς καὶ τὸ ἓν λέγειν αὐτὸν εἶναι παντελῶς παραιτεῖσθαι.

"Others, while they describe him (the Father) as 'snatching himself off' from all his creation, nevertheless accord him a Power and Intellect united to his simplicity, *and then again another Intellect*, and although they do not separate him from this triad, yet they seek to remove numeration from him, inasmuch as they absolutely refuse to denominate him The One."

This passage seems primarily to refer to Fr. 3 *Des Places*: ὁ πατὴρ ἥρπασσεν ἑαυτὸν,/οὐδ'ἐν ἑῇ δυνάμει νοερῇ κλείσας ἴδιον πῦρ, and to Fr. 4 *Des Places*: ἡ μὲν γὰρ δύναμις σὺν ἐκείνῳ, νοῦς δ'ἀπ' ἐκείνου, although it presents a somewhat different scheme, with a δύναμις— νοῦς (these two terms I take to describe one and the same entity) united with the Father, and another νοῦς in some undefined relationship to the Father less than unity. *Anon. Taur.* is in fact criticising the Oracles for establishing a triad which includes the Father and then trying to make the Father utterly transcendent to everything else. Assuming that *Anon Taur.* is Porphyry, as Hadot maintains (and even if he is not Porphyry, he is certainly Neoplatonic), we have here a Neoplatonic interpretation of the Chaldaean hierarchy which may not have correctly grasped the functions of the two νόες. The Neoplatonists saw a triad πατήρ-δύναμις-νοῦς, of which the δύναμις adhered closely to the Father, while the νοῦς went forth from him. Since *Anon. Taur.* calls the δύναμις also a νοῦς, it seems possible to connect these two νόες with the δυάς of Fr. 8.

There is evidence, then, for the existence within the Chaldaean hierarchy of Being of two entities which can be termed νοῦς, with a tendency for one, the outward- and downward-turning νοῦς, to be ranked below the other, but both being essentially, as I have said, on the same hypostatic level. The 'lower' νοῦς performs in relation to the world a *demiurgic* function.

In Numenius also, the near contemporary of Julian, the author of the Oracles, we find talk of two Intellects (Proclus, *In Tim.* I 303, 27 ff. and III 103, 28 ff = *Test.* 24 and 25 *Leemans*), but these are definitely on two different levels, the first being his supreme god, and the second the demiurge, so that, although the term δεύτερος νοῦς is used in connexion with Numenius, it has a different signification.

This δεύτερος νοῦς of Numenius is said to work directly upon the cosmos, which is described as Numenius' 'third god'. There seems here to be no place left for a World-Soul, whose function this would properly be, unless in fact we are to understand κόσμος in Numenius' scheme as being equivalent to ψυχὴ τοῦ κόσμου. In Plotinus and in subsequent Neoplatonism the World Soul was re-established as an hypostasis, and in the process the number of entities described as νοῦς was reduced to one.

In Calcidius' *Commentary on the Timaeus* (cc. 177 and 188, pp. 206, 3 and 213, 1 Waszink), in a passage which may be in fact nothing but Numenius,[4] we find a hierarchy of Being described which comprises (1) a *summus deus*, "qui est summum bonum ultra omnem substantiam omnemque naturam, aestimatione intellectuque melior", (2) *providentia*, "quae est post illum summum secundae eminentiae, quem *noyn* Graeci vocant." It is turned constantly towards the *summus deus*, in emulation of Him, and channels *bonitas* (ἀγαθότης) through itself from Him to all the rest of creation; (3) *secunda mens*, which follows in attendance upon (2). This 'second intellect', however, is described as 'anima mundi tripertita', the *tripertita* referring to the triple division of the sphere of the fixed stars, the sphere of the planets, and the sublunary sphere. Here we have a δεύτερος νοῦς identified with the ψυχὴ τοῦ κόσμου, while we have a πρῶτος θεός who certainly appears to be above intellection (either as subject or object), and thus very near to the Plotinian One.

We have, then, in the *Oracles*, in Numenius and in Calcidius (whom I take as representing pre-Plotinian Platonism; there is really no evidence — apart from passages like this, which beg the question — that Calc. is Neoplatonic), three schemata, all of which involve δεύτερος νοῦς, but only one of which (the *Oracles*) seems to provide two νόες

[4] See on this J. den Boeft, *Calcidius on Fate* (Philosophia Antiqua XVIII) pp. 85-98.

on the same level. It is the system of the *Oracles* which Arnobius is describing in *Adv. Nat.* II 25.

We may note that the concept of a dyad following upon a Supreme principle is not without parallels in earlier Middle Platonism. In the Pythagorean-influenced scheme of Eudorus of Alexandria (*ap.* Simpl. *In Phys.* 181, 7 ff), we find a Supreme One followed by a pair of Monad and Dyad, and in the philosophical scheme of Philo Judaeus we find God accompanied by a pair of supreme δυνάμεις, which in turn generate the Logos (*Cher.* 28, *Abr.* 119 ff.) Admittedly, in neither of these cases are we faced with a dyad of Intellects, but I am only concerned to provide an ancestry for the general concept of a dyad in this position.

How transcendent was the Father in the *Oracles* is open to dispute. Middle Platonism in general, on which the *Chaldaean Oracles* depend, although it is rich in assertions of the transcendence and unknowability of the Supreme Principle, and even of its superiority to a principle termed νοῦς, never seems to entirely renounce its right to describe the Supreme Principle as a νοῦς *of some sort* (He is, after all, repeatedly described as the πατρικὸς νοῦς). At any rate, in the *Oracles* the Father is the first cause of all creation, and he implants within Intellect the archetypal Ideas. These the First Intellect contemplates, while the Second Intellect uses them as patterns to create (presumably through the agency of the World-Soul (Hecate) and the planetary gods) the sensible universe.

The doctrine of two Intellects, however, did not take root as such in Neoplatonism. Plotinus was certainly prepared, on occasion, to distinguish between a higher and lower aspect of *Nous* (e.g. *Enn.* III 5, 9), but the lower aspect, that which descends towards the sensible universe through Soul, is the Logos, not a second *Nous*, and he condemns any duplication of *Nous* in III 9, 1, (see below). From Porphyry onward the realm of *Nous* becomes a triad, ὄν— ζωή— νοῦς, of which *Nous* itself is the outgoing principle, while τὸ ὄν is the object of intellection. Even within this triadic system, though, *Nous* performs both the function of contemplating the Ideas (τὸ ὄν) and applying them to the sensible world.

II

This, however, is not quite the whole story. In Proclus' *Commentary on the Timaeus* (II 154, 4 ff. *Diehl*), we have a curious passage. Proclus is discussing *Tim.* 35 A, the passage where Timaeus is describing the creation of the soul from the mixture of ἡ ἀμέριστος οὐσία and ἡ περὶ τὰ σώματα γιγνομένη μεριστή. The commentators take these two phrases as referring to various things, he says (153, 17 ff). All agree that the soul is intermediate between the physical and intelligible worlds, but (i) some see it as compounded of the monad and the indefinite dyad (Aristander and Numenius); (ii) others, as compounded from the point and the line (Severus); (iii) others take it as a mixture of the irrational and the divine souls (Plutarch and Atticus), and others (iv) take it simply as being a mixture of Intellect and Sense-Perception (Plotinus). But there is a fifth view:

οἱ δὲ ἀνωτέρω χωροῦντες δύο νόας πρὸ αὐτῆς θέντες, τὸν μὲν τῶν ὅλων τὰς ἰδέας ἔχοντα, τὸν δὲ τῶν μερικῶν, τούτων εἶναί φασι μέσην, ὡς ἀπ' ἀμφοῖν ὑφισταμένην. οὕτω γὰρ ὁ 'Ασιναῖος λέγει Θεόδωρος, εὑρὼν παρὰ τῷ Πορφυρίῳ τὴν δόξαν ὡς ἐκ Περσίδος ἥκουσαν. ταῦτα γοῦν 'Αντωνῖνον ἱστορῆσαι τὸν 'Αμμωνίου μαθητήν.

"Others, going further up the scale of Being (or simply, 'taking a more exalted line'), postulate the *two intellects* prior to the Soul, the one containing the forms of general concepts, the other those of individuals, and say that the soul is median between these, as deriving its existence from both. This is the theory of Theodorus of Asine, who found the doctrine in Porphyry, who said that it derived from Persia. At least that is what Antoninus, the pupil of Ammonius, relates."

First let us clarify the line of descent of this piece of information. As I understand it, Proclus says that Theodorus says that Porphyry says that Antoninus the pupil of Ammonius says that this doctrine of the two intellects comes from Persia. About this Antoninus we know nothing further, but Porphyry could perfectly well have been personally acquainted with him. Porphyry's information may well be oral, as is the case with his reports of Origen's views on the *Timaeus*.

It is next to be noted that Proclus does not himself like this theory. He regards it as another of Theodorus' eccentricities, and dismisses it pretty brusquely (154, 21-25). This he would hardly have done had he felt that he was faced with Chaldaean doctrine. We are not told that the doctrine is Chaldaean, but rather that it is said to have originated in Persia, the home of Magi rather than of Chaldaeans.

The question arises, nevertheless, as to whether this curious doctrine adopted by Theodorus can be related to the Chaldaean dyad of intellects. Bearing in mind that the role of the two minds may have been somewhat altered by Theodorus to suit his purposes, it seems to me that a connexion does present itself to view. There are, however, difficulties.

First, what are we to understand by τὰ ὅλα, of which the first Intellect contains the forms? In Neoplatonism this term normally refers somewhat vaguely, to the primary *genera*, either the five μέγιστα γένη of the *Sophist*, or the forms of the four elements, or to such general concepts as animal, plant, justice or plane figure. τὰ μερικά, on the other hand, are either individuals or the lowest species, in either case to be thought of as being immanent in matter. Now the precise delimitation of τὰ ὅλα may be vague, but at least it can be said that they are transcendent ideas, as opposed to μερικά, which are ideas in Matter. When this is realised, the distinction of roles between Theodorus' two Intellects comes very close to that of the Chaldaean Dyad.

The Soul is produced from the mixture of these. This would seem to imply that the second *nous* is somehow inferior to Soul, especially as the soul is said to be between the two. Certainly it is in the same position as the indefinite dyad in Numenius' interpretation, the ἄλογος ψυχή of Plutarch, and Plotinus' αἴσθησις, but the second *nous* need not, I think, be taken as an 'evil' or negative principle. It is simply the archetypal principle of the sense-world. Indeed Proclus' phrase ἀνωτέρω χωροῦντες may well relate in particular to the previous interpretation, that of Plotinus, and the second *nous* of Theodorus be seen as the noetic archetype of *aisthesis*. In *Enn.* VI. 7,6 Plotinus does talk about a sort of archetypal *aisthesis* in the intelligible realm, in a context where he is discussing three levels of Man, noetic, psychic and somatic. Even the noetic Man has a kind of *aisthesis*, and this could be related to Theodorus' second *nous*.[5]

[5] I am indebted to the anonymous reader for pointing out the relevance of the Plotinus passage. We may note that Philo of Alexandria already postulated an 'Idea' of sense-perception (*Leg. All.* I 19), but whether he found the notion in contemporary Platonism or invented it himself *ad hoc* is not clear. Prof. A. Henrichs points out to me that there may be a connexion between the *nous* which contains the forms of μερικά and the νοῦς ὑλικός which Macrobius (*In Somn. Sc.* I 12, 11) reports the Orphics as identifying with Dionysus. This Orphic *nous* projects itself from the undivided (transcendent) *Nous*, and divides itself among individuals (*in singulos*), the rending of Dionysus by the Titans being a mythological expression of this metaphysical fact. But the contrast which the Orphics are making appears to be between the Intellect in its transcendent aspect and the Intellect as *immanent* in individuals, whereas Theodorus' δεύτερος νοῦς is still transcendent. However, if the ὑλικὸς νοῦς is taken rather as the sum-total of the μερικοὶ νόες, the analogy becomes much closer, as it is then in fact an archetype of the individual intellects, which is very much what the

It remains uncertain in what sense this is a Persian doctrine. What use had the Magi for a doctrine of two intellects? W. Theiler, in his essay 'Ammonius der Lehrer des Origenes', assumes that Antoninus is giving an interpretation of Ormuzd and Ahriman, and this may well be so;[6] but even if so, the theory in its final form does not seem to make of the second *nous* an evil principle. We cannot be quite sure that Porphyry also used the theory of the two Intellects to explain *Tim.* 35 A. All Theodorus is reported as saying is that he found the theory in Porphyry. But Porphyry was no dualist, and he did not subscribe to the Plutarchan heresy about the ἄλογος ψυχή, so that if he used the doctrine here, he must have used it in the same way as Theodorus.

If the doctrine is indeed Chaldaean, why is it not described as such by Proclus? He has a definite way of alluding to the *Oracles*, after all, and an attitude of unqualified reverence towards them. Plainly he did not recognise this as a Chaldaean doctrine, (which, after all, makes it very unlikely that it was one). I can only suggest that, since Proclus did not much approve of Theodorus' innovations, and since Theodorus did not describe the doctrine as Chaldaean, Proclus did not recognise it as such. If the doctrine is in fact to be ascribed to some 'mage hellenisé', then we must face the fact that a very similar doctrine is simultaneously being propounded in the *Oracles*.

Perhaps if we address ourselves to the question of what purpose the postulation of two Intellects would serve in a system of metaphysics, it may be easier to see the coherence of the pieces of evidence that have been presented, and the relation of the theory to orthodox Neoplatonic teaching.

The role of the first *nous*, that which contains and contemplates the Ideas, hardly needs much discussion. It is the second *nous* whose position is open to question. Now it was always a problem in Platonism to account for the individuality of individuals. The Stoics had their

δεύτερος νοῦς appears to be. At the least, this Orphic concept fills another gap in this complicated jigsaw.

[6] *Forschungen zum Neuplatonismus*, p. 21, n. 1. Besides Theiler's rather obvious suggestion (based, no doubt, in part on Plut. *Is. et Os.* 369 D ff.), we may note that in the Avesta, *Yasna* 30. 3-6, there is a reference to two dualistically opposed Spirits as 'twins', which might lend significance to Arnobius' *mentes geminae*. Cf. H. S. Nyberg, *Die Religionen des alten Iran* (Leipzig 1938), p. 102 ff. (I am indebeted to Prof. A. Henrichs for this reference.) There remains, however, the problem that the two νόες with which we are concerned are not opposed to each other as good to evil.

doctrine of the ἰδίως ποιόν, that quality which makes an individual unique, but the Stoics did not have any problems about the intelligible world, and whether there are intelligible archetypes of individual qualities. It was this that Platonists had to face, and what Plotinus in fact deals with in his essay 'Whether there are Ideas of Individuals' (*Enn.* V 7). Not that Plotinus here makes any use of a concept of two intellects, but the sort of problem he was raising was possibly that to which this postulation of a second *nous* was an attempt to find an answer.[7]

Perhaps, after all, the need to postulate a second *nous* to attend to the world of particulars was obviated in later Neoplatonism by the use made of the image of the Charioteer and Pair of the *Phaedrus* Myth. It will be recalled that the Gods also have two horses, although they are both αὐτοί τε ἀγαθοί καὶ ἐξ ἀγαθῶν (*Phaedr.* 246 A), for which reason τὰ τῶν θεῶν ὀχήματα ἰσορρόπως εὐήνια ὄντα ῥᾳδίως πορεύεται (247 B). Nevertheless, there is this second horse, and for Iamblichus, at least, and later Proclus (*In. Tim.* II 309, 11 ff. = Iambl. *In Tim.* Fr. 59 of my ed.), the second horse of the divine chariot is that faculty by which the Gods can take note of the physical creation. This horse never misbehaves:

ἡ γνῶσις ἐν αὐτῷ μόνιμος ἀποτελεῖται, τὰ μὲν φερόμενα μονίμως , τὰ δὲ μεταρρέοντα καὶ ἐνδεχόμενα πιστῶς καὶ ἀραρότως ἐν ἑαυτῇ προειληφυῖα.

Iamblichus is here talking particularly about the All-Soul, ἡ ὅλη ψυχή, but the same goes for any divine entity. It seems to me that this second horse fulfils the same role as a δεύτερος νοῦς. Somehow a way had to be found for a transcendent God or gods to observe the physical world, albeit in a transcendent and non-temporal way. So this perhaps meaningless but metaphysically satisfactory formula was devised, that the gods view the world of flux and contingency μονίμως, πιστῶς καὶ ἀραρότως. The Church Fathers had the same problem with the Christian God, and settled it in the same way.

So then, the Second Intellect which turns up in Theodorus of Asine is by no means as superfluous as it might appear at first — far less so, indeed, than most of Theodorus' metaphysical innovations. But then this was not an innovation of Theodorus. He himself traces it back, through Porphyry, to the shadowy Antoninus, who alleges it to be

[7] In *Enn.* III 9, 1, commenting on *Tim.* 39 E, Plotinus adverts to the possibility of a separate entity, or phase of *Nous* which διενοήθη... ἃ ἐκεῖ ὁρᾷ ἐν τῷδε τῷ κόσμῳ ποιῆσαι, but rejects it.

Persian. I suggest that it is at least analogous to the Intellectual Dyad of the Chaldaean Oracles, and that under the guise of the Second Horse of the divine Chariot, it in fact finds a place of sorts in orthodox Neoplatonic doctrine.

XVII

The Platonizing of Mithra

R. Turcan, *Mithras Platonicus: Recherches sur l'Hellénisation philosophique de Mithra.*
(Études Préliminaires aux Religions Orientales dans l'Empire Romain, Vol. 47.) Brill,
Leiden, 1975: pp. xi and 145 (5 plates).

It is my intention here not only to give some account of the recent book of Robert Turcan,
but also to discuss, as they come up, some of the more interesting topics with which he
deals, so far, at least as they concern Platonism. The Persian and Mithraic side of his
investigations I am not competent to criticize, and can only express my gratitude to him
for presenting them. The purpose of his work is to examine the various stages, from the
first century B.C. on, by which the cult of Mithras was received into the framework of
Greek religious and philosophical speculation, and principally into the Platonic tradition,
under which Stoic and Pythagorean influences may be considered as subsumed.

Turcan divides his work into seven chapters, arranged chronologically. His first, entitled
Posidonius et les Pirates, deals with the first indications of a knowledge of a special cult of
Mithras in the West. It seems to have first imposed itself upon the notice of the Greco-
Roman world when Pompey tamed the Cilician pirates in 67/66 B.C. They worshipped
Mithra on their local Mt. Olympus (Plut. *Pomp.* 24, 7). Their curious beliefs and rites
became public knowledge when their lair was opened up, and the pirates were dispersed.
Some of these pirates Pompey settled in Calabria, where one of them, Turcan suggests
(following Servius, who identifies the *Corycius senex* of Vergil's *Georgics* IV, 125ff. as an old
pirate), may conceivably have told Vergil something of the new faith, which he could then
have worked into the Fourth Eclogue. Leaving that suggestion prudently to one side,
however, Turcan argues with more probability that Posidonius was the first Greek authority
to deal with the cult. Distrustful though one is of generalized attributions to Posidonius,
one must admit that this is a likely one. Posidonius certainly dealt with Pompey's campaigns
in the 60s in his *History*, and an excursus on the customs and beliefs of the Cilician pirates
would be entirely in character for that discursive man.

It is not clear that Posidonius himself made any attempt to fit Mithra into an Hellenic
theological framework, but as Turcan points out (13), at the same period we do find one of
the client kings of the Empire, Antiochus I of Commagene – a true bridge-figure between
Greece and Persia – making the connection Apollo–Mithras–Helios–Hermes in his
inscription at Nemrud-Dagh. Such an equation was to prove fruitful.

In his second chapter, Turcan turns to Plutarch. By Plutarch's time (let us say A.D. 100), certain developments in regard to Mithra were already well under way. First, he was being accorded both mediating (Hermaic) and demiurgic (Apollonian) functions, both character- istics fitting him comfortably into the Middle Platonic system, where he could be equated with the Demiurge of the *Timaeus*, and the Sun (as opposed to its noetic archetype) of *Republic* VI, or with the Logos of more Stoicizing Platonists, with which Hermes is already being identified by Varro in the first century B.C.

The second development is that Mithra becomes incorporated into the older Persian system with its two opposite principles, Ahura Mazda and Ahriman. At *De Iside* 369E, Plutarch describes Mithrēs as being μέcoc between these two, and being termed μεcίτηc by the Persians. It may have been the Mithraists themselves, rather than Greek philosophical observers, who effected this synthesis, but it is Greek speculation which makes the con- nection between Mithra as mediator and Mithra as demiurge. In the context of Platonism the development is easy enough to comprehend. In the very Stoicized Platonism of Antio- chus of Ascalon (Varro's master), the Stoic *logos* is both the force which holds the universe together, going all through it, and the force which effectively presides over its creation, by allowing it to unfold according to pre-ordained laws. Antiochus, as we know from Cicero, saw the Demiurge as the Stoic *logos*. In later Platonism, however, in which Stoic influence had somewhat receded, and had been overlaid by influences which may be termed Pytha- gorean, the Demiurge had become a second God in his own right (as he is for Numenius, for example), and the rôle of the *logos* is taken over rather more by the World Soul in its active, rational aspect. Mithra, in effect, had to choose what he most wanted to be. He chose Demiurge – Apollo rather than Hermes.

Not that this is not also a median position: in what we may term the 'underworld' of Middle Platonism, as Turcan suggests (20), Mithraic influence on the Demiurge may be clearer. The Valentinian Gnostic Ptolemy, in his *Letter to Flora*, puts his Demiurge in a very Mithraic position, between a Good and an Evil Principle, and gives him the title of μεcότηc. The relative weight of Platonist and Persian influences upon the various Gnostic systems is quite obscure, but Mithra happens to fit fairly plausibly into the Valentinian system, except that the world of the Valentinian system is an evil one.

It is probably after Plutarch's time, in the second century A.D. (though this is by no means certain) that there appear two works in Greek on Mithra, in which already, so far as we can see, the process of assimilation is well advanced. Turcan's third chapter is devoted to the very shadowy figures of Eubulus and Pallas (the former of whom wrote a multi- volume work περὶ τοῦ Μίθρα), for both of whom our only authority is Porphyry, in the *De Antro Nympharum* and the *De Abstinentia*. Turcan speculates about their relative chron- ology at some length (38–42), but the evidence is not there, and it hardly matters. Pallas mentions human sacrifices having been more or less universally given up by the reign of Hadrian (Porph. *De Abst.* II, 56), which puts him later than that. Eubulus might, *pace* Turcan, be the Platonic philosopher of that name who is attested in the mid-third century, though there is nothing to support this but the coincidence of names. What is more interest- ing is the degree of Platonization of Mithra that these writers reveal. For Eubulus, Mithras is a manifestation of the Platonic Demiurge – ὁ πάντων ποιητὴς καὶ πατὴρ Μίθρας, (Porph. *Antr.* 6). He also presents Zoroaster as the founder of the mysteries, a pious development that does violence to the facts, but which gives the cult a respectable ancestry among the ancient sages.

Of great interest, but again, I think, not susceptible of proof, is the relation between Eubulus' *interpretatio Platonica* and that of Numenius and Cronius, Porphyry's chief sources in the *De Antro Nympharum*. Turcan argues plausibly that Porphyry is actually quoting Eubulus through Numenius (which would dispose of the claim of the third-century Platonist). Numenius was certainly greatly interested in Eastern religion and wisdom in general, and certain details of language suggest that Porphyry is quoting Eubulus through another source (e.g. we find the genitive Μίθρου in passages where Eubulus is quoted, whereas it is plain from the title of his work that Eubulus used the genitive Μίθρα). It seems clear, at least, that the Platonizing of Mithra is not an invention of Numenius.

Turcan next turns to Numenius' slightly junior contemporary Celsus, author of the first philosophical anti-Christian polemic, the ᾿Αληθὴς Λόγος, probably in the 160s. I am surprised to find Turcan accepting the identification of this Celsus with Lucian's Epicurean friend (44). It seems to me most improbable that a sceptical Epicurean should turn himself into an orthodox school Platonist for the purpose of attacking the Christians, when sceptical and/or Epicurean arguments were readily available to him as well. This Celsus is a dogmatic Platonist, precisely the fact that baffled Origen, who also made this identification, when he came to reply to him more than half a century later. At any rate, Celsus, while somewhat confused as between orthodox Christians and assorted Gnostic sects, exhibits a good deal of knowledge of the mysteries. Indeed his interest in Eastern religions is closely akin to that of Numenius, and indeed to that shown by Diogenes Laertius, another approximate contemporary, in the Preface to his *Lives of the Philosophers*. It is plainly a characteristic of second-century Platonism, particularly of its Pythagorean wing. For instance, he gives quite a detailed – and, as Turcan shows (47ff.), accurate – account of the Mithraic doctrine of the soul's traversing (διέξοδος) of the heavenly spheres (Orig., *C. Cels.* VI, 22). What concerns us in the present context, however, is not so much the accuracy of his information, as the way in which he has Platonized it. The idea of a ladder with seven gates traversing the heavens, leading to an eighth gate, is not in itself Greek; the order of the planets, also, each with its proper metal, is quite peculiar, and, as Turcan shows, genuinely Mithraic. But the description of the two περίοδοι of the heavens, ἡ ἀπλανής and ἡ εἰς τοὺς πλανήτας αὖ νενμημένη, is Platonic, echoing *Timaeus* 35A, even down to the tell-tale αὖ. Celsus also introduced the Pythagorean theory of musical ratios into the mix, as Origen tells in the same passage.

The doctrine of the progress of the soul through the heavens is of peculiar interest, I think, as an example of cross-fertilization of ideas. On the one hand, we have the Platonic doctrine, or at least imagery, of the soul's heavenly ride in the *Phaedrus* myth, together with whatever one can derive from the myth of *Republic* X and the account of the soul's creation in the *Timaeus*, and on the other a doctrine of planetary influences which the soul acquires, in the form of χιτῶνες, 'garments', as it descends through the spheres to incarnation. This doctrine, which may be termed, rather vaguely, 'Chaldaean', is at the back of the doctrine of the Hermetic *Poemandres*, and at some stage in the development of Platonism (perhaps already in the second century, although Proclus' testimony at *In Tim.* III, 234, 8ff. actually leaves it rather unclear whether Atticus and Albinus held this doctrine in its full form), it was received into the Platonic system, the χιτῶνες, taken together, being identified with the ὄχημα, 'vehicle', into which the Demiurge sets the souls in *Timaeus* 41DE.

It is not this doctrine, however, as Turcan argues (50ff.), that Celsus is in fact describing here, but another, equally interesting one, the Chaldaean doctrine of the soul's cycle of reincarnations through the 'days', each a thousand years long, of the cosmic 'week', this being linked with the doctrine of cyclic renewal of the world at the end of each Great Week. The order of the planets which Celsus gives – Saturn, Venus, Jupiter, Mercury, Mars, Moon, Apollo (Sun) – is not their order in the (ancient) heavens, either Pythagorean or Chaldaean, but that of the days of the week, in reverse order. Origen, in his summary of Celsus, does not make it quite clear what Celsus is talking about, but he does 'accuse' him of bringing in the Mithraic doctrine to buttress his exegesis of Plato, so what Celsus was presumably basing himself on is the description of the cycle of lives in the *Phaedrus* myth, with which the Mithraic seven-stage cycle, with supra-celestial emancipation as the eighth stage, could be hammered into conformity. Celsus' purpose, certainly, is to ridicule the simplistic Christian doctrine of the immortality of the soul, by contrast with the Platonic and Mithraic doctrine of graduated reincarnations.

By the second century A.D., then, at the latest, we can observe considerable detailed knowledge of Mithraic doctrine in Greek philosophical circles, combined with a systematic effort to fit Mithra into the Platonic system. For Numenius at least, he was the Demiurge, the second God, creator and ruler of the physical world, and mediator between it and the supreme Deity. As far as possible, also, details of Mithraic worship are connected with Pythagorean precepts. The greatest effort of syncretism, however, is a work from the latter half of the next century, Porphyry's essay *On the Cave of the Nymphs in the Odyssey*, and it is to this that Turcan devotes his fifth chapter.

In fact, much of Porphyry's doctrine, and probably all of his information on the mysteries, is derived from the sources which we have been discussing, Pallas, Eubulus and Numenius (and/or Cronius). In fact, in discussing the doctrine of the *De Antro*, as Turcan discerns, we are still discussing Numenius. The first image to be considered, of course, is the Cave itself. It is natural that Mithraism should be introduced here by anyone acquainted with it, since caves are the characteristic centres of Mithraic worship. Of course, the Cave is a famous Platonic image – indeed, its presence in Empedocles (Fr. 120 D–K) makes it likely that it is Pythagorean – but the Platonic image has distinctly negative connotations. The Cave of *Republic* VII is not just the cosmos, but the *lower* world of illusion and slavery. The Mithraic *spelaion* is an image of the cosmos as a whole, and is a place of salvation rather than of deception. With its running water, its bees making honey in stone amphorae, and its two exits, the Cave of the Nymphs lends itself far more readily to allegorization on Mithraic lines, and that is what Numenius, it seems, gave it. The flowing water, again, had in Platonic tradition rather the connotation of the flux and turbulence of the material world, whereas in Mithraic tradition it represents purification and salvation. As for the bees and their honey, Plato has nothing obvious to contribute, whereas in Mithraic tradition they are a conspicuous aspect of the ritual of purification (cf. Turcan, 69ff.)

Such an *interpretatio Mithraica* does not have to be anti-Platonic or un-Greek, however; it simply lays emphasis on the Cave as a place of initiation, as most notably in the Eleusinian Mysteries. As Turcan points out (66), the spirit of the *Epinomis* (especially 986 CD), where the cosmos as a whole is treated as a mystery into which one must be initiated, is also an influence on later Platonism (he quotes a good passage from Dio Chrysostom, *Or*. 12, 33).

Turcan turns next (Ch. 6: *La Déesse aux Trois Visages*) to the *De Errore Profanarum*

Religionum of Firmicus Maternus, where, in §5, an interesting piece of Mithraic lore is preserved, concerning the female principle of the Persians, about which one does not hear anything clear from other Greco-Roman sources. According to Firmicus the Persians worship fire under two aspects, of which the male is Mithra, and the female is a figure with three faces, 'wound round with monstrous serpents'. This certainly sounds like Hecate, who is in fact found worshipped in certain Mithraea, but Firmicus puts no name on her. This notion of a female counterpart to a god is a concept reminiscent rather of Egypt than of Chaldaea, but Turcan shows that it is a Persian trait as well (91), and he identifies the goddess convincingly as Anahita (95 ff.), who is frequently attested as a consort of Mithra. She was the goddess of pure waters, and presumably the peculiar circumstance of having a wet substance which was also fiery (petroleum) gave rise to this association. What is interesting in the present context, however, is how Firmicus' source, whoever that was, has Platonized the lady. The three faces of the goddess represent the three parts of the Platonic soul, reason, spirit and desire, represented by Athena, Artemis, and Aphrodite. Indeed, as Turcan notes (97), Anahita is found identified in various Greek sources with each of these goddesses, though not elsewhere with all three together. It is plain that in Platonist terms Anahita has become a manifestation of the World-Soul in all its aspects, the counterpart of the Demiurge in the creation and preservation of the world. In this connection, the most interesting analogy comes, I think, in a source to which Turcan pays much less attention than he might have, the *Chaldaean Oracles*.

The *Oracles*, even more than Numenius (with whom they exhibit interesting connections), constitute a bridge between Platonism and Persian religion. The notion of a female principle in the universe, which has an interesting and varied history within Platonism itself (the Indefinite Dyad, the Evil Soul of *Laws* X, Athena as the thoughts of God, Philo's Sophia, the World-Soul of Middle Platonism) figures prominently in the *Oracles*, in the person of Hecate. Hecate is above all a linking entity. Whether she is to be identified also with the δύναμις situated between the Father and *Nous* is not quite clear, but she is certainly the entity which mediates between the creative force of the Father and the world. She is a triad (Frr. 28-9 Des Places), she receives fire from the Father into her womb, and sends it forth upon the world. Although mistress of life-giving fire (Fr. 32), she is also described as a fountain (πηγὴ τῶν πηγῶν, Fr. 30). In general, the emphasis upon fire as a creative force in the *Oracles* is a clear Persian influence, if not specifically Mithraic. Another possibly Mithraic image is the mixing-bowl (κράτηρ) in which this quasi-liquid fire is mixed (Fr. 42). This is also derivable, perhaps, from *Timaeus* 41D, but the line 'ὄφρα κεράccῃ/πηγαίους κρατῆρας ἑοῦ πυρὸς ἄνθος ἐπιςχών' seems to bring together impressively a number of images with Mithraic resonances. All in all, Turcan might, I think, have given more attention to the *Chaldaean Oracles*.

His final chapter, *Julien II, Héliolatre*, has a negative purpose, but is none the less salutary for that. It has been widely assumed (e.g. by Bidez, Cumont, and by one of Julian's most recent editors, Lacombrade, in the Budé series) that Julian was an initiated Mithraist, but, as Turcan shows, there is really very little evidence to support this 'strong' hypothesis, though there is no question that Julian knew of and honoured Mithra. Indeed, at the end of *The Caesars* (336C), he makes Hermes say to him: 'To you I have granted to know my father Mithra. Obey his commands, preparing for yourself a safe cable and mooring during life, and when you must depart from here, establishing for yourself, with Good Hope, a divine guide who will be benevolent to you.' The myth, or parable, which he tells in §22 of his treatise *Against Heraclius* involves his becoming the initiate and devotee of a Helios who sounds Mithraic enough, having a son Hermes and a consort Athena (who could be standing in for Anahita). All this shows a great reverence for the Sun-God, and at least a partial identification of him with Mithra, but the problem Turcan wishes to unravel (107) is a more difficult one: was Julian actually an initiate, or is he just celebrating a Platonized Mithra as another manifestation of his favourite deity?

Turcan thinks that he was not an initiate, despite Julian's many references to being an initiate of King Helios and to having received secret revelations from the god (e.g. *To King Helios* 130 B–C), and, despite the information (from Libanius and Himerius) that there was a shrine in the palace in Constantinople in which rites in honour of the Sun God were celebrated. Cumont and Bidez assume unhesitatingly that this was a Mithraeum, but they go somewhat beyond the evidence. Admittedly, the *titulus* of Himerius' address to Julian (*Or.* VII = XLI Colonna), in the MSS. R and B̆, describes it as 'a speech of thanks to the Emperor after being initiated into the mysteries of Mithra', but, as Turcan argues, there is nothing in the text to support this title, and it could well be an editorial deduction, similar to the assumptions of Bidez and Cumont.

Certainly something went on in this chapel, but on balance it seems more likely that Julian confined himself to religious practices more in accord with the ancient religion of Greece and of Empire, at least as he conceived of it. This was, after all, what he was trying to revive. Mithra was certainly a manifestation of King Helios, and, as a disciple of Iamblichus, Julian would recognize that any and all cult might be useful as an aid to putting the worshipper in contact with the Gods, but it is unlikely that, either for personal or for political reasons, he would so to speak have put all his eggs in this one basket.

There are other indications, at first sight persuasive, at closer examination not conclusive: Julian, in his autobiographical fable mentioned above, appears before Helios as a soldier, clad in armour, and is given more armour by Athena. Is this not a sign that he was a Mithraic *miles*? All through his life, also, he practised a regime of endurance, chastity and general asceticism such as Mithra enjoined upon his followers. But the military metaphor goes back in Platonism to the *Phaedo*, and was much used by Stoics such as Seneca and Epictetus, while the 'Mithraic' virtues mentioned are all those of the Platonic or Stoic sage.

What we have in Julian, I think, is a phenomenon much more interesting for our present purpose, namely a supreme example of that process of syncretism with Persian religion that had been going on for the previous three centuries and more. Helios-Mithra for Julian is the Demiurge, Athena is his consort, the World-Soul, Hermes is his servant, the Logos. Above Helios is a triad comprising Kronos, Rhea and Zeus, respectively *patēr*, *dunamis* and *nous* of the Chaldaean Oracles, this *dunamis* being the Mother of the Gods to whom Julian addresses one of his two main theological Orations. The theology here is essentially Iamblichean Neoplatonism, itself heavily influenced by the *Oracles*.

In conclusion, since this is a review, something should be said in praise of Turcan. He seems to me to perform his delicate task of evaluating influences and sources with great prudence and tact. His chapter on Julian is the only place where he is directly involved in challenging accepted beliefs, but everywhere he assembles and weighs the evidence with commendable judiciousness. It is indeed a complex operation to unravel the reciprocal influences of the Pythagorean-Platonic and the Persian traditions. After all, Plato (partly through Eudoxus) and Xenocrates after him – to say nothing of Pythagoras himself – were at least vaguely acquainted with something they knew of as the teachings of Zoroaster, who was later to be adopted as the founder of the mysteries. Hellenized Persians in the Hellenistic era, like Hellenized Jews, no doubt picked up a tincture of Greek philosophical thought, which was most likely to have been Stoic-influenced Middle Platonism. All this lies behind the actual arrival of Mithra on the philosophical scene. The profound urge to syncretize, animated as it was by the conviction that behind all diverse religious manifestations there reposed the same Truth, was a powerful force in favour of seeing connections between disparate religious traditions and glossing over substantial differences. All this is very annoying for us, no doubt, and makes Turcan's task, when he tries to estimate how much a given Greek writer actually *knew*, almost hopeless. In many cases the opportunity of learning the details of Mithraic worship and belief was no doubt present, but there was no desire to avail oneself of it. Turcan condemns Numenius, for instance (89), as an 'esprit confus et confusionniste', for trying to bring Platonism into accord with the doctrines of the Brahmans, the Jews, the Magi and the Egyptians, but his disapproval is somewhat anachronistic. Numenius, like Julian after him, knew very well what he was about. He was interested in the wood rather than the trees.

XVIII

PLOTINUS, PHILO AND ORIGEN ON THE GRADES OF VIRTUE

I.

My purpose in this essay, which I have much pleasure in offering as a small tribute to a giant in a field where I am a relative beginner, is to analyse the remarkable theory of grades of virtue which Plotinus advances in *Ennead* I 2, and then to see if anything answering to it can be found first in Philo of Alexandria, and then in the writings of Plotinus' great Christian contemporary Origen[1]. I am not one of those who hope to reconstruct the teachings of Ammonius Saccas from a comparison of the works of his two great pupils, but I remain interested in studying what each of them may have derived from their common heritage of second-century Platonism, and what they did with it. As for Philo, he serves as a useful and instructive foil to both later thinkers. I begin with Plotinus, though he is last chronologically, and deal with him at greatest length, since he gives the clearest rationale for the doctrine, and thus a thorough examination of him makes the traces of the doctrine in the two others easier to discern.

As so often, the Platonic doctrine which he inherited on the subject of Virtue presented Plotinus with a dilemma, though it is not one which seems to have greatly bothered his predecessors. On the one hand, we have the analysis of the four cardinal virtues in the *Republic* in terms of the tripartite soul, and the control exercised by the rational part over the irrational part or parts, and on the other we have the description of the path of virtue in the *Phaedo* as a purging away from the soul of all bodily concerns, including the passions, the proper contents of the irrational soul, and, in the same vein, the description of the purpose of life, or *telos*, at *Theaetetus* 176AB, as ὁμοίωσις θεῷ κατὰ τὸ δυνατόν – likeness to a god who, whatever his other characteristics, is certainly not possessed of an irrational element in his soul which requires rational ordering. Any concept of virtue, therefore, which involves such rational ordering of the irrational, can hardly be proper to likening oneself to God, if *homoiosis* denotes ›making oneself *homoios*‹ in any normal sense. To aggravate the contradiction between *Phaedo* and *Republic*, it would seem, Plato actually refers in a derogatory way in *Phaedo* 82A to a certain level of virtue as δημοτικὴ καὶ πολιτική, which is based on ἔθος and μελέτη rather than φιλοσοφία and νοῦς, and since πολιτική is the epithet of virtue in *Republic* IV (430C), later Platonists saw the makings of a contradiction here. What seems called for is a doctrine of grades or levels of virtue, but before this essay of Plotinus no clear account of one is to be seen. The contrast between what were called φυσικαὶ ἀρεταί or εὐφυΐαι, natural or unreflective excellences, such as we might share even with animals, and τέλειαι ἀρεταί, perfected virtues, had indeed been made, and is to be found in Albinus' *Didaskalikos* (ch. 30), and Apuleius' *De Platone*,

---

[1] The following works I have found useful in at least some degree: H. van Lieshout, *La théorie plotinienne de la vertu*, Paderborn, 1926; O. Schissel von Fleschenberg, *Marinos von Neapolis und die neuplatonischen Tugend-* *grade*, Athens, 1928; W. Capitaine, *de Origenis Ethica*, Münster 1898; B. J. M. Bradley, *Arete as a Christian Concept: The Structural Elements of Origen's Doctrine*, Unpubl. Doctoral Diss., Cambridge, 1976.

(ch. 6), but it is not the same contrast as we are concerned with here, though it is one that Plotinus makes in the very next tractate, I 3 (20) *On Dialectic.*

It is the apparent contradiction between the theories of virtue of the *Phaedo* and the *Republic,* and their reconciling with the long-since accepted Platonist definition of the *telos* derived from *Theastetus* 176AB to which Plotinus addresses himself in this tractate. What I propose to do first is to offer a commentary on the tractate, with a translation of the first chapter and of certain other sections, with a view to observing how Plotinus arrives at his distinctive theory. I will then turn to certain passages of, first, Philo, and then Origen, to see how they face similar problems about levels of virtue, though without arriving at a theory of anything like the elaboration of Plotinus.

Plotinus begins as follows:

»Since this realm here is where ›evils‹ are, and ›they must necessarily haunt this region‹, and the soul wishes to escape evils, ›we must flee hence.‹ (*Theaet.* 176A)

In what, then, does this flight consist? ›In becoming like unto God‹, Plato says. And *this* consists in ›becoming just and holy along with wisdom‹, and generally in acquiring virtue.

Now, if we ›become like‹ by virtue, does that imply that that to which we become like itself possesses virtue? And if so, what ›god‹ would that be? Would it be the one that particularly seems to possess these attributes, that is, the soul of the cosmos, and in particular the ruling element in this, which possesses marvellous wisdom?«

Plotinus is here raising a question which had plainly exercised Platonists before him, ever since any distinction had been made between a supreme, totally transcendent God and a Demiurge, and indeed between a Demiurge and a World Soul. We find in Albinos' *Didaskalikos* a recognition of this problem. In his discussion of the *telos*-formula ὁμοίωσις θεῷ, he says (ch. 28, p. 181,36–7 Hermann): »By ›god‹ is obviously meant the god in the heavens (ἐπουράνιος), not, by Zeus, the god above the heavens (ὑπερουράνιος), who does not possess virtue, but is superior to it«. In Albinos' system this will be the (demiurgic) Intellect of the World-Soul (ch. 10), as opposed to his ›First Intellect‹, which is entirely transcendent. Whether or not Plotinus has Albinos in mind in particular, this is the position on which he is basing his critique. He now turns to examine this position:

»The first problem is, are all the virtues properly attributable even to this entity? For instance, can he be self-controlled, or courageous, when there is nothing of which he might be frightened? There is nothing external to him, after all. Nor can there be any pleasurable sensation presented to him which he might desire to retain or acquire, since this would imply its not being present to him already.

On the other hand, if he himself is in a state of appetition towards the intelligible realm, towards which our aspirations are also directed, it is plain that our sense of order (κόσμος) and our virtues, as well as his, derive from that source. So, is that entity also to have these virtues?«

With a few quick strokes, borrowed from Aristotle, *EN* X 8 (1178b 8–15), Plotinus has undermined Albinos' complacent dismissal of the problem. The concept of ›becoming like‹ must imply some element of likeness in us to that entity to which we are becoming like. We are urged to ›become like‹ by the practice of virtue. Thence it would seem to follow that this entity must in some sense be virtuous.

Now the Middle Platonists, or some of them, had seen that to predicate the cardinal virtues of the supreme God was nonsensical, but they obviously felt that a demiurgic being, involved with the administration of the cosmos, could possess virtue without incongruity. The implications of even this, though, had not, as far as we can see, been properly thought out. Plotinus loses no time in setting them out here. First of all, the virtues, in the normal sense of the word, cannot be characteristics of a being which does not face the external circumstances which human beings face, and/or which does not have the sort of compound soul which human beings have (in Platonic theory, at least). Secondly, if the World Soul is itself an image of a higher being, then it should have the same relation of *homoiosis* to that as we have to *it,* and therefore, assuming that it resembles its model in respect of virtue, that model must itself be virtuous. So Albinos' qualification (ἐπουράνιος, not ὑπερουράνιος) does not have much substance, unless he is prepared to introduce certain other specifications, such as Plotinus himself now proceeds to do.

> »Certainly it is not reasonable to postulate that it should possess the so-called civic virtues – that is, wisdom in the rational part, courage in the spirited part, self-control manifested in a sort of agreement and justice consisting in the ›minding its own business‹ of each of these parts ›in respect of ruling and being ruled‹ (*Rep.* IV 434C).
> It is not, then, by civic virtues that we are made like, but by the superior ones which have the same names?
> In that case, though, do the civic ones have nothing to contribute to the process? It is unreasonable, surely, that we should not at all be made like by them, but that the likeness should be in respect of the superior virtues only. At any rate, men characterised by these virtues are certainly accorded in tradition the epithet ›divine‹, and must be said to have acquired such a likeness in some way or other. But in either case the result is that the entity possesses virtues, even if not the same ones as we have.«

Plotinus now attacks the problem that seems to arise if one admits that God (if we may take ›God‹ as signifying the ultimate object of our *homoiosis*) does not possess the ›civic‹ virtues. Is the possession of these virtues of any value whatever for one who wishes to attain likeness to God? That this was not an empty question is shown by the antinomian tendencies of certain of Plotinus' Gnostic contemporaries, and it is a thought that might occur to anyone of reasonably analytical mind. If one's salvation consists solely in cutting oneself off from things of this world, in purifying oneself of all passion, including compassion, then is there anything to be gained by helping an old lady across the road? To adapt the form in which the question is put by DAVID SACHS in his essay ›A Fallacy in Plato's *Republic?*‹[2] need Likeness to God involve Platonic Justice, any more than Platonic Justice need involve ›vulgar‹ justice? Plotinus would no doubt reply (as would have Plato) that it necessarily does, because the higher, purificatory virtues can only arise in a soul in which the civic virtues already hold sway. Nevertheless, it is not in respect of the civic virtues as such that we attain our *telos* of likeness to God.

As THEILER and BEUTLER point out, Herakles must have seemed a good example to illustrate that problem, and it is no doubt him that Plotinus has in mind when he refers to ›those whom tradition (φήμη) accords the epithet ›divine‹«. In the late tractate I 1 (sect. 12), he sees as a reason for Homer placing Herakles both in Hades and in Olympus the fact that on the one hand Herakles excelled in πρακτικὴ ἀρετή but was not at all θεωρητικός – and yet was accounted a god. In this passage his position is somewhat different: since Herakles *was* after all accounted a god, there must be something ›god-like‹ about practical or civic virtue.

At any rate, it is established that, whatever sort of virtues we may suppose God to have, it is not in respect of them that we assimilate ourselves to him, since our virtues are

---

[2] *Philosophical Review* LXXII (1963), pp. 141–158 (repr.   New York, 1971.
in *Plato II: Modern Studies in Philosophy,* ed. G. Vlastos,

of a different nature. Having conceded this, though, one can go a step further and suggest that it is possible that, by the practice of virtues proper to us, we can achieve assimilation to a being of whom virtue cannot meaningfully be predicated. And yet it goes against the grain for Plotinus to deny virtue altogether to God. The analysis must be carried a stage further.

»If, then, one is prepared to admit that likeness is possible even if it does not have the same virtues as us, we having a different relationship to a different set of virtues, there is no problem, even if we are not likened to its virtues, about our being likened by our own virtues to an entity that does not itself possess virtue.

How can this be so? Let us consider the following: if something is made hot by the presence of heat, is it necessary that that source from which the heat has come be also hot? Or more precisely, if something is hot through the presence of fire, is it necessary that the fire itself be also hot through the presence of fire?

In response to the former question, one could say that there is heat in the fire also, but innate, so that the argument, following out the analogy, would make virtue in the soul something adventitious, whereas in that from which it has it through imitation it is innate; while in response to the argument drawn from fire one could say that that makes it identical with virtue, whereas we want it to be greater than virtue.

But such an objection would only have force if we take that in which the soul participates as being identical to what it derives it from. In fact they are distinct. As an illustration, the house perceptible to our senses is not the same as the one in the mind, although it has a *likeness* to it. The sense-perceptible house partakes of structure of parts and order, whereas *there*, in the reason-principle, there is no structure of parts or order or symmetry. Even so, whereas we partake in order and structure and coherence from that source, and these are characteristics of virtue here, while things there have no need of coherence or order or structure, they would not have any need of virtue either, and yet we nonetheless can be assimilated to that realm through the presence in us of virtue.«

Plotinus' analogy is a most useful one, though he does not here seem to want to pursue it as far as he might. Let us consider the case of fire in particular. To say that fire is hot is to say something different from saying that we are hot, or that the coffee is hot. In the latter cases we are saying that the objects in question have been heated; in the case of fire, that it is capable of heating other objects. Other objects are hot by the presence in them of heat, or fire. But is fire itself hot by the presence in it of heat or fire? If we say yes to this, we must still, surely, mean something different from saying that the coffee is hot. ›Hot‹ if predicated of fire, must mean ›causing heat in others‹, rather than just ›heated‹. We might call this latter, normal use of the word ›hot₁‹ and the causative sense ›hot₂‹. In this way, God could be described as virtuous, but in the sense ›virtuous₂‹, ›causing virtue in others‹. To describe him as virtuous without this qualification is to introduce the confusion which Plotinus is criticising here.

I discern behind this argument a particular application of a principle first enunciated by Speusippus, that something which is an ἀρχή for other things cannot itself possess in the same way the quality or qualities which it bestows upon its products. This principle, the consequences of which are criticised rather tendentiously by Aristotle in *Met.* Λ 7 (1072b 30ff), is clearly stated only in a passage embedded (as PHILIP MERLAN has, I think, correctly discerned[3]) in Iamblichus' *De Communi Mathematica Scientia*, Ch. 4, and it is one which, I believe, was influential, whether immediately or indirectly, on the development of Plotinus' doctrine of the relation of the One to its products. What we would have here is a

---

[3] In *From Platonism to Neoplatonism*, The Hague, 1968 (3rd. ed.), ch. 5.

96

particular case of that principle, in the argument that what generates virtue in other entities cannot possess virtue itself, at least in the same way.

However, Plotinus does not really want to deny virtue to the gods absolutely. What he
does instead is to make use of this principle to develop a theory of grades of virtue, a
doctrine which he sees an occasion for in the apparent contradiction between the system of
›civic‹ virtues in the *Republic,* where the essential feature is control of the irrational element
in the soul, and the ›kathartic or ›purificatory‹ theory of virtue in the *Phaedo,* which involves the purging away of all bodily and irrational elements.

This doctrine was taken up enthusiastically by his successors from Porphyry on, and
built up to where we find Iamblichus[4] adding three more grades of virtue (one at the bottom, two more at the top) to the *four* – civic, purificatory, contemplative and paradigmatic-
which Porphyry, in no. 32 of the *Sententiae,* derives from this tractate. Porphyry discerns
the civic virtues as being discussed in ch. 1, the purificatory in ch. 3, with which we would
readily agree, but then the contemplative in ch. 6, and the paradigmatic in ch. 7. An
examination of how well this scheme accords with Plotinus' intentions will prove instructive, I think, in demonstrating how misleading Plotinus' method could be even for his
closest and most devoted follower, if that follower was possessed of an essentially scholastic
mind.

Having laid out his initial *aporia,* Plotinus ends ch. 1 with the remark: »So much for
the argument as to the necessity that there be virtue in that realm also, on the ground that
we assimilate ourselves to it by virtue. However, we must not rest content with enforcing
assent (βία); we must apply persuasion (πειθώ) to our logical argument«. His first attack
on the problem, then, he sees as βία, which may achieve grudging acquiescence, but not
full conviction. The rest of the essay he presents as πειθώ, supporting his initial position[5].

This would seem to imply that the rest of the essay is not on the same level of logical
rigour. This does not, on inspection, however, appear obvious, as I think we shall see. In
Plotinus' mind, I think, the πειθώ of the next six chapters consists rather in the adducing
of supporting arguments than in anything more subjective or rhetorical. It is rather the
same case as with the παιδιά we are promised at the beginning of *Enn.* III 8 – play,
perhaps, but pretty serious stuff.

Ch. 2 in fact starts out by establishing an important logical distinction, which forms
the basis for much of the later argument. We must distinguish, says Plotinus, between two
kinds of *homoiosis.* There is the likeness of one copy to another, which consists in the common possession of certain characteristics, relating both of them to an original; and there is
the likeness of a copy to its model, which cannot consist of such shared characteristics.
This, as ARMSTRONG suggests (note *ad loc.*), is plainly a distinction arising out of exegesis of
the *aporia* about likeness raised by Parmenides in *Parm.* 132D–133A. Proclus, in his commentary on that passage[6] makes the same distinction:

> »To this (sc. the difficulty raised by Parmenides) Socrates should have replied that ›like‹ has two
> senses, one, the likeness of two co-ordinate entities, the other, the likeness which involves sub-
> ordination to an archetype, and the one is to be seen as consisting in the identity of some one
> reason-principle, while the other involves not only identity, but at the same time otherness, when-
> ever something is ›like‹ as having the same form derived from the other, but not along with it.«

[4] ›Olympiodorus‹ (Damascius), *In Phaed.* p. 114, 16–25 Norvin.
[5] This contrast he is deriving, presumably, from Plato's use of it in *Laws* IV, where the necessity for backing up βία with πειθώ in lawgiving is repeatedly alluded to, e.g. 711 A–C, 720 A–722 B.
[6] *In Parm.* p.912, 31–8 Cousin.

It is not quite clear from the way Plotinus introduces the distinction (ἐπισημηνάμενοι) whether he is propounding it as something new. Probably not, as it must have formed part of any discussion of *Parm.* 132D which sought to salvage the Theory of Forms.

In this second sort of likeness, the likeness of the image for the model is not reciprocal (οὐκ ἀντιστρέφον). All that need be postulated is some formula or potency in the paradigm which produces the sense-perceptible image, and in the present instance, if one wishes to call that formula or potency ›virtue‹, then one must at least employ inverted commas.

Plotinus now turns to a definition of virtue in us, distinguishing first the civic virtues (in the remainder of ch. 2), and then (in ch. 3) the kathartic virtues corresponding to them. The civic virtues are actually concerned with setting us in order (κατακοσμοῦσι) by imposing μέτρον and κόσμος on our soul's appetitive part, which is a kind of ὕλη to their εἶδος. »In so far as they are measures in the matter of the soul«, he says, »they are ›like‹ the measure in that realm, and possess a trace of the Best there.« I do not think that Plotinus is actually referring here to an Idea of Measure, but rather to Nous as a whole, as the imposer of Form on Matter. He may even be referring to the One, as he goes on to say that Matter, in so far as it partakes of Form, is to that extent assimilated to that (source), which is itself formless (ἀνείδεον), an epithet only predicable properly of the One. His point is, presumably, that even as the imposer of Form in general must itself transcend Form, so must the imposer of Virtue transcend Virtue.

However, it is not the likeness which the civic virtues confer that Plato is concerned with at *Theaet.* 176AB, which is what we are discussing. There is a higher type of virtue than the civic, and it is that to which we must now turn. Here Plotinus works out, probably for the first time – to judge from the manner in which he presents it – a scheme of four kathartic, or purificatory, virtues, to match the four civic ones. He actually argues that these kathartic virtues are the *truer* forms, as being nearer the paradigm, and that Plato suggests this by explicitly denominating the virtues described in the *Republic* πολιτικαί. Plato does this at *Rep.* IV 430C, but Plotinus must be thinking primarily of *Phaedo* 82BC, where the contrast is made between those who practise δημοτικὴ καὶ πολιτικὴ ἀρετή and the ὀρθῶς φιλοσοφοῦντες who strive to be pure from all bodily concerns.

The higher forms of virtue, then, are not concerned with the ordering of the irrational soul or of the body, but rather with escaping from all entanglement with the sense-world. On this calculation, φρόνησις, in its higher form, is for the soul to act alone, without sharing at all in the opinions of sense (εἰ μήτε συνδοξάζοι, ἀλλὰ μόνη ἐνεργοῖ); σωφροσύνη will be refusing to share in bodily passions (μήτε ὁμοπαθὴς εἴη) – it sounds here as if Plotinus is relating μετριοπάθεια and ἀπάθεια to the lower and higher virtues respectively, an impression which is reinforced by his language later on (6, 25–6); ἀνδρεία consists in not fearing to depart from the body; and δικαιοσύνη in the unopposed rule of λόγος and νοῦς in the soul (3, 10–19).

Now all this might seem thoroughly tendentious and contrived, if we do not bear in mind that on Plotinus' theory there must be these four higher virtues, no more and no less, since they are actually paradigmatic for the lower, civic virtues, though themselves being only εἰκόνες of the Forms in Nous. A sage operating according to these virtues will indeed be like unto God, in that God is pure from all contact with Matter. »Why, then,« he asks, »is God not in this state?«, That is, why does God not have these virtues? »Because«, he replies, »the divine does not have any state at all (οὐδὲ διακεῖται); ›being in a state‹ is proper only to the soul.« Similarly, soul intelligises (νοεῖ), but it does so in a different way from Intellect itself, while the One does not intelligise at all.

Is the verb νοεῖν then, when applied to Nous and to Soul, used homonymously (3,25–6)? This question of homonymity concerns Plotinus a good deal in this context. It would not suit his picture of the relation between higher and lower to admit that ›virtue‹ was being used homonymously, in the Aristotelian sense, in respect of either the kathartic or the civic virtues. It is rather the concept of ›focal meaning‹ which he wants, and he establishes that with his example here of Nous intelligising πρώτως, while Soul intelligises παρ' ἐκείνου ἑτέρως. He adduces the difference between λόγος ἐνδιάθετος and λόγος προφορικός to reinforce his point. Ἀρετή proper, then – πρώτως – is in the soul in its pure state; secondarily it is in the ensouled body, the human being. In Nous or the One virtue has no place at all. This clear statement we must bear in mind when we come to consider the passages in chs. 6 and 7 which encouraged Porphyry to postulate higher grades of virtue at the level of the transcendent soul and of Nous.

I will pass over rather quickly the intervening chapters, 4 and 5, since they do not concern our present theme directly. I cannot, however, forebear to draw attention to the characteristically Plotinian *aporia* which largely occupies ch. 4: is the higher virtue identical with κάθαρσις or does it supervene upon the completed state of purification (τὸ κεκαθάρ-θαι)? Is it part of the process, or the result of the process? This enquiry, I think, shows Plotinus at his most acute. The importance of the enquiry is this: if virtue is simply the process of stripping away everything alien from the soul, then this would imply that the soul, when all accretions are stripped from it, is something entirely good. But this is not the case. If the soul were a nature entirely good, it would never have fallen in the first place. In fact, it has a natural tendency in both directions (πέφυκεν ἐπ ' ἄμφω). Along with purification, then, it must turn itself around (ἐπιστρέφεσθαι). Plotinus is careful to specify that the ἐπιστροφή does not follow on the κάθαρσις, but accompanies it, though being distinct from it: »Does it then turn itself after the purification? Rather, after the purification it is already turned. Is this, then, its virtue? No, it is rather that which results for ιτ from the conversion.« (4,16–18). The higher virtue, then, is rather like pleasure in Aristotle's formulation in *EN* X 4 (1174b31–3): ἐπιγινόμενόν τι τέλος, οἷον τοῖς ἀκμαίοις ἡ ὥρα.

In ch. 6, Plotinus returns to the main subject of the essay, and we can see, I think, what it was that gave Porphyry the excuse for his interpretation. Our purpose, says Ploti-nus, is not just to be free from sin; our purpose is to become god. Ὁμοίωσις θεῷ is here given a stronger sense than the original propounders of the formula, whether the Pythago-reans or Plato, intended. It is to be noted that Plotinus either tacitly disregards the Plato-nic qualification ›κατὰ τὸ δυνατόν‹, or else, as seems to me more probable, interprets it, as Eudorus of Alexandria, at least, had done before him[7], as meaning »in virtue of that element in us which is capable of this« – a strained, but possible, interpretation of the Greek. Plotinus sees divinisation as a natural *telos* for the sage, and the intellect as the element in us which can achieve this. But will this state involve virtue, or will the sage transcend virtue? Plotinus' language later in this chapter seems to indicate that the sage does in fact possess a set of virtues. How is this reconcilable with being a god?

---

[7] Cf. DILLON, *The Middle Platonists,* London and Cornell 1977, p.123.

In fact, Plotinus is distinguishing two stages of the sage's existence. The sage's object is to become a god, but this can only be fully achieved after he has freed himself from the body and the lower soul; so, only after death. Meanwhile, he is at best a god linked to a daemon (6,4), a double entity, and it is as such that he possesses the higher level of virtue.

»What, then, is each virtue for such a one? Well, wisdom and prudence (σοφία καὶ φρόνησις) consist in the contemplation of what Intellect contains (Intellect itself, of course, enjoys immediate contact (ἐπαφή) with this). Each of these (i.e. σοφία and φρόνησις) is double, one set in Intellect, the other in soul, but *there* (sc. in Intellect) they are not virtue, while in the soul they are. What, then, are they there? Its activity (ἐνέργεια) and what it is. *Here* (sc. in the soul) that which is from thence in an alien receptacle is (what is properly) virtue. For Justice Itself and each of the others are not virtues, but as it were paradigms; it is that which derives from each of them that is a virtue. For ›virtue‹.is something relative to some particular subject (τινὸς γὰρ ἡ ἀρετή); each of the essential Forms is in and for itself, not relative to anything else.«

There are a number of troubling things in this passage, and it is not difficult to see how from this and what follows it Porphyry managed to derive two further grades of virtue, despite Plotinus' caveats.

First, we find that the Ideas or Forms of the virtues are present at the level of Nous (which is the level of divinity towards which the sage is aspiring). But these, Plotinus is careful to say, are not themselves virtues. The reason he gives is not immediately easy to interpret. Virtue is τινός; the paradigms are ἕκαστον αὑτοῦ, οὐχὶ δὲ ἄλλου τινός. How are we to understand this? ARMSTRONG renders it: »Virtue is someone's virtue; but the exemplar of each particular virtue in the intellect belongs to itself, not to someone else.« HARDER says virtually the same, in German. BRÉHIER takes it as expressing more of a logical relation: »La vertu se dit d'un être;« whereas each of the examplars »se dit d'elle-même et non d'un être différent d'elle.« Stephen Mackenna is rather vaguer, but he may be right in that: »For Virtue is dependent, seated in something not itself; the Ideal-Form is self-standing, independent.«

As far as I can see, the point Plotinus is making is connected with something he said a littler earlier, that virtue is τὸ ἐν ἄλλῳ ἐκεῖθεν (6,16). I take it to mean that virtue is predicated, as a quality or characteristic, of an entity not itself (sc. the soul), whereas the Forms of the virtues are part of the essence of Intellect, and are not to be taken as predicated of it. At any rate, the principle that virtue must be ›of something‹ is intended to preclude the possibility that it should be present at the level of Nous, or of God.

So these paradigms are not virtues for Plotinus. And yet he does contrive to give some encouragement to a scholastic mind like that of Porphyry, for he goes .on to distinguish what their characteristics must be, once again in a way that must seem tendentious at first sight, but which is in fact entirely logical, once one accepts his premiss that any positive characteristic in a lower entity (that is to say, anything that does not arise from its greater involvement with Matter), must derive from its higher, and that therefore some analogue to it must be present in that higher. There are, therefore, paradigms of the four virtues in Intellect, and their characteristics are as follows: Wisdom, as we have seen, consists in direct contact with its own contents. Justice is οἰκειοπραγία in a special sense. To ›do one's own thing‹, Plotinus says rather defensively, one does not have to have a multiplicity of parts, as the definition of the *Republic* requires; in fact, the truest sort of οἰκειοπραγία is that of a unitary essence performing its essential act, and that is the Justice of Nous.

Σωφροσύνη, similarly, is a turning towards itself (τὸ πρὸς αὑτόν), while ἀνδρεία consists in immateriality (ἀϋλότης) and abiding pure by itself[8].

Porphyry unhesitatingly introduces all these as the paradigmatic virtues, which are in Nous (*Sent.* p. 28, 6ff. Lamberz). I find it impossible to believe that he is simply misunderstanding Plotinus (even as I find it difficult to believe, in many instances, that Aristotle is misunderstanding Plato). It must be rather, I think, that he feels he is introducing an improvement – ironing out an anomaly in Plotinus' thought. How much neater, after all, for virtues to appear in their appropriate form at each level of reality – and it also settles the uncomfortable paradox that the gods do not possess virtue. Iamblichus can then, in the same spirit, postulate henadic virtues, above these again, as being even more proper to the gods. Thus was the external form of Plotinus' system transmitted to posterity without the method or the spirit which informed it.

Similarly, the alleged third level of virtue, the theoretic or contemplative, which Porphyry discerns (*ibid.* p. 27,3ff.) as being described in this part of the essay, supervening upon the kathartic, is another scholastic wind-egg, induced by Plotinus' rather different way of presenting the higher virtues in ch. 6, when he is thinking of them in relation to their paradigms, rather than in relation to their lower manifestations, as he was in ch. 3:

> »So the higher Justice in the soul is its activity towards Intellect, its Self-control is its inward turning to Intellect, its Courage its freedom from affections (ἀπάθεια), according to the likeness of that to which it looks, which is free from affections by nature.« (ARMSTRONG's transl., 6,23–6).

Once again, Porphyry is probably not so much misunderstanding this as thinking that he can clarify what Plotinus has left indistinct – and indeed Plotinus could have made his intentions plainer!

Plotinus ends his essay with a characteristic *aporia*, the substance of which we have touched on previously, in ch. 1. It is admitted that he who possesses the higher virtues will have the lower ones *potentially* (7,11), but will he have them also in actuality? For instance, I suppose, the sage would tend to be the sort of person who would help old ladies across the road, if he happened to notice them, but he would in practice be most unlikely to do so. Again, the sage would possess the higher courage, which consists, as we have seen, in ἀπάθεια, but how would he function in the line of battle? Doubtless he would not be afraid of the enemy, but he might not notice them at all. Similarly for σωφροσύνη:

> »He will not make self-control consist in that former observance of measure and limit, but will altogether separate himself, as far as possible, from his lower nature, and will not live the life of a good man, which civic virtue requires. He will leave that behind, and choose another, the life of the gods: for it is to them, not to good men, that we are to be made like.« (7,23–8 ARMSTRONG's transl.)

---

[8] Porphyry, in relaying this text in *Sententiae* 32 (p. 29,6 Lamberz), interestingly produces for the hapax legomenon ἀϋλότης the plausible variant ταυτότης (that he really did so seems assured by the fact that Macrobius, at *In Somn. Scip.* I 8,10, follows him in this – *quod semper idem est*). Ἀϋλότης is certainly the *lectio difficilior*, and also seems to suit better, as the source and fount of a sequence which is characterised at the next stage by ›turning away from the body‹, which, as we have seen, is the kathartic virtue of ἀνδρεία. If Porphyry is really responsible for both readings, then one can only conjecture that, in his rephrasing in the *Sententiae*, he felt that ›sameness‹ sounded more like a virtue than ›immateriality‹. But the close likeness of the two readings may mean that he just misread his own handwriting.

On the other hand, Dr. Henry Blumenthal has suggested to me in conversation that the true reading may be αὑτότης, a word otherwise unknown, but quite plausible as a Plotinian *ad hoc* coinage. This would mean ›self-ness‹ rather than ›sameness‹, and is very much what Plotinus should want to say. But this must remain no more than a stimulating conjecture.

Not, of course, that the sage will behave disgracefully. It is just that he has rid himself of any element within the soul that requires control.

Plotinus ends with a return to the distinction that he made in ch. 2 between the two kinds of *homoiosis*. We are not concerned with the imitation of good men, because that would be the likeness of one image to another; we are concerned with likeness to our archetype, which is God, or Nous.

As Bréhier points out in his introduction to this tractate, Plotinus here manages to combine the Stoic doctrine that the virtues of the Sage are identical with those of God, and that those virtues are reciprocal (ἀνταϰολουθοῦσι), with the Aristotelian view that the virtues are proper to a certain type of being, to wit, Man, and that they thus cannot serve to assimilate us to the gods, to whom they are not proper. He does that, certainly, but he plainly does more. In this tractate, he explores the nature of assimilation to an entity which is quite other than the sense-world, and than ourselves as creatures of the sense-world, and speculates as to what such assimilation must be like. Of course, in his view our truest self is akin, if not identical, with that other, but the fact remains that it is not by being ›good‹ in traditionally human terms – even with the refinements to the concept of the virtues introduced by Plato in the *Republic* – that we become like that Other. The Stoics did not have this problem, since for them there were not two worlds, a material and a spiritual, but one. All one had to do was to comprehend as fully as possible the workings of this world, and school oneself to assent to them. That is the essence of ὁμολογουμένως τῇ φύσει ζῆν.

What Plotinus has done in this tractate, it seems to me, is to set out, perhaps for the first time in a coherent way, an ethic for the world-renouncing sage of later Platonism. Of course, the materials for such an ethic are present in Plato himself, particularly in the *Phaedo*, and at *Theaet.* 176AB, as Plotinus acknowledges, but Plato had not provided any clear connexion between the practice of the ordinary ›civic‹ virtues and the higher level of virtue. Such a connexion is certainly assumed, but it is not worked out. By his doctrine of the grades of virtue, Plotinus sets out a hierarchy of modes of behaviour, whereby the life of the sage is sharply differentiated from that of the ordinary man.

I have avoided bringing other Plotinian passages into the discussion, since I have not been concerned so much with Plotinus' philosophy in general as with his methods of philosophising in a particular context, but I will adduce his remarks on virtue and free will in chs. 5 and 6 of *Enn.* VI 8 (39), since they illustrate the problem with which he ends I 2: Will the sage in fact function according to the lower virtues? In VI 8,5–6, Plotinus says that he will if he has to, but, like a god, he will naturally prefer to have no occasion to exercise any of the civic virtues. And there are circumstances when all conventional claims must be subordinated to the sage's higher *telos* of divinisation:

»Virtue does not accommodate itself to events, as for instance saving someone who is in danger, but rather, if it seems necessary to it, it will even cast such a one aside, and bid life to be cast aside, and possessions, and children, and one's very fatherland, holding before itself the Good as its aim, but not the existence of anything subordinate to that.« (VI 8, 6, 14–18)

There is a hard streak in Plotinus, no doubt about it. It comes out with particular force in his discussion of Providence in III 2–3, and it stands in interesting contrast to his attested philanthropic behaviour as guardian and teacher. But it is severely logical. The sage is concerned with saving himself, with becoming a god, and any involvement with passions or other bodily concerns is a distraction from this great aim. The sage will, then, by preference not practise the civic virtues, though he will always possess them potentially.

II.

In *Enn.* I 2, then, Plotinus seems to me to articulate, with a coherence not visible in any extant previous treatment of the subject, an ethic for the late-antique holy man. The next most coherent attempts lie, I think, in the works of Philo of Alexandria and, later, of Origen, but compared to this analysis by Plotinus, they must inevitably appear somewhat vague and inchoate. Let us examine them in turn.

The only real suggestions of various levels of virtue in Philo occurs in the course of his exegesis of the Garden of Eden in *Allegories of the Laws* I 56–108, and in his comparison of the virtues of Aaron and Moses in *ibid.* III 125–144. VAN LIESHOUT accords Philo a chapter in his survey[9], but curiously fails to bring out the most interesting aspects of his doctrine.

What I find most interesting is how Philo, having put himself into a situation in the course of his exegesis where a theory of levels of virtue would seem called for, together with a discussion of what virtue at the paradigmatic or divine level would consist in, largely fails to grasp the implications of his own analysis, thus providing an instructive contrast with Plotinus.

At *LA* I 59, Philo reveals that ›some authorities‹ (τινές) recognise a Form of Virtue in general, which they denominate ἀγαθότης. Plato himself recognises no Form of Virtue as such, and certainly does not identify it with τἀγαθόν[10], so this will necessarily be a later Platonist development – if Philo is not simply inventing predecessors here. In Philo's scheme, this generic virtue, *agathotes*, is subordinated to the divine Logos, or Sophia (sect. 65), a Stoicising development which might be his own contribution.

The Forms of the four cardinal virtues (symbolised by the four rivers of Eden) derive from, or are at least logically subordinate to, that of generic Virtue. We have, therefore, in Philo's thought, Forms not only of the virtues (which would be perfectly Platonic), but of Virtue itself, which is not. What it does not occur to him to ask himself, however, is what it would mean to be a virtue on the divine level. He has no hesitation about applying these virtues to God (though not as part of his essence; rather as aspects of his Logos), but he does not make it clear what, for example, *phronesis* is within the Logos. When enumerating these virtues in the course of his allegory of the four rivers flowing out of Eden (66–76), he describes them in terms proper to virtues in the human soul, utilising the normal Stoic definition for these (65).

We can, however, I think, help Philo, on the basis of his own theory, to make a proper distinction. The Forms of the virtues are actually *logoi*, specialised aspects of the universal Logos, and thus are themselves not virtues in the proper sense so much as *causative principles* of virtue. There is an interesting passage in the *De Confusione Linguarum* (81) in which he actually seems to recognise such a class of entities. In the course of a discussion

---

[9] Op. cit. n. 1, pp. 44–54.
[10] Ἀγαθότης, the abstract noun, is not found before Philo himself – or the *Wisdom of Solomon* (1,1), if this is in fact earlier than Philo. On this question, see now DAVID WINSTON, *The Wisdom of Solomon* (translation and

commentary), Anchor Bible Series, New York, 1979, esp. 20–25. He argues for a late date, and dependence on Philo.
[11] *Clement of Alexandria: A Study in Christian Platonism and Gnosticism,* Oxford 1971, pp. 103–117.

of the doctrine of the sage as a ›sojourner‹ on this earth and a true citizen of the intelligible world, he refers to Isaac as being commanded by God, at Gen. 26,2–3, not to go down into Egypt (the realm of sense-perception and the passions), but to dwell ›in this land‹ (the intelligible world). Isaac, then, says Philo, as a *sophos*, »dwells in and has for his fatherland the virtues known to the mind (νοηταὶ ἀρεταί), which God ›speaks‹, and which are thus identical with divine *logoi*.« How exactly Philo conceives of these virtues is not clear, but his terminology is consistent with their being paradigms of the earthly virtues. If this is his theory, though, it is unfortunate that there is no passage where he develops it in any detail.

Similarly disappointing is the initially promising comparison of the virtues of Aaron and Moses in *LA* III 125ff. Basing his exegesis on Exodus 28,30, where, in the LXX version, ›the oracle of the judgements‹ is to be placed upon Aaron's breast, Philo (sect. 129) takes Aaron as the paradigm of the προκόπτων, ›the man undergoing improvement‹ in Stoic theory, who has not yet utterly excised the passions, or the lower parts of the soul, and thus still only *controls* them. His virtue is characterised by Philo as based on *metrio-*   * *patheia* – the Peripatetic ideal being here put to a strictly illegitimate use within a Stoic system. Philo's innovation here (if it *is* his) is thoroughly un-Stoic, as the Stoics would not recognise the *prokopton* as possessing virtue at all (at best he would possess ›sparks‹ or adumbrations of virtues), and the whole premiss upon which the Peripatetic (and Platonic) theory of virtue is based is alien to them, since it postulates a lower part, or parts, of the soul to be controlled.

However, this move gives Philo an opportunity to distinguish two levels of virtue, since with Aaron, who practises *metriopatheia,* he contrasts Moses, the achieved sage, who practises *apatheia*, basing himself for this purpose on Levit. 8,29 (ss. 129–30), where Moses removes the breast from the ram of consecration. This act Philo sees as symbolising the complete extirpation of those passions which reside in the breast, the *thymoeides* part of the soul – and *a fortiori*, it seems, the *epithymētikon* as well, residing as it does below the breast. Moses' level of virtue is therefore that of *apatheia*, the state proper to the Stoic sage.

Having got this far, however, Philo does not take the further step of distinguishing in detail between the virtues at either level, and there is no indication that the problem even occurred to him. It is not even clear whether he thought that Moses and Aaron each had a full set of four virtues. We have here, I think, a good contrast between the piercing logicality of Plotinus and the relative muddleheadedness of Philo.

Philo's opposition between the *metriopatheia* of the *prokoptōn* and the *apatheia* of the achieved sage is, as one would expect, fully reproduced by Clement of Alexandria. SALVA-TORE LILLA, in his most useful study of Clement,[11] sets out the relevant passages, and quotes parallels both from Middle Platonism and from Plotinus and Porphyry, though he does not bring out the important difference that Plotinus works out two parallel sets of virtues, whereas Philo and Clement do not. His work, however, and the fact that Clement is closely dependent in this matter upon Philo, enables me to pass over Clement in favour of Origen, who, though also dependent on Philo to a much greater extent than he would admit, is a man of considerably more originality than Clement.

Origen is a thinker in whom one might reasonably hope to find some theory of grades of virtue, since he in so many other ways betrays close acquaintance with contemporary trends in philosophy – if any such theory were current before Plotinus. However, any such expectation would be largely (though not completely) disappointed. Origen is certainly acquainted with the distinction between φυσικαί and τέλειαι or θεῖαι ἀρεταί. At *In Matth. comm. ser.* 69, for example, he makes a distinction between virtues ἐκ κατασκευῆς φυσικῆς, which many non-Christians can possess, and that enhancement of them that comes ἀπὸ θεοῦ. It is the addition of God's σοφία (Wisd. 9,6) that brings perfection and divinisation to virtues[12].

But this is not precisely what we want. Can we discern any trace in Origen of that peculiar working out of analogous levels of virtue which we have seen in Plotinus? Not, I think, as such, but there can be discerned in Origen the same Stoic-based distinction that we have found in Philo between the virtues of the *prokoptōn* and those of the achieved sage. In his exegesis of the wanderings of the Children of Israel in the Desert (Num. 33), in the 27th *Homily on Numbers*, he takes the wanderings as an allegory of the progress of the soul to perfection in virtue, and fixes on the transition from the Wilderness of Sin (which he etymologises as ›temptation‹) to Raphaca – the LXX misreading of Dophkah – (which he etymologises as ›health‹). At this point in its progress, the soul acquires ›discernment of heavenly things‹ and becomes πνευματική (*Hom.* XXVII 12). Its virtues thereafter are τέλειαι. All the ›stations‹ after Raphaca strengthen it in various ways. In connexion with the earlier stages, he uses the expression (in the Latin translation) ›virtutis gradus‹ (*ibid.* 3 ad fin.), and seems to envisage a series of grades being passed through before perfection (the *summus gradus*) is reached. This he depicts (*ibid.* 5 ad fin.) as being symbolised by the crossing of the river Jordan (»usque eo perveniatur ad ultimum, immo ad summum gradum virtutum, et transeatur flumen Dei ac promissa suscipiatur hereditas.«).

How does this relate to the transition from Sin to Raphaca? In fact, Origen seems to envisage two transitions, one from the status of *prokoptōn* to that of perfect virtue, the second from perfect virtue to divinisation. At the end of the homily (sect. 12, GCS Vol. VII, p. 279,3ff.), he says: »For when the soul has made its journey through all these virtues and has ascended to the peak of perfection, it crosses over from this sphere of existence (*saeculum*) and departs, as it is written of Enoch (Gen. 5:24); ›and he was not found, for God had translated him.‹« Such a person is no longer subject to human passions or concerns, and so will no longer exercise the ›lower‹ virtues; whatever virtues he exercises must be of a more exalted type.

Something more is said on this topic in a homily on Joshua (*In Iesu Naue* IV 4), commenting on the crossing of the Jordan in Jos. 4,19. Here we are told that »even though we may possess a single generic perfection, nevertheless, in the case of each species of virtue, ... if we can bring it to perfection, there will be a perfect state of that particular virtue.« And the example is given of anger being progressively quelled by *mansuetudo* (πραότης), until it is extinguished by *perfectio mansuetudinis*. Each virtue, then, has its perfect form, all of which are subsumed under *perfectio generalis*.

This, it must be admitted, is something short of the systematic ›mirroring‹ of the higher virtues by the lower which Plotinus propounds in *Enn.* I 2, and it indicates, I think, that this theory in its developed form is peculiar to Plotinus. But the concept of grades of virtue in general, and the notion that the pure soul, and even the gods, if possessed of virtue, as it was generally felt they were, must enjoy virtues of a quite different type from those exercised by ordinary men, may well have been aired by Middle Platonist thinkers, as well as by Philo and Origen.

---

[12] Cf. also *Exhort. ad Mart.* 5; *Comm. in Rom.* II 7.

It must be noted that the contrast we have been pursuing is not one between ethical and intellectual virtues, such as that made by Aristotle, nor yet the one between ›natural‹ and perfected virtues made by the Stoics, though it is not unconnected with those contrasts, and can be confused with them. It is rather the notion that a virtue like courage, for instance, in an achieved sage must be something different, though analogous to, the courage of an ordinary brave man, even of a *rationally* brave man. Plotinus' definition of kathartic courage is ›not fearing to depart from the body‹ (*Enn.* I 2, 3, 16.). This is certainly not the normal meaning of courage, but it plainly has some analogy to it. Of this interesting concept I discern some adumbrations in these passages of Philo and Origen, but no more.

If one accepts that the full working out of this theory is the distinctive contribution of Plotinus, then it can be seen to fit in with other aspects of his view of the way in which the noetic world ›mirrors‹ the sense-world (though of course it is properly the sense-world that is the mirror). One thinks in particular of the first sections of *Ennead* VI 7, where the sense-faculties are presented as dim correlates of a set of noetic ›senses‹[13], and even of *Enn.* III 8, where *praxis* is presented as a weak and diffuse form of *theoria*. This mirroring ›in a glass, darkly‹ of higher, noetic entities by lower, sensible ones is very much a feature of Plotinus' picture of the structure of the universe, which goes considerably beyond the rather vague provisions of what one might call the ›classical‹ Platonic Theory of Forms.

---

[13] Summed up by the epigrammatic remark in ch. 7, 29–31: εἶναι τὰς αἰσθήσεις ταύτας ἀμυδρὰς νοήσεις, τὰς δὲ ἐκεῖ νοήσεις ἐναργεῖς αἰσθήσεις.

XIX

AISTHÊSIS NOÊTÊ:
A DOCTRINE OF SPIRITUAL SENSES IN ORIGEN
AND IN PLOTINUS [1]

I

At *Contra Celsum* I 48, in an effort to refute a gibe of Celsus' about the absurdity of the report in the Gospel of Mark (1:10) — and the parallel stories in the other gospels — that Jesus saw the heavens opening and the Holy Spirit descending as a dove from heaven and settling on him, and that He heard the voice of God, Origen propounds a remarkable theory of noetic or spiritual analogues to the five senses. This enables him to explain away not only this troublesome passage, but a host of other awkward anthropomorphic descriptions of divine or supernatural activities in both the Old and New Testaments. It is notable that, in defending these passages, Origen is not content simply to declare them metaphorical or figurative, but prefers to maintain the existence of a set of 'spiritual' senses, by which our minds, or at least the minds of inspired saints here on earth, and of souls in general when free of the body, can apprehend various types of noetic impression.

He begins from a comparison with visions in dreams, the validity of which he accepts:

"All who accept the doctrine of providence are obviously agreed in believing that in dreams many people form images in their minds, some of divine things, others being announcements of future events in life, whether clear or mysterious. Why, then, is it strange to suppose that the force which forms an impression on the mind in a dream can also do so in the daytime for the benefit of the man on whom the impression is made, or for those who will hear about it from him?" (trans. Chadwick.)

---

[1] I am much indebted, for the part of this essay which pertains to Origen, to the most useful article of Karl Rahner, "Le début d'une doctrine des cinq sens spirituels chez Origene", in *Revue d'Ascétique et de Mystique* XII (1932), pp. 113-145. Rahner, however, sees no development in Origen's thought in this matter, and he may be right. I am prepared to argue for some development, however, as will be seen.

The argument Origen is using here is the Stoic one (accepted freely by later Platonists) that in sleep the mind is freed to attend to impulses from the Logos to which our working consciousness forms a barrier [2]. This argument can also be used to explain the power of 'natural' divination in certain people — they are able to break through that barrier when awake, by an effort of will, or by a gift of inspiration. However, this well-worn argument does not take Origen all the way he wants to go. It merely indicates that the mind, or *hegemonikon*, can receive impressions directly; no need to postulate a parallel set of 'spiritual' senses.

But he goes on :

"Anyone who looks into the matter more deeply will say that there is, as the Scripture calls it, a certain generic divine sense (θεία τις γενική αἴσθησις), which only the man who is blessed finds on this earth. Thus Solomon says (*Prov.* 2:5): 'Thou shalt find a divine sense (ὅτι αἴσθησιν θείαν εὑρήσεις)" [3].

Having found mention of a θεία αἴσθησις in such an unimpeachable authority as Solomon himself, Origen presses on :

"There are many forms of this sense : a sight which can see things superior to corporeal beings, the cherubim or seraphim being obvious instances, and a hearing which can receive impressions of sounds that have no objective existence in the air, and a taste which feeds on living bread that has come down from heaven and gives life to the world (*John* 6:33). So also there is a sense of smell which smells spiritual things, as Paul speaks of 'a sweet savour of Christ unto God' (2 *Cor.* 2:15), and a sense of touch, in accordance with which John says that he has handled with his hands 'of the Word of Life' (1 *John* 1:1)".

Origen has assembled here, to his own satisfaction, authorities as to the existence of a full set of five spiritual senses, although examples of sight and hearing are so common that he feels the need to produce references

[2] Cf. *SVF* II 1196-1206.

[3] We may note here the bizarre nature of this reference. It is a Greek version (not the accepted LXX) of *Proverbs* 2:5: "Then you will understand the fear of the Lord/ and find the knowledge of God". The LXX has for this latter phrase, "καὶ ἐπίγνωσιν θεοῦ εὑρήσεις", which is an accurate rendering of the Hebrew, *d'at' 'elohîm timṣā'*, and would never have given occasion to such an exegesis as that which Origen gives it. Presumably Origen's authority took *elohîm* as a descriptive, or subjective, rather than an objective, genitive (which, I am assured by those who know Hebrew better than I do, is *not* a possible interpretation here, and thus must be the work of someone who knew Hebrew imperfectly), and it is this that Origen can creatively misinterpret (that this is not his own translation is proved by the fact that Clement uses it before him (*Strom.* I 27,2), though without the particular interpretation). We have here, therefore, a good example of a piece of Origenist doctrine hatched from the wind-egg of a false translation. It is hard to believe that Origen did not have access also to the LXX version (if not to the Hebrew original), so that his use of this version may be seen as a conscious choice. It suited his theory.

only for the last three, smell, taste and touch. He goes on to quote *Ezechiel* 2:9-3:3, the remarkable passage describing Ezechiel's eating of a scroll presented to him by the Lord, and finding it 'as sweet as honey'; and Isaac's utterance to Jacob at *Gen.* 27:27: "See, the smell of my son is as the smell of a field which the Lord has blessed".

What must strike us about this assemblage of texts, and about the others which Origen gathers in the same cause at other passages to which we shall turn, is the extraordinarily perverse way in which he lumps together passages which are plainly allegorical or poetical with others which are plainly intended literally (e.g. 1 *John* 1:1, where John presumably means simply that he has touched Christ, who is the Logos) — and this from a man who is normally acutely alert to metaphor and allegory. Indeed, in a parallel passage later in the work (VII,34), he comes dangerously near to allegorising a number of such passages, but without, in his view, undermining his position:

> "Furthermore, when our Saviour says, 'he that hath ears to hear, let him hear!' (*Matt.* 11:15; 13:9, etc.), even the unintelligent man understands that this refers to spiritual ears. If Scripture says the word of the Lord was in the hand of Jeremiah the prophet (*Jer.* 1:9), or of anyone else, or the law in the hand of Moses (*Num.* 16:40), or that 'I sought the Lord with my hands and was not deceived' (*Ps.* 76:3 LXX), no one is such a blockhead as to fail to grasp that there are some hands which are given that name with an allegorical meaning"[4].

He then goes on to quote 1 John 1:1, and his special version of Prov. 2:5.

His talk of 'some hands being given that name with an allegorical meaning' seems to betoken a certain confusion. Either, surely, one is using the expression 'hands' *metaphorically*, or one is speaking *literally* about spiritual hands (as the organs of spiritual touch). However, it is not my purpose to dispute with Origen, so much as to try to comprehend his theory. It is plain that he has here developed a systematic theory of analogical, 'spiritual' senses for the intellect, or *hegemonikon*, apparently to solve a series of problems of exegesis posed by anthropomorphic expressions about the godhead and about spiritual life which abound in both the Old and New Testaments.

This doctrine of Origen appears to have developed over the course of his career[5]. If we turn back from these passages in the *Contra Celsum* to

---

[4] One might comment, in respect at least of the *Numbers* passage, that no one with any command of Hebrew should be such a blockhead as not to recognise the common idiom *beyad* as meaning simply 'through', 'by means of'.

[5] Rahner gives a comprehensive list of passages, *art. cit.* p. 114, n. 5. Besides those used here, they include *In Levit. Hom.* 31, 7; *In Ezech. Hom.* 11.1; *In Cant. Cant.* I and

the *De Principiis*, composed at the beginning of his exegetical career, we find the same proof texts employed (in particular *Prov.* 2:5), but with a somewhat different interpretation. For instance, at the end of Book I, ch. 1 (I 1,9), in the wake of a discussion of the absolute invisibility of God, and the question as to whether he is invisible even to the Son, we find the following:

"But if the question is put to us why it was said 'Blessed are the pure, for they shall see God in the heart'[6] (*Matt.* 5:8), I answer that in my opinion our argument will be much more firmly established by this passage. For what else is 'to see God in the heart' but to understand and know him with the mind, just as we have explained above? For the names of the organs of sense are often applied to the soul, so that we speak of seeing with the eyes of the heart, that is, of drawing some intellectual conclusion by means of the faculty of intelligence. So too we speak of hearing with the ears when we discern the deeper meaning of some statement. So too we speak of the soul as being able to use teeth, when it eats and consumes the bread of life who comes down from heaven. In a similar way we speak of it as using all the other bodily organs, which are transferred from their corporeal significance and applied to the faculties of the soul; as Solomon says, 'You will find a divine sense' (Prov. 2:5). For he knew that there were in us two kinds of senses, the one being mortal, corruptible and human, and the other immortal and intellectual, which he here calls 'divine'. By this divine sense, therefore, not of the eyes but of a pure heart, that is, the mind, God can be seen by those who are worthy. That 'heart' is used for mind, that is for the intellectual faculty, you will certainly find over and over again in all the scripture, both the New and the Old".

(trans. Butterworth, emended)

Here, in contrast to the *Contra Celsum*, passages speaking of the use of sense-organs in respect of the apprehension of divinity are regarded as metaphorical ("What else is 'to see God in the heart' but to understand and know him with the mind?"); *Prov.* 2:5 is quoted, but it is seen as referring to an 'immortal and intellectual' sense, which is simply the faculty of intellect (*mens*). Certainly, the reference to 'faculties of the soul' (*virtutes animae*) could be taken, in the light of what we know to be his doctrine later, to refer to spiritual sense-organs, but I submit that, in default of other *contemporary* evidence, there is nothing in this phrase, or in this passage, that would lead us to assume such a doctrine of

---

II passim; *In Luc.* Frs. 53,57; *In Joh.* X 279; In this last passage the spiritual senses are referred to as εἰ καλούμεναι θεῖαι αἰσθήσεις. This is probably just a reference to *Prov.* 2:5, but it shows the doctrine to be in Origen's mind by this time — shortly after his move to Caesarea.

[6] From what follows it is plain that Origen is taking τῇ καρδίᾳ with what follows it, rather than with καθαροί, a most perverse construal.

XIX

spiritual senses. What Origen is saying is that many expressions which appear to refer to activities of our sense-organs really refer to operations of the mind or soul; that is to say, they are metaphors. Some may feel that the fact that we are dependent here on Rufinus' translation may leave open the possibility that a doctrine of spiritual senses had been obscured or watered down, but there is no obvious doctrinal reason why Rufinus should indulge in 'laundering' here. I think we must accept the passage as it stands.

We have, after all, a similar passage at the very end of the work (IV,4, 10), where again *Prov.* 2:5 is appealed to:

> "We see, therefore, that men have a kind of blood-relationship with God; and since God knows all things and not a single intellectual truth can escape his notice ..., it is possible that a rational mind also, by advancing from a knowledge of small to a knowledge of greater things and from things visible to things invisible, may attain to an increasingly perfect understanding. For it has been placed in a body, and of necessity advances from sense-objects which are bodily, to sense-objects [7] which are incorporeal and intellectual. But in case it should appear mistaken to say as we have done that intellectual things are objects of sense, we will quote as an illustration the saying of Solomon: 'You will find also a divine sense'. By this he shows that intellectual things are to be investigated not by bodily sense but by some other which he calls divine".

> (trans. Butterworth, emended.)

Here we may see at least the beginnings of an 'analogical' theory in the mention of *sensibilia, quae sunt incorporea et intellectualia* (in Rufinus' translation), as the proper objects of the *sensus divinus*, but when it comes down to it, the *sensus divinus* seems just to be the *mens*, performing its proper operations. It seems to me preferable to assume that, at the time he wrote the *De Principiis*, Origen had not yet fully developed a theory of 'spiritual' senses.

In the *Dialogue with Heraclides*, however, which is of uncertain date [8], but almost certainly belongs to the period at Caesarea, we find the theory developed noticeably. In response to a question (10,16) as to whether "the soul is the blood", as stated in *Leviticus* 17:11 and *Deuteronomy* 12:23 — a question which was apparently causing great disquiet at this time in many

---

[7] The mss. here, and just below, admittedly read *insensibilia*, but this so spoils the sense as to almost certainly the work of an inept scribe (possibly already in the Greek — ἀναίσθητα). If so, this finds a most interesting parallel in Plotinus, *Enn.* VI 7, 6, 2, as we shall see below.

[8] See the useful discussion of J. Scherer, in the Introduction to his *Sources Chrétiennes* edition, pp. 19-21. He argues plausibly for a date between 244 and 249 A.D., because of its concern with the Arabian heresy, which flourished between those dates.

communities, because of the implication that the soul was mortal, or at least remained with the body in the tomb until the general resurrection — Origen launches into a comprehensive description of the inner, or spiritual, man, fitting him out not only with a full set of sense-organs, but with all other organs as well — hands, feet, entrails, bones, hair, and finally, of course, blood — in the process trampling with hobnailed boots over much of the finest poetry in the Old Testament (15, 28-24, 17).

What we have here is a doctrine of spiritual sense-organs subsumed into a more general theory, derived from Philo of Alexandria, of spiritual man, man 'in the image' (κατ' εἰκόνα) of God, as opposed to physical man, man 'in the likeness'[9], and Origen proceeds to fit out this 'inner' man analogically with every detail of the physical body.

If we turn next to the *Commentary on Matthew*, composed more or less contmporaneously with the *Contra Celsum*, between 244 and 249 A.D. (Eus. *HE* VI,36), we find the theory fully developed, if not so circumstantially presented as in the *Contra Celsum*. The parable of the Five Wise and the Five Foolish Maidens at *Matt.* 25:1-13 presents Origen with an excellent pretext for introducing a contrast between the five material sense-organs (which will naturally be 'foolish') and another set of five spiritual ones. We have his commentary, unfortunately, only in the Latin translation (Comm. ser. 63-4), and in a number of catena fragments, so that it is not entirely clear what his own terminology was, but he is clearly contrasting the senses as ordinarily understood (αἱ κοινῶς νοού-μεναι, *Cat.* no. 273), which he names, with another set of five, "referred to in *Proverbs*" (αἱ ἐν Παροιμίαις κείμεναι, *ibid.*). He then quotes *Prov.* 2:5.

Each set of senses receive their 'lamps', which are their proper organs. The soul, or mind, has therefore, not only five senses, but in some way also five sense-organs. He does not choose to develop this piece of doctrine here, however, as he does in the *Conversation with Heraclides* or the *Contra Celsum*. These senses, we learn, may be used well or badly, even as the bodily senses may be (*Cat.* no. 276)[10].

His nearest approach to discussing the different roles of the spiritual senses comes at the end of his exegesis of the parable[11], where he identifies

[9] Cf. *Opif.* 69; *Leg. All.* I 31; *Conf. Ling.* 62.3.

[10] Origen here seems to reveal a flaw in his exegesis. The proper contrast is, surely, between senses used well (who receive and store the 'oil', which is the teaching of inspired doctors and confessors), and senses used badly — not between physical and spiritual sense-faculties. He cannot, surely, have it both ways.

[11] *Comm. Ser.* 64, p. 150, 14-151, 3 Klosterman (*CGS* XI).

the 'adornment' or 'trimming' (κόσμος) of the senses as ἡ κατὰ τὰς
αἰσθήσεις εὐαγγελικὴ χρῆσις (*Cat.* no. 276), which I take to mean "the
use of the senses in an evangelical spirit"[12]. He then goes through his
favourite proof texts (*Is.* 33:15: seeing, hearing; *Mark* 7:34: hearing;
2 Cor. 2:15 and *Cant.* 1:3: smell; and *John* 1:1: touch), but strangely,
neither in the Latin translation nor in the Greek catena fragment is
there any mention of spiritual senses. To all appearances it is the ordinary
physical senses which profit from this spiritual stimulation. I find it
hard to believe, however, from all that has gone before, that Origen does
not in fact have his spiritual senses in mind here, though his mode of
presentation (at least in the form in which it has come down to us) is
regrettably obscure.

II

Enough has been said by now, I hope, to demonstrate the nature of
Origen's doctrine of spiritual senses. Whether he developed it himself,
or is borrowing from some source, Platonist or other, is unclear, though
my 'minimalist' interpretation of the doctrine as it appears in the *De
Principiis*, if accepted, would suggest that it is his own construction,
at least in its fully elaborated form.

On the other hand, we do find within the Platonist tradition, in the
person of Origen's younger contemporary Plotinus, a rather similar
theory, though arising from somewhat different stimuli. Origen, as I
have said, is provoked to this theory by the necessity of explaining a
whole series of scriptural passages which use expressions of an anthropomorphic nature about God, or which use physical imagery when talking
of spiritual apprehension of one sort or another. He could, one feels,
have explained these simply as metaphorical or figurative, but this easy
option obviously failed to satisfy him. What, he presumably asked himself, led the inspired authors to employ just these metaphors and figures?

Plotinus similarly has a problem of exegesis, of a rather more philosophical nature. It arises out of the discussion of a passage of the *Timaeus*,
45B, from which he begins his great treatise, *Enn.* VI,7. In this passage,
the Young Gods, under the orders of the Demiurge, are described as
fabricating eyes for the soul in the body (and, by implication, other

---

[12] The Latin *evangelicis usibus atque rectis* presumably means also "correct use of the
gospels".

organs of sense), to enable it to function successfully in the sensible world.

This seems to Plotinus to raise a major difficulty, at least for those who wish to take the creation-myth of the *Timaeus* literally — and even, as it turns out, for those, like himself, who do not. Are we to take it, he says, that before embodiment the soul had potentially the various sense-organs, or are these added at the moment of the fashioning of the organs themselves? Either way, he sees a problem :

"If he gave the souls senses at the same time as he gave them the organs, then, souls though they were, they had no sensations before; but if they were endowed with senses when they became souls, and they became souls in order that they might proceed into generation, then it is innate in them to proceed into process. So it would be against their nature to be apart from generation and within the realm of Intellect, and they were made that they should be involved with something alien to themselves, and that they might be in an evil state" (1, 14-19).

— all of which, needless to say, is repugnant to Platonism, as Plotinus understands it.

To preserve us from this conclusion, we must envisage some form of sense-faculties in the soul before it leaves the intelligible realm. It is this that leads Plotinus to raise his troublesome problem. If the nature of Man at the level of Form is to be complete, he says in ch. 3, no element of the physical make-up of Man can be excluded from it; but how, then, can we exempt Nous from the appearance of tending towards the sense-world? As he puts it :

"If, then, the possession of sense-perception, and sense-perception of just such a sort, is imposed upon the Form by eternal necessity, and by the (need for) completeness in Nous, which contains within it, for it to be complete, the causes (of everything), in such a way that we see later that all was correct all along — for there the cause is one and such as to complete (the essence), and so Man there was not only intellect, sense-perception being added when he was sent out into the realm of generation — how could it be that Intellect should not incline (ῥέποι) towards this realm? What is a faculty of sense-perception, after all, other than a faculty which grasps things perceptible by sense?"

It is, I think, the essence of Plotinus' greatness that, once he has taken up a problem bequeathed to him by the tradition, he worries away at it until he has, if not solved it (which he often fails to do), at least exposed every facet of it. Here the original *aporia* has become an enquiry into the contents of the world of Nous, and, specifically, how we can conceive of any analogue or paradigm of sense-perception being present at that level.

The problem had not been entirely ignored by his predecessors. In Albinus' *Didaskalikos*, ch. 26 (p. 178, 32 ff. Hermann), we learn that the souls of the gods have aspects corresponding to the two irrational parts of our souls, an appetitive (ὁρμητικόν) or 'dispositional' (παραστατικόν) element, corresponding to our θυμοειδές, and an 'appropriative' one (οἰκειωτικόν), corresponding to our ἐπιθυμητικόν. This is not quite the same thing as we have here, admittedly, but it gives evidence of some concern on the part of Platonists as to what could be the meaning of the detail in the *Phaedrus* myth (to which Plato probably did not want much significance attached) that the souls of the gods also have the form of a charioteer and pair, though both their horses are of equally impeccable lineage and behaviour. Despite Plato's qualification here, this schema for the divine souls inevitably gives occasion for speculation, in allegorically-inclined minds, as to whether pure souls also may not be intended to have some archetype of sense-perception, and even of the passions arising from sense-perception.

This, however, as Plotinus sees, does not solve the problem. It merely states it. If a pure soul has anything analogous to sense-perception, what can this quasi-sense-perception be deemed to perceive? The first sentence of ch. 6, in which this question is answered, plunges us into difficulties, compounded by the manuscript tradition, and an interesting reminiscence of a similar textual problem in Origen (see above, n. 7). The Greek mss., with one voice, say: ἢ τὸ αἰσθητικὸν τῶν ἐκεῖ ἀναισθήτων — 'the faculty of sense-perception is of the *im*perceptibles There', which makes some sense, but not much. The Arabic version, in the *Theology of Aristotle*, talks of 'the perceptibles There', and, that, as becomes plain from what follows, is what he must be saying[13]. So Plotinus is prepared to talk of αἰσθητά of some sort in the noetic realm. What he means becomes clear directly, though it remains strange. He is able, as often elsewhere, to resort to a general principle of his, that the phenomena of this world are just pale reflections of what exists, in a more real way, at a higher level. The civic virtues in *Enn.* 1 2, for instance, are simply distorted versions of the true, cathartic virtues; Time, in *Enn.* III 7, is an inadequate attempt to represent Eternity; Action, in *Enn.* III 8, is a dim equivalent of Contemplation. And so here, sensibilia are simply dim versions of higher, noetic 'sensibilia'. This is something more revolu-

---

[13] Henry and Schwyzer, in their edition, detach the ἀν- from αἰσθητά, and keep it as a kind of floating potential element. I must say I would prefer, with Ficino, Volkmann and others, to abolish it altogether, as a piece of scribal 'rationalising'.

tionary and peculiar, I think, than simply talking of forms or paradigms of sensibilia. He seems to mean, rather, noetic correlates of sensibilia, however one is to conceive of such entities. At any rate, we are concerned not so much with a process of participation as one of mirroring. He takes first the example of harmony perceived in this world, as being perceived by man as a reflection of harmony There; then fire here, as having a correlative Fire There. Then he says (6,7ff.), "for if there were these bodies There (presumably fire and so on), the soul would have perceptions, or apprehensions (ἀντιλήψεις) of them; and the Man There, being a soul of a particular sort, would have apprehension of these, whence also the subsequent man, the imitation, would have the *logoi* in imitation; and the man in Nous (is, *or* contains?) the man prior to all men".

Not infrequently, when I come to close grips with Plotinus (I do not venture to speak for anyone else in this matter), I find that suddenly, for whole sentences and even periods, I can no longer understand precisely what he is saying. This is one of those cases. I can derive no substantial help from translations or commentaries. And yet I suspect that he is saying something rather interesting.

First of all, however, there are grammatical and textual problems. The conditional clause, first, does not appear overtly counter-factual (there are aorist indicatives, but no ἄν in the apodosis — though Müller wished to insert one). I find it difficult, I must say, not to attach a counter-factual sense to these aorists, and I note that the Arabic paraphrase[14] does so too ("If there were in the upper world bodies like these bodies, the soul would perceive and attain them, and the men there would perceive and attain them too"), but Henry and Schwyzer set their faces against this, presumably on the grounds that in a way these bodies *are* in the noetic world. However, I still find the aorists peculiar. They presumably must mean "If in fact the bodies *are* there, then the soul *does* perceive them, and so does the Man".

Secondly, I take the καί in αἰσθήσεις καὶ ἀντιλήψεις to be epexegetic or specificatory ("perceptions, *or rather* apprehensions"), since Plotinus is rather conscious of using paradoxical language here, and is trying to modify it. Having used αἴσθησις initially, he goes on to use ἀντίληψις and ἀντιλαμβάνειν, as being vaguer.

Lastly, we see revealed here a hierarchy of grades of man, which he proceeds to expand on immediately afterwards. We are presented with

---

[14] *Theology of Aristotle* X 77 (printed in Vol. II of Henry and Schwyzer's big edition, p. 449).

(i) a noetic or archetypal Man, (ii) a man who is pure soul, not yet embodied, and (iii) an embodied man — or so I interpret them. I will pass over these rather lightly in the present context, except to suggest that they sound far more like a quasi-Gnostic sequence of pneumatic, psychic, and somatic or sarkic men than any traditional Platonic arrangement of archetype and image, though that terminology is being used here. Plotinus' purpose in producing them is to emphasise that all of them, up to the man in Nous, enjoy a full set of faculties answering to sense-faculties, and that they each contemplate or apprehend (again the all-purpose word ἀντιλαμ-βάνειν) appropriate objects. His main point, which he returns to at the end of ch. 7, is that we must not think of anticipations of the sense-world in the noetic world, but rather of the sense-world dimly mirroring the prior arrangements of the noetic. Thus the *aporia* raised at the outset of the tractate is dissolved. Plotinus concludes ch. 7 as follows (in MacKenna's trans., slightly adapted):

"What we have called the perceptibles of that realm enter into cognizance (ἀντίληψις) in a way of their own, since they are incorporeal, while sense-percep-tion here — so distinguished as dealing with corporeal objects — is fainter than the perception belonging to that higher world, but gains a specious clarity because its objects are bodies; the man of this sphere has sense-perception because existing in a less true degree and taking only enfeebled images of things There: percep-tions here are dim intellections, and intellections There are vivid perceptions."

This fine epigrammatic flourish at the end [15] serves to emphasise that we have here, in Plotinus' theory, a far greater degree of 'mirroring' of the noetic world by the sense-world than is traditional in Platonism. Everything here is also There, in another, more exalted, mode.

III

The question now arises, what is the inspiration for this theory, and what, if any, relation does it have to the theory propounded by Origen? I have mentioned already that Origen is provoked to his theory of spiritual senses by different considerations, more exegetical than philosophical, from those of Plotinus, but Origen can be discerned on other occasions adapting a piece of contemporary philosophic doctrine to his own pur-poses [16], and I think he may be doing so here.

[15] ὥστε εἶναι τὰς αἰσθήσεις ταύτας ἀμυδρὰς νοήσεις, τὰς δὲ ἐκεῖ νοήσεις ἐναργεῖς αἰσθήσεις.
[16] Cf. my article "Origen's Doctrine of the Trinity and Some Later Neoplatonic Theories", in *Neoplatonism and Christian Thought*, ed. D. O'Meara, SUNY Press, Albany, N.Y. 1982, pp. 19-23.

Plainly, he cannot be borrowing from Plotinus, so we must set out in search of a common Middle Platonist (or other) source. Now I have noted that we find in Albinus (*Did.* ch. 26) some adumbration of a doctrine that thè gods must enjoy some counterpart to the lower elements of the soul, and thus perhaps some correlate of sense-perception, but it is not much to go on. It may be more fruitful, I think, to look in another direction. In the Gnostic treatise *Zostrianos*[17], which we know from Porphyry's *Life of Plotinus* (ch. 16) to have been one of those read in Plotinus' circle, there are a number of descriptions of the noetic world (actually, of the contents of each individual aeon) which are most interesting. At VIII 48, we read :

"Corresponding to each of the aeons, I saw a living earth and a living water and (air) made of light, and fire that cannot burn (...) all being simple and immutable with (...) simple and (...) having a (...) in many ways, with trees that do not perish in many ways, and tares (...) this way, and all these and imperishable fruit and living men and every form, and immortal souls, and every shape and form of mind, and gods of truth, and messengers who exist in great glory, and indissoluble bodies, *and an unborn begetting and an immovable perception*" (italics mine).

This passage is unfortunately somewhat fragmentary, but this does not seriously impair its value in the present connexion. What we seem to have portrayed here is a comprehensive archetype of the physical world (right down, it seems, to the tares among the wheat!). Of particular concern to us is the presence of noetic archetypes or correlates, of bodies, of 'begetting' (presumably γένεσις), and of 'perception' (presumably αἴσθησις). This description occurs again at 55, 15-25, with more or less the same list, though this time including 'animals'.

We have here, then, in a document of Valentinian Gnosticism known to Plotinus, a view of the contents of the intelligible world (or at least its Gnostic equivalent, the Pleroma) remarkably similar to that presented by Plotinus in *Enn.* VI 7. 'Immovable perception' (αἴσθησις ἀκίνητος?) is a peculiar phrase, certainly, but seems to be a sub-philosophic attempt to describe a noetic equivalent of sense-perception.

I am not suggesting that either Plotinus or Origen were actually influenced by the doctrine of *Zostrianos*, or even by Valentinian speculation, though that is not impossible. What seems to me more probable, however, is that the rather incoherent effusions of *Zostrianos*, like much else in

[17] Published in *The Nag Hammadi Library in English*, ed. J.M. Robinson, Harper and Row, New York, 1977. The projected edition of the Coptic text of Codex VIII is unfortunately not yet available.

Gnosticism, are a reflection of Gnostic use of contemporary Platonist doctrine, from which Origen and Plotinus also are drawing inspiration. Plotinus' philosophic motive for postulating a noetic correlate of sense-perception is plain enough — he was seeking a solution to the dilemma that either the Demiurge was creating additional faculties for the soul especially to facilitate its incarnation, or pure soul was fitted with faculties which only actualised themselves when it entered upon a worse state; but one must be left wondering why Origen, himself the great advocate of allegorising, should have chosen to take literally a series of passages speaking of sense-perception which, one would think, lent themselves readily to allegory. It makes his procedure at least somewhat less peculiar if one postulates that he knew of Platonist speculation about an intelligible correlate of sense-perception, and chose to make use of it for his own purposes, rather than assuming, as does Rahner (*art. cit. supra* n. 1, p. 114), that he invented it *ad hoc*.

The evidence at our disposal is miserably slim, but we do find Philo, two hundred years earlier, at *Leg. All.* I 21-27, postulating an Idea of αἴσθησις, along with an Idea of νοῦς, in the mind of God. He even speaks, rather tentatively, just before this (in I 19) of ἡ κατὰ τὰς ἰδέας τεταγμένη νοητή, εἰ οἷόν τε τοῦτο εἰπεῖν, αἴσθησις. And we cannot even assume that Philo concocted such a concept himself, since, as we have seen, it has a possible role to play in Platonist speculations about the contents of the noetic realm, and about the mode of divine knowledge of the physical world. This would push the development of the concept back at least to the 1st Cent. B.C.E. — although it must be said that Philo shows no sign of envisaging a set of *spiritual senses* for the soul[18].

Enough evidence has been produced, however, I think, to suggest that a complex of interlocking speculations concerning a noetic correlate of sense-perception was part of the Platonist heritage on which both Origen and Plotinus could draw. I would suggest that meditation on the implications of the portrayal of the structure of both divine and human souls in the myth of the *Phaedrus* provided the initial stimulus to these speculations, but who may have been their first begetter I do not venture to guess.

---

[18] A number of interesting passages, quoted by Rahner (*art. cit.* p. 115, n. 8) show, as he says, that Philo is simply using sense-language metaphorically, e.g. *Conf. Ling.* 100; *Spec. Leg.* I 272 (ʹοὓς θεῖον, 'the ear of God'); III 6 (οἱ τῆς ψυχῆς ὀφθαλμοί); the θεῖα ὄψις of *Praem.* 165 is not relevant; it means a divine *vision*. Philo is largely influenced by Platonic talk of the 'eye of the soul', and he plays variations on this in his characteristic manner.

The Theory of Three Classes of Men in
Plotinus and in Philo

I

Plotinus begins his early tractate, Ennead V 9 [5], On Intellect and the Ideas and Being, with a fine passage contrasting three classes of men. It runs as follows (in Armstrong's Loeb translation):

> "All men from the beginning, as soon as they are born, employ sense-perception before intellect, and sense-objects are necessarily the first which they encounter. Some of them stay here and live through their lives considering these to be primary and ultimate, and since they consider what is painful and pleasant in them to be evil and good respectively, they think this is enough, and pass their lives pursuing the one and contriving to get rid of the other. And those of them who claim rationality make this their philosophy, like the heavy sort of birds who have taken much from the earth and are weighed down by it and so are unable to fly high although nature has given them wings.
>
> Others have risen a little from the things below because the better part of their soul has urged them on from the pleasant to a greater beauty; but since they were unable to see what is above, as they have no other ground to stand on, they are brought down, with the name of virtue, to practical actions and choices of the things below from which they tried to raise themselves at first.
>
> But there is a third kind of godlike men (*theioi anthropoi*) who by their greater power and the sharpness of their eyes, as if by a special keensightedness, see the glory above and are raised to it as if above the clouds and the mist of this lower world, and remain there, overlooking all things here below and delighting in the true region which is their own, like a man who has come home after long wandering to his own well-ordered country."

Modern editors, such as Bréhier, Harder, Henry and Schwyzer, Cilento, and Armstrong, are united in their identification of these three classes of person with the Epicureans (the earthy birds that cannot fly), the Stoics (those that rise only a little above the ground), and the Platonists (the divine men) respectively, and I would not seek to dispute that[1]. Certainly Plotinus repeatedly begins an essay with a doxography of this sort[2], and he no doubt has Epicureans and Stoics primarily in mind in this passage. While granting this, however, I want to suggest here that another influence is making itself felt, in the form of the particular triadic structure which Plotinus is employing.

It is apposite in this connexion, I think, to turn back in the first instance to a similarly peculiar passage in the works of Philo of Alexandria, towards the end of his short treatise *On the Giants* (ss. 60-61)[3], where a three-fold division of humankind likewise appears:

> "So then it is no myth at all of giants that he (sc. Moses) sets before us; rather he wishes to show you that some men are earth-born, some are heaven-born, and some God-born. The earth-born are those who take the pleasures of the body for their quarry, who make it their practice to indulge in them and enjoy them and provide the means by which each of them may be promoted. The heaven-born are the votaries of the arts and of knowledge, the lovers of learning -- for the heavenly element in each of us is the mind, as the heavenly beings are each of them a mind. And it is the mind which pursues the learning of the schools and the other arts one and all, which sharpens and whets itself, aye and trains and drills itself solid in the contemplation of what is intelligible by mind (*ta noeta*).
>
> But the men of God are priests and prophets who have refused to accept membership in the commonwealth of the world and to become citizens therein (*kosmopolitai*), but have risen wholly above the sphere of sense-perception and have been translated into the world of the intelligible and dwell there registered as freemen of the commonwealth of Ideas (*ideōn politeia*), which are imperishable and incorporeal." (trans. Colson, Loeb Classical Library ed.)

Once again, it is an obvious suggestion that Epicureans, Stoics and Platonists (or rather, perhaps, 'Mosaics') are being referred to, but Philo's categories have a much broader reference than that. The 'men of Earth' are simply 'les hommes moyen sensuels', for whom the world of the senses is all that there is. The 'men of Heaven' are a more interesting category. They are those who are skilled in 'the wisdom of this world', in Paul's words (cf. I Cor. 1, 18-25) -- in all branches of *enkyklios paideia*. There is probably also a reference to the Stoic view that there is nothing that transcends the material world, but no sort of school philosopher is necessarily being referred to at all. These people value the life of the mind; they employ the 'heavenly' part of us, *nous*, but they use it for the amassing and enjoyment of this-worldly knowledge and skills -- they are 'lovers or sound and spectacle', in the words of Plato (Rep. V 475E).

The 'men of God', finally, are not said to transcend intellect, but they employ it to turn away from this world altogether, realising that Reality lies elsewhere. They do not deign even to become *kos-*

mopolitai -- a crack here, surely at the Stoics -- but depart mentally from this world, and take their place as citizens of the 'commonwealth of Ideas', a reference to the realm of the Platonic Forms.

This theme of withdrawal, of alienation, recurs, as we see, in Plotinus in very similar terms. Plotinus' divine men are portrayed, with a reference both to the allegorical interpretation of the *Odyssey* and, perhaps, also to Plato's use of *Iliad* 9, 363 in *Crito* 44B, as returning 'to their well-ordered country', the intelligible world. In the case of both philosophers, the myth of Plato's *Phaedo* (109Bff.) seems to be exercising an influence. Philo's description of the men of God as 'rising above' (*hyperkypsantes*) the sense-world echoes the *anakypsas* of *Phaedo* 109d2 (cf. also 109e3), while Plotinus talks of rising above the clouds and mists of this realm in language strongly reminiscent of *Phaedo* 109b5, where "water and mist and air have run together" into certain hollows in the real earth where we live, "like ants or frogs about a pond"[4].

But if this explains, as I think it does, the coincidence of imagery, it does not explain the triadic schema. Since I am not one of those who believe that Plotinus was acquainted with the works of Philo, I am under the necessity of supposing that any coincidence of doctrine or imagery between them is either just that, a coincidence, or that it betokens some third source, either common to both, such as Plato, the Old Academy, or the Stoics, or intermediate between them, such as, perhaps, Numenius of Apamea.

II

In the case of the three classes of men, the situation is rather troublesome. On the one hand, the idea of such a triadic division could be seen as going back to Pythagoras and his famous image of the three classes of people whom one may find attending a festival, as told by Plato's pupil, Heraclides of Pontus[5]. Heraclides presents Pythagoras as engaged in conversation with Leon, tyrant of Phlius. Being asked by Leon what was his profession, Pythagoras declares that he is a 'philosopher', and when Leon, who is not familiar with this Pythagorean coinage, asks what is meant by a philosopher, Pythagoras explains by way of an image:

"Pythagoras replied that life seemed to him like the gathering when the great games were held, which were attended by the whole of Greece. For there some men sought to win fame and the glory of the crown by exerting their bodies, others were attracted by the gain and profit of buying and selling, but there was one kind of man, the noblest of all, who sought neither applause nor profit, but came in order to watch and wanted to see what was happening and how. So too among us, who have migrated into this life from a different life and mode of being, as if from some city to a crowded festival, some are slaves to fame, others to money; but there are some rare spirits who, holding all else as nothing, eagerly contemplate the universe; these he calls lovers of wisdom (*philosophoi*); and as at the festival it most becomes a gentleman to be a spectator without thought of personal gain, so in life the contemplation and understanding of the universe is far superior to all other pursuits."[6]

There is considerable irony in this image, I should say, since it is precisely the humblest, and most *numerous*, element in any festival or games, the spectators, who are being singled out as the noblest and *rarest* element, while the competitors, who would naturally be regarded as the most noble by ordinary men, are relegated to the lowest rank, because they have paid attention to their bodies rather than their minds. Even the despised hucksters and assorted charlatans who attend to make money are preferred to them, since they are making at least *some* use of their minds.[7]

III

This Pythagorean account of the three types of life, however, only gets us part of the way. In that story, the philosophers are presented primarily as contemplators of this world and its wonders (though in Iamblichus' version, at least, such contemplation is linked with the contemplation of intelligible reality; but this may be Iamblichus' own contribution), whereas in the scheme which we are investigating, the second level of men, the 'heaven-born' of Philo, and the 'higher-flying birds' of Plotinus, are already contemplators of the beauties and the order of this world, while the highest level transcend it altogether.

The closest analogy, in fact, to the scheme of Philo and Plotinus is to be found in the well-known triadic distinction found in many Gnostic systems between 'corporeal' or 'material' (*sarkikoi, choikoi, hylikoi*), 'psychic' (*psychikoi*), and 'spiritual' (*pneumatikoi*) men[8], such as we find set out in Irenaeus, *Adv. Haer.* I 1, 14, or Hippolytus, *Ref.* X 9-10 (Naassenes and Peratae), but most clearly, perhaps, in the *Excerpta ex Theodoto* of Clement of Alexandria (preserved in Book VII of the *Stromateis*), which are notes of an account of Valentinianism "according to the oriental teaching" (i.e., as opposed to that of the Italian school), composed by a certain Theodotus[9]. Exc. 54 runs as follows:

> "From Adam three natures are begotten. The first was the irrational (alogos), which was Cain's, the second the rational and just, which was Abel's, the third the spiritual (pneumatikê), which was Seth's. Now that which is earthly (choikos) is 'according to the image' (Gen. 1:26), that which is psychical (psychikos) is 'according to the likeness' of God (ibid.), and that which is spiritual is 'according to the Form' (kat' idean, Gen. 5:3); and with reference to these three, without the other children of Adam, it was said: "This is the book of the generation of men" (Gen. 5:1). And because Seth was spiritual he neither tends flocks nor tills the soil but produces a child, as spiritual things do. And him, "who hoped to call upon the name of the Lord" (Gen. 4:26), who looked upward and whose "citizenship is in heaven" (Phil. 3:20) -- him the world does not contain."
>
> (trans. R.P. Casey)

Here, the natures of Cain, Abel and Seth are distinguished hierarchically, on the basis of Gen. 4. Philo, it must be admitted, knows nothing of a special ranking for Seth above Abel. For him, both Abel and Seth are representatives of virtue and *nous*, over against Cain, and Seth is simply a reincarnation of Abel (*De Post. Caini*, 172-3). The exaltation of Seth seems to be a distinctively Gnostic development. It is in respect of the quotation of *Philippians* 3:20 ("for our citizenship is in heaven") that a point of contact with Philo arises. The whole final section, with its reference to "looking upward" (*anô bleponta*) and transcending this world, is reminiscent of *Gig.* 61, where the Men of God rise into the intelligible world and become enrolled in the *politeia* of the Forms. Similar imagery is employed by Plotinus, the 'third class' being portrayed as coming home to their true fatherland outside this world.

IV

If some similarity be granted between these three passages, what are we to make of it? Where does this triadic division of mankind originate? Who is influencing whom? That Plotinus knew some Gnostic writings is attested by Porphyry (*Vit. Plot.* ch. 16), and at least two of these have turned up in the Nag Hammadi Corpus, *Zostrianus* (VIII 1) and *Allogenes* (XI 3), with which treatises another is closely connected in doctrine, *The Three Steles of Seth* (VII 5). While Plotinus emphatically disapproved of their doctrines, and of their general attitude to the world and to Hellenic culture (as we can see from his attack on them in *Ennead* II 9), it is quite possible that he was prepared to borrow from them a concept such as this, stripped of its objectionable aspects -- notably the exclusiveness of the pneumatic class, and the notion that the Elect are exempt from, as being superior to, conventional law and custom. In fact, Theodotus accepts (*Exc.* 56, 3) that, since the psychics have free will, some of them are capable of being saved, but the material men are beyond salvation. Of course, Platonists believed that very few people ever became 'godlike', but there is no predestined number or class of these, and nothing very terrible, in any case, happens to those who do not qualify, provided that they behave themselves reasonably.

Plotinus, then, could be seen as having borrowed this concept from Gnostic sources, but what of Philo? One can, of course, push the birth of Gnosticism back before Christianity, to dissident Jewish sects such as the Samaritans, the Essenes or the Therapeutae, all of whom had a belief in the salvation of a small body of the Elect, and with the latter two of whom Philo had some contact, as we know. The apostle Paul, after all, can be seen both to react to and to reflect these beliefs (e.g. 1 *Cor.* 8; 10, 15; *Rom.* 8), with a strong antithesis between those of the Flesh and those of the Spirit. This gives one the basic antithesis between pneumatic and sarkic man, though not the triadic distinction. If, however, you combine with this an antipathy to the 'wisdom of this world', represented both by the orthodox Jewish establishment and by the Greek philosophical tradition, one has, I think, the makings of the triadic distinction which we have before us. Whether the older Pythagorean schema had any influence on this is unclear, but it is not necessary, I think, to postulate that it did, well-known though it would have been to both Philo and Plotinus.

Philo, then, I would suggest, may have picked up this concept of the three levels of man from his contacts with the Essenes or Therapeutae, and Plotinus from a later stage in the Gnostic tradition. It is clear, admittedly, that whoever was an influence on Philo had not yet elevated Seth to the position of archetype of pneumatic man, since we find no sign of such a development in his writings, but that is no great problem. The triadic schema is not dependent on the status of Seth, though it fits the trio of Cain, Abel and Seth very well, even as it can be adapted to the sequence of Epicureans, Stoics and Platonists. In the hands of Philo and Plotinus, it constitutes an interesting case of cultural cross-fertilisation.

Notes

1. The reference, in particular, to practical actions and choices (*praxeis kai eklogai*), in the case of the second class of 'birds', is a pretty clear reference to Stoic terminology and doctrine, cf. *SVF* III 64; 118, but the reference to those who rationalise and philosophise pleasure-seeking also refers plainly enough to the Epicureans.

2. E.g. *Enn.* II 4, 1; III 1, 2; IV 7, 2-3.

3. Commented on recently by David Winston and myself, in *Two Treatises of Philo of Alexandria*, ed. David Winston and John Dillon, Scholars Press, Chico, 1983.

4. Although the word Plotinus uses for 'mist' (*achlys*, instead of *homichlē*), he borrows from a famous passage of the *Iliad* (5, 127), where Athena removes the mist from Diomedes' eyes, so that he can "discern both god and man".

5. Fr. 88 Wehrli, preserved by Cicero, in *Tusc. Disp.* V 3, 8-9. Cf. also Iamblichus, *Vita Pythagorica*, 58-59.

6. Trans. J.E. King (Loeb Classical Library). The form of this doubtless owes something to Cicero's stylistic elaboration, but there is no reason not to attribute the content to Heraclides.

7. In the version given by Iamblichus, the competitors, in their desire for fame, are ranked above those who are merely seeking material gain, but Cicero's version seems closer to Heraclides', whether or not *that* is the original version of the story.

8. There are also traces of this distinction in the Hermetic tradition, which does in general recognise a clear distinction between soul and 'spirit' (*pneuma*), or, in Platonic terms, intellect (*nous*), e.g. *CH* I passim, X 19-21. In IX 9, in fact, we find a triadic distinction of types of thing generated by God, "some exercising their activity through bodies, others that move themselves by means of psychic substance, and others that vivify themselves by means of spirit." This is not a division of classes of men, however, but something broader.

9. Edited by R.P. Casey, *The Excerpta ex Theodoto of Clement of Alexandria*, London, 1934.

2

Origen's Doctrine of the Trinity and Some Later Neoplatonic Theories

In Chapter 3 of Book I of his *Peri Archon*, Origen advances a remarkable doctrine concerning the varying extent of the influences of the three persons of the Trinity. It is one of the doctrines that involved him in some posthumous trouble, a fortunate consequence of which is that we have a statement of it by Justinian, in his *Letter to Menas*,[1] as well as an accurate Latin version by Jerome in his *Letter to Avitus*,[2] a circumstance which frees us from reliance upon the circumlocutions and prevarications of the loyal but cautious Rufinus.

From a Platonist perspective, this doctrine is of great interest, but poses something of a puzzle, as will become apparent presently. First, however, I should like to set out the doctrine as it is presented to us by Justinian who, though hostile, is sufficiently bald and factual to inspire in one the confidence that he is truer to Origen than is Rufinus:

> "[Origen declares] that God the Father, in holding together all things, extends his power to every level of being, imparting to each from His own store its being what it is; while the Son, in a lesser degree than the Father, extends only to rational beings

[for he is second to the Father]; and to a still lesser degree the Holy Spirit penetrates only to the saints" [i.e., to the consecrated members of the Christian community]. "So that according to this theory, the power of the Father is greater than that of the Son and the Holy Spirit, and again that of the Holy Spirit is superior to the other holy agencies."[3]

Jerome's only significant variant from this is his description of the Son as actually "less" (minorem) than the Father, and the Holy Spirit as "inferior" (inferiorem) to the Son,[4] which I take to be, a tendentious distortion of Origen's meaning. Justinian, with creditable attention to accuracy, speaks only of the Son as ἐλαττόνως . . . φθάνων, and the Holy Spirit ἔτι ἡττόνως, which does not, I would maintain, imply the sort of essential subordinationism of which Jerome is certainly accusing him.

Rufinus, of course, is concerned to soften the effect of this troublesome doctrine as far as he, in good conscience, can. If we were dependent on Rufinus alone, we would derive a very muted impression of Origen's theory. Here is his version (De Princ. I, 3, 5):

"I am of the opinion, then, that the activity of the Father and the Son is to be seen both in saints and in sinners, in rational men and in dumb animals, yes, and even in lifeless things and in absolutely everything that exists; but the activity of the Holy Spirit does not extend at all either to lifeless things, or to things that have life but yet are dumb, nor is it to be found in those who, though rational, still lie in wickedness and are not wholly converted to better things. Only in those who are already turning to better things and walking in the ways of Jesus Christ, that is, who are engaged in good deeds and who abide in God, is the work of the Holy Spirit, I think, to be found."[5] (Trans. Butterworth)

The distinction in extent of power between the Father and the Son, as we can see, has been here thoroughly obscured. They are both represented as being concerned with the whole of creation, as opposed to the Holy Spirit's exclusive concern with "the saints." With the help of our other evidence, however, we can, I think, discern what doctrine Rufinus was faced with. The Father alone extends his power "to lifeless things and to absolutely everything that exists," whereas the Son's power extends to all living things, both rational and irrational. The influence of the Holy Spirit, in turn, extends only to that class of rational beings which Origen's Gnostic predecessors classed as "pneumatics," those "saved" individuals endowed not only with soul but with pneuma. Origen is prepared to recognize such a class of person; his only objection to the Gnostic position, and it is a vehement one, is that he denies that this class is a closed one—any human being may acquire pneumatic status.

However, I am concerned in this paper not primarily with the significance of this doctrine in Origen's thought, but rather with its possible sources or analogues in contemporary Platonism.[6] To throw any light on this it is unfortunately necessary to move on approximately two centuries, down to the time of Proclus, and then to see if we can work our way back from there to the early decades of the third century.

In Proposition 57 of his *Elements of Theology,* Proclus advances a general principle concerning the range of activity of causal principles that, it seems to me, bears a remarkable resemblance to the doctrine of Origen. For our present purpose, I fear that it will be necessary to quote it in full:

> *Every cause both operates prior to its consequent and gives rise to a greater number of posterior terms.*
>
> For if it is a cause, it is more perfect and more powerful than its consequent. And if so, it must cause a greater number of effects: for greater power produces more effects, equal power, equal effects, and lesser power, fewer; and the power which can produce the greater effects upon a like subject can produce also the lesser, whereas a power capable of the lesser will not necessarily be capable of the greater. If, then, the cause is more powerful than its consequent, it is productive of a greater number of effects.
>
> But again, the powers which are in the consequent are present in a greater measure in the cause. For all that is produced by secondary beings is produced in a greater measure by prior and more determinative principles. The cause, then, is cooperative in the production of all that the consequent is capable of producing.
>
> And if it first produces the consequent itself, it is of course plain that it is operative before the latter in the activity which produces it. Thus every cause operates both prior to its consequent and in conjunction with it, and likewise gives rise to further effects posterior to it. [*Corollary:*] From this it is apparent that what Soul causes is caused also by Intelligence, but not all that Intelligence causes is caused by Soul: Intelligence operates prior to Soul; and what Soul bestows on secondary existences Intelligence bestows in a greater measure; and at a level where Soul is no longer operative Intelligence irradiates with its own gifts things on which Soul has not bestowed itself—for even the inanimate participates Intelligence, or the creative activity of Intelligence, in so far as it participates Form.
>
> Again, what Intelligence causes is also caused by the Good, but not conversely. For even privation of Form is from the Good, since it is the source of all things; but Intelligence, being Form, cannot give rise to privation.[7] (Trans. Dodds)

The theory presented here can be traced back, as Dodds points out in his excellent note *ad loc.,* as far as Syrianus, who enunciates it in his commentary on the *Metaphysics* (p. 59, 17 Kroll),[8] but no further. Iamblichus, as we shall see in a moment, has a rather different theory, and neither Porphyry nor Plotinus seems to make any use of it.

Proclus' theory is a consequence of certain other principles of his metaphysics. First, the principle that *every productive cause is superior to that which it produces* (Prop. 7); then, the immediately preceding proposition to the present one (56), that *all that is produced by secondary beings is in a greater measure produced from those prior and more determinative principles from which the secondary were themselves derived.* His doctrine is securely underpinned by a rigorous logical framework. The supreme principle, which he here terms the Good, rather than the One, in recognition, perhaps, of its causal role, extends its *energeia* to the lowest reaches of creation, even to what is unformed, negations (*stereseis*), and the chiefest of *stereseis,* matter itself (this is made clear by Syrianus, in the passage quoted in note 8). The second hypostasis, *Nous,* extends its influence not just to rational beings, as one might expect, but, precisely by virtue of the fact that it is a higher principle than Soul, which is the life principle, it extends also lower than Soul, to all entities that have Form, animate or inanimate, by reason of its role as bestower of Form. Soul itself, being the lowest of the hypostases, extends least far, taking in only what has life, be it rational or irrational.

It should be plain that, while there are striking similarities between the schemes of Origen and of Proclus (or should we say, of the Athenian school?), there are also considerable differences. The ranges of influence of the three hypostases are quite different in each case. What remains to be decided is, first, whether this theory can be traced in Platonism any further back than Syrianus, and on the other hand, whether Origen's doctrine sounds like something that he devised himself from the whole cloth, or is rather an adaptation of an already existing theory to his own particular requirements.

To take the second problem first, it is surely noticeable that, particularly in the case of the range of influence of the Holy Spirit, Origen's demarcation of influence does not seem to correspond to a natural division in the universe. Traditional divisions would be rather between rational and irrational animals, animate and inanimate objects, material and immaterial being; at the top of the scale pure Unity, at the bottom unformed, undifferentiated matter. Within this scale, and within the known metaphysical scheme of second-century Platonism, it is not difficult to fabricate a plausible triad of principles with concentric spheres of influence. Both Albinus, in the *Didaskalikos,* and Numenius, in his surviving fragments, present us with a triad of First God or Father, Second God or Demiurge (both of these, admittedly, being Intellects of a sort, but the First God being, according to Albinus, also "nobler than Intellect,"[9] according to Numenius Intellect "at rest"[10]), and finally World Soul. It would be easy to construct a Platonic theory of spheres of influence, according to which the Father extended his activity to all creation, even as far as matter—there is, after all, a school of thought in Platonism, traceable back to Eudorus of Alexandria,[11] and appearing in the *Chaldaean Oracles,*[12] according to which God is the creator even of matter, while the power of the Demiurge extends to all that which is endowed with Form, it being the Demiurge's particular task to create the material cosmos; the Soul would then extend to all that had soul. The only problem with such a construction is that there is absolutely no evidence for it. And yet Origen's scheme has a distinct look of being adapted to a special purpose. He was presented with a third principle which was precisely not Soul, but Spirit, and Soul and Spirit were sharply distinguished in the tradition from which Origen sprang, going back to St. Paul. The *hagion pneuma* could not be responsible for all that had soul; it could only be responsible for the *pneumatikoi,* the "saints." So Origen had to adapt, even at the cost of incurring the Platonist reproach of splitting up reality like a bad butcher, not at the joints.

Let us turn back to our first problem: what is the ancestry of this theory in the Platonic tradition? I have come upon only one clue, and it is not a very satisfactory one.

In the course of a comment on *Alcibiades* I, 115A, Olympiodorus reports, first, the theory of Proclus concerning the extension of influences of the hypostases, and then, in contrast to it, that of Iamblichus:[13]

> But the divine Iamblichus does not distinguish the higher principles from the lower by the greater extent of their influence (for all the principles, in his view, extend downwards as far as matter; for this is a dogma of his, that, irrespective of at what point a principle begins to operate, it does not cease its operation before extending to the lowest level; for even if it is stronger, nevertheless the fact of its greater separation can create a balancing factor, rendering it weaker), but he distinguishes them by the fact that the influence of the higher principles is more piercing (*drimutera*). For we strive for Being more basically than for Life, and for Life more basically than for Intelligence.

Iamblichus is actually talking here, not of the three basic hypostases, but rather of the three moments of the hypostasis of *Nous*, Being, Life, and Intelligence, but this does not affect the nature of his argument. The language of Olympiodorus does not admit of certainty, but it sounds to me rather as if Iamblichus is here presented as arguing against a previous view (he is actually presented as arguing against Proclus, which is impossible). If this were so, it would be evidence that the theory goes back at least to early Neoplatonism, and was only revived by Syrianus. Now, in his comments recorded elsewhere, Iamblichus is frequently to be found in opposition both to Amelius and to Porphyry, and with either of these we can find linked the name of Numenius.[14]

However, at this point the trail gives out. We cannot be sure that Iamblichus is in fact contradicting anyone. We are left with the reflection that there is much that we do not know about the doctrines of the three last-mentioned figures, and even less about the mysterious figure who provides a link between Numenius and Neoplatonism on the one hand, and Origen on the other, Ammonius Saccas. All one can say is that the doctrine would fit, not uncomfortably, into what we know of second-century Platonist speculation.

There is another aspect to this theory which, it must be noted, had no attraction for Origen, but did for the later Platonists, and this is the theurgic aspect. The theory speculates that, in a powerful sense, the lower down the scale of nature an entity is situated, the more closely it is linked with higher principles. This provides an excellent philosophical justification for making use of stones, plants, and animals in the performance of magical rituals; they are actually nearer to one god or another than we are, being direct products of the divine realm. Such a theory would accord well with the doctrines of the *Chaldaean Oracles*, another major influence on Neoplatonism from Porphyry onwards, and themselves a second-century production more or less contemporary with Numenius, but once again the available sources fail us. All we find attested, and that only in Psellus' summary of Chaldaean doctrine, is a doctrine of *sympatheia*.[15]

I remain convinced, however, that Origen's theory and Proclus' theory are applications of the same doctrine, and that this doctrine was not invented by Origen. Further than that, at the moment, I cannot go.

Notes

ORIGEN'S DOCTRINE OF THE TRINITY AND SOME LATER NEOPLATONIC THEORIES

1. *Ep. ad Menam.* p. 208, 26–32 Schw. = Fr. 9 Koetschau.
2. *Ep.* 124, 2, p. 98, 1–6 Hilberg.
3. Ἐκ τοῦ πρώτου λόγου τοῦ Περὶ ἀρχῶν βιβλίου. Ὅτι ὁ μὲν θεὸς καὶ πατὴρ συνέχων τὰ πάντα φθάνει εἰς ἕκαστον τῶν ὄντων, μεταδιδοὺς ἑκάστῳ ἀπὸ τοῦ ἰδίου τὸ εἶναι ὅπερ ἐστίν, ἐλαττόνως δὲ παρὰ τὸν πατέρα ὁ υἱὸς φθάνων ἐπὶ μόνα τὰ λογικά (δεύτερος γὰρ ἐστι τοῦ πατρός), ἔτι δὲ ἡττόνως τὸ πνεῦμα τὸ ἅγιον ἐπὶ μόνους τοὺς ἁγίους διικνούμενον ὥστε κατὰ τοῦτο μείζων ἡ δύναμις τοῦ πατρὸς παρὰ τὸν υἱὸν καὶ τὸ πνεῦμα τὸ ἅγιον, πλείων δὲ ἡ τοῦ υἱοῦ παρὰ τὸ πνεῦμα τὸ ἅγιον, καὶ πάλιν διαφέρουσα μᾶλλον τοῦ ἁγίου πνεύματος ἡ δύναμις παρὰ τὰ ἄλλα ἅγια.
4. "Filium quoque minorem a patre eo quod secundus ab illo sit, et spiritum sanctum inferiorem a filio in sanctis quibusque versari, atque hoc ordine maiorem patris fortitudinem esse quam filii et spiritus sancti, et rursum maiorem filii fortitudinem esse quam spiritus sancti, et consequenter ipsius sancti spiritus maiorem esse virtutem ceteris, quae sancta dicuntur."
5. "Arbitror igitur operationem quidem esse patris et filii tam in sanctis quam in peccatoribus, in hominibus rationabilibus et in mutis animalibus, sed et in his, quae sine anima sunt, et in omnibus omnino quae sunt; operationem vero spiritus sancti nequaquam prorsus incidere vel in ea, quae sine anima sunt, vel in ea, quae animantia quidem sed muta sunt, sed ne in illis quidem inveniri, qui rationabiles quidem sunt sed 'in malitia positi' nec omnino ad meliora conversi. In illis autem solis esse arbitror opus spiritus sancti, qui iam se ad meliora convertunt et 'per vias Christi Iesu' incedunt, id est qui sunt 'in bonis actibus' et 'in deo permanent.'"
6. The former question is well discussed in an article by Manlio Simonetti, "Sull' interpretazione di un passo del *De Principiis* di Origene (I 3, 5–8)," in *Riv. di Cult. Class. e Med.*, 6 (1964), pp. 15–32, but he does not concern himself with possible Platonic analogies.
7. Πᾶν αἴτιον καὶ πρὸ τοῦ αἰτιατοῦ ἐνεργεῖ καὶ μετ' αὐτὸ πλειόνων ἐστὶν ὑποστατικόν.
   εἰ γάρ ἐστιν αἴτιον, τελειότερόν ἐστι καὶ δυνατώτερον τοῦ μετ' αὐτό. καὶ εἰ τοῦτο, πλειόνων αἴτιον· δυνάμεως γὰρ μείζονος τὸ πλείω παράγειν, ἴσης δὲ τὰ ἴσα, καὶ τῆς ἐλάττονος ἐλάττω· καὶ ἡ μὲν τὰ μείζονα ἐν τοῖς ὁμοίοις δυναμένη δύναμις καὶ τὰ ἐλάττονα δύναται, ἡ δὲ τὰ ἐλάττονα δυναμένη οὐκ ἐξ ἀνάγκης τὰ μείζω δυνήσεται. εἰ οὖν δυνατώτερον τὸ αἴτιον, πλειόνων ἐστὶ παρακτικόν.

ἀλλὰ μὴν καὶ ὅσα δύναται τὸ αἰτιατόν, μειζόνως ἐκεῖνο δύναται. πᾶν γὰρ τὸ ὑπὸ τῶν δευτέρων παραγόμενον ὑπὸ τῶν προτέρων καὶ αἰτιωτέρων παράγεται μειζόνως. συνυφίστησιν ἄρα αὐτῷ πάντα ὅσα πέφυκε παράγειν.

εἰ δὲ καὶ αὐτὸ πρότερον παράγει, δῆλον δήπουθεν ὅτι πρὸ αὐτοῦ ἐνεργεῖ κατὰ τὴν παρακτικὴν αὐτοῦ ἐνέργειαν. ἅπαν ἄρα αἴτιον καὶ πρὸ τοῦ αἰτιατοῦ ἐνεργεῖ καὶ σὺν αὐτῷ καὶ μετ' αὐτὸ ἄλλα ὑφίστησιν.

ἐκ δὴ τούτων φανερὸν ὅτι ὅσων μὲν αἰτία ψυχή, καὶ νοῦς αἴτιος, οὐχ ὅσων δὲ νοῦς, καὶ ψυχὴ αἰτία· ἀλλὰ καὶ πρὸ ψυχῆς ἐνεργεῖ, καὶ ἃ δίδωσι ψυχὴ τοῖς δευτέροις, δίδωσι καὶ νοῦς μειζόνως, καὶ μηκέτι ψυχῆς ἐνεργούσης νοῦς ἐλλάμπει τὰς ἑαυτοῦ δόσεις, οἷς μὴ δέδωκε ψυχὴ ἑαυτήν. καὶ γὰρ τὸ ἄψυχον, καθόσον εἴδους μετέσχε, νοῦ μετέχει καὶ τῆς τοῦ νοῦ ποιήσεως.

καὶ δὴ καὶ ὅσων νοῦς αἴτιος, καὶ τὸ ἀγαθὸν αἴτιον· οὐκ ἔμπαλιν δέ. καὶ γὰρ αἱ στερήσεις τῶν εἰδῶν ἐκεῖθεν (πάντα γὰρ ἐκεῖθεν). νοῦς δὲ στερήσεως ὑποστάτης οὐκ ἔστιν, εἶδος ὤν.

8. τὸ γὰρ ἓν καὶ ὑπὲρ τὸ ὂν καὶ σὺν τῷ ὄντι καὶ ἐπὶ τάδε τοῦ ὄντος, ὡς ἐπὶ τῆς ὕλης καὶ τῆς στερήσεως.

9. *Did.* ch. X, 2: τούτου δὲ (sc. the Active Intellect) καλλίων ὁ αἴτιος τούτου καὶ ὅπερ ἂν ἔτι ἀνώτερω τούτων ὑφέστηκεν. οὗτος ἂν εἴη ὁ πρῶτος θεός, . . .

10. Fr. 15 Des Places: ὁ μὲν πρῶτος θεός . . . ἑστώς. The πρῶτος νοῦς is also termed αὐτόον in Fr. 17, as being an object of contemplation for the Demiurge.

11. Alex. Aphrod. *In Metaph.* p. 59, 1 Hayduck, *ad Met.* 988a10–11.

12. *Fr.* 34 Des Places: Ἔνθεν ἀποθῴσκει γένεσις πολυποικίλου ὕλης. Matter is also described as πατρογενής by Psellus in his *Hypotyposis*, sect. 27, p. 201 Des Places.

13. *In Alc.* p. 110, 13ff. Creuzer = Iambl. *In Alc.* Fr. 8 Dillon.

14. Amelius, e.g., *In Tim.* Fr. 39; Fr. 54; Fr. 57 (with Numenius); Porphyry, Fr. 16; Fr. 70, Dillon.

15. *Expos. Chald.* 1153a10–11, p. 191 Des Places: συμπαθῆ δὲ τὰ ἄνω τοῖς κάτω φασὶ καὶ μάλιστα τὰ ὑπὸ σελήνην.

XXII

LOOKING ON THE LIGHT: SOME REMARKS ON THE IMAGERY OF LIGHT IN THE FIRST CHAPTER OF THE *PERI ARCHON*

This essay is an attempt to address a general question, that of Origen's relation to the Greek philosophical tradition, by concentrating on one particular issue, which I hope will prove adequately illustrative.

As we all know, the battle has long raged between partisans of Origen the systematic philosopher, such as Adolf von Harnack, Eugène de Faye, Hal Koch and Hans Jonas, and those who see him as essentially an exegete of scripture and Christian apologist, such as Walther Völker, Henri de Lubac, Henri Crouzel, or Marguerite Harl. To a certain extent one's attitude is conditioned by how far one concentrates on a text such as the *Peri Archon,* or rather on the *Homilies* and such works as the *Exhortation to Martyrdom* and the treatise *On Prayer,* but these emphases are themselves plainly conditioned by the overt or covert prejudices of the authorities concerned, in their anxiety to maintain either the originality and philosophical standing of Origen or alternatively, if not his orthodoxy, at least his essential Christianity. Part of the problem, I think, has been that the alternatives are stated too starkly. Either Origen is presented as a Platonist with a superficial veneer of Christianity, or he is not to be a systematic philosopher at all. The truth may rather be that he is indeed a philosopher, but one who, rather than adopting Platonism or the doctrine of any other Hellenic school, has forged a system of his own out of the Christian scriptures and tradition, to which he lays Platonism tribute for concepts and formulations which he finds useful, without surrendering to the Greeks any principle whatever.[1] I would suggest that Origen's relation to primitive Christianity is somewhat analogous to that of Plotinus to Plato and earlier Platonism. He draws his inspiration from the tradition, and genuinely aspires to be faithful to it, but his genius drives him to the creation of a new system, built upon what he has inherited. In a word, Origen only wishes to be a Christian, as does Plotinus to be a Platonist, but if we persist in calling Plotinus, in recognition of his achievement, a Neoplatonist, then we must denominate Origen a 'Neochristian'.

What I want to do in this paper is to consider one dominant image of which Origen makes much use in his discussion of the nature of God in

---

[1] We may recall that, as he tells it himself (*ap.* Eusebius *HE* VI.19, 12-13), Origen only began to attend the lectures of "the teacher of philosophy" (sc. Ammonius Saccas) when he himself was already an established, if precocious, teacher of Christian doctrine. He went to Ammonius, not to be converted to Platonism, but rather to pick up useful technical information, to aid in his apostolate to the Alexandrian intelligentsia, a number of whom, such as Heraclas and his brother Plutarch, he actually lured away from Ammonius. This he could not have done, I submit, without a system to offer. The system need not be worked out in every detail, nor even free of contradictions, but one cannot reasonably deny, I think, that it is there. Without going into details, I see it as involving, above all, the concept of a cosmic process of procession (or 'fall') and return, involving the pre-existence of souls and, inevitably, some form of reincarnation and sequence of worlds (though I doubt that Origen ever quite made up his mind on these questions). All other aspects of his thought seem to me to be conditioned by this grand conception, which is itself the product of his concern with the problem of God's providence and our free will. To that extent I remain sympathetic to Hal Koch, in *Pronoia und Paideusis* (Berlin and Leipzig, 1932), and even to Hans Jonas.

the *Peri Archon*, and see how his use of Platonic imagery and doctrine may be seen to support my thesis.[2]

On the vexed question of the nature of the *Peri Archon*, on which much has been written in recent years,[3] I must say that I am inclined to view

---

[2]Origen's use of light imagery in general is comprehensively examined in a thesis by M. Martinez-Pastor, *Teologia de la luz en Orígenes* (Comillas, 1962), but Martinez does not address himself to the particular problem that concerns me here. See also H. Crouzel, *Origène et la 'Connaissance mystique'* (Paris/Bruges, 1961), pp. 130-154, for a good account of the uses to which Origen puts the imagery of light.

[3]Cf. B. Steidle, "Neue Untersuchungen zu Origenes" περί Ἀρχῶν', *ZNW* 40 (1942), 236-243; M. Harl, "Recherches sur le περί Ἀρχῶν' d'Origène en vue d'une nouvelle édition: la division en chapitres," *Studia Patristica* 3 (= TU 78; Berlin, 1961), pp. 57-67; H. Crouzel, Intro. to *Origène Traité des Principes*, Tome 1 (SC 252), pp. 15-22. The precise meaning of ἀρχαί intended by Origen in this context has been the object of some uncertainty (Cf. Crouzel's discussion *op. cit.* pp. 12-15, and "Qu'a voulu faire Origène en composant le Traité des Principes?," *BLE* 76 (1975), pp. 161-186, and 241-260). It seems probable to me that he sees himself as meaning what any Platonic philosopher would mean by this, viz. a discussion of the three acknowledged "first principles", God, Idea(s), Matter, together with topics arising out of those, and that is the subject-matter of the first section of the work (to II.3), *mutatis mutandis* (e.g. for "Ideas", we have "rational beings", for Matter, the World). How well the title fits the other portions of the work is more problematic (a reference back to the discussion of free will in III.1 in the *Comm. in Rom.* (VII.15, PG XIV 1145A) as a separate *libellus* would seem to indicate that Origen thought of the work rather as a collection of essays).
    Some light may be thrown on what particular connotation Origen attaches to the term ἀρχαί by his remarks at *Comm. in Joh.* XIII.46, 302, where he presents the ἀρχαί of any science or art as what the first discoverer, or "sower", lays down, to be developed further and brought to completion (τέλος) by later generations ("reapers")--all this by way of exegesis of John 4:36. This "dynamic" concept of the ἀρχαί of a science imports another dimension, I think, into the traditionally static philosophical meanings of the term, as immutable basic principles, or ultimate principles of reality. Certainly Origen is to some extent "transposing" the traditional Platonic meaning of the term, as Crouzel suggests; the connotation "principles of the Christian faith" is superimposed on the basic meaning "first principles of reality." Cf. also *De Princ.* 4, 1.7, where ἀρχή is significantly glossed by στοιχείωσις.

the work as an attempt by Origen to state a reasoned Christian position on the topic of ἀρχαί, or 'first principles', arising out of his attendance at the lectures of Ammonius Saccas. I am led to this view, not just by a consideration of the subject matter, but by looking at the very way in which the work starts out. Origen begins abruptly, not with a positive statement of God's nature,[4] but with an answer to an accusation, plainly from a Platonic source, that Christians regard God as having a *corporeal* nature.[5] In combating this accusation he has to face a series of passages of Scripture which seem to attribute to God material substance or characteristics.[6]

For instance, Moses says at Deut. 4:24: "Our God is a consuming fire",[7] and Jesus says to the Samaritan woman at John 4:24: "God is spirit (πνεῦμα), and those who worship him must worship in spirit and in truth". Now Origen's general line of defense is plainly that such passages must be taken figuratively, but that is not the first point that he makes. This first

---

[4]As one would expect in a statement of First Principles. On the immateriality of God, Cf. Aetius, *Placita* I.7, 31 (p. 304 Diels, *Dox.Gr.*), Apuleius, *De Plat.* I.5, 190-1; Numenius, Fr. 3 des Places. (Albinus in *Did.* ch. 10 asserts, certainly, God's immateriality, but only at the *end* of his discussion).

[5]In the Preface, also, he begins, rather defensively, by identifying himself with Moses, who preferred, in the words of the author of Hebrews (11:24-26), "the abused state (ὀνειδισμός) of Christ to the treasure-houses of the Egyptians", these latter being the much-vaunted doctrines of contemporary philosophy.

[6]These passages may well have been adduced by anti-Christian polemicists, (and even by Ammonius, whom Porphyry, at least, maintained to have started as a Christian himself), though here Origen only says that they *might* do so (*scio quoniam conabuntur*).

[7]He also describes him there as "a jealous God", but Origen leaves that aside in the present context.

point I find rather interesting, and it is that which I wish to start from, since I think that it serves as a good instance of Origen's complex relationship to contemporary Hellenic[8] philosophy.

"These men," says Origen, "will have it that fire and spirit are body and nothing else. But I would ask them what they have to say about this passage of Scripture: 'God is light,' as John says in his epistle (1 John 1:5), 'and in him is no darkness.' "

The point of adducing this passage about light is presumably that, in later Platonism, light is agreed to be incorporeal. But this is, strangely enough, not a point which Origen cares to make explicit. Instead, he goes on:

> He is that light, surely, which lightens the whole understanding of those who are capable of receiving truth, as it is written in the Thirty-fifth Psalm, 'In thy light shall we see light.' For what other light of God can we speak of in which a man sees light, except God's spiritual power ($\delta\acute{v}\nu\alpha\mu\iota\varsigma$) which when it lightens a man causes him either to see clearly the truth of all things or to know God himself, who is called the truth? (trans. Butterworth).

Origen here has slipped unobtrusively from making one point to making another. The original purpose of introducing the example of light, to counter the references to fire and to $\pi\nu\epsilon\hat{v}\mu\alpha$, has been passed over in favour of an argument which applies to all three epithets equally, that they are not to be taken literally but metaphorically.

---

[8] I use "Hellenic" here instead of the commonly-used term "pagan," which I find objectionable.

Why should Origen make such an apparently inconsequential move? I wish to propose two reasons, both of which illustrate his complex relationship to contemporary Platonism. The first is that, while he was well aware of contemporary Platonic doctrine on the incorporeality of light, he did not necessarily accept it himself; the second is that he also has very much in mind the Sun Simile of *Republic* VI (507a-509c), which certainly since Alexander of Aphrodisias had been brought into conjunction with Aristotle's doctrines of the Active Intellect in *De Anima* III.5 and of the Unmoved Mover in *Metaphysics* XII, and had thus been incorporated in a coordinated Peripatetic and Platonist doctrine of God as Pure Activity (ἐνέργεια) and as the *noetic* analogue of the Sun, bestowing both intelligibility and existence on all things, as well as knowledge on rational souls.

Let us explore each of these points in turn. First of all, the incorporeality of light. This is not a Platonic doctrine--neither in the *Republic* nor in the *Timaeus* is light presented as something incorporeal--but it is at least derivable from Aristotle, who, in *De Anima* II.7, declares light to be "the actuality of the transparent *qua* transparent."[9] Aristotle simply wants to make the point that light is not a substance of any kind, but a condition of a substance (countering the doctrine of Empedocles), but for later Aristotelians and Platonists this incorporeality of light became something rather special, being connected with its preeminent role in the operation of the sense of sight, the most 'honourable' of the senses (cf. Plato, *Tim.* 45B-D), and then being used as an analogy for the role of the Good (or in Alexander's theory, *Nous*) in the activation of the human intellect in its cognising of True Being.

---

[9]148b9-10: φῶς δέ ἐστιν ἡ τούτου ἐνέργεια, τοῦ διαφανοῦς ἧ διαφανές.

Thus it is that in Alexander's *De Anima* we find, first, at pp. 42, 19-
43, 11 Bruns, a straightforward paraphrase of Ar. *De An*. III.7, but then, at
88, 26-89, 6, the use of the analogy of light to illustrate the principle that
"whatever is eminently some kind of being imparts this kind of being to
everything which is less eminently the same kind of being," to quote Philip
Merlan's formulation.[10]   The Active Intellect, being preeminently
intelligible, imparts intelligibility to the "material" intellect (that is, the
immanent human intellect), which becomes intelligible by intelligising the
proper objects of intellect, the forms in matter.   Similarly, light, being
preeminently visible, is the cause of the visibility of everything visible, as
well as of the seeing ability of the eyes.

This comparison of Alexander's plainly owes much to the Sun
Simile of the *Republic*, and it in turn can be seen to have had considerable
influence on Plotinus' view of the status of light in such passages as *Enn*.
IV.5, 6-7, II.1,7 and I.6,3.[11] The evidence of Origen would seem to indicate
that this identification of light as ἀσώματον, against the indications of
Plato's doctrine in the *Timaeus*, goes back to Middle Platonism, perhaps to
Numenius, or at least to Ammonius Saccas.

For a Platonist, Aristotle's doctrine as presented in *De An*. II.7 is
not satisfactory, since Aristotle declares light not to be a body, not for the
purpose of exalting it, but simply to deprive it of any independent existence.
Quite a different connotation can be put upon this bodilessness of light if one

---

[10]In *Monopsychism, Mysticism, Metaconsciousness* (The Hague,
1969[2]), p. 39.

[11]See A. H. Armstrong, *The Architecture of the Intelligible
Universe in the Philosophy of Plotinus* (Cambridge, 1940; repr. Hakkert,
1967), pp. 54-57; F. M. Schroeder, "Light and the Active Intellect in
Alexander and Plotinus," *Hermes* 112 (1984), pp. 239-245.

chooses to take this, as does Alexander, and later Plotinus, as indicating that light is pure Form without an admixture of matter. In Alexander this is actually only implied in the comparison of light with the Active Intellect, but in Plotinus it is quite explicit.[12] For Plotinus, ordinary, physical light is, by reason of its freedom from admixture with body, the noblest element in the material universe.

Now as I say, Origen seems to recognize the existence of this doctrine of light, but he is not prepared to approve it. When it comes to employing the similes of the Sun and the Cave of the *Republic*, however, he has no such hesitation, although he employs them in a suitably disguised form. At *De Princ*, I. 1.5, we find the following:[13]

> Having then refuted, to the best of our ability, every interpretation which suggests that we should attribute to God any material characteristics, we assert that he is in truth incomprehensible and immeasurable.[14] For whatever may be the knowledge which we have been able to obtain about God, whether by perception or reflection, we must of necessity believe that he is far and away better than our thoughts about him. For if we see a man who can scarcely look at a glimmer or the light of the smallest lamp, and if we wish to teach such a one, whose eyesight is not strong enough

---

[12]E.g. *Enn.* I 6, 7, 17-18: light is $\dot{a}\sigma\omega\mu a\tau o\nu$ $\kappa a\dot{\iota}$ $\lambda\acute{o}\gamma o\varsigma$ $\kappa a\dot{\iota}$ $\epsilon\tilde{\iota}\delta o\varsigma$.

[13]I use Butterworth's translation, unless otherwise noted.

[14]*Incomprehensibilis* here translates $\dot{a}\kappa a\tau\acute{a}\lambda\eta\pi\tau o\varsigma$; *inaestimabilis* may render $\dot{a}\pi\epsilon\rho\acute{\iota}\mu\epsilon\tau\rho o\varsigma$, an epithet, which, though Greek, is only found in Apuleius' *De Plat.* ch. 5, but $\dot{a}\delta\iota\epsilon\xi\acute{\eta}\tau\eta\tau o\varsigma$ or $\dot{a}\pi\epsilon\rho\iota\acute{o}\rho\iota\sigma\tau o\varsigma$ are also possibilities.

to receive more light than we have said, about the brightness and
splendour of the sun, shall we not have to tell him that the
splendour of the sun is unspeakably and immeasurably better and
more glorious than all this light he can see?

Here, and in what follows, the influence of the Simile of the Cave is
palpable enough, I think,[15] but there is another element here also, which is
not present in Plato's image. Plato stresses the shock and discomfort of
being brought from one's comfortable viewing of the shadows on the wall
cast by the fire, first to the realization that the fire is only a fire, and the
figures only cardboard cutouts, and then to a view of the outside world
dominated by the sun, but the end result is that one *can* view the sun, one
does attain to a knowledge of the Good. For Origen, God is of such a
nature as "the human mind, however pure or clear to the very utmost that
mind may be, cannot gaze at or behold" (*ibid.*).

Now this is very much a part of the Christian doctrine of the
"invisibility" of God, but it finds an echo also in a passage of Numenius'
dialogue *On the Good* (Fr. 2, des Places), a work which Origen certainly
knew (since he quotes from it in the *Contra Celsum*),[16] to the effect that we
can gain the notion of anything bodily from comparison with things of a
similar nature, but in the case of the Good, "no object present to us nor any

---

[15]Though long since formalized in Middle Platonic tradition, the
Sun Simile is given by Albinus in *Did.* ch. 10 as prime example of the "way
of analogy", while of the "way of ἀναγωγή" (*via eminentiae*), of which the
Cave is certainly an instance, he actually gives Diotima's speech in the
Symposium as the example. Origen uses the comparison of the light of a
lamp with the light of the sun elsewhere, at *Comm. in Joh.* II.120-121 and
C.Cels. V.II.

[16]I.15; IV.51.

sensible object similar to it gives us any means of grasping its nature." However, Numenius is actually leading up here to his lively description of the mystical vision of the Good, which he compares with a little fishing-boat which by close attention one can just pick out bobbing between the waves. Origen gives no such promise of a mystical vision in this life. The important thing is, though, that Numenius seems here to be giving an interpretation of the negative aspect of the Sun Simile--after all, Socrates *does* emphasize at the outset, in 506 C-E, that he cannot give an account of the Good itself, but only a series of images.

In the very next section (I.1.6), Origen seems to make further use of the Cave Simile, though sufficiently altered as to make identification less than obvious:

> But it will not appear out of place if to make the matter clearer still we use yet another illustration. Sometimes our eyes cannot look upon the light itself, that is, the actual sun, but when we see the brightness and rays of the sun as they pour into our windows, for example, or into any small openings for light, we are able to infer from these how great is the source and the foundation of physical light.

This seems to owe something to *Rep*. VII.515e-516b, where the prisoner, newly freed from the Cave, cannot yet look upon the sun or bear the sunlight: "he would find it painful to be thus dragged out, and would chafe at it, and when he came out into the light, his eyes would be filled with its beam so that he would not be able to see even one of the things which we call real," and a gradual process of habituation is required. The difference, of course, is, once again, that in Plato one does come eventually to a vision of the Good, whereas in Origen one does not, at least in this life.[17] In fact,

Origen has here subtly blended the imagery of the Cave with the later Stoic

argument for the existence of God from the contemplation of his works (cf.

Sextus Empiricus, *Adversus Mathematicos* IX.75-87), which suits him

rather better, especially as St. Paul himself had referred to it at *Rom.* 1:20:

"Ever since the creation of the world his invisible nature, namely, his eternal

power and deity, has been clearly perceived in the things that have been

made." But for Origen the force of this argument, in relation to the Cave

Simile, is that we can get no further than inference from God's

manifestations and effects to His nature; we cannot know Him as He is.

Origen certainly approves of the central images of the *Republic*, as

we can see from *Contra Celsum* VII.45-6, where he first quotes Celsus

making use of the Sun and the Line, and then says, "We are careful not to

raise objections to good teachings, even if the authors are outside the faith,"

but he is not committed to the full implications of the doctrine behind them,

nor does he feel constrained from modifying them with other doctrines of his

own. For instance, in the next chapter of Book I (2, 7) dealing with the Son

or *Logos*, he identifies the process of habituation(συνήθεια) mentioned in

Rep. VII.516 a with the activity of the *Logos* (who is, after all, "light from

light"):[18]

> . . . for it is through his brightness that the nature of the light itself
> is known and experienced. This brightness falls softly and gently on

---

[17]There seems almost an explicit contradiction of *Rep.* VII.516B,
αὐτόν καθ' αὐτόν ἐν τῇ αὐτοῦ χώρᾳ δύναιτ' ἂν κατιδεῖν in I.1, 6:
mens nostra ipsum per se ipsum deum sicut est non potest intueri.

[18]*Splendor ex luce* (presumably translating ἀπαύγασμα ἐκ
φωτός) a phrase inspired by Wisdom of Solomon 7:26 and Hebrews 1:3.

the tender and weak eyes of mortal man and little by little trains and accustoms (*adsuescens*) them to bear the light in its clearness; and when it has removed from them all that darkens and obstructs their vision, . . . it renders them capable of enduring the glory of the light, becoming in this respect even a kind of mediator ($\mu\epsilon\sigma\acute{\iota}\tau\eta\varsigma$, 1 Tim. 2:5) between men and the light.

Here, indeed, it seems as if, through Christ, we *are* enabled to see the Father, which would be fully in the spirit of the imagery of the Cave, but in fact Origen is allowing himself to be carried away slightly. This impression is severely qualified in what follows (sects. 8-10), particularly by the striking image of the immense statue, which is too big for us to view, and the miniature statue which is its faithful copy, which we can see, and which gives us a true image ($\epsilon\grave{\iota}\kappa\acute{\omega}\nu$, *similitudo*), but still only an image, of what we cannot see.[19]

In all this we cannot, unfortunately, be sure that Rufinus is not indulging in a certain degree of censorship and "laundering" of the text (as he certainly is seen to be doing in the few places where the original is available to us), but Origen seems to be struggling with the problem of how far God is knowable or unknowable, and to what extent Christ is the means to that knowledge, and Platonic imagery is both a help and a hindrance to him in this.

This is not quite the whole story, however. Origen gives ample indication, in ch. 1 of the *Peri Archon*, that he is aware of the considerable development that had taken place over the previous centuries in the Platonic

---

[19]This is very much in the spirit of Origen's view of Christ as the "image of the invisible God" (Col. 1:15)--one of Origen's favorite texts (119 citations listed in *Biblia Patristica* 3).

doctrine of the nature and the knowability of God. He is influenced not only
by his knowledge of the speculations of such Pythagoreanising Platonists as
Moderatus and Numenius, and also possibly of the more "main-line"
Platonist Albinus, but also by his acquaintance with the works of Philo, who
was himself influenced by contemporary Platonism. The consensus that
appears to have been reached by 200 A.D. or so was that God was both
absolute Unity (μονάς, εἷς, ἕν) but also an Intellect--an Intellect, however,
which is to be distinguished from a second, active, demiurgic intellect or
λόγος (Moderatus, Numenius and Albinus favour a second νοῦς, Philo,
Plutarch and Atticus a λόγος), by being "static" (Num. Fr. 15 des Places) as
opposed to "in motion", a fount and first principle of νοῦς, or, more vaguely
"something higher" (ἀνωτέρω) than νοῦς (Albinus, Didaskalikos, ch. 10).

Such an entity can be known, if at all, only in some rather special
way. Plato's famous dictum at Timaeus 28c about the difficulty of
discovering the nature of God and the impossibility of communicating it to
the general public gave much stimulus to negative theology of various kinds
in later times, but it was not until the second part of the Parmenides was
given a metaphysical interpretation, from the 1st century A.D. on, that the
problem of how the First Principle could be cognised became an acute one for
Platonists. At the end of the first hypothesis (142A), we reach the
conclusion about the One that "it cannot have a name or be spoken of, nor
can there by any knowledge or perception or opinion of it. It is not named or
spoken of, not an object of opinion or knowledge, not perceived by any
creature."

If it is to be cognised at all, then, it cannot be by any 'normal'
cognitive process, such as αἴσθησις, δόξα, or ἐπιστήμη. It will require a
distinct supra-noetic faculty, termed poetically by the Chaldaean Oracles (Fr.
1.1DP) "the flower of the mind" (ἄνθος νοῦ), recognized by Plotinus as the

νοῦς in a state of sober intoxication (*Enn.* III 5, 9; VI 7, 35), and also perhaps by Numenius in his eloquent description of the vision of the Good in Fr. 2 (mentioned above).

Origen, however, does not seem to have arrived at a formula for this special faculty. In his exhaustive study of Origen's terminology and doctrine of the modes and levels of knowledge (*Origène et la 'connaissance mystique'*),[20] despite the promising title (which he does, admittedly, enclose in inverted commas), Henri Crouzel cannot come up with any clear reference to a direct vision of God himself *in this life*. The term which best expresses the sort of direct intellectual contact envisaged by Origen for the beatific vision to be enjoyed by the saints after death is προσβολή,[21] but the significant thing here is that this same term is used by Plotinus, along with ἐπιβολή and ἐπαφή, for the sort of supranoetic contact which is attainable by the νοῦς while still in the body.[22] This is not to deny that Origen had mystical experience (Crouzel makes an eloquent case for his having had some, quoting in particular his first Homily on the Song of Songs (sec. 7),[23] but the fact remains, I think, that for theological reasons he denied that

---

[20]Paris/Bruges, 1963, pp. 496-508.

[21]Interesting passages are *Fragm. In Joh.* XIII (GCS, IV p. 495), κατὰ προσβολὴν νοήσεως, *Exh. ad Mart.*. XIII, where the "friends of God" will enjoy direct knowledge ἐν εἴδει, προσβάλλοντες τῇ τῶν νοητῶν φύσει καὶ τῷ τῆς ἀληθείας κάλλει; *P. Euch.* XXV, 2 ὁ νοῦς προσβάλλει τοῖς νοητοῖς.

[22]E.G. *Enn.* III.8, 10, 33 προσβολή; VI.7, 35, 21 ἐπιβολή; V.3, 10, 42 ἐπαφή.

[23]*Origène*, pp. 162-4. Even here, though, as Patricia Cox points out to me, Origen may after all only be talking about the frustrating experience of having at one moment a vision of the spiritual meaning of a certain text, only to lose it again on further reflection.

the human soul or mind, while still in the body, could achieve the equivalent, in Platonic terms, of looking directly at the sun.

* * * * * *

This has been, I fear, a rather superficial study, based only on one particular series of connected passages in one work (though a major one), of a very prolific and many-sided thinker, but, such as it is, it serves to bear out Crouzel's characterization of Origen as a "transformer" of Platonism, rather than a crypto-Platonist of any sort. One could, obviously, pursue this theme much further, in various directions. One direction that occurs to me is the paradoxical presentation of God as "darkness" ($\sigma\kappa\acute{o}\tau o\varsigma$) in the *Commentary on John* (II.172), arising out of the exegesis of John 1:5, where precisely God is, after all, declared to be "light shining in darkness". By way of going one better, it would almost seem, than the traditional Platonic image of God as light and standing it on its head, but also in order to explain certain troublesome passages of the Old Testament, such as Exodus 19:9, 16, and 20:21, where God is described as enveloped in a thick cloud, and Psalm 18:11: "He made darkness his covering around him, his canopy thick clouds dark with water" (passages which, it seems, Gnostics such as Marcion had fastened on to support their argument that Jahweh was an evil Demiurge), Origen presents this "darkness" and "cloudiness" as a symbol of God's unknowability to the human intellect; in himself, of course, he remains Light.[24]

But this is just by way of coda to my main theme. It seems suitable that a discussion of Origen's use of light imagery should end, paradoxically, with a discussion of God as darkness. My main purpose has

---

[24]Cf. Crouzel, *Origène et la 'connaissance mystique'*, pp. 91-95.

been to suggest that Origen, while making extensive use of Platonic images and formulations, is never enslaved by these, but subordinates them always to his own independent purposes. In view of that I would like to substitute for the misleading notion of Origen the Neoplatonist what I hope is the more accurate picture of Origen as "Neochristian".

XXIII

THE MAGICAL POWER OF NAMES IN ORIGEN AND LATER PLATONISM

One of the basic presuppositions of magical practice, both in Greco-Roman antiquity and elsewhere, is that there is power in names, or to be more exact, in the magician's knowledge of names. This applies to knowing the proper name or names of a given god or daemon, or to being in possession of formulae of power, strings of meaningless[1] words or sounds designed to capture the attention and compel the services of some supernatural or natural force.

Such beliefs can be illustrated readily from the Greek Magical Papyri[2]. For instance, at *PGM* IV, 275, at the end of a prayer to Typhon, we have this: "Mighty Typhon, hear me, and perform for me the task (*mention it*); for I speak your name IO ERBETH[3] IO PAKERBETH IO BOLSOCHETH OEN TYPHON ASBARABO BIEAISE" — and so on, for another two lines. "Hearken to me, and perform such and such a task". The beginning of this sequence, IO ERBETH, IO PAKERBETH, IO BOLSOCHETH (together with five other IO's) is found at *PGM* III, 75ff, addressed to "the powerful and mighty spirit of this animal in this place" (a cat has just been sacrificed by drowning); and the spirit is adjured also by the titles IAO, SABAOTH, ADONAI, ABRASAX, and the great god IAEO, followed by a formula including the recognisable names

---

[1] Meaningless, that is, to the magician uttering them. Often enough, such sequences of words in the magical papyri can be analysed as garbled versions of meaningful utterances in Egyptian, or, more rarely, Hebrew or Chaldaean, but they seem to have been used as gibberish in the formulae we have.

[2] Ed. KARL PREISENDANZ, Leipzig and Berlin, 1928-41. (2nd ed. revised and edited by A. HENRICHS, Stuttgart, 1971). A team of scholars, the present author among them, under Prof. H.-D. BETZ of the University of Chicago, has recently completed a translation, with notes, of the whole PGM corpus, due to be published in 1982.

[3] It has been the practice of the Chicago team to print *voces magicae* in capitals, and I reproduce that here.

or titles SESENGEN BARPHARANGES, MITHRA and DAMNA-
MENEUS. The IO invocation recurs shortly after this, in a prayer
to Mithra (*ibid* 100ff.), followed by: "I adjure you in the Hebrew
language, and by virtue of the Necessity of the Necessitators (?)
MASKELLI MASKELLO; accomplish this for me".

A little later again, Mithra or the Sun is adjured by Iao, Abaoth,
Adonai, Michael, Souriel, Gabriel, Raphael and Abrasax, all of
whom are denominated gods (*ibid* 145ff.) At the same time, the
magician calls himself Adam — "I am Adam the forefather; my
name is Adam".

At *PGM* III, 494-611, in a prayer to the Sun, we find a most
elaborate sequence of symbols and sacred names recited, one for
each of the twelve hours of the day, followed by the adjuration:
"I have said your signs and your symbols; therefore, O Lord, do the
specified thing for me by necessity, lest I shake the heaven". The
implication here, and frequently elsewhere, is that the magician's
knowledge of the god's true name or names (and the magician's
conferring upon himself of certain names of power) gives him control
over the god in question.

Examples of this could be multiplied endlessly from the papyri,
but enough, I think, has been quoted by now to establish the point.
I wish to turn next to certain texts, no longer explicitly magical,
but inhabiting the same thought-world with the magical papyri —
the Gnostic texts of the Nag Hammadi corpus. We find here also
great attention paid to naming, and many of the names agree with
those in the magical papyri. In *Zostrianos* (VIII, 1,6)[4], we find
the following sequence of sacred names, in connexion with an account
of a spiritual baptism:

I was baptised in the name of the Self-begotten God by these powers
which are upon the living waters, Michar and Michea. I was purified
by the great Barpharanges. Then they revealed themselves to me and
wrote me in the glory. I was sealed by those who are on those powers,
Michar and Micheus and Seldao and Elenos and Zogenethlos ... With the
souls I blessed the Self-begotten God and the forefather, Geradamas ...
the self-begotten, the first perfect man, and Seth Emmacha Seth, the

---

[4] I use the translation published by the Claremont team under JAMES
ROBINSON, *The Nag Hammadi Library in English*, Harper and Row, New
York, 1977.

son of Adamas, the father of the immovable race, and the four lights . . .
and Mirothea, the mother . . . and eminence . . . of the lights and De . . .

Although this is not made explicit, the purpose of this litany of
powerful helpers is presumably to attract power to the reciter or
the text. He shows that he knows the names of the operative spirits.
Later on, in sect. 47, we find a list of "the keepers of the immortal
soul", and other beings:

> These are keepers of the immortal soul: Gamaliel together with
> Strempsouchos, and Akramas together with Loel, and Mnesinous. These
> are the immortal spirits: Yesseus, Mazareus, Yessedekeus . . . . Kamaliel
> is the spirit-giver. They stand before us, Isauel and Audael, and Abrasax,
> the the thousand Phaleris, with Phalses and Eurios. The keeper of the
> glories is Stetheus with Theopemptos and Eurumeneus and Olsen —
> and so on.

These names are revealed to Zostrianos by "the child of the child"
Ephesek (a variant of the spirit Esephech, which turns up elsewhere
(e.g. *Gospel of the Egyptians*, 50, 53; 55), and a lot of the same
characters appear also in the *Gospel of the Egyptians*, 64-5. These
litanies constitute a kind of guide to the ruling spirits of the universe,
but the purpose of knowing their names is, surely, to be able to
dominate them, or to protect oneself against them.

The Hermetic writings also believe in the power of the word,
though they do not make use of magical names and incantations.
There is, however, a notable passage at the beginning of *Tractate 16*[5],
where Asclepius warns King Ammon against translating this treatise
(which was almost certainly originally composed in Greek) into
Greek:

> As far as you can, O King — and all things are possible for you —
> preserve this discourse untranslated, in order that neither such mysteries
> as these come to the Greeks, nor the over-confident and careless and,
> as it were, overdecorative language of the Greeks render ineffective the
> awesome strength and powerful phraseology of the words. For the
> Greeks, O King, have empty language, good only for logical demonstra-
> tion, and this is the philosophy of the Greeks, the sounding-off of argu-
> ments. We do not use arguments, but rather utterances filled with power.

It is against such a background that I wish to examine certain
at first sight surprising statements of Origen, first in the *Contra*

---

[5] *Corpus Hermeticum* XVI, 2, p. 232 Nock-Festugière.

Celsum, where he is responding to attacks by Celsus on the Christian use of sacred names, and secondly in the *Homilies on Joshua* (XX), where he is discussing more generally the value of Old Testament sacred names [6].

The question is first raised at *CCels*. I, 6, in response to an allegation by Celsus that "Christians get the power they possess by pronouncing the names of certain daemons and incantations" [7].

If we expect Origen to repudiate this allegation indignantly and *in toto*, we shall be somewhat surprised. What he actually says is rather that Celsus misrepresents the situation:

> For they do not get "the power which they seem to possess" by any incantations, but by the name of Jesus, with the recital of the histories about him. For when these are pronounced they have often made daemons to be driven out of men, and especially when those who utter them speak with real sincerity and genuine belief. In fact the name of Jesus is so powerful against the daemons that sometimes it is effective even when pronounced by bad men. Jesus taught this when he said: "Many shall say to me in that day, In thy name we have cast out daemons and performed miracles" (Mt 7,22). (tr. Chadwick) [8].

The most interesting aspect of this passage for our purposes is the statement that the name of Jesus has power independent of the virtue of the person using it. It has, thus, a truly *magical* power. The efficacy of a magical incantation is not dependent on the moral state of the person using it, but solely on the correct performance of the associated ritual (including the observance of ritual purity, if so required).

The matter arises again at I,24, in response to a statement by Celsus "that it makes no difference whether one calls the supreme god by the name used among the Greeks, or by that, for example,

---

[6] There is a good brief discussion of Origen's doctrine on this matter in R. P. C. HANSON, *Allegory and Event*, London 1959, pp. 205-7, to which I am indebted.

[7] Later, at VI, 40, Origen reports Celsus as saying that "he has seen among certain elders who were of our opinion books containing barbarian names of daemons, and magical formulas". It sounds very much as if Celsus has been consorting with Gnostics such as those whose works we have been surveying.

[8] This and all subsequent translations from the *Contra Celsum* are from Henry Chadwick's excellent version, Cambridge Univ. Press, 1953.

used among the Indians, or by that among the Egyptians". To this aggressively syncretistical suggestion Origen feels it necessary to make an elaborate reply, involving the whole question of the power of names:

> My answer to this is that a profound and obscure question is raised by this subject, that concerning the nature of names. The problem is whether, as Aristotle thinks (*De Int.* 2, 16 a 27), names were given by arbitrary determination; or, as the Stoics hold, by nature, the first utterances being imitations of the things described and becoming their names; or whether, as Epicurus teaches (*Fr. 334* Usener), . . . names were given by nature, the first men having burst out with certain sounds descriptive of the objects [9]. Now if by a special study we could show the nature of powerful names (*onomata energe*), some of which are used by the Egyptian wise men, or the learned men among the Persian magi, or the Brahmans or the Samanaeans among the Indian philosophers, and so on according to each nation, and if we could establish that so-called magic is not, as the followers of Epicurus and Aristotle think, utterly incoherent, but as the experts in these things prove, is a consistent system, which has principles known to very few; then we would say that the names Sabaoth, and Adonai, and all the other names that have been handed down by the Hebrews with great reverence, are not concerned with ordinary created things, but with a certain mysterious divine science (*theologia aporrhetos*), that is related to the creator of the universe.
>
> It is for this reason that when these names are pronounced in a particular sequence that is natural to them, they can be employed for certain purposes; and so also with other names in use in Egyptian which invoke certain daemons who have power only to do certain particular things; and other names in Persian which invoke other powers, and so on with each nation.

Origen here relates the question of the efficacy of magical formulae to the philosophical debate as to the origin and nature of language, with which it is not unconnected. Stoic etymological theory, which is largely derived from an interpretation of Plato's *Cratylus*, and which was borrowed back from the Stoics by later, dogmatic Platonists, provided an excellent theoretical basis for a theory of the magical power of names, especially in combination with the doctrine of cosmic sympathy. It is plain that Origen accepts this Stoic and

---

[9] The Epicurean theory differs from that of the Stoic in that the initial sounds which men made, though natural, were not purposive, but, as Epicurus is reported as saying, rather of the nature of coughs or sneezes (*Fr. 335* USENER = Procl. *In Crat.* XVII).

Platonist theory, and that he is well acquainted with the practice of the Egyptian magicians whose prescriptions we can read in the *PGM*. We have seen that the sacred names Sabaoth and Adonai were very popular with the magicians, and they are precisely used to invoke, not the Supreme God, but rather "daemons who have power only to do particular things". These two names were also popular in Gnostic circles, as names of archons. In the *Apocryphon of John* (10), for example, we find "Adonaiou, who is called Sabaoth", as the fifth of a series of ten inferior archons appointed by Ialdabaoth, and Sabaoth is the offspring of Ialdabaoth in the *Hypostasis of the Archons* (95), being placed in charge of the seventh heaven. In the treatise *On the Origin of the World*, Sabaoth and Adonaios appear among a group of seven androgynous beings in Chaos.

Origen does not admit these names are used of any inferior beings of this sort, but he can hardly have been oblivious to this. He talks of them as being connected with "a certain *theologia aporrhetos* that is related to the creator of the universe", and is aware also of the importance of pronouncing the names in a certain natural sequence. He is in fact admitting fully, in a different context, what Celsus had been reported earlier, at I 6, as accusing Christians of doing. And he is not finished with the subject yet. He goes on, in I, 25:

> On the subject of names I have to say further that experts in the use of charms relate that a man who pronounces a given spell in its native language can bring about the effect that the spell is claimed to do. But if the same spell is translated into any other language whatever, it can be seen to be weak and ineffective. Thus it is not the significance of the things which the words describe that has a certain power to do this or that, but it is the qualities and characteristics of the sounds . . . .
> Much more might be said on the subject of names to those who think that it makes no difference how they are used. And if Plato is admired for his words in the *Philebus*, "My reverence, Protarchus, for the names of the gods is profound" (*Phil.* 12C), when Philebus had called pleasure a god in his discussion with Socrates, why should we not give even more approval to the Christians for their carefulness not to apply any of the names used in mythologies to the creator of the universe?

Origen here enunciates the theory which we can see operating behind the use of magical formulae in the *PGM*, and which is stated explicitly by the author of *Corpus Hermeticum* XVI, quoted above.

The *Chaldaean Oracles*, also, forbid the alteration, and *a fortiori* the translation, of *barbara onomata* (*Fr.* 150 Des Places). We shall have more to say of this prohibition presently.

The mention of *Philebus* 12C in this context is most interesting, since it provides evidence, a hundred years and more earlier than we have from other sources, of an exegesis of this passage which supports the doctrine of the magical power of names. The only formal commentary we have on the passage is that of Damascius, in his *Lecture-Notes on the Philebus*[10], delivered in the first quarter of the sixth century, where we find the following entry (sect. 24):

> Why this great reverence of Socrates for the names of gods? Because from of old apposite names have been consecrated to each, and it would be wrong to change what should not be changed (*kinein ta akineta*); or because they are naturally appropriate to them, according to the teaching of the *Cratylus*; or because they are vocal images (*agalmata phoneenta*) of the gods, as Democritus says.

We have here presented to us a conjunction of old and respectable Platonic reasons for respecting the names of the gods, together with some rather less respectable ones which appear to have arisen from other sources. Not to *kinein ta akineta* is a sentiment proper to Platonic conservatism (*e.g.* Laws III 684D, XI, 913B); but what should we make of the statement that such names "are naturally appropriate" (*physei okeiotai*) to the gods, and the reference to the *Cratylus* 391DE, where Socrates remarks, following on his initial statement at 390DE of Cratylus' thesis that names are *physei*, that the gods, at any rate, call things by their right names. If we turn to Proclus' *Commentary on the Cratylus* (LXII, p. 29, 21ff. Pasquali), we find that he chooses this passage to launch into a general discourse on the power of names, and this discourse contains pronounced magical elements.

He distinguishes, first, two views among "the ancients": some think that names only begin at the level of superhuman (but subdivine) beings (i.e. daemons, heroes and so on), the gods being beyond such specification; others claim, however, that names are proper to the gods as well. Names, they say, are only one type of the many *symbola* and *synthemata* which the gods have sown in the

---

[10] Ed. L. G. WESTERINK, Amsterdam, 1959.

210

world, at all levels of existence. They are, in a way, meta-symbols, or the subjective correlatives of the symbols the gods have laid down. If one gets them right, one has the key to the understanding and manipulation of the world, and if one has the gods' names right, one has achieved access to the gods. Theurgy teaches us how to represent the structure of the *symbola* in the physical world by means of inarticulate utterances (*adiarthrotoi ekphoneseis*, p. 31, 27). These would presumably be the apparently meaningless strings of syllables, often just sequences of vowels, which we find employed so frequently in *PGM*. But over and above these there are the divine names proper (p. 31, 28ff.), which come down to us directly from the intellectual *hypostases*, by means of which the gods may be called upon and hymned. Proclus, however, has a more tolerant view of the variety and possibilities of translation of names than does Origen (or, as we shall see, than does the Chaldaean tradition). The Egyptians, he says (p. 32, 5ff.), have received a share of the divine power of naming in their native tongue, as have the Chaldaeans, the Indians and the Greeks. All their sacred names have validity. The god who among the Greeks is called Briareus, for instance, is called something else by the Chaldaeans, but each of these names must be deemed an offspring (*engonos*) of the gods, and indicative of that particular divine nature. If some names are more efficacious (*drasteria*) than others, we should not be astonished; this merely reflects the relative power of the entities being named — angels, daemons or others.

This vindicates, as we should expect from a Hellene and a Platonist, the efficacy of the Greek language, in contrast to the chauvinistic attack made on it in *Corpus Hermeticum* XVI, quoted above. The magical tradition, in fact, is quite prepared to use Greek names, such as Apollo, Helios or Hecate, along with a multiplicity of barbarian ones. There is, however, a tradition within later Platonism, deriving its inspiration, it would seem, from the *Chaldaean Oracles*, which accords a much higher status to barbarian names than to Greek ones, and in this connexion the third reason for respecting divine names given by Damascius above, and attributed to Democritus — that they are "vocal images" of the gods — is relevant. As WESTERINK points out in his note *ad loc.*, "Democritus" can hardly be the great atomist, since he is attested as holding that names are "by convention" (B26 D-K). Unless Damascius is gravely confused, he must be referring to a rather eccentric Platonist of the mid-third century A.D. called Democritus Chnous, who was much addicted to numerology and the numerical significance of names, including his own (cf Olymp. *In Alc.* p. 105, 13 Creuzer). *Agalmata phoneenta* must mean, in this context, something like "phonetic correlates of images"; that is to say, they represent in words what the *symbola* and *synthemata* sown by the gods in the world, described by Proclus, represent in nature, or what properly constructed and consecrated statues of the gods would represent in theurgical art.

The Chaldaean-influenced doctrine of divine names in later Platonism goes back to a tag from the *Oracles* (*Fr.* 150 Des Places), mentioned above, which is quoted explicitly only by Michael Psellus, in the eleventh century, in his *Exegesis of the Chaldaean Oracles* (*PG* CXXII, 1132) [11]. *Onomata barbara mepot' allaxes* ("Never change barbarian names!"). His exegesis of this oracle is of interest:

> That is, there are god-given names among all races, which have unspeakable power in magic rites. *Do not,* therefore, *change* these into the Greek language, e.g. Seraphim and Cherubim and Michael and Gabriel. For these when uttered in the Hebrew form have unspeakable power in magic rites, but if changed into Greek words, they lose it.

Origen, as we shall see, makes very much the same point later in the *Contra Celsum* (V, 45). The main statement of this doctrine in Platonism, however, comes about half a century after Origen, in Iamblichus' *De Mysteriis* (VII, 4-5), where he is answering a query of Porphyry's — or rather, two connected ones: (1) What is the point of meaningless names (*asema onomata*)?, and (2) why, among meaningful names, are we to honour barbarian names above those proper to our own language? Only the second of these questions is really relevant to our enquiry, but Iamblichus' replies to both are interesting.

The *asema onomata* are the sequences of syllables and of vowels found in all magical texts. Iamblichus maintains that the gods know the meanings of these, meanings that could not be expressed in human speech in any case, and that we should not even attempt to apply conceptions or rational explanations to them,

---

[11] Included by DES PLACES in his Budé edition of the *Chaldaean Oracles*, pp. 189-195.

as any such attempt gets in the way of their usefulness. As for the barbarian names, he gives this explanation: certain ancient and holy races, such as the Assyrians and the Egyptians, have had a whole vocabulary suitable to divinity (*theoprepes*) revealed to them by the gods, and their modes of address to them are therefore to be preferred to more recent ones. These races are also extremely conservative, by contrast to the Greeks, who are always innovating (*neoteropoioi*) and dashing after new experiences, which involves them in unremitting linguistic development (*astatos heuresilogia*).

This last remark is strongly reminiscent of the complaint made in the preface of *CH* XVI, and indeed Iamblichus' influences in the *De Mysteriis* seem more Hermetic than Chaldaean (which is, after all, in keeping with his persona as the Egyptian High Priest Abammon). Porphyry, in his *Letter to Anebo* which provoked this reply from Iamblichus, is in fact being, for polemical purposes, rather more sceptical than the Platonist tradition as a whole would justify, and so, for similar purposes, is Celsus a hundred years earlier. The fact that Origen can quote at him the proof text from the *Philebus* seems to me to indicate that already in Origen's time there existed in the Platonic tradition a theory of the magical efficacy of divine names, though not perhaps with all the elaborations given to it in the later period. However, if the Democritus of Damascius' commentary is indeed the third-century Platonist of that name, the theory is attested for the Platonism of Origen's time, even if Porphyry, in a certain mood, professes scepticism of it.

But let us return now to Origen, because he has more to add to his theory, both in the *Contra Celsum* and in a most significant passage from the *Homilies on Joshua* (which are of uncertain date, but seem at least to be later than the Decian Persecution of 249-51, to which there is a fairly clear reference in *Homily IX*, which would place them a few years later than the *Contra Celsum* (248)).

At *Contra Celsum* IV, 33-4, reacting to a derogatory reference by Celsus to the propensity of the Jews to trace their ancestry back to remote and obscure personages, Origen points out that Abraham, Isaac and Jacob (to whom Celsus appears to be referring) are names so powerful that they are widely used by magicians who are not Jews at all (e.g. in the formula "God of Abraham, God of Isaac, God of Jacob"), and that this sort of formula is most efficacious for exorcising demons.

This claim is borne out by the evidence of *PGM*, where we find, for instance, at XII, 285ff a most elaborate invocation of "the greatest god" as, among other things, "Iao, Sabaoth, Adonai . . . Abraham, Isaac, Jacob", while at XIII 817 the magician declares that he has taken on the power of Abraham, Isaac and Jacob, "and of the great god-daemon Iao". Origen mentions also such formulae as "the God of the Hebrews", which we find at *PGM* XIII b 18 as an invocation, after Sabaoth and Adonai. Plainly, Origen concludes, these names and formulae have power, even in the mouths of unworthy practitioners.

At V, 45, he is again provoked by the syncretistic remark of Celsus' that had provoked him at I, 24, but this time he presents some further thoughts on the divine origin of language. He begins again by a rejection of Aristotle's view that names are by convention, in favour of an interpretation of Plato's *Cratylus*:

> For the languages in use among men have not a human origin, which is clear to those able to give careful attention to the nature of spells which were adapted by the authors of the languages in accordance with each different language and different pronunciation. We briefly discussed this question above when we said that if names whose nature it is to be powerful are translated into another tongue, they no longer have any effect such as they did with their proper sounds. This phenomenon is also to be found with men's names. For if we translated the name of some man or other who from birth has had a name in the Greek language into the language of the Egyptians or the Romans or some other nation, we would not bring about the experience or action which would happen if he were called by the name first given to him. Nor, if we translated into the Greek language the name of a man called in the first instance by a Roman name, would we effect what the spell is professed to do if the first name by which he was called is preserved.
>
> If this is true of human names, what ought we to think in the case of names that are applied for whatever reason to God? For example, something of the word Abraham may be translated into Greek, and something is signified by the name Isaac, and there is a meaning in the sound Jacob. If anyone who utters an invocation or oath names "the God of Abraham, and the God of Isaac, and the God of Jacob", he would effect something, either because of the nature of these names, or even because of their power; for daemons are overcome and made subject to him who says these things. But if he were to say "the God of the chosen father of the echo, and the God of laughter, and the God of the man who strikes with the heel" [12], in this case the recitation would

---

[12] All translations taken over by Origen from Philo.

have no effect, as it would be no different from the names which have no power at all.

We see here again a linking of semantic with magical theory such as could well have been resorted to by contemporary Platonists. The meaning of a man's name cannot be properly translated; or, to adapt, perhaps illegitimately, a modern distinction, you may render the *sense* of it in another language (Deborah may be translated as Melissa, or Malchus as Basileus), but you lose the *reference*. The power of a divine name resides, or may be seen as residing, in the fact that it is a means of "referring to" the god, and thus binding him to do one's will.

Origen goes on to discuss the names Israel, Sabaoth and Adonai, and the loss of power that results from the translation of any of them. What we do not yet have from him, though, is an explicit statement of just how such "powerful" names work on the human psyche or body. This we find in a remarkable passage from the *Homilies on Joshua* (XX, 1), which is fortunately preserved in the original Greek, in the *Philocalia*, ch. 12. He is seeking here to justify the large number of names of towns and individuals and tribes which are found throughout that work:

> Even as magical incantations have a certain natural power, such that he who utters them, even when he is not conscious of their meaning, derives something from the incantation by virtue of the nature of the sounds in the incantation, whether for the harm or the healing of his body or his soul; so you must recognise that more powerful than any incantation is the naming of the names in the Holy Scripture. For there are certain powers (*dynameis*) within us, of which the better are nourished by these, as it were, incantations, since they have a natural affinity (*syngeneis*) with them, even if we are not conscious of it; those powers, understanding what is said, become more powerful within us for assisting our lives.
>
> That there are certain invisible forms within us, and indeed a multitude of them, is revealed to us by the psalm which says (102 (103), 1): "Praise the Lord, O my soul, and let all the things within me praise His holy name!". So there are a multitude of powers within us which have been assigned to our souls and bodies, which, if they are holy, when the Holy Scripture is read, are benefitted and become stronger, even if "our mind be unfruitful", as it is written about "him who speaks with tongues" (1 Cor. 14,14): "My spirit prays, but my mind is unfruitful". You must recognise that even when "the mind within us is unfruitful", the powers which work with the soul and the mind and the whole of us are nourished by the rational food from the holy writings

and these names, and, being nourished, are made more powerful to assist us. And even as the better powers are, as it were, charmed and aided and made more powerful by such writings and names, so the opposite powers within us are, as it were, depressed and overcome by the incantations of God, and, being overcome, are put to sleep. (My trans.)

He goes on to compare the whole process to snake-charming, an activity with which he could count on the audience being familiar. Furthermore, he says, even as certain drugs — for instance, one to improve eyesight — will work away within us without our noticing, and the effects emerge, perhaps, after a few days, so hearing the words of Scripture may have a delayed effect on us, without our noticing at the time. But some good effect they must have.

Here we find Origen drawing on the notion of *sympatheia* to explain what physical effect powerful names can have on us, or on others when we make use of them. The resonances they give forth set up favourable vibrations within us, rather as the Pythagoreans felt was done by the right sort of music. Such resonances are independent of the purpose or state of mind of the utterer; they have a natural power independent of meaning.

With this passage in turn we may compare an important statement on magic which Plotinus makes in his great essay *Problems of the Soul* (*Enn.* IV, 3-4), in the course of a discussion as to whether the souls of the stars have memory and sensation, and, if not, how prayer and magical practices can have the effects they do (*Enn.* IV, 4, 30-45). "How", he asks at the beginning of sect. 40, "do magical incantations work?" The answer he gives is *sympatheia,* "the concord of like things and the mutual repulsion of unlike ones, and in general the variety of the many potencies all combining to make one single living being."

This is essentially the same theory as Origen is expounding in the 20th *Homily on Joshua.* Plotinus goes on to say that it is by drawing on this unifying force in Nature that the magician achieves his effects. Nature itself, indeed, is the primal magician (40, 6-7) (*ho goes ho protos kai pharmakeus*). The utterances of the magician, performed with the proper gestures and intonations, have a powerful effect at least on the irrational part of the soul — the reason, Plotinus maintains, can rise above these influences. He ends by adducing the image of a man fascinated by a snake (40, 28ff), a comparison interestingly similar to Origen's image of the snake-charmer. The man's intellect may be unaffected by the fascination, but it can be temporarily neutralised, and this gives the snake its chance to strike.

What may be concluded from this investigation? Simply, I think, that here, as often elsewhere, we find Origen showing a comprehensive acquaintance with trends in contemporary Platonism, and even with what we might call the Platonic "underworld" of magic and theurgy, and indeed himself constituting the best available evidence for contemporary Platonist doctrine. The theory of the magical efficacy of names was not in fact a subject of dispute between the Christianity which he is representing and the Platonist tradition. Even the learned Psellus, as we have seen, in eleventh century Byzantium, is not prepared to dismiss the theory out of hand, though he is uncomfortable about it. It is intimately bound up with the wider doctrine of *sympatheia* and of "the Great Chain of Being", which was common ground to philosophers and magicians of Late Antiquity and beyond, though they made different applications of it, and with this Origen, as a Christian philosopher, has no quarrel.

XXIV

JOHN DILLON : PLOTINUS
AND THE TRANSCENDENTAL IMAGINATION

I

The status and role of *phantasia*, or imagination, in Platonism generally is low. The nearest thing to a definition of it by Plato is to be found at *Soph.* 264AB,[1] and Aristotle's discussion in *De Anima* III 3 is essentially a development of the Platonist position.[2] It is a faculty or activity of the 'lower' soul, dependent upon sense-perception, from which the soul must purify itself in the course of its ascent to knowledge of, and unity with, the divine. Only outside the philosophical tradition, in the spheres of rhetoric and of art-criticism is there any sign of a higher valuation of what the imagination can be.[3]

However, that is not quite the whole story, and the exception arises from a quarter from which one should expect it, the fertile mind of Plotinus.[4] Plotinus of course also assigns to *phantasia* its normal Platonic role,[5] and as such recommends that we transcend it, but his profound speculations on the consequences of postulating immortality for the individual soul, and the survival, in some form, of the personality, involves him, especially in *Enneads* IV 3, 23–32 (in the course of his major enquiry, *Problems of the Soul*, divided by Porphyry into three tractates, *Enn.* IV 3–5), in a discussion of memory, and thus of the faculty of imagination, on which he finds memory to be based.

The conclusion that the disembodied, 'purified', soul must retain memory of at least some aspect of its earthly existence necessitates, it seems to him, there being a faculty of imagination dependent on the activities of the higher soul, as well as those of the lower (IV 3, 30–1). At this point, it may be useful to quote from IV 3, 30, where Plotinus raises the question, 'Is imagination involved also in mental acts?' He answers as follows: 'If in fact every mental act is accompanied by an image (*phantasia*), we may well believe that when this image, which woud be as it were a picture of the thought, remains on, this would explain how memory of an object of knowledge would take place. But if this is not the case, another suggestion may be made. Perhaps memory would be the reception into the imagination of the discursive sequel[6] (*logos*) to an act of intuitive thought (*noêma*). The thought itself, being indivisible and never, as it were, rising to the exterior of the consciousness, remains hidden within, but the *logos*, unfolding and

56

proceeding from the thought into the imagination, displays the thought as it were in a mirror,[7] and thus results the apprehension of it, its continued presence, and consequently memory.'

For our present purpose it does not much matter whether the *noêma* itself or its *logos* is 'mirrored' in the imagination. The main thing is that the imagination is clearly recognised as receptive of images from 'above' as well as of sense-data.[8] The imagination is thus situated interestingly at the border, as it were, between the two levels of soul. This Janus-like position for the imagination bothers Plotinus, and he would prefer to postulate *two* imaginative faculties, one serving either level of memory. He then was faced with the problem of how these two would coordinate while the soul is in the body (IV 3, 31).

They cannot, he agrees, simply operate side by side, or we would have some consciousness of this fact—of throwing a mental switch, as it were, to activate one or the other. His solution involves conjuring up one of those vivid images for which he is noted, and about which I will have more to say presently: 'when the two souls are in harmony, and the two imagining faculties do not stand apart, but that of the superior soul is dominant, then a single image only is perceived, the less powerful being like a shadow on the other, like a lesser light merging into a greater.'

The image is that of a stronger and a weaker light focused on a common field, so that the weaker light is not noticed. When the two imaginations are in conflict, he goes on to say, we notice the two lights as separate, though we are still not conscious of the presence of two levels of soul. This image is both striking and apt, as it portrays exactly the sort of double life Plotinus envisages for the imagination. He gives no illustrative examples, but we may propose one. Suppose one is engaged in meditation, conjuring up, perhaps, just such an image of light as he has suggested to us here, and one's bodily organs and senses are totally under control, providing no distractions; the 'lower' imagination is not inoperative; it has simply subordinated its activity completely to that of the higher. On the other hand, if one is an unsuccessful meditator, then conflicting images—perhaps of a friend, or of one's garden, or of a gin-and-tonic—may come crowding in. Here the second 'spotlight' is no longer focused on the same spot as the first; it begins to wander here and there, and distracting images impinge upon the central one.

This image, as I say, is striking, but it may also involve Plotinus in certain problems.[9] Do we really need two imaging faculties? Is it not better to see *phantasia* as a pivotal faculty of the soul, able to serve both the reason and the passions? Possibly, but not for Plotinus, since he is concerned here with preserving *phantasia* in the disembodied soul, without being able to deny its traditional Platonic role as the servant of *aisthēsis* and the passions. We can salute his acuity, I think, without necessarily adopting his particular solution. What his speculations have led to, for the first time, as far as we can see (our knowledge of Middle Platonic speculation is sadly deficient), is the opening of a rôle for *phantasia* as the servant of intellectual (and theological) speculation, such as was not open to it in traditional Platonism.

It may be helpful at this point to confront Plotinus' theory of the imagination with that of Kant. In the *Critique of Pure Reason*, in the course of his 'Deduction of the Pure Concepts of the Understanding' (pp.A115ff),[10] Kant distinguishes between the 'productive' and the merely 'reproductive', the transcendental and the empirical, imagination. The former he describes as follows (A120):[11]

> What is first given to us is appearance. When combined with consciousness it is called perception . . . Now, since every appearance contains a manifold, and since different perceptions therefore occur in the mind separately and singly, a combination of them, such as they cannot have in sense itself, is demanded. There must therefore exist in us an active faculty for the synthesis of the manifold. To this faculty I give the title, imagination.

The role of the transcendental imagination is, then, 'the synthesis of the manifold' of experience. To decide whether Plotinus' higher imagination has anything in common with this, we must consider what it does when the soul is in the body (which is the situation Kant is addressing himself to, and the only one in which we are interested at the moment). An interesting text in this connexion is III 6, 4, 19–21 (discussed by Blumenthal, pp.92–3), where Plotinus makes a distinction between 'imagination in the primary sense (*prôtê phantasia*) which we call opinion (*doxa*)', which is the faculty in the soul which synthesises the data of sense-perception (in this case, that there is or is not something to be feared), and delivers an opinion on the basis of them, and a lower imagination, involving no synthesis or judgement (*anepikritos*) which presumably just takes in the data as discrete images.[12]

Although III 6 (26) immediately precedes IV 3–5 (27–9) in Porphyry's chronological list, there is no mention here of two levels of soul, with one imagination each, but this would be explained by the fact that Plotinus is here talking exclusively of the soul in the body, where the distinction between the two levels is not clearly discernible. At any rate, Plotinus' *prôtê phantasia* here seems to have very much the role of Kant's transcendent imagination.

However, there is more to the higher imagination than that. Besides synthesising the reports of the senses, it is also the recipient, the 'mirror', of the operations of the intellect. In *Enn.* I 4, a late treatise (46), in the course of a discussion as to why we are not always conscious of the activity of *nous* within us, Plotinus presents *phantasia* as a mirror for intellectual activity (I 4, 10, 7ff), which only performs properly when the 'surface' of the soul, so to speak, is unruffled by

58

passion, and thus 'smooth'. 'But when this is broken because the harmony of the body is upset, thought and intellect operate without an image, and then intellectual activity takes place without *phantasia*. So one might come to this sort of conclusion, that intellectual activity takes place with the accompaniment of *phantasia*, though it is not identical with *phantasia*.'

Here, as in IV 3, 30 (quoted above), the imagination is the receptacle for *noêseis*, intellectual acts. One might well ask, what are these intellectual acts which the imagination, if the soul is in a harmonious state, can mirror? No doubt Plotinus has various types of intellection in mind—solutions to mathematical or geometrical problems being one possible example, a witty riposte that one failed to make in the Common Room last night being another—but there is one particularly interesting type that I would like to focus on, and that is Plotinus' well-known 'dynamic images',[13] those spiritual exercises which he prescribes for us at various points in the tractates in order to make vivid some knotty point of doctrine. These require the active, creative use of the imagination for the clearer grasping of a truth which transcends all sense-perception, though one must start from physical images in one's ascent to understanding.

One example is to be found at *Enn.* V 8, 9, where Plotinus explains to us how to imagine the intellectual world:

> Let us, then, grasp with our mind (*dianoia*) this cosmos, each member of it remaining what it is, distinct and apart, yet all forming, as far as possible, a complete unity, so that whatever comes into focus, say the outer orb of the heavens, shall bring immediately with it the image (*phantasia*), on the one plane, of the sun and of the other planets, with earth and sea and all living things, as if exhibited upon a transparent globe.

> Let there be, then, in your soul the gleaming image (*phantasia*) of a sphere, a picture holding all the things in the universe whether in motion or at rest, or rather, some at rest and others in motion. Keep this sphere before you, and from it imagine another, a sphere stripped of magnitude and of spatial differences; cast out spatial conceptions and the image (*phantasma*) of matter within you; do not simply substitute an image reduced in size, but call on God, the maker of the sphere whose image you now hold, and pray him to enter. (translation by MacKenna, emended)

Here we are being called upon to use our imagination creatively, to attain to a purely intellectual conception. It is worth while, perhaps, to try to perform the exercise as Plotinus prescribes. I have attempted it repeatedly, and the sticking-point is always the instruction, once one has conjured up the universe (as a luminous, diaphanous globe, with all its parts distinct and functioning), then to think away the spatiality ('*aphelōn ton onkon labe*')—and not just by shrinking it! It is in fact an

excellent spiritual exercise. Calling upon God here is no empty for-
mality. If done effectively, it has a quasi-theurgic result: 'He may
come, bringing his own cosmos, with all the gods that dwell in it—He
who is the one God, and all the gods, where each is all, blending into a
unity, distinct in powers but all one god, in virtue of that one divine
power of many facets.'

In other words, if you perform the exercise correctly, you will
achieve a mystical vision of the noetic cosmos. And Plotinus knew
what he was talking about.

Let us consider another passage, this time from *Enn.* VI 4, where
Plotinus is trying to convey to us how an immaterial force, such as
Soul, may be present equally at all points in the universe. In chapter 7,
he adduces two images. The first is that of a hand carrying a long
plank. The hand supports the whole plank, though its actual contact
with it only covers a fraction of its length. 'Now,' says Plotinus, 'think
away the corporeal mass of the hand, but retain the same power as it
exerted previously. Is not that same power, indivisible, present in-
tegrally over every part of the object?'

He follows this up with another image, characteristically involving
light, in this case a flame lighting up a translucent globe:

Or imagine a small luminous mass serving as centre to a transparent sphere, so that the light from within shows upon the entire
outer surface, otherwise unlit: we surely agree that the inner core
of light, intact and immobile, reaches over the entire outer extension; the simple light of that small centre illuminates the whole
field. The diffused light is not due to any bodily magnitude of that
central point which illuminates not as body but as body lit, that is
by another kind of power than corporeal quality: let us then
abstract the corporeal mass, retaining the light as power: we can
no longer speak of the light in any particular spot; it is equally
diffused within and throughout the entire sphere. We can no
longer name the spot it occupied so as to say whence it came or
how it is present; we can but seek, and wonder as the search shows
us the light simultaneously present at each and every point of the
sphere. (translation by MacKenna)

Here again, the imagination is being asked, first to construct a model of
a physical object or situation, and then to 'abstract the corporeal mass'.
That is a job for a creative imagination, and one in the service of
intellect, not of the senses.

II

Having seen the 'transcendental' imagination at work (in one of its
rôles, at least), let us return to the problem of the two imaginations. As
I have said, the chief reason for postulating this duality in *Enn.* IV 3 is
that Plotinus feels that the disembodied rational soul will retain a

60

(selective) memory of its earthly existence, and that the prerequisite of memory is a faculty of imagination. We, however, are discussing the embodied soul, where the imagination behaves, at least, like a unitary faculty. As such, it both reproduces and produces (synthesises) images derived from both sense-data and from purely intellectual operations.

One might ask, though, will the two imaginations ever concern themselves with the same object? Plotinus addresses this question in *Enn.* IV 3, 32, and answers in the affirmative. Once again, he is thinking of the disembodied soul remembering *without passion* (*apathōs*) events or people (a wife, for example) which evoked passionate images in its bodily existence. But we frequently have the experience, surely, of being able now 'calmly and dispassionately' to conjure up the memory of a past event, such as the death of a wife, an old love-affair, an act of injustice that enraged us, and consider it free from the passionate feelings that came with it, or even accompanied earlier memories of it. In such a case, would we not be justified, using Plotinus' formulation, in saying that we are now contemplating the event with our 'higher' imagination?[14] This is certainly, in his view, how we would contemplate it after death.

But the proper rôle of the higher imagination is plainly the representation of mental acts, and of intelligible reality. We hear more of this in the first chapters of *Enn.* IV 4, still in connection with memory. Plotinus, it must be said, does not accord memory or imagination a place of unalloyed honour. Neither the higher beings, even down to the heavenly gods, nor the human soul in its highest state (in contemplation of the intelligible realm), have any use for either memory or imagination. These only arise when the soul descends from its highest state, and then reflects upon it:

> But it leaves that conjunction (sc. with the Intelligible); it cannot suffer that unity; it falls in love with its own powers and possessions, and desires to stand apart; it leans outwards, so to speak; then, it appears to acquire a memory of itself. (*Enn.* IV 4, 3, translation by MacKenna)

And where memory arises, there the imagination necessarily is also. This less-than-perfect status for the imagination explains Plotinus' unwillingness earlier (IV 3, 30, 5–6) to allow intellectual acts themselves to be mirrored in it, but rather their *logoi*, or projections.

Memory, and thus imagination, are only possible for beings whose state changes, and who are thus creatures of time rather than eternity. In the next few chapters of IV 4, Plotinus explains why it is inappropriate to postulate memory of various classes of higher being, even down to the World Soul, which, though the originator of time, is not properly itself *in* time. In chapter 13, in connection with a description of Nature (*Physis*) as the lowest emanation of the World-Soul, and too dim an entity to have memory or imagination, he places imagination interestingly at the mid-point, in some sense, of the Soul's life:

> For this reason Nature does not possess even imagination. Intellection (*noêsis*) is superior to imagination. Imagination is between the levels of Nature and of Intellection. Nature, after all, does not have apprehension or consciousness of anything, while Imagination has consciousness of what is external to it; for it allows that which has the image to have knowledge of what it has experienced. Intellection, on the other hand, is a generation and activity from the active (intellect) itself.

It is not clear to me whether Plotinus is positing a level of the World-Soul which employs imagination—if so, we should hear more of it—or whether he is really just thinking of the levels of the individual soul, and brings in imagination here just to show how far *physis* is inferior to *noêsis*. I would prefer the latter alternative, but I cannot be sure. In any case, we are not concerned here with the anatomy of the World-Soul, and what he says is true of the individual, that the imagination is a median faculty, on the borderline (*methorion*, IV 4, 3, 11) between the intelligible and the sensible.

III

Finally, a word on the subject of the imagination as an organ of artistic creativity. Plotinus was, of course, not interested in art for art's sake, but he was concerned with both beauty and art in the service of theology. The famous ascent to the Beautiful Itself set out in Diotima's speech in Plato's *Symposium* (210A–212A) is an important exercise of the imaginative faculty, which he celebrates in *Enn.* III 5 and elsewhere. But in one important respect Plotinus goes beyond, and indeed against, Plato, and that is in the value he places on the artistic imagination—or at least in the imagination of *some* divinely-inspired artists, such as Phidias.[15] His doctrine here was a great consolation later to Platonically-minded artists of the Renaissance, such as Michelangelo, to whom Plato would have given short shrift. In an important passage near the beginning of his tractate *On the Intellectual Beauty* (V 8 (31)), he says the following (chapter 1, 36–40):

> Still, the arts are not to be slighted on the ground that they create by imitation of natural objects; for, to begin with, these natural objects are themselves imitations; then we must recognise that they give no bare reproduction of the thing seen, but go back to the Reason-Principles from which Nature itself derives, and, furthermore, that much of their work is all their own; they are holders of beauty and add where nature is lacking. Thus Pheidias wrought the Zeus (in Olympia) upon no model among things of sense, but by apprehending what form Zeus must take if he chose to become manifest to sight. (translation by MacKenna)

In other words, Phidias used his transcendental artistic imagination, to

62

mirror forth a true representation of Zeus himself.

IV

What we see here, I think, in the case of Plotinus, is a significant broadening and upgrading of the concept of the imagination by comparison with the norm of ancient philosophic thought, a development which has considerable significance for later Neoplatonism. By way of appendix to this paper, I will present a few significant passages.

First, a notable statement by Iamblichus, in the *De Mysteriis* III 14 (132), in the course of replying to remarks of Porphyry's about that branch of divination called *phôtagogia* or 'drawing down of light':

This (activity) illuminates the aetherial and luminous vehicle (*ochêma*) of the soul with divine light, in consequence of which divine images (*phantasiai*) take hold upon our faculty of imagination (*tēn en hēmin phantastikēn dynamin*), stimulated by the will of the gods. For the whole life of the soul and all the faculties in it are subject to the gods and moved by them, in accordance with the wish of its conductors (*hêgemones*).

Porphyry said that in this type of divination, the practitioners remain conscious (*parakolouthountes heautois*), in other respects, while being divinely possessed as to their imaginative faculty (*kata to phantastikon epitheiazousi*). Iamblichus is not basically quarrelling with this statement, merely elucidating it. He goes on to say (133) that the divine light does not fasten on the *dianoia*, or reflective consciousness, but rather on the imaginative faculty, because it allows itself to be stimulated by the gods directly, where the *dianoia* would interpose a degree of self-consciousness.

This is admittedly not to grant a very exalted role to the *phantasia*. It is favoured by the gods precisely because it is subrational. But it is allowed by Iamblichus to have direct access to divine inspiration, which makes it a faculty open to influences from above as well as from below, as it is in Plotinus.

The double nature of *phantasia* is a doctrine preserved also by the Athenian School, though in a less radical form. Plutarch of Athens is reported by Pseudo-Philoponus (Stephanus?) on the *De Anima* (p.515, 12–15 Hayduck, *CAG* xv) as follows:

Plutarch considers the imagination to be double, and that its upper boundary, which is to say its originative principle (*archē*), is the (lower) boundary of the discursive intellect (*dianoêtikon*), while its other boundary is the upper limit of the senses.

This duality, as Blumenthal points out (*art. cit.* p.134), is one of function rather than of essence. The commentator goes on to report Plutarch's comparison of the imagination to a point where two lines meet, one coming from above, the other from below. What we have here, then, is not two *phantasiai*, but rather a Janus-faced figure, such as Plotinus in fact presents us with, in *Enn.* IV 3, 30 and I 4, 10, but rejects in favour of his double *phantasia*, for special reasons which I have explained.

Proclus' position on *phantasia* is a good deal more complicated, probably simply because we have so much more of him,[16] but in most cases he gives it its traditional low ranking, as something dependent on *aisthesis*, and a function of the lower soul, and associates it closely, and confusingly, with *doxa*. Only in his *Euclid Commentary* do we find a more exalted role being accorded it. At p.141, 4ff Friedlein, Proclus speaks of the soul, 'while acting cognitively, projecting upon the *phantasia*, as upon a mirror, the *logoi* of (geometrical) *schemata*', which the *phantasia* processes, and, as it were, throws up on a screen for the soul to contemplate.[17]

The circumstance that we are concerned with the contemplation of geometrical constructions presumably accounts for this promotion of the *phantasia*, but it is still, here, no more than a 'two-faced', median faculty, not really part of the rational soul, but rather acting as a 'mirror' to it, and there is no trace in Proclus, any more than in Plutarch, of the distinctive Plotinian theory of two imaginations.

V

On the whole, then, Plotinus' successors, as in a number of other areas, tend to back off from his more adventurous innovations, in the direction of a more orthodox Platonic, and indeed Aristotelian, position. Nevertheless, the concept of the imagination as receptive of noetic perceptions as well as of sense perceptions does persist in the tradition, and leave the way open for a higher valuation of it among Renaissance Platonists.

NOTES

1. Other relevant passages are *Tim.* 52A and *Phileb.* 39B.
2. Aristotle also touches on *phantasia* in *De An.* III 7, and in *De Memoria* I, 449b31ff, in both of which places he makes the troublesome statement that no *noêsis* takes place without *phantasia*, but this does not imply either that *phantasia* is a faculty of a higher part of the soul, or that any *phantasia* derives from *nous*.
3. The fullest pre-Plotinian discussion of *phantasia* in the Platonic-Aristotelian tradition occurs in Alexander of Aphrodisias' *De Anima*, pp.66, 9-73, 13 Bruns (*CAG*), and it is merely an amplification of Aristotle's remarks in *De An.* III 3, embellished with some Stoic terminology. A key passage for the sophistic revaluation of *phantasia* occurs in Philostratus, *Life of Apollonius of Tyana* VI 19 (Philostratus being more or less a contemporary of Alexander).
4. See the useful article of E. W. Warren, 'Imagination in Plotinus', *CQ* n.s. 16 (1966), pp.277-85. (The remarks of H. von Kleist, in *Plotinische Studien*, Heidelberg, 1883, p.87, are still valuable.)

64

5. Plotinus gives succinct definitions of *phantasia* in its more traditional sense, e.g. *Enn.* I 8, 15, 18-19: 'Imagination is brought about by the irrational part (sc. of the soul) being struck from outside. But (the soul) receives the blow on account of its divisible nature'. *Enn.* VI 8, 3, 10-12: 'But as for ourselves, we call imagination, strictly speaking, what is awakened from the passive impression of the body'.

6. Adopting here the formulation of Henry Blumenthal (*Plotinus' Psychology*, Nijhoff, The Hague, 1971, chapter 7, p.88). No straightforward translation of *logos* will quite do here, as what Plotinus seems to mean is a 'projection' of the original intuition (*noēma*) onto the discursive level of thought, which involves mental images. Bréhier's 'formule verbale' is harmlessly uninformative, as is Harder's 'Begriff', and Armstrong's 'verbal expression'.

7. This 'mirroring' role for the *phantasia* is to some extent anticipated by Plato's interesting presentation of the rôle of the liver, in *Tim.* 71B-D, as receiving 'as in a mirror' images of *dianoemata* from the intellect. But, of course, these images are not themselves rational, nor does the liver indulge in rational activity.

* 8. This is actually adumbrated as a possibility by Aristotle in *De An.* III 3, but nothing much is made of it.

9. Such as are raised by Blumenthal, op. cit. pp.94ff.

10. Using Norman Kemp Smith's edition (A before the page number refers to Kant's first edition pagination).

* 11. Quoted by Mary Warnock on p.28 of her *Imagination*.

12. The close connection here between *phantasia* and *doxa* is noteworthy, since the relation of these two faculties is quite tortuous, both in Plotinus himself and in later Platonists, such as Plutarch of Athens and Proclus. See on this Blumenthal, 'Plutarch's *De Anima* and Proclus' in *De Iamblique à Proclus: Entretiens sur l'Antiquité Classique*, XXI, Vandoeuvres-Genève, 1975, pp.123-51.

13. By 'dynamic image' is meant an image which is designed to develop as one contemplates it, thus leading the mind to a deeper comprehension of reality.

14. Plotinus' distinction here is reminiscent of that made by Aristotle between *doxa* and *phantasia* in *De An.* III 3, 427b21ff, where he describes *doxa* as being accompanied by *pathos*, while *phantasia* is free of this, 'as if one were contemplating terrible or encouraging things in a painting'.

15. The use of Phidias as an exemplum goes back at least to Cicero (*Orator* 7ff) but it occurs, significantly, in the discourse of Apollonius of Tyana on *phantasia* composed by Philostratus (see n.3 above).

16. I am indebted here to Blumenthal's discussion of Plutarch's and Proclus' doctrine in the article quoted above n.9.

17. The *phantasia* is described as a mirror for the *dianoia* also earlier, at p.121, 5-6.

XXV

PLOTINUS, *ENN.* 3.9.1, AND LATER VIEWS ON THE INTELLIGIBLE WORLD

Plotinus' short note on the internal composition of the Intellect, which Porphyry has placed as the first of the ἐπισκέψεις διάφοροι (*Enn.* 3.9 [13]), gave rise in later Neoplatonism to a variety of interpretation. In particular, Amelius Gentilianus and Porphyry, both of them pupils and companions of the Master for many years, seem to have drawn quite different conclusions from it. They are each criticized for their conclusions by Iamblichus, and then by Proclus, each of whom himself took the passage differently, bringing the total of interpretations to four. I wish, therefore, after recording in turn Amelius' and Porphyry's doctrine on the Demiurge, to turn to a detailed examination of the short passage from which all this bewildering variety appears to have sprung,[1] and to consider how their very various interpretations could have arisen from it.[2]

The stimulus for the doctrine, for Plotinus and Amelius at any rate, was Plat. *Tim.* 39E:

ἥπερ οὖν νοῦς ἐνούσας ἰδέας τῷ ὃ ἔστι ζῷον, οἷαί τε ἔνεισι καὶ ὅσαι, καθορᾷ, τοιαύτας καὶ τοσαύτας διενοήθη δεῖν καὶ τόδε σχεῖν,

---

[1] We cannot, of course, ignore the probability that Plotinus' pupils based their views of his doctrine equally much on unpublished discussions with the master—Amelius explicitly refers to such in another connection (Procl. *In Tim.* 2.213.9 ff. Diehl)—but their positions are in fact adequately derivable from *Enn.* 3.9.1. Porphyry puts 3.9 among the first group of treatises, written before his time, which would mean that he cannot have participated in the discussion which led to it. Amelius, on the other hand, very probably did.

[2] I am not here concerned with the occasion for the writing of 3.9.1, which was the thesis that the Ideas are outside the Intellect—a view to which Porphyry himself adhered (*Vit. Plot.* 18) when he first arrived in Plotinus' circle. These matters are discussed adequately by Bréhier and Armstrong in the introduction to the tractate in their respective editions (Budé and Loeb). Indeed, a look at either or both of these editions of the tractate is recommended before one proceeds further.

XXV

64

although the main discussion, as recorded by Proclus (*Comm. In Tim.*
1, pp. 305–10 Diehl),[3] is based on *Tim.* 28C, no doubt because that
is where Porphyry and Iamblichus, in their commentaries, first raised
the subject.

Let us take Amelius first. He is the senior disciple, his commentary
on the Timaeus preceded that of Porphyry (cf. μετὰ δὴ τὸν ᾿Αμέλιον
ὁ Πορφύριος, Pr. 1.306.31 f.), and he was very probably present when
the discussion that led to *Enn.* 3.9.1 took place. Porphyry must be
taken as reacting to him, rather than he to Porphyry.

For Proclus, the triad of Demiurgic Intellects was Amelius' most
distinctive doctrine. He reports it in two contexts, apropos of
Timaeus 28C and 39E, which latter passage is the one from which
Plotinus takes his start. Proclus' evidence is as follows: (1) *In Tim.*
1.306.1 ff. Diehl (ad *Tim.* 28c):

᾿Αμέλιος δὲ τριττὸν ποιεῖ τὸν δημιουργὸν καὶ τρεῖς νοῦς, βασιλέας
τρεῖς, τὸν ὄντα, τὸν ἔχοντα, τὸν ὁρῶντα. διαφέρουσι δὲ οὗτοι, διότι ὁ
μὲν πρῶτος νοῦς ὄντως ἐστὶν ὅ ἐστιν, ὁ δὲ δεύτερος ἔστι μὲν τὸ ἐν αὐτῷ
νοητόν, ἔχει δὲ τὸ πρὸ αὐτοῦ καὶ μετέχει πάντως ἐκείνου καὶ διὰ τοῦτο
δεύτερος, ὁ δὲ τρίτος ἔστι μὲν τὸ ἐν αὐτῷ καὶ οὗτος· πᾶς γὰρ νοῦς τῷ
συζυγοῦντι νοητῷ ὁ αὐτός ἐστιν· ἔχει δὲ τὸ ἐν τῷ δευτέρῳ καὶ ὁρᾷ τὸ
πρῶτον· ὅσῳ γὰρ πλείων ἡ ἀπόστασις, τοσούτῳ τὸ ἔχειν ἀμυδρότερον.
τούτους οὖν τοὺς τρεῖς νόας καὶ δημιουργοὺς ὑποτίθεται καὶ τοὺς
παρὰ τῷ Πλάτωνι τρεῖς βασιλέας καὶ τοὺς παρ᾿ Ὀρφεῖ τρεῖς, Φάνητα
καὶ Οὐρανὸν καὶ Κρόνον, καὶ ὁ μάλιστα παρ᾿ αὐτῷ δημιουργὸς ὁ Φάνης
ἐστίν.

"Amelius conceives the Demiurge as triple, and says that there are three
Intellects, three Kings, he who *is*, he who *possesses*, and he who *sees*.
The first intellect *is* really what he is; the second *is* the Intelligible which
is in him, but he *possesses* the Intelligible which is prior to him, and in
all ways participates solely in him, and is for this reason second;
and third too *is* what is in him—for all Intellect is identical with the
Intelligible linked to it—but he also *possesses* the contents of the second
Intellect, and *sees* the first element; for the intensity of possession becomes
dimmer according to the degree of remoteness. These three Intellects and
Demiurges he also identifies with the three Kings in Plato (*Ep.* 2.312E),

³ Proclus Diadochus, *In Platonis Timaeum Commentaria*, ed. E. Diehl, 3 vols. (Leipzig
1904–6).

and the Orphic triad, Phanes and Uranos and Cronos (fr. 96 Kern), and according to him the Demiurge par excellence is Phanes."

(2) *In Tim.* 3.103.18 ff. Diehl (ad *Tim.* 29E):

Ἀμέλιος μὲν οὖν τὴν τριάδα τῶν δημιουργικῶν νόων ἀπὸ τούτων μάλιστα συνίστησι τῶν ῥημάτων, τὸν μὲν πρῶτον ὄντα καλῶν ἀπὸ τοῦ "ὅ ἐστι ζῷον," τὸν δὲ δεύτερον ἔχοντα ἀπὸ τοῦ "ἐνούσας" (οὐ γὰρ ἔστιν ὁ δεύτερος, ἀλλ' εἴσειοιν ἐν αὐτῷ), τὸν δὲ τρίτον ὁρῶντα ἀπὸ τοῦ "καθορᾶν."

"Amelius relies particularly on this passage in constructing his triad of Demiurgic Intellects, calling the first 'he who is' from the 'really existing living being,' the second, 'he who possesses,' from the phrase, 'existing in' (for the second does not exist, so much as that they exist in him), and the third 'he who sees,' from the word 'behold.'"

Of the three, ὁ ἔχων perhaps presents the most difficulty. What does ὁ ἔχων possess? The ideas, we must say, the *content* of τὸ ζῷον, rather than τὸ ζῷον itself. The curious statement οὐ γὰρ ἔστιν ὁ δεύτερος, ἀλλ' εἴσεισιν ἐν αὐτῷ must mean that ὁ ἔχων is no more than the sum of the ἐνοῦσαι ἰδέαι. It is hard to regard ὁ ἔχων as conscious at all. As soon as he begins to contemplate the ideas within him, he becomes ὁ ὁρῶν.

But we must turn now to Porphyry (*In Tim.* 1.306.31 ff.):

μετὰ δὴ τὸν Ἀμέλιον ὁ Πορφύριος οἰόμενος τῷ Πλωτίνῳ συνᾴδειν, τὴν μὲν ψυχὴν τὴν ὑπερκόσμιον ἀποκαλεῖ δημιουργόν, τὸν δὲ νοῦν αὐτῆς, πρὸς ὃν ἐπέστραπται, τὸ αὐτοζῷον, ὡς εἶναι τὸ παράδειγμα τοῦ δημιουργοῦ κατὰ τοῦτον τὸν νοῦν.

"Following on Amelius, Porphyry, considering himself to be in accord with Plotinus, calls the hypercosmic Soul the Demiurge, and its Intellect, towards which it is turned, the Essential Living Being, so that the Paradigm of the Demiurge is for him the Intellect."

Proclus protests against this. Where, he asks, does Plotinus make the Soul the Demiurge? (p. 307.4–5). This is a question that I hope to answer in what follows.

Plotinus, as we have said, begins his enquiry from a consideration of *Tim.* 39E (rather loosely quoted):

"Νοῦς," φησίν, "ὁρᾷ ἐνούσας ἰδέας ἐν τῷ ὅ ἐστι ζῷον· εἶτα διενοήθη,"

66

φησίν, ''ὁ δημιουργός, ἃ ὁ νοῦς ὁρᾷ ἐν τῷ ὅ ἐστι ζῷον, καὶ τόδε τὸ πᾶν ἔχειν.''

The first *aporia* raised is: Are the *eidê* then prior to *Nous*, if *Nous* sees them as already *onta*? In replying to this, he says, we must first of all consider the possibility that the *Zôon* is not Nous but other than Nous. That which beholds is Nous, so that the Zoon in itself will not be Nous, but the object of intellection (*noêton*), and thus Nous will be beholding objects outside itself. But in that case Nous will immediately cognize not reality, but *eidôla*, which is intolerable.[4] We must therefore consider *Nous* and *to Zôon*, Intellect and its object, as being distinguished only in theory:

οὐδὲν κωλύει, ὅσον ἐπὶ τῷ λεγομένῳ, ἓν εἶναι ἄμφω, διαιρούμενα τῇ νοήσει, εἴπερ μόνον ὡς ὂν τὸ μὲν νοητόν, τὸ δὲ νοοῦν· ὁ γὰρ καθορᾷ οὔ φησιν ἐν ἑτέρῳ πάντως, ἀλλ᾿ ἐν αὐτῷ τῷ ἐν αὐτῷ τὸ νοητὸν ἔχειν.

"There is nothing in the statement to prevent us from taking these two elements as one, although they may be distinguished conceptually, if only to the extent that there is one element which is cognized, and another which cognizes; for Plato does not mean that the element which cognizes beholds in any sense something outside itself, but that it contains the cognized element within itself."

The ideas, and τὸ ὅ ἐστι ζῷον, must, then, be *in* Nous, or absurdities result. This conclusion was more fully worked out later in *Enn.* 5.5 [32], where the relation of Intellect to the Ideas is the primary problem. Here it is only the first part of the enquiry. *To Zôon*, then, is analyzed (albeit somewhat tentatively: οὐδὲν κωλύει) as νοῦς ἐν στάσει καὶ ἑνότητι καὶ ἡσυχίᾳ, while the νοῦς ὁρῶν ἐκεῖνον τὸν νοῦν is envisaged as ἐνέργειά τις ἀπ᾿ ἐκείνου, ὅτι νοεῖ ἐκεῖνον. This distinction is important as a source for two of Amelius' νόες (and Demiurges), the first and the third, ὁ ὤν and ὁ ὁρῶν. The second νοῦς, ὁ ἔχων, is, however, readily deducible from the conclusion that Nous possesses the Zoon within it (ἐν αὐτῷ ... τὸ νοητὸν ἔχειν). Nous *qua* possessor can be reasonably distinguished from Nous *qua* beholder, especially if, as was the case with Amelius, one has a weakness for triads.

Plotinus, however, does not propose ὁ ἔχων in so many words in

---

[4] Porphyry's equating of τὸ ὅ ἐστι ζῷον with the Paradigm and with Nous (see above) would be open to this criticism.

XXV

PLOTINUS, ENN. 3.9.1   67

this passage.   Instead, he produces another possible third element, *to dianooumenon*.[5]

τοῦτο (ὁ νοῦς ὁρῶν) οὖν ἐστι τὸ "διανοηθέν," ἃ ἐκεῖ ὁρᾷ, ἐν τῷδε τῷ κόσμῳ ποιῆσαι ζῴων γένη τέσσαρα.   δοκεῖ γε μὴν τὸ διανοούμενον ἐπικεκρυμμένως ἕτερον ἐκείνων τῶν δύο ποιεῖν.

"This then is that being which 'planned' to create in this lower Universe what it sees there, the four classes of living beings.   He seems, certainly, to make the planning element tacitly distinct from the other two."

So, as he says in the next line, we seem to have three elements, τὸ ζῷον αὐτὸ ὅ ἐστιν, ὁ νοῦς, and τὸ διανοούμενον.   Some, he says, may see all these as one, others as three; it depends how you look at it.   If, however, one postulates τὸ διανοούμενον as a distinct element, what would be its role?

Its role, as it turns out, would be distinctly demiurgic.   Its task is ἐργάσασθαι καὶ ποιῆσαι καὶ μερίσαι all those things which νοῦς beholds in τὸ ζῷον.   The energies of Nous are turned inward upon itself; those of τὸ διανοούμενον are turned outward, upon the world. A triad has emerged.

At this point, however, we reach a starting point for Porphyry's doctrine.   Porphyry equated the Demiurge with the ὑπερκόσμιος ψυχή, and its Nous with the Autozoon and the Paradigm.   As between the two disciples, we see the representation of two extreme views—on the one hand, an urge to schematize each moment of each hypostasis (triadically), in the case of Amelius; on the other, an impulse to simplify, as represented by Porphyry, who often in this respect seems to look back to Middle Platonism.

At any rate, Plotinus here goes on to raise another *aporia*:

ἢ δυνατὸν τρόπον μὲν ἄλλον τὸν νοῦν εἶναι τὸν μερίσαντα, τρόπον δὲ ἕτερον τὸν μερίσαντα μὴ τὸν νοῦν εἶναι· ᾗ μὲν γὰρ παρ' αὐτοῦ τὰ μερισθέντα, αὐτὸν εἶναι τὸν μερίσαντα, ᾗ δ' αὐτὸς ἀμέριστος μένει, τὰ δ' ἀπ' αὐτοῦ ἐστι τὰ μερισθέντα—ταῦτα δέ ἐστι ψυχαί—ψυχὴν εἶναι τὴν μερίσασαν εἰς πολλὰς ψυχάς.

"It is possible that in one way Intellect is the divider (producer of partial

[5] We get a clue, however, to Amelius' interpretation from a passage of Proclus (*In Tim.* 1.242.23–24): νοῦς μὲν γάρ ἐστι τὸ νοητόν, αἴσθησις δὲ ὁρᾷ τὸ αἰσθητόν, διάνοια δὲ ἔχει ἐν ἑαυτῇ τὸ διανοητόν.   This is an application of what must have been Amelius' formulation.   τὸ διανοούμενον is then ὁ νοῦς ἔχων.

existences), while in another the dividing agent is not Intellect; that to the extent that the partial existences proceed from it, it is the divider, while to the extent that it itself remains undivided, its products being what is divided—these products being souls—it is the Soul that is the agent causing division into many souls."

And he seems to appeal at this point to *Tim.* 35A, where the creation of the Soul is connected with the creation of divided Nature (τρίτον ἐξ ἀμφοῖν ἐν μέσῳ συνεκεράσατο οὐσίας εἶδος etc.):

διὸ καί φησι τοῦ τρίτου εἶναι τὸν μερισμὸν καὶ ἐν τῷ τρίτῳ, ὅτι διενοήθη, ὃ οὐ νοῦ ἔργον—ἡ διάνοια—ἀλλὰ ψυχῆς μεριστὴν ἐνέργειαν ἐχούσης ἐν μεριστῇ φύσει.

"Which is why he says the separation is the work of the third element and begins in it, because it thinks discursively, which is not a characteristic of Intellect, but of Soul, possessing as it does a dividing activity within divided Nature."

Porphyry thus had ample excuse from this passage for positioning Soul as the Demiurge. That Proclus credits Porphyry with identifying the Demiurge not just with ψυχή, but with ἡ ὑπερκόσμιος ψυχή (1.307.1), or ἡ ἀμέθεκτος ψυχή (1.322.1–3), would seem to indicate that Porphyry already had postulated an unparticipated Soul-Monad, to preside over the psychic order, the multitude of partial souls, a development which on other grounds I would prefer to attribute to Iamblichus. We need not, however, assume that, even if Porphyry used these terms to describe his Demiurge-Soul, he had developed the whole system as we find it in Proclus.

Iamblichus and Proclus are thus unreasonable in condemning Porphyry's interpretation as un-Plotinian, at least as regards the interpretations derivable from this seminal passage, 3.9.1.

It remains to consider Proclus' and Iamblichus' own interpretations of the passage, to appreciate the full extent of the ambiguities therein contained.

Proclus declares (1.305.16 ff.) that Plotinus assumes the Demiurge to be double (διττός), τὸν μὲν ἐν τῷ νοητῷ, τὸν δὲ τὸ ἡγεμονοῦν τοῦ παντός, which doctrine he himself commends. He must, then, take the two Demiurges as νοῦς and τὸ διανοούμενον, τὸ ζῷον being merely the object of intellection. *Νοῦς* in contemplating τὸ ζῷον produces the ideas, the content of the Intelligible Realm, τὸ διανοούμενον beholds the Ideas and "divides" them in the Universe. Again, an interpretation surely derivable from the text as we have it.

Iamblichus, at least in his Timaeus Commentary,[6] takes the whole Intelligible Realm as the Demiurge, roundly condemning Porphyry as un-Plotinian (we must accept Kroll's insertion of μή in 307.16), and claiming himself to follow Plotinus. Proclus quotes him as follows:

τὴν ὄντως οὐσίαν καὶ τῶν γιγνομένων ἀρχὴν καὶ τὰ νοητὰ τοῦ κόσμου παραδείγματα, ὅν γε καλοῦμεν νοητὸν κόσμον, καὶ ὅσας αἰτίας προυπάρχειν τιθέμεθα τῶν ἐν τῇ φύσει πάντων, ταῦτα πάντα ὁ νῦν ζητούμενος θεὸς δημιουργὸς ἐν ἑνὶ συλλαβὼν ὑφ' ἑαυτὸν ἔχει.

"Real Existence and the origin of created things and the intelligible paradigms of the Universe, which we term the Intelligible Universe, and those causes which we posit as pre-existing all things in Nature, all these things the Demiurge God who is the object of our present search gathers into one and holds within himself."

ἡ ὄντως οὐσία will be τὸ ὅ ἐστι ζῷον, while ἡ τῶν γιγνομένων ἀρχή and the intelligible paradigms of the Universe are the Ideas. Both of these the beholding and possessing and apportioning element contains within itself, and one is perfectly entitled, according to Plotinus, to take the whole combination as one or as three (ἄλλοις δὲ δόξει τὰ τρία ἓν εἶναι, ... ἢ ὥσπερ ἐν πολλοῖς, προτείνων ἄλλως, ὁ δὲ ἄλλως, νοεῖ τρία εἶναι). Iamblichus takes the former alternative. It might seem that for the Demiurge to "contain within himself" the whole noetic world need not imply identity with it, but Proclus is quite clear, in the preceding passage (πάντα τὸν νοητὸν κόσμον ἀπο-καλεῖ δημιουργόν), that that is what Iamblichus meant.

This is not the whole story of the identification of the Demiurge by the successors of Plotinus. Amelius, for instance, derives another triad, ὁ βουληθείς, ὁ λογιζόμενος, and ὁ παραλαβών, from the passage Tim. 30A (Proclus, In Tim. 1.398.16 ff.).[7] My purpose, however, has

---

[6] Ap. Proc. In Tim. 1.307.14 ff. D. Proclus quotes against him a much more elaborate categorization of the Demiurge which he made in an essay Περὶ τῆς ἐν Τιμαίῳ τοῦ Διὸς δημηγορίας, where, very much under the influence of the Chaldaean Oracles, he gives the Demiurge τὴν τρίτην ἐν τοῖς πατράσιν τάξιν, ἐν τῇ νοερᾷ ἑβδομάδι (1.308.17 ff.).

[7] The doctrines of Theodorus of Asine (1.309.9 ff.) and of Syrianus (1.310.3 ff.) are not immediately derived, I feel, from 3.9.1. Theodore elaborates on Amelius' triad, and Syrianus postulates a Demiurgic Monad presiding over a triad of demiurges. At this stage the doctrine has developed its own momentum.

XXV

70

been merely to demonstrate, in this one instance, the openness of Plotinus' philosophizing, the openings it gave for further developments by his successors, and the use made of these openings. It really does seem as if we have, in 3.9.1, a record of the results of one of the discussions that took place in Plotinus' circle, transmitted to us by Porphyry from Plotinus' papers in a more unfinished, tentative state than that of any completed tractate. It is, more truly than in the case of the finished tractate, a piece of "work in progress," work in which Amelius had a hand, but (if Porphyry's own chronological listing is accurate) not Porphyry himself.[8]

[8] I am grateful to Prof. T. G. Rosenmeyer for reading over this paper, and making helpful suggestions on presentation. One might remark in conclusion that a proper study of the philosopher Amelius is an obvious desideratum in Neoplatonic studies.

XXVI

Iamblichus and the Origin of the Doctrine of Henads

E. R. Dodds, in his great edition of Proclus' *Elements of Theology*[1], devotes some pages of his commentary (pp. 257-260) to a discussion of the origin of the doctrine of divine henads, and their identification with the traditional gods. He traces this doctrine to Syrianus. Later, in the *Addenda and Corrigenda* (p. 346), he correctly retracts one point in his argument, observing that Syrianus cannot be referred to by Proclus at *In Parm.* 1066, 21 Cousin, as τινὲς τῶν ἡμῖν αἰδοίων, since he places the gods in the Second Hypothesis of the *Parmenides*, whereas the figure or figures referred to there place them in the First. At this point he gives up, merely noting that the doctrine of henads must be earlier than Syrianus.

It seems to me that by a somewhat closer examination of the existing evidence we can come to a more definite conclusion than this, and in fact attribute the origin of the doctrine with virtual certainty to Iamblichus.

Proclus, in Book VI of his *Commentary on the Parmenides* (1054, 34 ff. Cousin), sets out what can be identified with certainty, on the basis of a scholium and correspondences in Damascius, *Dubitationes et Solutiones*, as the view of Iamblichus as to the subject matters of the various Hypotheses.[2] His account of the first one is as follows:

Οἱ δὲ μετὰ τούτους κατ'ἄλλον τρόπον εἰσάγοντες τὰ ὄντα, τὴν μὲν πρώτην λέγοντες εἶναι περὶ θεοῦ καὶ θεῶν· οὐ γὰρ μόνον περὶ τοῦ ἑνός, ἀλλὰ καὶ περὶ πασῶν τῶν θείων ἑνάδων αὐτὴν ποιεῖσθαι τὸν λόγον.

It might be doubted here whether the amplification mentioning the 'divine henads' is Iamblichean or due to Proclus. Regarded by itself, all this testimony can be taken to affirm with certainty is that Iamblichus took the First Hypothesis to concern not only God (that is, ὁ πρώτιστος θεός, which Porphyry had made the subject of it – 1053, 40 Cousin), but the gods in general. Even if we confine ourselves to this passage alone, however, the question still arises as to what status

[1] Oxford 2nd Ed. 1963.
[2] See the excellent survey in the Introduction to the Budé edition of Proclus' *Platonic Theology*, (edd. Saffrey and Westerink, Vol. I pp. LXXV-LXXXIX).

Iamblichus envisaged for this multiplicity of gods. Would they not inevitably be 'henads', in the sense in which the term was later understood? But we do not in fact have to confine ourselves to this passage. Later, at *In Parm.* 1066, 16 ff., we find the following passage, which seems to me to refer inevitably to Iamblichus:

Ἀνάγκη τοίνυν, εἴπερ μόνον καὶ ἅπαν τὸ θεῖον ὑπὲρ οὐσίαν ἐστίν, ἢ περὶ τοῦ πρώτου θεοῦ μόνον εἶναι τὸν παρόντα λόγον, ὃς δὴ μόνος ἐστὶν ὑπὲρ οὐσίαν, ἢ περὶ πάντων θεῶν καὶ τῶν μετ' ἐκεῖνον, ὥσπερ ἀξιοῦσί τινες τῶν ἡμῖν αἰδοίων.

'The present argument' is the First Hypothesis. A phrase such as 'certain of those whom we revere' would have been suitable to Syrianus, as Dodds points out (*loc. cit.*), but for the fact, above mentioned, that Syrianus puts the gods in the Second Hypothesis (*In Parm.* 1061, 33 ff.). The phrase must therefore refer to someone else, and only one other philosopher is recorded as explicitly placing the Gods in the First Hypothesis, to wit, Iamblichus.

Proclus continues, presumably now paraphrasing or elaborating on Iamblichus' explanation (1066, 22 ff.):

ἐπειδὴ γὰρ πᾶς θεὸς καθὸ θεὸς ἑνάς ἐστι (τοῦτο γάρ ἐστι τὸ πάσης οὐσίας ἐκθεωτικόν, τὸ ἕν), διὰ δὴ τοῦτο συνάπτειν ἀξιοῦσι τῇ περὶ θεοῦ τοῦ πρώτου θεωρίᾳ τὴν περὶ θεῶν ἁπάντων ὑφήγησιν· πάντες γάρ εἰσιν ἑνάδες ὑπερούσιοι, καὶ τοῦ πλήθους τῶν ὄντων ὑπερανέχουσαι, καὶ ἀκρότητες τῶν οὐσιῶν.

It was Porphyry, as we have seen, who declared Hyp. I to be about 'the first god', and Iamblichus who chose to add '(all) the gods'. If we consider for a moment how he will have defended his innovation, we must conclude, I think, that it was very much along the lines laid down here by Proclus.

At this point one may suitably introduce a passage of Damascius, *Dub. et Sol.* (ch. 100, I 257, 20 ff. Ruelle), where he is contrasting Iamblichus with his predecessors in his treatment of the gods:

Τί δεῖ πολλὰ λέγειν ὅτε καὶ τοὺς θεοὺς οὕτως ὑποτίθενται τοὺς πολλοὺς οἱ πρὸ Ἰαμβλίχου σχεδόν τι πάντες φιλόσοφοι, ἕνα μὲν εἶναι τὸν ὑπερούσιον θεὸν λέγοντες, τοὺς <δ'> ἄλλους οὐσιώδεις εἶναι, ταῖς ἀπὸ τοῦ ἑνὸς ἐλλάμψεσιν ἐκθεουμένους, καὶ εἶναι τὸ τῶν ὑπερουσίων πλῆθος ἑνάδων οὐκ αὐτοτελῶν ὑποστάσεων, ἀλλὰ τῶν ἐλλαμπομένων ἀπὸ τοῦ μόνου θεοῦ, καὶ ταῖς οὐσίαις ἐνδιδομένων θεώσεων.

From which we may reasonably conclude that Iamblichus held that the rest of the gods were also 'superessential', that they *were* 'independent hypostases', and that they were *not* simply entities (of a lower order) divinised by the supreme and only God.[3]

It should be plain from this that Iamblichus had worked out at least the substance of the later doctrine of henads. Whether or not he termed these gods 'henads' is less important, but it seems somewhat perverse, in face of these various pieces of evidence, to deny him the term. Iamblichus needed these henads as links between the supreme and ineffable One and his creation. All of his very complicated systematising of the Realm of the One, including his postulating of two Ones (Dam. *Dub. et Sol.* ch. 43, I 86 Ruelle), is prompted by the desire to bridge the great gap between a completely transcendent First Principle and everything subsequent to it. He could also defend the introduction of henads on the analogy of the multiplicity of intellects co-existing with Intellect itself, and the souls co-existing with Soul, each multiplicity being inferior to its monad, but not being mere ἐλλάμψεις thereof. And this indeed is the argument developed by Damascius throughout ch. 100.

The henads, which may be equated with the traditional gods on their highest level, are not then simply 'illuminations' of the One, but they are not to be regarded as properly distinct from it either. Such distinction would be intolerable, after all, in the henadic realm. Sallustius, in ch. 2 of the *De Diis et Mundo*, is probably being Iamblichean when he says of the Gods:

οὐδὲ τῆς πρώτης αἰτίας ἢ ἀλλήλων χωρίζονται, ὥσπερ οὐδὲ νοῦ αἱ νοήσεις οὐδὲ ψυχῆς αἱ ἐπιστῆμαι οὐδὲ ζῴου αἱ αἰσθήσεις.

[3] Of the predecessors of Iamblichus in this context the most distinguished was Plotinus himself. In *Enn.* II 9, 9, for instance, he makes it clear that the Supreme God produces the multiplicity of gods as emanations of himself. They are in the noetic world; he is above it:

ἐντεῦθεν δὲ ἤδη καὶ τοὺς νοητοὺς ὑμνεῖν θεούς, ἐφ' ἅπασι δὲ ἤδη τὸν μέγαν τῶν ἐκεῖ βασιλέα καὶ ἐν τῷ πλήθει μάλιστα τῶν θεῶν τὸ μέγα αὐτοῦ ἐνδεικνύμενον· οὐ γὰρ τὸ συστεῖλαι εἰς ἕν, ἀλλὰ τὸ δεῖξαι πολὺ τὸ θεῖον, ὅσον ἔδειξεν αὐτός, τοῦτό ἐστι δύναμιν θεοῦ εἰδότων, ὅταν μένων ὅς ἐστι πολλοὺς ποιῇ πάντας εἰς αὐτὸν ἀνηρτη- μένους καὶ δι' ἐκεῖνον καὶ παρ' ἐκείνου ὄντας. Cf. also *Enn.* V 1, 8 ff, which points in the same direction. If the Demiurge is in the noetic world, and is represented in the second hypothesis of the *Parmenides*, then *a fortiori* so are the gods in general. Plotinus recognises no gods above the Demiurge, only The One.

Porphyry followed Plotinus in all this, as we see from the fact that he placed 'the gods' in the Second Hypothesis, and only the Supreme God in the First. Iamblichus' break with this doctrine is thus of considerable importance in the development of later Neoplatonism.

I do not think that one should necessarily conclude from this, as Dodds does (*op. cit.* p. 259, n. 1), that Sallustius is here representing the Gods as simply Philonic 'powers' of the First Cause; he is simply, I think, using a vivid comparison, perhaps a somewhat unfortunate one, to express an inexpressible relation.

To return to Proclus, he continues to discuss the placing of the other gods in the First Hypothesis until 1071, 8. The criticism he levels against the doctrine is not of a type which he would have used against Syrianus, whom he never disagrees with as directly as this.[4] He firmly rejects the notion, and the reason he gives first is most useful for the understanding of Iamblichus' reason for postulating henads. (1066, 33 ff.):

εἰ δὲ τὸ μὲν πρώτιστον ἕν, ὡς δοκεῖ που καὶ αὐτοῖς μάλιστα, πάντων μόνως ἐστὶ καὶ ἀσύντακτον πρὸς τὰ ἄλλα πάντα καὶ ἀμέθεκτον, φασίν, αὐτὸ ἀρπάσαν πρὸς τῶν ὅλων, καὶ ἄγνωστον τοῖς πᾶσιν <καὶ> ἐξῃρημένον, ἑκάστη δὲ τῶν ἄλλων ἐνάδων μεθεκτή πώς ἐστι, καὶ οὐ μόνον ἑνὸς ἀλλὰ καὶ πλήθους οἰκείου μετέχουσα, καὶ οὐσίας ἢ νοητῆς ἢ νοερᾶς ἢ ψυχικῆς ἢ καὶ σωματικῆς (μέχρι γὰρ ταύτης πρόεισιν ἡ μέθεξις), τί χρὴ τὸ μὴ συναριθμούμενον τοῖς οὖσιν ἕν, μηδὲ συναττόμενον ὅλως τοῖς πολλοῖς, εἰς μίαν ὑπόθεσιν ἀναφέρειν ταῖς μετεχομέναις μὲν ἀπὸ τῶν ὄντων, συνεκτικαῖς δὲ τῶν πολλῶν ἐνάσιν;

This may be a powerful argument against Iamblichus' doctrine, but it also tells us why he should have wanted to propound it, and what role his henads were to play. It seems from this evidence very much as if Iamblichus saw each henad, or god, as the head of a sequence of manifestations of itself at various levels, from the intelligible down to the bodily, by each of which it is participated. This is nothing less than a σειρά, and indeed the doctrine of henads seems to involve the doctrine of *seirai* for the henads to govern. Proclus does not, of course, object to the doctrine, simply to the idea of associating these participated entities too closely (i.e. in the same Hypothesis) with the imparticipable One.

To conclude, it seems plain that the 'revered' individual who is the object of criticism from *In Parm.* 1066, 16 to 1071, 8 had a doctrine of henads and of their participation by *seirai* of entities right down

---

[4] Proclus had enormous respect for Iamblichus, but he is nonetheless prepared to contradict him on occasion, something he does not do to Syrianus, e.g. *In Tim.* I 153, 28 ff; 218, 13 ff; II 105, 28 ff; III 247, 27 ff. In all these cases the original contradiction is really made by Syrianus; Proclus merely endorses it. In one passage (I 147, 29 ff), Proclus even backs Porphyry against Iamblichus, without mentioning Syrianus.

the scale of being, and it seems equally plain that this individual can only have been Iamblichus. The doubt that has hung over of the question of the origins of the doctrine of divine henads should therefore be dispelled, and Iamblichus should be given the credit which his successors of the Athenian School certainly did not grudge him, though they were frequently less than specific in acknowledging the extent of their debt.

XXVII

PROCLUS AND THE *PARMENIDEAN* DIALECTIC

Before embarking on his "vast and various sea[1] of discourse", in the latter part of Plato's *Parmenides*, Parmenides outlines the method he proposes to follow, emphasising its comprehensiveness, as compared to that of Zeno (136 A-C):

"Take, if you like, the supposition that Zeno made: 'If there is a plurality of things'. You must consider what consequences follow both for those many things with reference to one another and to the One, and also for the One with reference to itself and to the many. Then again, on the supposition that there is not a plurality, you must consider what will follow both for the One and for the many, with reference to themselves and to each other. Or, once more, if you suppose that 'Likeness exists', or 'does not exist', what will follow on either supposition both for the terms supposed and for other things, with reference to themselves and to each other. And so again with Unlikeness, Motion and Rest, Coming-to-be and Perishing, and Being and Not-Being themselves. In a word, whenever you suppose that anything whatsoever exists or does not exist or has any other character, you ought to consider the consequences with reference to itself or to any one of the other things that you may select, or several of them, or all of them together; and again you must study these others with reference both to one another and to any one thing you may select, whether you have assumed the thing to exist or not to exist, if you are really going to make out the truth after a complete course of discipline." (Cornford's trans.)

He thus lays down the principles of a dialectical method which cannot fail, as he says, κυρίως διόψεσθαι τὸ ἀληθές, a project central to the concerns of most ancient philosophers. Yet Proclus, writing about

---

(1) It is worth noting, perhaps, that the colourful πέλαγος, which Burnet adopts in the OCT for the πλῆθος of all the mss., is taken by him from Marsilio Ficino, though he should have noted that, although Proclus' *lemma* reads πλῆθος, Proclus reads πέλαγος in the body of his text (cols. 1018,13, and 1020,19 Cousin). Proclus' *lemmata* are often "corrected" by the scribe from a manuscript of Plato.

900 years later, almost at the end of the ancient philosophical tradition, is able to say, in Book V of his *Commentary on the Parmenides* (p. 1020, 31-5 Cousin[2]):

"A sign of the difficulty involved in making use of this method is the fact that none of those who followed Plato set out any of their own works in this form (leaving aside Ammikartos, whoever he was[2])."

That is why, Proclus continues, he himself has decided to exercise the method on a number of examples, which he has just been giving us. My purpose in this paper is not to contribute further to the extensive discussion as to what Plato's purpose may have been in the second part of the *Parmenides*, or to that about the validity and usefulness of the dialectical method set out in 136 A-C, but simply to present and discuss what Proclus understood that method to be. Proclus, of course, considered the second part of the *Parmenides* to be a dialectical exposition of the total structure of reality, from the One, down through Intellect and Soul, to embodied Form and Matter. He also felt the method of "Parmenides" to be the ideal one for the fulfilment of this task. We do not have to share in either of these dogmas, I think, to find interesting his application (and indeed, if we are to believe him, his pioneering application) of the method.

Proclus discerns in Plato's description an elaborate structure of propositions (*In Parm.* p. 1000, 34ff. Cousin). In order to find the true attributes of any given subject, such as Unity, Likeness, Providence, Soul—or, indeed, to test the truth of any proposition, such as "that the soul is immortal" (p. 1014, 7ff.)—one must proceed as follows. The first division is into asserting or denying the existence of the entity (or affirming or negating the proposition) to be examined. One then divides each side into what is true for itself and what is true for others. This gives one four subdivisions. Depending upon each of these subdivisions is a set of six propositions: (1) true[3] in relation to itself; (2) not true in relation to itself; (3) true and not true in relation to itself; (4) true in relation to others; (5) not true in relation to others; (6) true and not true in relation to others. One arrives thus at a total of twenty-four propositions, arranged in four sets of six.

In Proclus' view, this treatment inevitably brings to light the truth about intelligible entities—far more surely, he feels, than does the Aristotelian syllogistic (p. 1007, 10ff.). In particular, he sees it as a weakness of the syllogistic method, as it was of Zeno's method (p. 998,

---

(2) I can find no mention of this personage anywhere. The name sounds Semitic, which may betoken a Phoenician, a Carthaginian, or possibly a Cyrenaic. At least we may assume that Proclus has not invented him, since the claims to know nothing about him either.

(3) The Greek is ἕπεται, "follows". I have ventured to render this as "is true", as expressing the meaning more idiomatically.

7ff.), that it only considers what follows, or does not follow, if something exists, or is the case. To get a complete picture of reality, however, we must also consider what follows and does not follow if something is *not* the case. In other words, to gain a full understanding of something's role in the universe, and thus of its essence, we must contemplate the results of its non-existence as well as of its existence.

This is all very well, but it cannot be denied that there are difficulties. The method, as he sets it out, involves a great deal that appears arbitrary and subjective. The user of the method must choose, on the basis of intuition, what attributes are appropriate to the entity in question at each stage of the dialectical process, and, indeed, must also have a clear idea of what the conclusion is going to be. It is hard to see how the method can be used for the generation of any new truth, and easy to understand why, even if Plato ever intended it to be used, his followers never took it up. Proclus might, admittedly, argue that metaphysical truths are by nature analytic, and that this method is simply a method of ordering one's intuitions about Unity, or Motion, or Providence, in such a way as to produce the most comprehensive view of the entity concerned. His defence of the method, at any rate, could be interpreted in this sense (p. 1007, 10ff., quoted below, p. 170). Proclus here maintains, in effect, that this method provokes us to the systematic summing-up of true propositions about the given entity, and the sum-total of these, when surveyed, in turn provokes us to an intuition of the truth.

What I would like to do here is to see how the method actually works with respect to one of the entities which Proclus picks out for full treatment, namely Soul (p. 1004, 8ff.). I choose Soul, since it is arguably, after the One, the entity of central importance to Proclus' philosophy.[4] I will set it out schematically, to make clear the various subdivisions. Proclus presents the attributes in each case either as neuter singulars or as articular infinitives, both being subjects of ἕπεται or οὐχ ἕπεται, which I, as stated in n. 3 above, have chosen to render "is, or is not, true of ...". Sometimes idiomatic translation involves altering the structure even further, but this will not affect its accuracy for our present purpose. It is plain that there is no set number of attributes which one must think up at each stage, though Proclus usually comes up with three. At later stages of his exercise, however, he tends to tire somewhat, and we may find only one at a given stage. The category "is

(4) See on this the illuminating essay of Jean Trouillard, *L'âme et l'un selon Proclos*, Paris 1972. Proclus also picks out for the same treatment Zeno's own hypothesis "That there are many", and then Likeness and Unlikeness, Motion and Rest, Generation and Corruption (1008, 4 - 1013, 20), followed in turn by a subject-predicate proposition "The Soul is immortal" (1014, 16 - 1017, 33). I will consider these latter two below.

and is not true of ..." gives him the most trouble in general, and is thus often followed by a sentence or two of explanation. We may note also that Proclus feels free to alter the reference of τὰ ἄλλα ("the field", as Gilbert Ryle has wittily termed it), to represent whatever is the accepted "opposite" to the entity under consideration, in this case "bodies".[5]

Let us now proceed to our dialectical exercise:

IA: If Soul exists, (1) there is true of it, in relation to itself, self-motion, essential life, and self-substantiation;

(2) not true of it are self-destruction, total ignorance of itself, and non-recognition ot its own attributes;

(3) true and not true of it are divisibility and indivisibility (for in a way it is divisible, in a way indivisible), and eternity and non-eternity (for in a way it is eternal, in a way subject to change), and everything that pertains to it as a property of its median nature is of this sort.

IB: Again, *if soul exists,* (4) there is true of it, in relation to bodies, that it is productive of life, that it initiates motion, that it holds together bodies, as long as it is present to bodies, that it lords and rules over them by nature;

(5) not true of it are being moved externally (for it is property of ensouled bodies that they are moved from within), and being the cause for bodies of rest and changelessness;

(6) true and not true is its being present in them and apart from them (for it is present in them though its providence, but separate from them in its essence.)

IIA: If Soul exists, the following is true for other things—in this case, bodies:

(7) in relation to themselves, self-awareness (for it is by reason of the life-giving causal principle that these have a mutual awareness);

(8) not true is lack of sensation (for it is necessary that in the presence of soul everything should have a sensation, on the one hand as individuals, on the other as parts of the universe);

(9) true and not true is that ensouled bodies move themselves and do not move themselves (for in one sense they move themselves, in another not; there are many modes of self-motion).

IIB: Again, *if Soul exists,* then (10) there is true for bodies, in relation to it, being moved from within by it, being vivified by it, and being preserved and held together through it, and in general being dependent upon it;

(5) He makes this clear at 1015, 20-24, where he states that the one or more things selected as τὰ ἄλλα must be cognate (συγγενῶς ἔχειν) with the subject under consideration —as for instance, the equal with the unequal, or Motion and Rest with Being. Such a principle is vague enough to cause problems, but at least it provides a guideline.

(11) not true are being dispersed by it and being filled with lifelessness by it (for it is from that source that it partakes in life and cohesiveness);

(12) true and not true are participation and non-participation in it (for both are true, both that in a way bodies partake of it, and that in a way they do not).

IIIA: If Soul does not exist, (13) there is true of itself, in relation to itself, lifelessness, non-being and mindlessness (for if it does not exist, it will not possess either being or life or mind);

(14) not true will be the powers of self-preservation, self-creation, self-motion, and all such attributes;

(15) true and not true will be being an object of knowledge and reasoning to itself (for if it does not exist it will in a way be unknowable and irrational, inasmuch as it will not know or reason about itself at all, whereas in a way it will be neither irrational or unknowable, if these attributes imply having some nature which is not rational nor participant in knowledge).

IIIB: Again, *if Soul does not exist*, (16) there are true of it, in relation to bodies, being incapable of generating them, being unmingled with them, having no care of them;

(17) not true of it are the powers of moving them, of giving them coherence;

(18) true and not true are its being other than bodies and having no relation to them (for this is in a way true and in a way not true, if one takes otherness an implying existence, but total difference—in this way it would be other—but not other, on the other hand, as not existing at all, and other than this, because non-existent).

IVA: if Soul does not exist, (19) there are true of bodies, in relation to themselves, immobility, non-differentiation in respect of life, lack of feeling for each other;

(20) not true are being sense-perceptible by one another, being self-mobile;

(21) true and not true is being able to affect one another (for in a way they will experience influences, and in a way not; they will experience them only as material bodies, not as living things).

IVB: if Soul does not exist, (22) there is true for other things, in relation to it, not being watched over or being moved by it;

(23) not true is being vivified or being held together by it;

(24) true and not true is being like and unlike it (for in so far as, if it does not exist, they would not exist either, they would be like it—for they would be in the same state as it—but in so far as it is not possible for something which does not exist to be like anything, in this respect likeness of them to it will not be true).

What, we may ask, have we learned about the nature of the soul from this laborious exercise that we did not already know? I do not think, in fact, that Proclus would claim that we are deriving new truths about the soul (any more than, as he would claim, we do from an Aristotelian syllogism); we are simply ordering our intuitions in a rational way. This method, by directing our attention in turn to the soul and to its opposite, and to their relation to themselves and to each other, and to the conseqences of the soul's non-existence as well of its existence, ensures that we leave out no essential characteristic of our chosen entity. This, at any rate, is how he summarises his conclusions (p. 1006, 17ff.):

"So now we have gone through the method for our example in all the proper modes, and we conclude from these arguments that Soul is the cause of life and motion and interaction for bodies, and in general of their existence and preservation. For on the assumption that Soul exists, these things follow, and in the case of its non-existence the negation of these follow.[6] Only, then, from Soul and through Soul are these qualities present to bodies. This is the purpose of the whole method, to discover the propertiesof a thing, and of what things it is the cause both to itself and to other things."

A little further down, he compares the "Parmenidean" system with that of Aristotle (p. 1007, 10ff.):

"I know, certainly, that Aristotle, in his imitation of this system, aims in the case of his categorical syllogisms to set out the predicates and the subjects and what is contrary to the subject and the predicate, stating what is true and what is not true of them. The system set out here, however, is far more complete, setting out as it does by the process of division all the modes through which one must proceed if one proposes to exercise one's intellect on each aspect of being ... When we are in pursuit of metaphysical truth, we are more likely to discover it through this system than through that of Aristotle, since through this multiplicity of hypotheses we can track down more accurately the subject of investigation."

For Proclus, then, Aristotle's syllogistic is inadequate to isolate the true essence of any intelligible entity, in a way that the method of Parmenides is ideal. Let us examine this remarkable claim, by asking certain pertinent questions.

What difference is there, really, for Proclus, between syllogistic and diaeresis, in the form in which it is employed here? How is this system "far more complete"? As far as I can see, Proclus' claim amounts to this, that Aristotle's syllogistic appears as a collection of logically

---

(6) It might reasonably be objected that there is a logical incoherence about postulating attributes of, or consequences following from, something non-existent. Proclus actually sees this problem, and tries to counter it (at p. 999, 13ff.) by distinguishing various senses of not-being, but he does not seem to solve adequately the problem raised by saying, e.g. "if soul does not exist, there is true of it, in relation to itself, lifelessness", etc.

independent units, e.g. "If A belongs to all B and B belongs to all C, then A belongs to all C"; "If A belongs to no D and D belongs to all E, then A belongs to no E", and so on, from which one could derive a series of truths about the Soul, for example, such as "All soul is automotive"— (from e.g. Self-motion belongs to all life, and life belongs to all Soul) or "No soul is material" (from e.g. "Mortality belongs to no soul, and mortality belongs to all material things"), but such a procedure cannot guarantee that one covers every aspect of the soul's essence systematically, since no hierarchy of propositions is set out.[7] Now Aristotle would protest, no doubt, that he would start from first principles (though it is a notorious aspect of Aristotle's philosophy that he never seems to employ the syllogistic method either to establish the axioms of any science or to derive propositions from those axioms),[8] but Proclus might ask in reply how one can be sure that one has arrived at the relevant first principle or principles on a given subject, without a method such as the "Parmenidean". The curious thing is that Aristotle does actually, in *An. Pr.* I 28, set out in some detail how one should go about selecting the premisses (προτάσεις) in relation to each subject (50 b 1-12):

"We must set down (1) the subject itself, its definitions and all its properties (ἴδια), (2) all the concepts which are consequents of the subject (ὅσα ἕπεται τῷ πράγματι), (3) the concepts of which the subject is a consequent, and (4) the attributes which cannot apply to the subject (we need not select the concepts to which it cannot apply, because the negative premiss is convertible). We must also distinguish among these consequents those which are included in the essence (ἐν τῷ τί ἐστι), those which are predicated as properties, and those which are predicated as accidents, and of these we must distinguish those which are supposedly (δοξαστικῶς) from those which are really associated with the subject, for the greater our supply of the latter, the sooner we shall arrive at a conclusion, and the truer they are, the more convincing will be our proof." (trans. Tredennick. LCL).

And he goes on, further, to specify that the consequents must be of the correct degree of generality. This surely, one would think, with its distinctions of essential and accidental properties and its specifications about the relations between consequent and subject, is a more effective analytical method than the Parmenidean. But Proclus has just this passage in mind (as Cousin discerned), and he is not impressed. His

---

(7) This is not a fair criticism, perhaps, since in *An. Pr.* A 25, Aristotle discusses sequences of syllogisms, but he is not there concerned to build up an axiomatic system on the basis of such sequences; rather, he is concerned to establish the distinctness of each syllogism.

(8) To quote Jonathan Barnes, "Aristotle's Theory of Demonstration", in *Articles on Aristotle I*, London, 1975, p. 66: "If the *Organon* were lost, we should have no reason to suppose that Aristotle had discovered and was mightily proud of the syllogism." As he says, just above: "In the whole of the Aristotelian corpus there is not, as far as I am aware, a single perfect example of a demonstration" (i.e., a syllogistically-based proof).

objections seems to be that without going through all the consequences of the non-existence, as well as the existence, of the entity in question, one cannot be sure of achieving the admirable goal which Aristotle sets himself. Proclus sees the Parmenidean method as a sort of master-method, to which the other traditional Platonist logical procedures are subordinate.[9]

But one might ask, how far is this method applicable to every aspect of reality?—It might seem as if the method is only applicable to existential statements about Forms or general concepts ("Soul exists", "Motion exists", "Generation exists"), but at 1014, 6-15, Proclus extends the method to subject-predicate propositions (though still about purely intelligible entities):

"There are two ways in which we undertake the examination of things. Sometimes we consider whether each thing exists or does not exist, sometimes whether such and such an attribute applies or does not apply to it —as for instance, whether the soul is immortal. On this occasion we are enquiring not only as to existence or otherwise of all the attributes of the thing hypothesised, itself with respect to itself and to others, and for others with respect to themselves and to it, but also as to their applicability or otherwise."

Admittedly, the results of this investigation (truncated to just *eight* stages instead of twenty-four) do not seem greatly different from the results of the analysis of the proposition "that Soul exists". For instance, as we saw, "if Soul exists", there follows, in its relation to bodies, "that it is productive of life, that it initiates motion, that it holds together bodies, that it lords and rules over them by nature", whereas "if soul is immortal", there will be true, in relation to bodies, "ruling over them, preserving each one of them, containing the beginnings and the ends of all things, bringing everything perfectly to its conclusion". But one cannot expect too much difference in this case, after all, since the soul's immortality is very much a part of its essence, for a Platonist at least.

More interesting would have been an attempt by Proclus to work out the consequences of giving the "Parmenidean" treatment to some controversial doctrine in the area of ethics or physics—let us say, "Virtue is sufficient to Happiness", or "There is such a thing as total mixture". The method should, after all, be able to function in any area of philosophical enquiry, and to reveal flaws in a proposition as well as confirming its correctness. In this capacity it could be seen as an illustration of the otherwise unexemplified method propounded by Socrates at *Phaedo* 101 DE, which calls for a working-out of all the

---

(9) *In Parm.* p. 1003, 6-29 Cousin.[2] Here he shows how the four traditional procedures of definition, division, demonstration and analysis may be seen as subordinate to the Method.

consequences of one's hypothesis before finally accepting it or rejecting it. A good way of ensuring that one had done this might seem to be proceeding through all the twenty-four steps of the "Parmenidean" system, thinking through, let us say, in the case of the proposition that Virtue is sufficient to Happiness, what propositions seem to follow and not to follow, both in relation to itself and to its opposite, or 'other' (presumably Vice), from both the postulation of this hypothesis and from its denial.[10]

It is unfortunate that Proclus does not attempt anything of this sort (though one could, I think, do it for him, by the expenditure of a little ingenuity); nor does he attempt to illustrate the vaunted superiority of the method over that of Aristotle by taking a distinctively Aristotelian doctrine (e.g. "Form is always immanent in Matter" or "Soul is the primal entelechy of a living being") and showing its incoherence (though admittedly Aristotle never uses the syllogism to establish such a doctrine). Instead, feeling that the method could still do with a little more illustration, he decides to provide another example of an existential proposition, "that Providence exists" (p. 1016, 4 - 1017, 33).

Providence is perhaps slightly different from Soul, in that Soul is a substance, while Providence is an activity (though a frequently hypostatised one), but it is in this really no different from Motion or Rest or Generation or Corruption, all of which have been "done" earlier, so it is not easy to see why he should add it here, except, perhaps that it is a somewhat controversial proposition, being opposed, in varying degrees, by both Peripatetics and Epicureans. At any rate, he gives it the full 24-part treatment, leading to the conclusion (which he does not, however, explicitly draw) that Providence is the cause of the preservation and orderly interrelationships of all things, without which all would be randomness and disorder.

Once again, it is not easy to see he *proves* anything here, for example to an Epicurean. All he does is to tease out the implications inherent in the concept of Providence, if one already believes in such a concept. But then he does not really claim to be doing more than that. All he is claiming for the method is that it is the best way to articulate and test the validity of one's conceptions, and that in this

---

(10) It might also be seen as having some connexion with the method of diaeresis practised by Speusippus, since he is reported (Fr. 63 Taran = 38-42 Isnardi Parente) as maintaining that it is impossible to define, and therefore to know, any entity unless one can identify its relationships to all other entities—a task impossible to realise, one would think, but we know that this did not deter Speusippus from attempting definitions. A method such as the "Parmenidean" would be suited to such a project, but we have no evidence that Speusippus used anything but normal Platonic diaeresis (if one can speak of such thing!). If he did, Proclus has no knowledge of it, at any rate.

respect it is superior to the syllogistic method, which does not after all claim to do any more than that either.

What does Proclus see as the ideal result of the exercise of the method? I quote his own words, at 1015, 33-41:

"But what has he (sc. Parmenides) set before us as the end of this exercise? "The vision of the truth", he says (136 C). Let us not understand "truth" here in a general sense, but as being precisely that intelligible truth about which he has taught us elsewhere, for the sake of which there is the great struggle to see "the plain of truth" (*Phaedr.* 248 B). So all our life is an exercise in preparation for that vision, and the "excursion" through dialectic strives towards that goal."

And that, perhaps, is the best that can be said for the Parmenidean Method. What use Ammikartos put it to we shall, alas, never know.

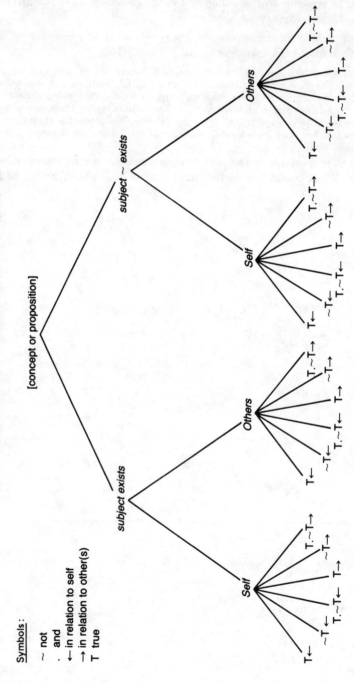

FULL SCHEMA OF THE 'PARMENIDEAN' DIALECTIC

Symbols:
~ not
. and
↙ in relation to self
→ in relation to other(s)
T true

XXVIII

Image, Symbol and Analogy: Three Basic Concepts of Neoplatonic Allegorical Exegesis

I

The contemporary relevance of this subject is, perhaps, not great. Allegory, as such, is rather out of fashion. But for much of European history allegory has been indulged in freely, in all forms of art, and any discussion of the rules of allegory in any age or culture should be of general interest. Even today, the search for Freudian motifs and Jungian archetypes must have its rules – that is to say, ways of judging when a false analogy has been made.

This paper is simply an attempt to sort out, through an examination of some individual contexts, the possible difference of meaning between two basic terms of Neoplatonic allegory, *eikon* and *symbolon*, and in this connexion the use of the term *analogia/ analogon*. In such company as this, I do not come so much to instruct as in the hope of learning more. There are, after all, many nooks and crannies of Neoplatonism into which I have not yet penetrated. What chiefly concerns me is the question of the *rules* of Neoplatonic allegory. By what system does one recognise in a given text an image or symbol of metaphysical reality? How can one learn to recognise the correct *'analogia'*? I do not find these rules stated anywhere in the writings of the Neoplatonist commentators. That is not to say that they are not there, however, and I would be glad to have pointed out to me some passage which I have overlooked.

It is possible, on the other hand, that the rules of Allegory cannot be stated precisely, but must simply be derived from experience – sitting at the feet of one's master – and from personal inspiration. I myself, after all, feel that I can now recognise a symbol in a given text and observe the correct analogy, but I would be somewhat at a loss to say on what precise principles I was proceeding, except the simple discernment of points of similarity. This may well seem to be an intolerably vague conclusion, and I would be glad to have the whole question made more definite.

II

That said, let us turn to a few texts. Near the beginning of his *Commentary on the Timaeus*, in connexion with the exegesis of the lemma *Tim.* 17BC (where Socrates declares his intention of giving a recapitulation of his discourse of the previous day on the Ideal State), Proclus makes the following comment (*In Tim.* I 29, 31ff. Diehl):

"Some (sc. Porphyry), taking the recapitulation of the *Republic* in an ethical sense (ἠϑικώτερον), say that it reveals to us that we must enter upon the contemplation of the Universe in an ethically ordered frame of mind; others (sc. Iamblichus) consider that it has been placed before the whole enquiry into Nature (φυσιολογία) as an image (εἰκών) of the organisation of the Universe; for the Pythagoreans had the habit of placing before their scientific instruction the revelation of the subjects under enquiry through similitudes (ὅμοια) and images (εἰκόνες), and after this of introducing the secret revelation of the same subjects through symbols (σύμβολα), and then in this way, after the reactivation of the soul's ability to comprehend the intelligible realm and the purging of its vision, to bring on the complete knowledge of the subjects laid down for investigation. And here too the relating in summary of the *Republic* before the enquiry into Nature prepares us to understand the orderly creation of the Universe *through the medium of an image* (εἰκονικῶς), while the story of the Atlantids *acts as a symbol* (συμβολικῶς); for indeed myths in general tend to reveal

the principles of reality (τὰ πράγματα) through symbols.
So the discussion of Nature in fact runs through the whole
dialogue, but appears in different forms according to the
different methods of revelation."
This, I think, is a good passage from which to start, as it sets out
– or seems to set out – a clear distinction between an *eikon*
and a *symbolon*, and, further, links the whole theory of allegory
firmly with Pythagoreanism. I believe Iamblichus to be responsible for introducing this theory in its developed form into
Neoplatonism, and he will have derived it from his Neopythagorean sources of inspiration, Numenius, Nicomachus of
Gerasa, or even Apollonius of Tyana. I am not, however,
concerned here with the origins of the theory, but rather with
the nature of it.
  We see, then, a three-level system of exegesis set out. The
Pythagoreans, it seems, before revealing directly the truths of
their doctrine, would take the disciple through two preliminary
stages. First, they would present to him *homoia* and *eikones* of
reality. Obviously these were not their famous 'symbols' (of
which Iamblichus gives an extended account at the end of his
Protrepticus); the very word used for them precludes that. An
eikon must be something simpler and more straight-forward.
The only clue we have from this passage is that, in relation to
the doctrine presented in the *Timaeus*, the recapitulation of the
Republic is an *eikon*, while the Atlantis Myth is a *symbolon* (it
is also suggested here that *all* myths are *symbola*). But it is just
here that the difficulties begin. It is not clear, to me at any rate,
nor is it made clear by Proclus, how the recapitulation of the
Republic, or the description of the Ideal State in general, differs
generically, as a representation of cosmic truths, from the
Atlantis myth, or from myths in general. Indeed, a little earlier
in the work (p. 4, 7ff.), Proclus speaks of both the recapitulation of the Republic and the Atlantis myth as representing the
order of the universe δι' εἰκόνων, the Republic being an *eikon*
of its unity (ἕνωσις), the Atlantis myth of its division
(διαίρεσις) and of the opposition of the two basic orders
(συστοιχίαι) within it – or, alternatively, the *Republic* can be
seen as being like to (ὁμοιοῦσθαι) the heavenly realm, the
Atlantis myth to the realm of *genesis* below the Moon. Not only
are both here *eikones*, but they may be seen as images of rather

different things, in one case of unity and diversity extending all through the Universe (a vertical distinction, one might say), or, alternatively, or the superlunary and sublunary realms (a horizontal distinction).

Let us for the moment confine ourselves to *eikones*, and consider in what respect they might reflect reality. For an *eikon*, in fact, 'reflecting' should be the key word. An *eikon* is, after all, properly a mirror-image, or a direct representation, of an original, its *paradeigma*, whereas a *symbolon* merely 'fits together' with some corresponding reality in a higher realm. One might use the comparison of a statue of Winston Churchill, say, on the one hand, with Churchill's cigar – or perhaps, a picture of Cinderella with Cinderella's slipper. The statue and the picture are plainly *eikones*, the cigar and the slipper *symbola* – particularly the slipper. These examples are certainly crude, but perhaps they will do as preliminaries.

If we return for the moment to the statue of Churchill, we can immediately see the difficulties. The statue, if it is a good one, will have a one-to-one correspondence with the various (external) features of its model. But at least the model, the *paradeigma*, is a physical object; we can compare image and archetype with the same faculty. If one takes the most obvious Platonic example, the comparison of the Sun as *eikon* with the Good as *paradeigma*, we have arrived at the point of difficulty. Why is the Sun an *eikon* (*Rep.* 509a9), and not a *symbolon*? Following Plato, we maintain that there is a one-to-one correspondence between Sun and Good. Both are a source of visibility, and even of existence, to the entities subordinate to them, the world of sensible objects and the world of intelligible objects. In the case of the Ideal State of the *Republic*, the three classes therein described must correspond exactly to the triple division of Gods, Daemons and Men in the Universe, and their mutual relations and activities must also correspond. But then, we say, the battle of the Athenians with the Atlantids seems to correspond well enough to the constant struggle in the Universe between the forces of order and disorder, unity and diversity, represented at the highest level by the archetypal opposition of Monad and Indefinite Dyad. What, if anything, makes the one an *eikon* and the other a *symbolon*?

III

For further elucidation of this, I would like to turn from Proclus' *Timaeus Commentary* to his *Commentary on the Republic*, and specifically to the essay in which he discusses the theory behind Homer's mythologising (*In Remp.* I pp. 71-96 Kroll). Here Proclus is seeking both to defend Homer from the charges made against him in the *Republic* and to defend Plato against the charge of inconsistency in his attitude to Homer. This essay makes an important distinction between *eikon* and *symbolon*,[2] and it is a rather unexpected one. How, asks Proclus (72, 9ff), can such stories about the Gods as Homer, Hesiod and even Orpheus tell – rapes, thefts, bindings, castrations and so on – bear any relation at all to divine realities? Must not stories that are to represent (ἀπεικάζεσθαι) things divine imitate the order and unspeakable transcendence of these entities? Here, I think, we have a clue. An Homeric tale, such as, say, the story of Ares and Aphrodite, does not precisely mirror the intellectual calm and unanimity in which the Gods must live. If it in fact resembles that reality in any way, it must do it indirectly. In the course of presenting the common criticism of Homeric myth, Proclus says the following (73, 11ff):

". . for these *symbola* have obviously no resemblance (οὐ ... ἐοικότα) to the essential natures of the Gods. But myths must surely, if they are not to fall short utterly of representing the truth, have *some* resemblance to the nature of things (ἀπεικάζεσθαί πως τοῖς πράγμασιν), the contemplation of which they are attempting to conceal by means of the screens of appearance (τοῖς φαινομένοις παραπετάσμασιν)."

On the other hand, he continues, Plato in many places instructs us mystically about divine matters through *eikones*, bringing in nothing shameful or disorderly or materialistic into his myths, but, while concealing his transcendent intuitions about the Gods, yet presenting by way of concealment visible images (ἀγάλματα) which accurately represent the realities of the secret theory hidden within them.

Now what is the distinction being made here? Surely it is simply that Plato's myths, and indeed the purified myths which

Socrates would propose for the poets, have in them no feature that is *prima facie* discordant with our conception of divine nature. That is to say, they bear on their face the signs of being representations of *some* divine reality — though without authorised exegesis the layman cannot say precisely what. A poetic myth, on the other hand, with its rapes and conflicts, does not mirror the divine nature in this direct way. Nevertheless, it does represent truths about the universe in an indirect way, as Proclus explains further on (81, 28ff). The binding of Kronos, for instance, represents the uniting (ἕνωσις) of the whole creation to the intellectual and paternal transcendence (ὑπεροχή) of Kronos (82, 14ff). These myths, we learn at 83, 9, are *symbola*. The Gods, Proclus asserts, actually enjoy hearing these stories about themselves; that is why such tales are a feature of mystical rites and ceremonies (83, 18ff).

IV

But let us halt at this example of the binding of Kronos. Why, one asks, is this a *symbolon* and not an *eikon*? As far as I can see, the actual distinction centres round the subject matter. It is not so much a question, I think, of whether or not the story is discreditable or obscene on the surface — though the myths in question normally are — as whether or not the story seems to have a self-contained meaning, not directly pointing to any truth beyond itself, in the way that a conscious allegory should. A Platonic myth, or some purified (and thus allegorised) poetic myth, we would have to maintain, is plainly representative of something else, even as a statue is plainly a statue of someone or something, whereas an unreformed poetic myth appears just to be a good story in its own right, as for instance the Tale of Ares and Aphrodite.

This distinction may or may not seem cogent to us, but it is at least, I think recognisable. The issue of immorality in the non-iconic myths seems to me to be secondary, although in fact both Plato and Proclus dwell on it a good deal, and of course this 'scandal' of immoral stories had been used ever since the beginnings of allegory as a compelling reason why these stories *must* be allegorised. If we return to our original text in the *Timaeus* Commentary, we may now say that the Atlantis Myth, if it is a *symbolon* and not an *eikon*, must be taken as being a story which does not directly point to any meaning beyond itself—it is a tale of a great war of long ago, and can be regarded as simply history— whereas the recapitulation of the *Republic* has an obvious allegorical signification. We *should* also be able to add that the Atlantis story portrays divine truths in a *prima facie* discordant way. This would imply that the elements of the universe do not fight each other in the same way as the Athenians fought the Atlantids. The problem here is that in fact the elements—or rather the conflicting forces of Form and Matter—*are* fighting each other in very much this way. Why is the portrayal of their mutual relations in the *Republic* iconic, while this is symbolic?

V

But I do not wish to raise difficulties at this stage. If we are to try and confirm the distinction, the *symbolon*, in the Pythagorean system, must be seen as a higher stage of allegory than the *eikon*, first of all, perhaps, because it is more difficult to discern as being allegorical at all, but secondly, I assume, because it tends to represent more ineffable truths, truths which are not susceptible of full representation through *eikones*.

If Proclus himself observed these distinctions in an entirely consistent manner, our task would be much easier, but he does not. In an attempt to shed some further light on the question, I would like to turn now to the consideration of the allegorisation of the characters in the two dialogues *Timaeus* and *Parmenides*, together with the allegorisation of the whole introductory situation in the *Parmenides*, to see if any consistent pattern emerges.

First let us ask ourselves whether we expect the characters (πρόσωπα) of the dialogues to be *eikones* or *symbola*? In the sense that they do not *prima facie* suggest − to the normal reader − that they are representations of any 'higher' truth, one might take them to be *symbola*; on the other hand, they themselves, and their mutual relationships, might be thought to mirror Reality in the same way that the various classes in the Ideal State of the Republic do, and thus qualify as *eikones*. We

must now see how the case actually stands. When the
identifications of the characters are first made in the *Timaeus*
Commentary (I 9, 13ff), the arrangement of the characters –
that is, a trio of auditors listening to a single speaker – is
described as an *eikon* of the organisation of the Universe:

> "The father of the discourse should correspond (ἀνάλογον
> ἑστάναι) to the father of Creation (for the creation of the
> cosmos in discourse is an *eikon* of the creation of the
> cosmos by the (demiurgic) intellect); while to the demi-
> urgic triad which receives the unitary and generic creation
> of the Father, there should correspond the triad of those
> who receive the discourse, of whom the summit is
> Socrates, joining himself directly to Timaeus by reason of
> contiguity of life-force, even as in the paradeigmatic realm
> the first principle is united to that which is prior to the
> triad."

On the other hand, when the matter is taken up again later (I
198, 25ff, *ad Tim.* 27AB), the arrangement of speeches among
the characters is described as a *symbolon* of the creation of the
Universe, and the passage ends (200, 2-3) with the sentence:
"These things then one may understand in some such symbolic
* sense as this (οὑτωσὶ συμβόλων) , without, perhaps, reading
too much into them."

The sad fact is that, if one checks assiduously through
Diehl's index under *eikon* and *symbolon* right through Book I
of the commentary one will find the two terms used indiscrim-
inately for characters, events, and even words and phrases. In
one passage at least (94, 27f) we find both delightfully
combined. The causal principles of creation are said to be
represented in the Atlantis Myth 'in images through symbols'
(ἐν εἰκόσι διά τινων συμβόλων). Plainly it is only when he is on
his very best behaviour that Proclus maintains any strict
distinction between the two terms.

In the *Parmenides* Commentary the situation is much the
same. At 660, 26ff *Cousin*, the allegorical significance of the
places of origin of the various characters is set out:

> "Ionia is a *symbolon* of Nature, Italy of intelligible being;
> Athens is symbolic of the median position between these,
> through which an ascent can be made from the realm of

Nature to that of Intellect for souls who are stimulated to such an ascent."

However, after a good deal more of such identifications, during which neither of our key terms is in fact used, we have the phrase 'presents an *eikon* (εἰκόνα φέρει)', employed in two successive sentences of summing up: "The above-mentioned presents an *eikon* of these realities to those not entirely incapable of observing such things." (661, 21), and, a little further down (662, 10), "All these (situations and characters) present an *eikon* of the Gods themselves, and would provide no problems to those who are willing to follow out the *analogia.*"

VI

The third basic term in our investigation has now presented itself forcefully, and we may profitably turn to an examination of it, especially as the allegorisation of the characters in the *Parmenides* Commentary makes use of it more than of either of the other terms. *Analogia* in Neoplatonic terminology always retains something of its mathematical sense of 'geometrical proportion', and is frequently so used in the course of Proclus' commentaries, but in the context of allegorical exegesis proper it signifies the correspondence between the surface meaning of the text (or of the characters, things and actions mentioned in the text) and the metaphysical truths of which it, or they, are the expression. This must have been seen as a sort of fixed mathematical relation, but it is not the sort of relation that could be stated in any kind of formula.

We may at this point suitably reintroduce the Pythagoreans. They are reported by Proclus (*In Tim.* I 33, 4ff), again in connexion with the recapitulation of the *Republic* (*ad Tim.* 17c), as follows:

"The account of the Ideal State and the condensed and succinct summary of the classes within it contributed to the general presentation of these descriptions, taken as *eikones*, to (the appreciation of) general truths. And indeed this is precisely how the Pythagoreans used to go about things, tracking down the points of similarity (ὁμοιότητες) in the world on the basis of *analogiai*, and passing from *eikones* to their respective *paradeigmata.*"

The Pythagoreans, then, as we might expect of such mathe-matically-minded folk, employed *analogiai* to discern what the surface phenomena they dealt with were *eikones* (and presum-ably *symbola*) of. Once again, however, there is no clue as to what precise rules are to be followed in fixing the *analogiai*, and I would suggest that there were in fact none that could be formulated. That is not to say that the resulting allegory is arbitrary, as Fr. Amandus Bielmeier would suggest ("*Die Wilkür hat hier im einzelnen freies Feld*", op. cit. p. 76); it is surely plain that it does in fact follow a fairly strict system. All I would suggest is that the discerning of the correct 'analogies' had to be learned by experience.

That there was a distinct sense of correctness and incorrectness in this area is made plain by a number of passages. At *In Tim.* I 165, 16ff, for instance, Porphyry is reported as being criticised by Iamblichus, *à propos Tim.* 24D, for situating Athena, as described in the passage, in the Moon. Iamblichus' criticism is that Athena must be ranked higher than the Moon, ' which is simply one of her emanations. Porphyry 'has not correctly preserved the *analogia* (οὐ καλῶς τὴν ἀναλογίαν διασῴζεσθαι). In the context this seems to mean something like: 'the correct *analogia* is 1:100; Porphyry has made it 1:10'). At another point, Proclus himself, once again *à propos* the recapitulation of the *Republic*, makes a remarkable state-ment. It is possible, it seems, to have various correct *analogiai* to a given surface phenomenon (*In Tim.* I 57, 22ff):

"And if we formerly took the πόλις (of the *Republic*) here below as representing the realm of generation, and now take it as representing the cosmic conflict, that should be no cause for astonishment. For it is safe to understand the same thing according to various *analogiai* in relation to different contexts."

– since, that is, the same thing by virtue of different aspects of itself can show an *analogia* to different elements of reality. It is possible, then, to postulate a multiplicity of correct 'analogies', ·as well, of course, as a multiplicity of wrong ones.

When we turn to the allegorisation of the *personae* of the *Parmenides* (*In Parm.* 628. 1ff), we find in fact that the terms *analogon* and *analogia* are those chiefly used (628, 2, 21, 31,

40), though *eikon* is used once (in the phrase εἰκόνα φέρει). Parmenides is to be taken as *analogon* to the unparticipated and divine *Nous*, the summit of the noetic world; Zeno is analogous to that *nous* which is participated by the divine Soul, and Socrates represents (here ἔοικε is used, which may be taken as a verbal form of εἰκών) the individual *nous*, capable of receiving the divine forms. Parallel with this scheme, however, Proclus declares that these three figures seem to him to 'preserve' (διασῴζειν) another *analogia*, according to which they represent respectively the three moments Being, Life and Mind within the hypostasis of *Nous*. Either of these *analogiai* are acceptable, it seems. They both represent great metaphysical truths.

    Analogia then, is the principle on which allegorical exegesis is based, but when one has said that one has still not fathomed the principles on which it is applied. If one had the rules according to which one preserved the *analogia*, one would have the rules of allegorical exegesis set out before one. As I say, I do not see these rules stated anywhere in the Neoplatonic corpus, and I do not believe that they can be stated, even though they can plainly be learned. In the *Anonymous Prolegomena to Platonic Philosophy*, ch. IX, we find an elaborate set of ten rules for recognising the subject, or *skopos*, of a dialogue; if there had been set rules for allegorising, it would be in such a work as this that one would expect them to be set out.

VII

    This survey has not been particularly comprehensive, I fear, but I hope that it is at least representative enough to give a fair picture of the complexities of the situation. It seems to me to be the case that we have, on the one hand, evidence of a three-tiered system of Neopythagorean allegorical interpretation, perhaps first connected with the exegesis of Plato's dialogues by Iamblichus, which Proclus reports but does not himself follows very strictly — and which, indeed, could not be followed very strictly in the exegesis of a Platonic dialogue — and on the other hand, more normal Greek usage, in which the terms *eikon* and *symbolon*, together with *analogia*, could be used interchangeably with each other and in combination with a good many other terms (e.g. ἐκφαίνειν, μιμεῖσϑαι, ἀπεικάζειν) to express the relation between the surface meaning of the text and the truths it allegedly represented. I am concerned with trying to distinguish the essence of the Pythagorean system from the looser usage that obscures it.

It seems fairly plain that some authority on Pythagoreanism did describe the school as educating its neophytes first through images, then through symbols, and then by the direct revelation of (mystical) truth. The symbols are plainly the well-known Pythagorean Symbols, of which, as I have mentioned already, we have a comprehensive survey at the end of Iamblichus' *Protrepticus* (ch. XXI). What might the *eikones* have been? Iamblichus' *Vita Pythagorica* might reasonably be expected to throw some light on this question, especially if, as I have suggested, he is the source of the application of this theory to Platonic exegesis, but in fact this work proves disappointing. There is indeed a good exposition of the Pythagorean theory of *symbola* in cc. 103-105, in which it is explained how the Pythagoreans veiled the truths of their doctrine with the deceptive appearance of the apparently foolish *symbola*, but there is no mention of *eikones* in this connexion, nor any suggestion of a three-tiered system, as opposed to a simple contrast of symbolic and direct instruction. Elsewhere, however, in cc. 64-67, there is a discussion of the use of music in philosophic training, in the course of which music is twice (in c. 66) spoken of as an *eikon* of reality, in this case of the harmony of the universe. This may give us some idea as to what might have been regarded as an *eikon* in a three-tiered system of Pythagorean instruction, but the fact remains that there is no explicit statement of such a system in the *Vita Pythagorica*. The exact provenance of the system, as well as its proper contents, remain, as far as I am concerned, something of a mystery, on which I would welcome enlightenment from this gathering. As regards the application of it to the allegorical exegesis of the Platonic dialogues, this is all that I can find to say at present.

APPENDIX
C. S. Peirce on Icon and Symbol

While not wishing to embark on a full historical survey of the meanings of these terms in Western Literature and philosophy, I think it not unsuitable to make a brief reference to one modern authority who makes notable use of the terms 'icon' and 'symbol', the American philosopher C. S. Peirce.

In an essay entitled *Logic as Semiotic: The Theory of Signs*,[3] Peirce produces an elaborate set of technical terms for the various possible types of sign. The only aspect of this with which I will concern myself is his definition of Icon, Index and Symbol (I include Index because it is linked closely by him with the other two, and shares in the distribution of characteristics which I find relevant to the understanding of the Neoplatonic distinction):

"A sign either an *icon*, an *index*, or a *symbol*. An *icon* is a sign which would possess the character which renders it significant, even though its object had no existence; such as a lead-pencil streak as representing a geometrical line. An *index* is a sign which would, at once, lose the character which makes it a sign if its object were removed, but would not lose that character if there were no interpretant. Such, for instance, is a piece of mould with a bullet-hole in it as sign of a shot; for without the shot there would have been no hole; but there is a hole there, whether anybody has the sense to attribute it to a shot or not. A *symbol* is a sign which would lose the character which renders it a sign if there were no interpretant. Such is any utterance of speech which signifies what it does only by virtue of its being understood to have that signification." (*op. cit.* p. 104)

Before entering upon a discussion of these definitions, I will append some further basic definitions, for those (like myself) who may be unfamiliar with Peirce's terminology:

"A sign, or *representamen*, is something which stands to somebody for something in some respect or capacity. It addresses somebody, that is, creates in the mind of that person an equivalent sign, or perhaps a more developed sign. That sign which it creates I call the *interpretant* of the first sign. The sign stands for something, its *object*." (p. 99).

First, let me reformulate what I take to be the Neoplatonic, or Neopythagorean, definitions of εἰκών and σύμβολον in terms analogous to those of Peirce. It seems to me that an εἰκών in the three-tiered Pythagorean system is a sign which would lose the character that makes it a sign if its object were removed, *or* if there were no interpretant. It seems to me, in fact, that, rather than answering to Peirce's *icon*, it combines the characteristics of his *index* and *symbol*. An *eikon* clearly points outside itself to some other thing – in Neoplatonic metaphysics, to some noetic reality. Churchill's portrait loses its specific character if *either* there is no such person as Churchill *or* if no one any longer recognises Churchill. It is still a painting, but it is not, properly, a portrait of anyone. If we take the Pythagorean use of music as an example, a certain sequence of notes is only a soothing or mind-clearing sound if (as they thought) it accords with the harmony of the spheres and/or there is a mind such as to be soothed or cleared by it. Whether or not the examples from the Platonic dialogues that we have examined fit it uncomfortably, if at all. But perhaps Iamblichus (rather than Proclus) may have seen the ordering of the characters in the *Timaeus*, for instance, as having no significance at all apart from the metaphysical realities they are representing, whereas the Atlantis Myth has a clear and self-contained (historical) meaning, apart from its allegorical use.

What Peirce would call an *icon*, on the other hand, I would want to call a σύμβολον, that is, a sign which would possess the character which renders it significant, even though its object had no existence. A cigar, for instance, which could in certain circumstances stand as a symbol of Churchill, is still a cigar, even if there were no such person as Churchill. I am somewhat bothered by the distinction that Peirce makes here between an icon and an index. The mark of the pencil on the paper is a pencil mark even if there were no such thing as a geometrical straight line. It does, however, imply the previous presence of a pencil. The bullet-hole (*qua* bullet-hole) implies the previous passage of a bullet. If, however, there appears someone (a child, say) who does not understand about bullets, the hole is for him just a hole. But for a person who does not understand about pencils, there is still a mark on the paper.

I do not want to get into an argument with Peirce, however his purposes in definition are somewhat different from mine. What I find useful is his basic distinction between a sign which has no basic meaning apart from its object or interpretant, and one which has. A Pythagorean symbol, it seems to me, has an independent meaning, such a meaning as would conceal from the ordinary public that it is a sign at all. Exhortations to make one's bed when one gets up in the morning, or to avoid main roads, seem perfectly straightforward. Even pieces of advice which might seem eccentric, such as not to let swallows into the house, or not to stir the fire with a fork, do not point in any particular direction to a meaning beyond their surface one. They have a more devious, or more hidden, relation to reality than does an *eikon*, and are thus properly introduced to the neophyte at a later stage.

In conclusion, I must confess to being by no means convinced myself that there is, normally, any clear distinction between εἰκών and σύμβολον in Proclus' system of allegory, but I hope that this investigation, together with the brief survey of Peirce's terminology, has made some contribution to the elucidation of the problem of those passages where such a distinction *is* being made.

NOTES

1. The only secondary sources which I have been unable to uncover that are of immediate relevance to the subject under discussion (and even these are of limited usefulness) are: A. Bielmeier, *Die Neuplatonische Phaidrosinterpretation*, Paderborn 1930; and A. R. Sodano, 'Porfirio Commentatore di Platone', in Entretiens Hardt XII, *Porphyre*, 1965. Works on allegory in general have not proved helpful in this particular enquiry.

262

2. There is an interesting discussion of myths in chapters III and IV of Sallustius *On the God and the World*, as Professor John Whittaker reminds me, but, although Sallustius makes a division of myths into various types, theological, physical, ethical and so on, he nowhere makes a distinction between eikon and symbolon.

3. Printed in *Philosophical Writings of Peirce*, sel. and ed. J. Buchler. Dover Publications, 1944.

Since writing this paper, I have come across an article by R. A. Marcus 'St. Augustine on Signs' (*Phronesis* 2:1, 1957), which contains much of interest on general questions of terminology, and which also, in an appendix (pp. 82-3), makes use of Peirce.

ADDENDA AND CORRIGENDA

I.

p. 53: This is supported by Plutarch, *De Exilio* 10, 603B: "The Academy, a little plot of ground (*khôridion*) bought for three thousand drachmas, was the dwelling of Plato and Xenocrates and Polemon, who taught and spent their lives there, except for the one day every year when Xenocrates went down for the new tragedies at the Dionysia." Plutarch cannot be referring to the public park.

p. 59: Essay III in this collection.

III.

p. 69: I would now accept that the author of the *Didaskalikos* is not certainly to be identified with the Platonist Albinus, and is best left as 'Aicinous'. The author of the *Eisagôge* or *Prologos*, however, is Albinus.

IV.

p. 108: I must admit to side-stepping here the awkward fact that *mens*, the most basic Latin word for 'mind', is *feminine*. However, the contrast of *animus* and *anima* is, I think, significant.

p. 113: Essay VI in this collection.

p. 114: I deal with this problem more fully in Essay VII.

V.

p. 54: Kind readers have since produced a few more instances, notably *Phaedo* 114c3: ἄνευ τε καμάτων ζῶσι Eusebius, for ἄνευ τε σωμάτων ζῶσι of the mss., where one might suspect Eusebius, as a Christian who nevertheless admired Plato, of emending the text to conform with the Christian doctrine that the blessed would never be without bodies (Prof. J.V. Luce); *Soph.* 240b7: οὐκ ὄντως οὐκ ὄν of mss. B and W, and Proclus (*In Parm.* 816, 19 and 842, 7 Cousin), as opposed to the οὐκ ὄντως ὄν of T favoured by modern editors (cf. also οὐκ ὄν ἀραοὐκὄντωςκ of all mss. below at b12, where the second οὐκ is excised by Badham), where one might see efforts by Platonists, by introducing the second οὐκ, to bring Plato into conformity with the Aristotelian 'square of opposition' (Prof. D.B. Robinson); and *Soph.* 258e2 τὸ ὂν ἕκαστον Simplicius (*In Phys.* 238, 26 – though at 135, 26 he reads ἑκάστου!), for τὸ ὂν ἑκάστου of B and T, an 'emendation' designed, presumably, to bring Plato's text into line with later theories of matter (cf. Plotinus, *Enn.* II 4, 16, 1–3, who is paraphrasing the "emendation'). (Dr Denis O'Brien)

VI.

p. 325 (title): On Speusippus' metaphysics, see now the useful article of R.M. Dancy, 'Ancient Non-Beings: Speusippus and Others', *Ancient Philosophy* IX (1989), 207–44.

VII.

p. 47: Now published, as *Knowledge of God in the Graeco-Roman World*, ed. R. van den Broek, T. Baarda, and J. Mansfeld, Leiden: Brill, 1988, 43–68.

VIII.

p. 510: On this see further Essay X.

XIV.

p. 130: Westerink has since edited the 'B' and 'C' commentaries, identifying them as notes taken at Damascius' lectures, *The Greek Commentators on Plato's Phaedo*, II, Amsterdam: North Holland Publ. Co., 1977. Westerink in fact adopts my numeration of the fragments, but accidentally omits this article from his bibliography, which must give rise to confusion.
p. 132: See now Westerink's translation and discussion of this passage in *The Greek Commentators* . . . II, pp. 88–9. He manages to derive a satisfactory meaning from the text as it stands.
p. 140: for 'Plut. *Quod Deus.* . . .' read 'Philo, *Quod Deus* . . .'

XV.

Leonardo Tarán, 'Nicomachus of Gerasa', *Dictionary of Scientific Biography* 10 (1974), 113, n. 1, dismisses my argument on the ground that Proclus is nowhere attested to have paid any attention to the properties of the number 216, even in his exegesis of the account of the creation in the *Timaeus*, where he might well have mentioned it. This is a good point, certainly, but not, I think, absolutely compelling. The number of incarnation was well enough known. I admit, however, that Nicomachus is more comfortably placed a generation earlier than this date implies.

XVI.

p. 181: It is possible that this man is the same as the 'Antonius of Rhodes' who accompanied Porphyry from Athens to Rome when he came to study with Plotinus (*V. Plot.* 4), but even this, if accepted, would not greatly advance our knowledge.

XVII.

p. 83: See on this topic Essay IV.

p. 85: On this subject, see now the excellent study of David Ulansey, *The Origins of the Mithraic Mysteries*, Oxford, 1989.

XVIII.

p. 103: On this subject, see also Essay VIII.

XIX.

p. 453: I now feel that the Gnostic comparison is inapposite. What Plotinus is referring to is, surely, (a) the Form of Man, (b) the *logos* of Man at the level of Soul, and (c) the embodied man.

p. 453: Essay XXI in the present collection.

XXIV.

p. 55: This reference should read '*Enn.* IV 3, 25 – 4, 12'.

p. 64, n. 8: The reference should be to *De An.* III 7.

p. 64, n. 11: Mary Warnock's *Imagination* was published by Faber, London, 1976.

XXVIII.

p. 254: For οὐτωσὶ συμβόλων read οὐτωσὶ συμβολικῶς.

p. 257: See my remarks in the Introduction, p. x.

p. 260: Line omitted here. Text should read: ". . . fit <this scheme is another matter. My view is that they fit> it . . ."

INDEX

(I have included here all references of any substantial importance, even if the figure is only mentioned once. I have omitted casual references, and simple citations of authorities.)

Academy, Platonic: I *passim*; II 66; III *passim*
Adrastus (Peripatetic): V 67n.
Aeneas of Gaza: XIV 136, 138, 146
Aenesidemus: II 198n.
Aetius: IV 114–6, VII *passim*
Albinus (Alcinous): II 61, 66; III 70, 74–5; IV 118–9; V 58–9, 61, 67; VIII 515–6; IX 5; XII 359–60; XIII 219, 224–7; XIV 216–7n.; XVII 81; XVIII 92–4; XIX 451, 454; XXI 22; XXII 218n.; 223n., 227
Alexander of Aphrodisias: II 69; III 74; V 59–60; XIII 225; XXII 220–22; XXIV 63n.
Alexander Polyhistor: I 51; III 64
Amelius Gentilianus: III 73–5; IV 109n.; XIV 143n.; XXI 23; XXV *passim*
Ammikartos: XXVII 166, 174
Ammonius (teacher of Plutarch): II 66; III 66–7, 72; XIII 218
Ammonius Saccas: III 74; V 51n.; XVI 181; XVIII 92; XXII 216n., 218
Andronicus: II 64
Anniceris of Cyrene: I 52–3
Anonymous Parmenides Commentary: XVI 178
Anonymous Theaetetus Commentary: II 198n.; V 52; XIV 125–6
Antigonus of Carystus: I 57
Antiochus of Ascalon: II 62–5, 74; III 65–6; IV 117; VIII 510–1; XII 363; XIII 219; XVII 80
Antiochus I of Commagene: XVII 79
Antoninus (Platonist): XVI 181
Apuleius: III 72; VIII 515–6; XIII 224–5; XVIII 92
Arcesilaus: I 57–8; II 61–2, 68; III 64n.
Archytas, Pseudo–: IX 2–4
Ariston of Alexandria: II 65
Ariston of Ceos (Stoic): VIII 509
Aristotle: I 51, 53; II 60–1, 64; IV 109, 113; V 55–6, 66–7; VI *passim*; VIII 508; IX

2, 7; XIII 224; XIV 142–3; XVIII 93, 95, 98, 105; XXII 210; XXIII 207; XXIV 55, 63n., 64n.
Aristoxenus: XV 274
Aristus: III 66
Arius Didymus: II 198n.
Armstrong, A.H.: XIII 217; XVIII 96, 99; XX 69; XXV 63n.
Arnobius: XVI 176, 180
Attalus of Pergamum: III 64n.
Atticus: II 67; III 74; XIII 219, 224; XIV 126, 136, 141–3, 145–6; XVI 181; XVII 81; XXII 227
Augustine: II 63, 68, 74

Baltes, M.: VII 47–8, 50; IX 2n.
Basilides: XIV 145
Bernays, J.: V 65, 71
Bidez, J.: XVII 84
Blumenthal, H.: XVIII 100n.; XXIV 57, 62
Boethus of Sidon: XIV 137
Boyancé, P.: IV 116; VII 49
Bréhier, E.: X 17; XVIII 99, 101; XX 69; XXV 63n.
Brotinus: IX 3
Burkert, W.: 198n.; IX 2

Calcidius: V 55n., 56n., 60, 71; XIV 215; XVI 179
Cameron, A.: III 63n.
Carneades: II 62–3; III 64–5
Castricius Firmus: III 72
Celsus (Platonist): II 69–71; V 54; XVII 81–2; XIX 443; XXII 225; XXIII 206, 208
Chaldaean Oracles: II 73; IV 107, 121–2; XIII 227–8; XVI *passim*; XVIII 81, 83–4; XXI 22–3; XXIII 209, 211; XXV 69n.; XXII 227
Cherniss, H.: III 64n.; IV 109n., 110n., 113n.

Christians, Christianity: II 66, 69–73; XVII 81; XXII 215–6
Chrysippus: VIII 509, 512–6
Cicero: I 58; II 63–4; III 65; V 60, 68, 70; VIII 510; X 21; XII 363
Clement of Alexandria: XVIII 103; XX 73
Clitomachus: II 63; IV 109n.
Cornford, F.M.: IV 110n.; V 55, 67, 71
Crantor: I 57
Crates: I 57; II 62
Cratippus: II 65
Cratylus: I 51–2
Cronius: II 72; III 74; XII 361; XIV 137, 141–2; XVII 81–2
Crouzel, H.: XXII 215, 217n., 228–9
Cumont, F.: XVII 84

Daemons: VII 50; XIII 220; XXIII 206
Damascius: II 69; III 77n.; V 54; XIV 130, 135, 138, 146; XXIII 209–10; XXVI 102–4
De Lacy, P.: II 198n.
Demiurge: IV 109–11, 118, 123; XIV 142; XVI 177; XVII 80–2; XVIII 93; XIX 455; XXV passim
Democritus (Platonist): XIV 138; XXIII 209–12
Des Places, E.: IV 122
Deuse, W.: IV 119n.
diairesis: II 61; XXVII passim
Dio Chrysostom: XVII 82
Diocles of Cnidus: II 68
Diogenes Laertius: I 51–2, 58; II 62; III 64; VII 49; XVII 81
Dionysius the Areopagite: IX 8
Dionysus: XVI 182n.
Dodds, E.R.: IX 4n.; XIII 223; XXI 21; XXVI 102–3
Dörrie, H.: VI 329n.; VII 47–8
Dyad, Indefinite: II 65; IV passim; VII passim; IX passim; XIII 228; XVI 180–2; XXVIII 250

Egyptian religion: XXIII 208, 210, 212
Empedocles: XII 359; XVII 82; XXII 220
enargeia: II 62
Epicureans, Epicureanism: II 66–7; XIII 222, 225; XX 69–70, 75; XXIII 207; XXVII 173
Epicurus: I 54
Epistemology: II 62–3
Eubulus (Platonist): III 71, 75–6; XVII 80–2
Eudorus: II 65; IX 4, 6; X 20; XIII 219; XVI 180; XVIII 98; XXI 22

Eusebius of Caesarea: II 68; V 60–1; XIII 226

Favorinus of Arles: I 52; II 67
Festugière, A-J.: XII 358n.; XIV 129n.
Firmicus Maternus: XVII 83
Fowden, G.: III 76n.
Frede, M.: VIII 516; IX 7–8

Gaiser, K.: IV 109n.
Gaius (Platonist): II 66; III 74–5; XIV 145
Galen: II 70–1; V 71; VIII 516–7
Gallienus: III 72
Gellius, Aulus: II 66, 69; III 68–9, 72; VIII 516n.
Glucker, J.: I 51, 56; II 62–3, 66
Gnostics, Gnosticism: II 71–2; IV 107, 117, 119–22; XII 357, 360–4; XIII 216–7; XIV 145; XVII 80; XIX 454; XX 72–5; XXI 20; XXII 229; XXIII 204–5, 208
God: II 65–6; IX passim; XIII 215–6, 223–5; XVIII 93; XXI 19–20, 22
Goodenough, E.R.: II 74
Guthrie, W.K.C.: I 55; III 64n.; VII 47

Hadot, P.: XVI 178
Harder, R.: XVIII 99; XX 69
Harl, M.: XXII 215, 217n.
Harpocration of Argos: XII 361; XIV passim
Hecate: II 70; IV 117, 121–2; XVII 83
Heinze, R.: IV 116; VII 47–8
Henrichs, A.: XVI 182n.
Heraclides Ponticus: XII 359; XX 71
Heraclitus of Tyre: III 65
Hermeias: V 54; XIV 125, 139–41
Hermetica: V 61–2; XIII 222; XVII 81; XX 76n.; XXIII 205, 210
Herodes Atticus: III 69, 72
Hesiod: II 73; IV 116; VII 49
Hierocles: V 51n.
Himerius: XVII 84
Hippolytus: IV 120; XX 73
Homer: II 73; V 50, 59; XI 183; XVIII 94; XX 71; XXVIII 251

Iamblichus: II 69, 75; III 70; IV 113; V 53, 57, 59, 65–6; VI 325, 329, 331; IX 7; XII 358–62; XIII 223; XIV 126–7, 129, 132–3, 137, 140–1, 146; XVI 184; XVIII 95–6, 100; XX 72, 76n.; XXI 21, 23; XXIII 211; XXIV 62; XXV–XXVI passim; XXVIII 248–9, 256–8
Indian philosophers (Brahmans, etc.): XXIII 207, 210

Intellect (*Nous*): IV 109–10, 116–7, 120; XIII 220–2; XVI *passim*; XVIII 98–9; XXI 21–3; XXV *passim*
Irenaeus: IV 120n.; XX 73
Isnardi Parente, M.: VII 47–8

Jerome, St.: XX 19–20
Jews, Judaism: II 70–2; XIII 226–7; XX 74; XXIII 207; 212
John Philoponus: III 69n.; V 58–60, 71
Jones, R.M.: IV 121n.
Julian (Emperor): II 69, 71; V 71; XVII 83–4
Julian (Theurgist): II 73; IV 121n.; XIII 227; XVI 179
Justin, Pseudo–: V 60
Justinian (Emperor): XXI 19–20

Kant, I.: XXIV 57
katalêpsis: II 62
Koch, H.: XXII 216n.
Krämer, H-J.: IV 109n., 115; VIII 47–8

Lacydes: III 64n.
Lewy, H.: XVI 177
Libanius: XVII 84
Lieshout, H. van: XVIII 92n., 102
Lilla, S.: XVIII 103
Logic, Aristotelian: II 61, 65; XXVII 170–2; Stoic: IV 118
Logos: IV 117–8; XI *passim*; XII 218; XVI 180; XVII 84; XVIII 102; XIX 444; XXIV 55
Longinus: III 71; XIV 130
Lucian: I 53; II 69; XVII 81
Lucius (Platonist): II 67
Lynch, J.P.: I 51, 55; II 66; III 63, 77n.

MacKenna, S.: XVIII 99
Macrobius: XVI 182n.; XVIII 100n.
Magic: II 73, 75; XXIII *passim*
Marcus Aurelius: II 69, 73; III 76; XIII 227
Marcus, R.: X 17, 23n.; XXVIII 262n.
Marinus: XV 274
Matter: IV 109, 115, 117; IX 3; XII 357; XIV 141; XXI 23
Maximus of Ephesus: II 73
Maximus of Tyre: II 70; XIII 224–5
Merlan, P.: III 66n.; IV 113n.; VI 325; IX 7; XVIII 95; XXII 221
Mithras: II 70; XI 184–5; XVII *passim*; XXIII 204
Mithridates VI of Pontus: II 63; III 63
Moderatus of Gades: XIII 226; XXII 227
Monad: II 65; IV 114–5; VI 328; VII

passim; IX *passim*; XVI 180–1; XXVIII 250
Moraux, P.: II 198n.
Moses: III 70–2; VIII 515; XI 183–4; XIII 227

Nemesius of Emesa: XIV 137
Nicomachus of Gerasa: V 60; XV *passim*; XXVIII 249
Nicostratus: II 67; XIV 130
Numenius of Apamea: II 68–9; III 74–5; IV 118, 120; V 60; XII 361; XIII 218, 226–8; XIV 136–8, 140–6; XVI 179, 181–2; XVII 81–3, 85; XX 71; XXI 22; XXII 221, 223–4, 227; XXVIII 249
Nutton, V.: III 77n.

Ocellus Lucanus: IX 5
Olympiodorus: XIV 126–31; XXI 23
One, The: II 65; IV 114–5; VI 326–8; IX *passim*; XII 357; XIII 227; XXVI 105
Origen (Christian): II 69; XVII 81; XVIII 102–5; XIX 443–9, 453–5; XXI–XXIII *passim*
Origen (Platonist): III 73; XVI 181
Orpheus, Orphism: II 73; XII 50, 52n.; XVI 182n.; XXV 64–5

Pallas (author on Mithraism): XVII 80, 82
Paul, St.: XX 74; XXI 22; XXII 225
Peirce, C.S.: XXVIII 259–61
Pépin, J.: XI 183n.
Persian religion: XI 185; XIII 218; XVI 181, 183
Philo of Alexandria: II 66, 74; IV 108, 117–8; V 64, 70; VIII 515, 517n.; IX–XI *passim*; XII 362–3; XIII 227; XVI 180, 182n.; XVIII 102–5; XIX 448, 455; XX *passim*; XXII 227; XXVI 105
Philo of Larisa: II 61–4, 68; III 65
Philodemus: VII 50
Philolaus: IV 115; VII 48; IX 3–5
Plato: I 51–3, 56; II 62; III 64, 72, 74; IV 108–112; VIII 508; IX 3–4, 6, 8; XII 357–8, 361; XIII 217, 227; XVII 81, 85; XVIII 97, 101; XX 71; XXII 220, 223; XXIII 209; XXIV 55; XXVII 165; XXVIII 250
Plotinus: II 65–6, 69; III 63, 71–6; IV 109n., 114, 121; V 62–3, 66, 68n.; IX 6; XII 357, 364; XIII 227; XVI 179–82, 184; XVIII *passim*; XIX 449–55; XX *passim*; XXII 216, 221–2, 227; XXIII 215; XXIV *passim*; XXV *passim*; XXVI 104n.

Plutarch of Athens: II 75; XIV 138, 140; XXIV 62
Plutarch of Chaeronea: I 57; II 61, 67, 74; III 66–8; IV 111, 116–22; V 60–1, 67–9; VII 48, 51n.; VIII 511–5; X 20; XI 184; XII 358, 361; XIII 214–23; XIV 125, 136, 141–2; XVI 181–2; XVII 79–80
Plutarch, Pseudo–, *De Fato*: V 63; XIII 225; XXII 227
Polemon: I 57–8; II 62
Porphyry: II 66; III 71–6; V 57, 59, 65–6; XIV 125–6, 129, 137, 144–6; XVI 178, 180–1, 183; XVII 80–2; XVIII 96, 98–100; XX 74; XXI 21, 23; XXIII 211; XXIV 62; XXV *passim*; XXVI 104n.; XXVIII 248, 256
Posidonius of Apamea: VIII 511; X 21; XII 363; XIV 140; XVII 79
Proclus: II 69, 73–5; III 76; IV 122; V *passim*; IX 1; XIV–XV *passim*; XVI 181–2, 184; XVII 81; XVIII 96; XXI 21–3; XXIII 209–11; XXIV 63; XXV–XXVIII *passim*
Psellus, Michael: IV 122; XVI 177; XXI 23; XXIII 211, 216
Pythagoras: II 70; VII 50; XIII 216; XVII 85; XX 71
Pythagoreans, Pythagoreanism: II 65, 68, 70; III 66, 70; IV 123; V 56; VII 48, 50; IX *passim*; XI 183; XIII 219, 226; XV *passim*; XVII 81; XX 72; XXIII 215; XXVIII 248–9, 253, 255–8

Rahner, K.: XIX 443n., 445n., 455
Reitzenstein, R.: V 62
Riginos, A.S.: I 59
Rist, J.M.: VIII 516n.; X 23n.
Rufinus: XIX 447; XXI 19–20; XXII 226

Sallustius: II 73; XXVI 104–5; XXVIII 262n.
Sandbach, F.: VIII 516
Schleiermacher, F.: III 66
Schuhl, P-M.: IV 110–1
Severus: III 74; XIV 143; XVI 181
Sextus Empiricus: II 68; V 60; VI 329n.
Simplicius: II 69; V 54, 63; IX 4
Sophia: IV 110, 117–22; XII 362–3
Soul (World–): IV *passim*; VII 48–50; XIII 218; XVI 179–80; XVII 83–4; XVIII 93, 98; XXI 21–2; XXIV 59–60; XXV 65, 68; XXVII 167–70
Speusippus: I 53–7; II 60; IV 110, 113–6; V 56; VI *passim*; IX 1–2, 6–8; XIV 140; XVIII 95; XXVII 173n.

Stobaeus, Johannes: V 63, 65, 71; VII 47; XII 358n.
Stoics, Stoicism: II 61–9; III 66; VIII *passim*; X *passim*; XIII 219, 225; XIV 140; XVI 183–4; XVII 85; XVIII 101–5; XIX 444; XX 69–71, 75; XXII 225; XXIII 207
Syrianus: IX 3; XIV 139, 143n.; XXI 21–3; XXV 69n.; XXVI 102–3

Tarán, L.: I 59n.; IV 113n.; VI *passim*
Tarrant, H.: IV 113n., 119n.
Taurus, L. Calvenus: II 66–7; III 67–9; V 58–9; VIII 515; XII 359–60; XIII 219, 223; XIV 142
Theiler, W.: XVI 183; XVIII 94
Themistius: II 69
Theodorus of Asine: XIV 137–8, 143n.; XVI 181, 183–4; XXV 69n.
Theomnestus of Naucratis: III 66
Theon of Smyrna: II 74; V 67n.; XIV 215
Theophrastus: VI 327–9; VII 51
Thesleff, H.: IX 2
Theurgy: II 73; XXI 23; XXIII 210
Thrasyllus: III 70
Tigerstedt, E.N.: III 66n.
Timaeus Locrus: V 69; IX 2
Trouillard, J.: XXVII 167n.
Turcan, R.: XVII *passim*

Valentinus, Valentinianism: IV 117, 120–2; XII 358, 362–3; XVII 80; XIX 454; XX 73
Varro, C. Terentius: II 64; IV 117; VIII 510
Vlastos, G.: XIII 217

Walzer, R.: II 71
Waszink, J.H.: XIV 125n.
Westerink, L.G.: XIV 130; XXIII 210
Whittaker, J.: V 51n., 57, 60–1, 63; XIII 228n.; XXVIII 262n.
Wilamowitz-Moellendorf, U. von: I 55
Winston, D.: IV 118n.; X 21; XVIII 102n.

Xenocrates: I 53–4, 57; II 60; III 65; IV 108–10, 113–6; V 57, 69n.; VII *passim*; IX 2; XIV 140; XVII 85

Zeno of Citium: VIII *passim*
Zoroaster: XVII 80, 85
Zumpt, C.G.: II 66; III 63